The Politics of Aircraft

Modern War Studies

Theodore A. Wilson
General Editor

Raymond A. Callahan
J. Garry Clifford
Jacob W. Kipp
Jay Luvaas
Series Editors

THE POLITICS
OF AIRCRAFT

Building an American
Military Industry

JACOB A. VANDER MEULEN

University Press of Kansas

Photographs courtesy of National Air and Space Museum,
Smithsonian Institution

Published by the University Press of Kansas (Lawrence, Kansas 66049),
which was organized by the Kansas Board of Regents and is operated and
funded by Emporia State University, Fort Hays State University, Kansas
State University, Pittsburg State University, the University of Kansas, and
Wichita State University

Library of Congress Cataloging-in-Publication Data

Vander Meulen, Jacob A.
  The politics of aircraft : building an American military industry
/ Jacob A. Vander Meulen.
        p.   cm. — (Modern war studies)
Includes bibliographical references and index.
ISBN 0–7006–0505–3 (hard cover)
  1. Aircraft industry—Government policy—United States.
2. Aircraft industry—Military aspects—United States. 3. Military-
industrial complex—United States. I. Title. II. Series.
HD9711.U6V36   1992
338.4′762913334′0973—dc20   91–19616

British Library Cataloguing in Publication Data is available.

Printed in the United States of America

10   9   8   7   6   5   4   3   2   1

The paper used in this publication meets the minimum requirements of the
American National Standard for Permanence of Paper for Printed Library
Materials Z39.48-1984.

TO WILLIAM C. BERMAN

CONTENTS

TABLES, FIGURES, AND ILLUSTRATIONS

TABLES

FIGURES

ILLUSTRATIONS

PREFACE

This study is based on a 1989 doctoral dissertation prepared for the Department of History at the University of Toronto. It would not have been completed without the intellectual and emotional support of many people as well as the financial aid and other practical help of various institutions. To acknowledge this help is as much a pleasure as it was to engage in what it made possible—the endless discoveries, surprises, and ideas for further work that are an inevitable part of concentrated research in American history. That basic, animating feature of the historian's work was only amplified by a subject as neglected, yet as richly textured and filled with broad implications for the contemporary experience, as the aircraft industry and its relations with the United States government.

For an ideal mixture of basic, detailed, and hands-off guidance, I am especially grateful to William Berman and John Ingham, my supervisers at Toronto. They, along with William H. Nelson and the members of my thesis committee, Robert Accinelli, Michael Bliss, Robert Cuff, and Jean Smith, forced me to truly "defend" my dissertation and thus helped me both to sharpen and to blunt my interpretations. Also critical were fellow students and friends, especially Jennifer Clibbon, Michael Barrier, Susan MacDonald, Duncan Macintyre, Patrice Gilbert, and Mark Tamminga. If this study has any strengths, they are due to the help of these and others; its weaknesses and limitations, many of which they would quickly point out, are my responsibility.

The early stages of this study were supported financially by the University of Toronto Connaught Fellowships, the University of Toronto Associates, the Social Sciences and Humanities Research Council of Canada, the Henry J. Kaiser Fund at the Walter Reuther Library in Detroit, and the Truman Presidential Library in Independence. Financial aid during the latter stages was provided by the United States Information Service and through fellowships from the Smithsonian Institution and the National Air and Space Museum. My debt to NASM is substantial. Its constant visual reminders of my subject; its location "on the Mall" within the finest infrastructure for scholarship; the knowledge and accessibility of its staff and other fellows; the wide berth allowed for provocative ideas— these added up to an otherwise unimaginable situation for a historian. Special thanks go to Dom Pisano, Von Hardesty, Peter Jakab, Anita Mason, Joanne Gernstein, Robert Vander Linden, Tom Crouch, Phil Edwards, Larry Wilson, Tom Dietz, Richard Muller, John Morrow, Russell Lee, and Tami Davis-Biddle.

Four archivists and librarians stand out as instrumental in the process of wading through the various sources used here: Jerry Hess, Will Mahoney, and Karl Weissenbach—names that will be fondly recognized by many other researchers—at the National Archives; and Mrs. Billie Perry of the Aerospace Industries Association in Washington, D.C. Without Ms. Perry's openness and cheery patience, a key source would have remained obscure and some of the major questions raised here, even if they are incompletely answered, could not have been posed. I am also indebted to the collections and interlibrary loan staffs of Robarts Library at the University of Toronto and to the staff of the University Press of Kansas who prodded the manuscript along and mustered some sharp critics to point out errors and incoherencies. As for any that still remain, I hope they can be avoided in future work.

CHAPTER ONE

Introduction

Every society is shot through with currents, bristling with obstacles, with obstinate relics of the past that block the way, with long-lasting structures whose permanence is their most revealing feature for the historian.

—*Fernand Braudel*, Wheels of Commerce[1]

Thinking about aeronautics, aviation, and aerospace is difficult without thinking a good deal about politics, as anyone with a sense of the military and political roles of air power in the contemporary world knows. Surely the art of powered flight is driven by certain technological imperatives—speed, range, payload—and has served a host of human needs and desires. But the central fact in the development of aeronautics is its enlistment as a weapon, an instrument of international politics. The key to understanding why most aircraft look and perform the way they do is the way they were understood in terms of national security. Each captures in material form a compromise between technology and military doctrine in which the latter predominates.

For those with a sense of how extensively the modern state also uses aerospace to intervene in social and economic life at home, the claim that politics explains a great deal about aeronautics and the aircraft industry would seem equally obvious. For them, airplanes, helicopters, and missiles capture in material form a compromise among technology, military doctrine, and the needs and interests of various markets, constituents, and bureaucracies. Again, the latter seems predominant, so much so that technological processes and military doctrine often appear to be of minor importance.

This study began as an attempt to outline the early links between U.S. politics and high-technology weapons industries during the twenty-five years before World War II, when such weapons first appeared in the form of military aeronautics. Conceived in the mid-1980s when the United States was engaged in its largest peacetime military buildup, the goal seemed clear—to trace the origins of the American military-industrial complex and to sketch the political and institutional roots of a dangerous arms race. Work in the archives, however, quickly revealed that serving the particular needs of business, military, and political interests—now so often cited as the major function of the Pentagon and defense industry—had little to do with the formative years of the aircraft industry, which today constitutes the core of the military-industrial complex.

That is not to say that a military-industrial complex for aircraft was absent during these years. It did exist and featured many of the familiar corporate names—Bell, Boeing, Douglas, Grumman, Lockheed, Martin, Northrop, United, and so on. But it existed only in the term's neutral descriptive sense—the sense of military institutions and industries highly dependent on one another. Nor is it to say that the early aircraft industry was not the origin of the contemporary military-industrial complex; the industry served as the base for massive expansion during World War II and the cold war. Further, it is not suggested that the early complex for aircraft was not an expression of domestic politics. On the contrary, this study confirms the centrality of domestic politics in the development of modern defense industries. It shows how deeply politicized were the aircraft industry, its technology, and its relations with the army and navy.

But during the interwar years, the aircraft industry and its relations with the military served a type of politics quite different from those of the pork barrel and bureaucratic interests that critics complain of today. Then, the aircraft military-industrial complex served as a high-profile and highly charged forum for political conflict and debate over what ought to be the reach and role of federal power in American society, over how political economy ought to be reformed to accommodate changing and more demanding circumstances. The industry's formative years paralleled and complicated a critical period during which Americans struggled to shape and adapt themselves to the challenges of an advanced industrial society. As these challenges mounted everywhere, people reluctantly looked to the federal government for solutions and direction. Social, economic, and technological change, it seemed, compelled reconsideration of the state-society relationship, which in theory, if not always in practice, Americans had tried to keep as distant as possible.

The conservatism and tensions in the approaches Americans have taken to their evolving state are projected into sharp relief by the aircraft industry's early development. Its history is a microhistory of the American state. Aircraft manufacture was reliant on the federal government, which could not ignore the industry since aircraft were rapidly becoming a key measure of power and prestige among nation states. But if a close, mutually dependent relationship seemed predetermined by technological and military necessity, the actual nature of the relationship was not. The policies and institutions that would define this forced relationship depended on how much of the old Americans were willing to abandon to the challenges of the new. The industry's early decades thus encapsulate a basic dilemma of modern American political economy: the need for state solutions to the complex problems of change yet the obstacles to such solutions posed by tradition. The aircraft industry's structure, its technology and products, and the state that needed them more and more were stamped by this dilemma, by the tensions between new institutional needs and a conservative political culture that revered past practices and old republican, antistatist values.

During the two and a half decades before World War II, private and public managers of aeronautics sought ways to order their affairs and cope with rapid change. But dependence on the military meant that congressmen were able to use funding and the rules of military contracting to determine the industry's structural development and shape it in accordance with their ideological visions. They wanted the industry to serve as a bastion of republican political economy, a preserve for economic individualism, free-market enterprise, the small firm, the independent inventor, and the limited state. They insisted that aircraft manufacture serve these goals whatever the severe handicaps they posed for the industry and for military aviation and in spite of the consensus among military and business groups that aeronautics required a much different approach.

William H. McNeill has noted the irony of modern weaponry in modern democracies. The more sophisticated weapons become, the more difficult it is to subject their production, development, and military roles to rational control. Military "command technologies" depend on careful state cultivation through close and active links between industry and the military. As the numbers and complexity of these technologies relentlessly grow, along with their claims on public funds, so too does the state's administrative role in national economies. Especially in democracies, that expanding role is inevitably politicized and comes to serve a host of purposes well apart from supplying seemingly objective military needs.[2] McNeill's correlation between the sophistication and the politicization of military technologies defines America's response to aeronautics. Since this technology's foundation in private enterprise was never seriously questioned, radical steps in business-government relations were necessary. But these proved more than usually difficult for American political culture to condone.[3]

Historically unique in its complexity and dynamism, aeronautics was always racing against obsolescence. Military aeronautics presented a continuum of technical and funding problems that had to be addressed jointly by industry and the aviation wings of the army and navy. It required constant mobilization of part of the most advanced sectors of the nation's industrial base and technical elite for the complicated tasks of designing and producing warplanes. To assure itself a dependable supply of "state of the art" aircraft, the government needed to fund, direct, and protect producers. Air power meant governmental regulatory power exerted upon private industry in the most detailed way, a new and permanent public-private enterprise.

But it was because the industry was both public and private that the effort to impose order upon it was so difficult and resulted in so much confusion, waste, and discord. At the outset, the effort was greatly complicated by a technology that was evolving very rapidly and that would have been difficult to cope with even under the most controlled circumstances. This dynamism made a mockery of attempts to provide state of the art warplanes during World War I, a time in which the industry's managers made plans with a relatively free hand. But even then, and especially so during the interwar years, when the pressures of war were absent, the public-private nature of this new military enterprise ensured that it would be a vehicle for politics and ideology. All attempts to order the process of producing aircraft and to use limited funds efficiently to develop military aeronautics were constrained because the aircraft industry's market, structure, financing, and performance were subject to Congress's control and its attempts to set the terms for an evolving state-society relationship.

Federal regulation of business—the imposition of political directives on markets and production—was unique in aircraft mainly because those being regulated had so little influence over regulatory policy. Despite its plainly negative results for the industry and the overwhelming hostility to it among manufacturers, the regulatory framework in aircraft remained strikingly consistent over a period of more than twenty years. This framework was not the outcome of the fluid political give-and-take among competing interests that made regulation in other industries so elastic. Nor was it the product of special-purpose legislation, the passage or implementation of which were processes that various interests could shape.[4] Instead, federal regulation came to the aircraft industry informally, as a result of the government's command over the aircraft market.

The aircraft business was largely Congress's business, which has always dominated the market for aircraft through its agents in the military.[5] From its pre–World War I beginnings through the interwar years, aircraft industry meant military aircraft industry. Aircraft industrialists were obliged to defer to a congressional-military client that controlled their industry through its power as a virtual monopoly buyer.[6] All the key decisions in the business were made on Capitol Hill. When on occasion the views of manufacturers on how their industry should be regulated were solicited, they were ignored. Congress dictated terms to aircraft makers. It determined market size by appropriating funds for military aviation in amounts that it deemed necessary. Through its contracting rules, Congress determined how the market was apportioned among firms, the sizes of firms, and the way they related to one another. It did so in ways intended to uphold price competition, equal access to federal contracts, and minimal interaction between businessmen and military officers.

For an industry driven by complex, endless, and costly technological change, such regulation proved a crippling burden to bear. Until World War II, most firms absorbed almost steady losses, while others operated only marginally. Only subsidies provided by manufacturers, investors, workers, and foreign buyers carried the development of aeronautics and military aviation in the United States. The enthusiasm of manufacturers and designers and their commitments to aeronautics; the thousands who bought aviation stocks during the investment bubble of the late 1920s; the steadily overworked, underpaid, and unorganized aircraft workers; and in the 1930s, the foreign governments that provided a profitable market for American warplanes—together and despite Congress these kept the U.S. industry and technology at least competitive on the world scene and capable of frequently spectacular successes.

Manufacturers continually but unavailingly attacked the rules governing their business as wasteful of public funds and as exploitative of private initiative. Congress denied the industry the alternative "corporatist" or "associationalist" industrial framework and planning mechanisms that many of those familiar with the problems of producing advanced military aircraft concluded were necessary. Most critically, Congress refused to permit an industrial structure that featured relations between aircraft firms on any basis other than price competition. Because of the clear wastefulness and futility of price competition in this new field, manufacturers and their military and civilian allies in the various administrations urged that it be abolished. They called for the restriction of military aircraft contracts to only a handful of companies and argued that manufacturers be allowed to aid one another in the development of aeronautics and that competition be limited to product performance. In these ways, cooperation among firms, between firms and the military, and between firms and their employees would replace the secrecy and hostility generated all around by price competition. America would get the most for its tax dollars and military aeronautics would develop evenly and quickly into a sophisticated, subtle weapon.

But for congressmen, particularly on the Naval Affairs and Military Affairs committees in the House and Senate, such steps violated long-standing individualistic values of political economy, values that became closely associated with aeronautics in part because of how this technology evoked impressions of independence, resourcefulness, heroism. Many congressmen recognized aeronautics as a powerful agent of the future and were bent on using their power over it to ensure that that future reflected their sense of American values. They hoped aeronautics would reinvigorate those values at a time when economic, social, and technological change seemed to threaten them so. They wanted aeronautics to be a democratic technology, out of the hands of big business and its research and development bureaucracies. They wanted it to preserve the "independent" whom they perceived as still the true source of innovation. They were committed to limiting executive federal power and keeping it firmly under congressional control. They regarded the industry's proposals as a prescription for monopoly—an "Aircraft Trust"—and for a powerfully independent military-industrial clique that would fleece the taxpayer and foment war.

Denial of the manufacturers' property rights to their designs for military aircraft was the primary lever among the many regulatory tools congressmen wielded to make the industry conform to their vision. After World War I, the army and navy were obliged to regard privately funded designs as public property and to let production contracts in open competition. Without rights to their designs, manufacturers could never be sure of recovering the costs of research and development. Nor could they contain price competition or make their affairs and those of the military as predictable as an unpredictable technology would allow. When designing aircraft, they were compelled to think primarily about defending their shares of the production market. Only in repetitive production might adequate profits be made to cover design costs. Congress thus shaped technical decisions, the air weapon that emerged from them, and the way its use in warfare came to be understood.

Aside from a small assortment of personal papers left by aircraft manufacturers themselves, this study could not benefit from company records. The records of almost all the early aircraft firms sadly have been either lost or destroyed, and access to the few corporate archive collections that are being preserved was denied. Fortunately, much can be learned about the early industry from the records of the industry's trade association and aircraft worker unions. But since this was so much a public industry, even more was gleaned from the public record—the records of the War and Navy Departments and the National Recovery Administration, as well as congressional archives.

Chapter 2 traces the industry's experiences during World War I when military aircraft first appeared and when aircraft manufacture and its technology first became vehicles of ideological and political conflict. Chapters 3 through 5 outline the industry's early evolution as determined by the nature of its product, its manufacturing process, and by congressional manipulation. They trace the manufacturers' attempts to break Congress's grip over them—through legislated change in the mid-1920s, through the creation of a commercial-market haven from congressional abuse during the late 1920s, and through a "code of fair competition" under the New Deal's National Recovery Administration. Each of these attempts failed to end the artificial competitive regime imposed upon the industry. These chapters focus on the industry's problems from the perspectives of the manufacturers and the military and try to place these issues in a larger context of the development of American political economy during the period. Chapter 6 traces the industry's problems from the perspectives of aircraft workers during the early New Deal. Since wages represented the bulk of the costs of producing aircraft, these skilled workers bore a significant share of the industry's competitive burdens as devised by Congress. Their inability to organize effective unions denied the industry a potentially stabilizing force. Chapter 7 describes Congress's business during the latter half of the 1930s, which served as the base for the great aircraft production complex erected for World War II.

CHAPTER TWO

A New Dilemma: Military Aircraft Production during World War I

FUTURE VISIONS

During their involvement in the Great War, Americans put much of their hope, resources, and money into the new weapons of the air. They also granted a large measure of trust, confidence, and discretion to a group of progressive businessmen and engineers to supply them. Adherents of the latest thinking in the organization of production and in relations between business and government, these men persuaded the nation that mass air power was needed to defeat Germany and claimed the ability to manage aircraft production on the necessary huge scale. Congress accepted the claims of these "experts" and provided them a blank check, wide latitude, and a unique opportunity to act on their ideas.

The period from late July 1917, when Congress approved a massive military aircraft program, to the Armistice in November 1918 marks the only period in the American aircraft industry's pre–World War II history when its organization was not directly determined by Congress. Implicit in Congress's mandate to these World War I progressives were the traditional, clearly demarcated spheres of public and private authority. Also implicit were restraints on the power of government agencies and the rearrangement of power among them. But the aircraft program's managers accepted these limits, often insisting upon them, and considered the new space for experimentation within them adequate to the task. Their use of this space to produce little more than disappointment, waste, and embarrassment meant that until the next war, Congress's detailed scrutiny and control over all things to do with the supply of military aircraft would not be abdicated again. A high technology industry over-whelmingly reliant on the federal government, aircraft manufacture required radically new approaches in the organization of industry and in business-government relations. The failure of the World War I aircraft program helped ensure that any such new approaches would not be tolerated by a suspicious Congress.

Because it was so new and seemed to hold so many keys to the future, those with power over the early aircraft industry sought to stamp it with their particular views of how that future should look. During the war progressive businessmen and engineers sought to use their influence over aircraft production to make it serve their visions. For them, aircraft would help open the way to a future of large-scale, mass-production, technology-driven industries guided by private managers and engineers like themselves who would work cooperatively with government under the rules of an active but limited voluntary state.

Unfortunately, the manufacture of advanced aircraft cruelly exposed the limits of the techniques of mass production. The system of standardized, assembly-line production by large firms, numerous subcontractors, and unskilled labor that had recently emerged in the automobile industry under the name of "Fordism" was much too inflexible for aircraft. Rapid technical change, inherent in aeronautics and greatly accelerated during the war, made mass-produced state of the art combat aircraft a contradiction in terms. Even if technical change could be ignored, aircraft were too complicated and dependent upon assembly at tolerances too strict for mass production. Aircraft were made of delicate wood and fabric parts of often large, unwieldy, curving shapes. Carefully strung together with wires, turnbuckles, sheet-metal fittings, screws, and glue, they required the skilled handwork and constant fitting of craftsmen. They were quite unlike consumer durables such as Henry Ford's Model Ts, which consisted of simple, rigid parts of low-quality metal and repetitively produced by special-purpose machinery, assembly lines, and unskilled workers. Later, with the development of less intricate and more durable all-metal aircraft during the 1930s, the limitations of Fordism to aircraft manufacture became less severe. But even the great production lines of World War II could bear few resemblances to the Fordism that many hoped would be America's contribution to Allied air power during both world wars.

Like most Americans who contemplated the new air weapon, the businessmen and engineers who conceived and managed the wartime aircraft program seriously erred when they imagined air power as best applied in "waves" and again when they imagined that the new "Detroit methods" were applicable to aircraft.[1] But even when the latter error became plain, alternative approaches were barred by institutional momentum, the preservation of reputations, a sense by mid-1918 of inevitable German defeat, and an unwillingness on the part of planners to rethink their visions of social management and of the role of air power and the aircraft industry in bringing them about. As was suggested by some small, neglected aircraft firms that used methods more appropriate to complex production, a solution might have been to reorganize the program and industry in ways that could better accommodate the intricacies of state of the art aircraft: a decentralized structure of small- to medium-sized firms relying on the flexibility of skilled workers and shared information to cope with technical sophistication and rapid change.[2] Fewer aircraft would have been constructed than the numbers imagined in the mass-production program but far more of quality and lower cost than those that were actually produced. Instead the program's managers pursued the opposite extreme and blamed the failure of mass production on the lack of centralized power behind their vision. They thus gave up the other half of the social vision they had hoped aeronautics would vindicate—that of cooperative and voluntary relations between large-scale private industry and a limited state—and sought a much stronger application of federal authority behind the program.

But this was not a solution and it went well beyond the roles of the state as Congress and the Wilson administration defined them or would tolerate. The aircraft program's outcome was thus deadlock, frustration, waste, and muddle, as well as a suspicion of the aircraft industry that endured on Capitol Hill through the interwar years. Most congressmen and the press did not identify the program's failure with its contradictory goals of mass-produced air power. As explanations they preferred graft, corruption, and a conspiracy by manufacturers and their agents in government to swindle the taxpayer, destroy free competition, and monopolize control over a new technology. The lesson for the interwar years was that the program's managers had been granted too much power; Congress had to carefully ensure that further interaction between government and the industry was kept minimal and that aircraft development and manufacture was kept strictly price competitive.

Neither did other analysts, some of whom were directly involved with it, blame the program's failure on an overblown conception of air power's capacity or on the attempts to mass-produce aircraft. Instead they blamed congressional parsimony and a conservative attitude toward aviation within the military establishment prior to 1917. These, they argued, left the nation without an aircraft industry and inexperienced and unprepared for wartime needs. They suggested, and many historians agreed, that if not for the need to create an industry "where none existed," the mass-production challenges would have been met and, had the war gone on a little longer, the program would have been fully vindicated. Thus the link between air power and mass production remained fixed through the interwar years.[3]

Graft and the size of the prewar aircraft industry explain much less of the program's failure than the ambitions of those who came to dominate it. In April 1917 the American aircraft industry was tiny, widely dispersed, and quite unequal to the task of suddenly producing large numbers of advanced military aircraft; but it did exist and was quite active. However, an aggressive and vocal group of business progressives used investment and semiofficial government positions to gain a strong influence over it and prepare it for what they hoped would be an enormous and profitable proving ground for the latest in American manufacturing techniques and political economic thought. Most in Congress and the Wilson administration were delighted that private industry, under the guidance of men with stellar production performances who aired confidence in their unlimited ability, obviated the need for distastefully radical state initiatives or reorganizations to create and oversee a large military aircraft industry.

During the period from the Wright brothers' 1903 flight at Kitty Hawk to the beginning of World War I, the American aircraft industry consisted of a series of small workshops scattered across the nation and operated by pioneers who experimented and constructed a handful of airplanes per year mainly for wealthy sportsmen. A larger market for military aircraft developed slowly but perceptibly. Under pressure from President Theodore Roosevelt, an apathetic War Department made its first call for bids on aircraft, and a $30,000 contract was signed with the Wrights in February 1908. Beginning in 1909, small but regular appropriations were made for army and navy aviation. The army and navy were indifferent to the possibilities of air power, but aviation gained institutional bases within the services largely because of pressure on Congress from enthusiasts and the National Guard. A coordinator for naval aviation was appointed in late 1913 and a tiny aviation section was created in the Army Signal Corps in July 1914. In 1915 Congress established the National Advisory Committee for Aeronautics. Thereafter, rapid advances in Europe were given much attention in the press and Congress substantially increased appropriations and personnel for military aviation.[4]

A basic feature of the aircraft industry through its first decades, and a key explanation for why it survived despite its punishment through the interwar years by Congress, was its powerful noneconomic attractions to participants. Venturesome, usually young spirits with an eye for the extraordinary were drawn to the industry along with craftsmen and engineers attracted to the unique technical problems of conquering air. A knowledge- and craft-based activity, aircraft manufacture did not require significant start-up capital and offered wide space to new entries with new ideas. To compete in this prestigious, labor-intensive industry, one simply needed basic aeronautical expertise, a reasonably large building, adequate hand tools, and a group of skilled workers to use them.

Before World War I, the industry's attractions were supplemented more and more by the profit motive as visions of the airplane's commercial possibilities developed, and more particularly, as Allied purchasing agents scoured the United States for new aircraft suppliers after the war in Europe began. Spurred on by their generous orders as well as the investments of those who anticipated large profits and also genuinely fretted over America's security and place among the new air powers, the pioneer workshops were transformed into small factories. By the end of 1916 at least fourteen firms employing 10,000 workers were competing for foreign and U.S. military aircraft contracts. Two firms—Curtiss Aeroplane and Motor Company and Wright-Martin Corporation—were capitalized at $10 million each, were the focus of heavy stock market speculation, and were under the control of Wall Street syndicates that reflected the manufacturing perspectives of the auto industry.[5]

These larger firms, like the industry's two trade journals, also came to reflect the perspectives of a group of promoters, engineers, and business progressives who had little experience with aircraft manufacture but had eclipsed in influence the pioneers who did. Led by Howard E. Coffin of the Hudson Motor Company and including Sydney Waldon of Packard Motor Car; Edward A. Deeds of National Cash Register and DELCO; F. G. Diffin of the Society of Automotive Engineers; and C. D. Walcott, secretary of the Smithsonian Institution and the National Advisory Committee for Aeronautics, this group persuaded business, Congress, and the public that hordes of American military aircraft mass-produced under their expert guidance could win the war and demonstrate to the world, all in a matter of a few months, the superiority of America's technology, industry, and voluntarist system of political economy.[6]

"The American Flag That Will Fly over Germany." This illustration, which appeared in the journal *Flying*, August 1917, combines two powerful new ideas, air power and "Fordism," the system of assembly-line mass production that had recently and spectacularly emerged in America's auto plants. Similar cartoons were common in magazines and on the editorial pages of newspapers during 1917 as part of a national campaign directed by Howard Coffin. To link air power with mass production was to connect it with a basic source of national self-confidence, and in both world wars a mass-production program for warplanes was crucial in mobilizing popular commitment.

The aircraft program began as a centerpiece of the nation's efforts to mobilize for the war. Prodded by a publicity campaign coordinated by Coffin among the nation's leading newspapers, air power and mass production became fixed together in the public mind and in the perceptions of military and civilian experts. Images abounded of European skies suddenly blackened by waves of mass-produced American "battleplanes" forcing a quick end to the conflict.[7] Congressmen hailed air power as "America's opportunity" to display its industrial prowess, as military power on the cheap, and as a quick fix for a "world that seems to be in a deadlock" of trench warfare and imperial decrepitude. With expressions of confidence in the assurances of military and business experts and of fears that detailed discussion would only give "comfort and aid to the enemy," the House approved without a single dissenting vote $640 million for army aviation on July 14, 1917. Signed by President Wilson on July 24, the "Aero Bill" is notable both as the largest single appropriation made by Congress to that point, and for the lack of partisan politics that plagued other wartime legislative initiatives during the Wilson administration.[8] The enthusiasm and confidence of House Minority Leader James R. Mann was shared by most congressmen, though not his accurate sense of the great gamble being taken on military aircraft:

> Here is an unknown quantity—the use of flying machines . . . did you ever buy a pig in a poke and take a chance on it? Sometimes it turns out very fortunately; sometimes with the loss of the money invested. I believe that the time has arrived in our country when we can afford to spend an immense sum of money in trying out the control of the air [applause] . . . If I had my way about it I would pass this bill without saying a word [Loud applause and cries of "Vote!", "Vote!"][9]

A handful of congressmen worried about the "appalling magnitude" of the program and Congress's abdication of control over it to an unproven industry and an unenthusiastic army. The General Staff was unimpressed by dire warnings of German air superiority. Hostile to military aviation, it blocked submission of the $640 million plan to Congress. But Congress's eagerness and the media clamor for air power compelled Secretary of War Newton D. Baker to submit it despite the General Staff's opposition. Cong. Fiorello H. LaGuardia and Senator Morris Sheppard proposed a new Department of Aeronautics where all facets of the government's aviation activities would be concentrated, but their bills died in committee after the strong opposition of Secretary Baker and Secretary of the Navy Josephus Daniels and after assurances by Coffin and his associates that existing arrangements were adequate. Along with President Wilson, Baker and Daniels were loath to take such radical steps and insisted that their departments retain full control over their aviation programs.[10]

More than just bureaucratic interests prevented such proposals and similar ones during the interwar years. In America, aviation has always served as a powerful ideological vehicle, a way of looking into and coping with the future. Paradoxically, aviation was and is widely perceived as a redemptive force, an agent for the preservation of institutions and values which seem threatened by modern society.[11] Aeronautics as the creator of a new, unbounded frontier for the independent American inventor, entrepreneur, craftsman, adventurist, and warrior; as the harmonizer of the individual and the machine age; as the guarantor of international stability and peace—these elements of the faith in early aeronautics and the antagonism and blame that their disappointment produced shaped in key ways the political context in which the aircraft industry had to develop during its first decades.

The World War I aircraft program was the first major manifestation of this popular mysticism. From a different but equally conservative perspective, those involved with the program's planning and management also saw aeronautics as something more than a quick technical fix to the war. To them it seemed a unique opportunity to demonstrate that old republican values of free enterprise and the limited state could be squared with the organizational needs of large-scale undertakings in a complex, technologically advanced national economy. To progressive capitalists, managers, and engineers involved with industrial mobilization generally, the war was as much a struggle for conservative reform at home as it was a war to defeat Germany. To them, the emergency seemed to provide the immediacy and sense of national purpose that both the reform and rejuvenation of traditional values required.[12]

Business progressives feared that basic values of competitive individualism and a political economy of democratic voluntarism were being overwhelmed by concentrated economic power and the social and political turbulence that accompanied the rise of modern industrialism in America. As a solution, many espoused what a contemporary called the new competition, what William Appleman Williams described as an American variant of corporatism, and what Ellis Hawley labeled associationalism. The corporatist vision of political economy was common among western nations, particularly after the war, but its American version placed special

stress on business prerogatives and the limited state. American corporatists believed that old republican values could be preserved if regulatory and coordinating mechanisms were set in place and if primary
control over these mechanisms were left in private hands. For them,
there was no necessary contradiction between the organizational needs of
modern industrial society and values that long predated its rise, only tensions, waste, and discord that could be offset by better management and
information, more efficient methods, greater consultation and promotion,
and the replacement of short-term parochial and class interests by a clear
sense of society's collective goals. The individual needed to grasp his or
her place and role within a new society defined as the corporate whole of
its interdependent parts—capital, labor, farmers, and government. Each
part would be represented by experts from associations and unions,
where key decisions, with the assistance of a supportive state in the
background, could be achieved cooperatively, voluntarily, and in accord
with scientific principles. Only in these ways, it was thought, could harmony emerge, assumed to be latent in American society. The chaos of
laissez-faire could be avoided on the one hand and the tyrannies of business monopoly and coercive statism on the other.[13]

To Howard Coffin and his associates, the aircraft industry seemed an
ideal laboratory for this vision. Public and private officials would jointly
and scientifically manage industrial change. Traditional rights of private
enterprise and values of competition would be preserved but modified to
encourage cooperation and technical advance. Coffin was an industrial
engineer who had become the leader of a national movement to standard-
ize manufacture and eliminate waste and conflict through data collection,
publicity, and industrial self-regulation. He and his associates perceived
aircraft manufacture as a great mass-production industry of the future,
soon to rival "even the spectacular rise of the horseless road vehicle" and
thus a perfect forum for their crusade for efficiency and expert guided
progress.[14]

Aeronautics meant a new technology and an industry free from the
vested interests that had thwarted progressive experimentation in the
past, keeping the engineer-business progressives outside the centers of
power.[15] Its high profile meant an opportunity for broad reform by example. The technical complexity of aircraft manufacture seemed to make
cross-firm cooperation and standardization of methods imperative while
the supportive relations that would have to be developed between the
industry and government would stimulate similar positive but limited
state intervention elsewhere. On behalf of this message Coffin used his

various positions as governor of the Aero Club, member of the Naval Consulting Board and the Council for National Defense, and later, as chairman of the Aircraft Production Board.

For Coffin and his associates the military program would have the convenient effect of telescoping the aircraft industry's development, which in their views would always be primarily commercial. They shared in the fantasy of air power as the key to the war's rapid end and as a final deterrent to future war. Thus in their minds the military orientation of aeronautics was only temporary and the aircraft program just an initial primer for a postwar commercial aviation industry that would rival the auto industry and act as an engine for future commerce generally. In the meantime the rapid creation and management of a huge, technically advanced industry by experts acting in accord with voluntarist values would serve as a model for the reform and preservation of the values basic to American institutions. Corporatist wartime management, it was hoped, would set precedents and lay the foundations for socioeconomic management with the return to peace. At the same time it would display to a world desperately in need of new models the workings of a superior American social system that did not subsume the individual in such horrors as trench warfare and state bureaucracy.

These optimistic men came to staff the wartime civilian and military agencies for aeronautics and to set the agenda for the aircraft program. The initial approaches to mobilizing the industry were thus taken with the primary goals of imposing Fordist mass production on aeronautics and of preserving its independent, private structure for postwar business by limiting federal and especially military control over the industry. During the program's early stages, these men were confident that the relationship between individual manufacturers and the military could be kept as distant as possible and successfully and noncoercively mediated by a buffer zone made up of an industry trade association and a federally appointed clearing house of civilian advisers with pseudogovernment authority.

THE LIMITS OF VOLUNTARISM

Beginning as early as 1913 several steps within the framework of voluntary associationalism were taken toward facilitating consultation between manufacturers and public aeronautical bodies with the aim of disseminating technical information, increasing productivity, and stan-

dardizing aircraft specifications and materials. Efforts by such bodies as
the National Advisory Committee for Aeronautics (NACA), the Naval
Consulting Board (NCB), and the Society of Automotive Engineers
(SAE) were made with a short-term view of the brief demands of war and
a long-term view of private, large-scale commercial aviation. A role for
the federal government was recognized, but the goal of minimizing it as a
complement of private effort was paramount. NACA was barred by Congress and its own prejudices from offering membership to private manufacturers but was nonetheless strongly committed to nurturing healthy,
free-enterprise aviation through technical advice. Along with Coffin at
the NCB it pursued its goals in 1915 and 1916 through meetings with manufacturers and the SAE. It helped manufacturers gain access to the testing facilities of the Bureau of Standards and served as an informal
mediary between them and the services as they sought to address deficiencies in American aeronautics, particularly in aircraft engines.[16]

Coffin and the members of NACA also moved to shore up private aircraft manufacture in ways that would fulfill their aspirations of cooperative, expertly managed commercial aviation for the postwar period. Its
preservation could not be taken for granted, given the overwhelming military demand for aircraft and, later, the growing suspicions of the industry in the military and in Congress. But even well before American entry
into the war, the industry clearly did not lend itself to the prescriptions of
voluntary associationalism, which, to Coffin and his associates, were essential to its viability. According to these prescriptions, intraindustry
conflict was an aberration in fundamentally harmonious capitalist relations. It resulted from ignorance and the lack of a common forum such as
a trade association where mechanisms for cooperative self-regulation,
supposedly latent in every industry, could be developed and implemented. The key, theoretically, was to explain the benefits of a trade
association to an industry's members who would then willingly fall into
line behind it. But the government's advisers vainly tried to persuade
separate aircraft manufacturers that their true interests lay in cooperat-
ing toward an ideal future. Their eventual imposition of an association
violated voluntarism and, more importantly for the aircraft program,
created an atmosphere of suspicion among all concerned, which the program's planners eventually blamed for the program's failure rather than
its conflicting goals of mass producing state of the art aircraft.

Aircraft manufacturers were bitterly divided and mutually hostile. The
industry's attractions as a technological vanguard, as an easy field to enter, and increasingly, as a potential machine for war profits combined to

produce a chaotic competitiveness that during the second half of 1916 expressed itself in the hoarding of scarce accessories and material, in the piracy of elite workers, and in tight bidding for foreign orders and the handful of army and navy contracts.[17] To Coffin's chagrin, it also produced a range of unstandardized aircraft, even though they had been designed for identical contract specifications. Adding to the mistrust among manufacturers were ongoing patent wars. The patent issue remained unsettled and did not deter new entries, but as its resolution by the Supreme Court loomed, so did the prospect of an industry monopoly. Against this possible outcome, manufacturers strove to position themselves as favorably as they could.

Patent disputes had endured since the Wrights received their 1906 patent on the wing-warping technique, a basic innovation that gave an airplane lateral stability and made possible the great breakthrough at Kitty Hawk. The Wrights' main struggle was with Glenn Curtiss, who, with Alexander Graham Bell, had developed and patented the aileron in 1911. A hinged flap on each wing, the aileron was more effective and dependable than the Wrights' technique; but the court granted the Wright patent a liberal scope, and it won the verdicts in a long series of suits. For his part, Curtiss defended claims to some thirty patents on seaplanes. By the fall of 1915 Orville Wright had tired of litigation and sold his interests to a group of investors who concentrated on engine manufacture. At about the same time Curtiss sold out to a New York syndicate that built seaplanes and trainers for the Allies at its Buffalo, Toronto, and Hammondsport plants. In the summer of 1916 the two new firms sought a merger as a solution to their disputes and as the basis for a powerful, integrated manufacturer of engines and airframes, but their lawyers advised that a merger would not survive an antitrust suit. The Wright Company, seeking a counter to Curtiss's position in the promising seaplane market, merged instead with the Glenn L. Martin Company of Los Angeles, a builder of seaplanes primarily for export.[18] As the patent dispute moved up through the courts and as competition grew, both firms heavy-handedly asserted their claims against eager newcomers. In late 1916 Wright-Martin announced a patent-license scheme in which all manufacturers would pay a 5 percent royalty on their gross business, with a minimum of $10,000 annually. Curtiss retaliated with a similar demand on builders of seaplanes for which the navy had just announced a $3 million spending program.[19]

More lawsuits and appeals resulted, along with the first expression of the Aircraft Trust myth, which at least until World War II held such great appeal for populist legislators who had not made their peace with big business and continually disrupted attempts to use political economic reform to accommodate it. Suspicions were raised by National Guard spokesmen and manufacturers victimized by the patent claims. In an argument that would resonate for decades, they insisted that the primary source for aeronautical innovation was in the independent inventor and the small firm and that a patent-wielding trust would destroy it. Antimonopoly sentiment was particularly attracted to aviation because of its high profile, its dependence on the government, and the great hopes placed in aeronautics as a redeemer of American individualism and as a democratizer of technology. In June 1940, when France fell to the Nazis, Congress at last relented on its faith in antitrust military-contracting laws. Until then, populist republicanism had thwarted all efforts to rationalize the industry and systematize its relations with the military in ways that seemed essential for the development of military aeronautics.[20]

Growing criticism, the industry's disorder, and the scale of the patent problem—192 aeronautic patents had been approved by mid-1917—led Coffin and NACA finally to use the government's contracting power to impose a patent pool on the industry. Their actions suggest the willingness of Wilson's war managers to violate the tenets of voluntarism when they had little bearing on the realities of certain industries.[21] Nevertheless, these steps were taken on behalf of the broader vision. Coffin and NACA wanted a commercially oriented aircraft industry that would be protected from both extremes of chaotic competition and monopoly control by interfirm cooperation directed by experts, particularly on technical matters and in dealings with the government. They wanted the patent disputes settled so that hesitant automobile firms—Ford, Fisher Body, Willys-Overland, and others—would enter the business with their expertise in mass production. They hoped the industry would generate cooperative mechanisms on its own but were willing to use federal power when it did not. Yet their solution only encouraged more suspicions of an Aircraft Trust and new limits on the room they came to believe they needed to make the aircraft program work.

Coffin and Waldon suggested a trade association to manage a patent pool in fall 1916. Coffin despised the "senseless patent litigation" and attacked Wright-Martin for its "short-sighted tax." He warned the manufacturers that they risked military confiscation of the patents and tried to impress upon them the insignificance of minor patent advantages in relation to the potential gains of cooperation in a seemingly limitless market, first in military, then in commercial, aviation. He tried to persuade them to form a cross-licensing scheme modeled on the auto industry's patent pool. For him, technological complexity should have been a source of business cooperation, not discord. The value of patents was a "rallying point about which to organize the manufacturing interests. . . . It is only through some such arrangement as will permit the free extension of the commercial possibilities of aircraft through civilian channels."[22]

But manufacturers would surrender nothing to cooperation until they were assured positions in the market. The suggestion of a trade association built around a patent pool was taken up by Henry B. Mingle, a New York City lawyer and president of the Standard Aircraft Corporation, established in 1916 by Mitsui and Company of Japan at Elizabethtown, New Jersey. Coffin had organized an exposition of commercial aeronautics in New York for February 1917 to advance his vision of the industry's future. He and Mingle used the occasion to promote their Aircraft Manufacturers' Association (AMA). Most manufacturers agreed to join but gave the new trade association little support since Wright-Martin declined to join. It held the controlling patent and saw no reason to abdicate it for the good of its competitors.[23]

As war loomed the industry's disorder attracted greater attention from government officials and the press. Royalty payments were increasing the costs of airplanes to the army and navy by $600 to $900 apiece, nearly 25 percent of the average airplane's cost. In March Secretary Daniels proposed government purchase of the patents, but NACA's chairman, C. D. Walcott, opposed this as "indicating an unreasonable attitude" and as a threat to commercial aeronautics. He worked for a private patent pool initiated and managed by the industry, even while admitting that until individual firms were assured large and profitable contracts, particularly Wright-Martin, they would surrender little for the abstract interests of industry cooperation and the prevention of a possible federal takeover of the industry.[24]

Negotiations among NACA, Coffin, members of the new Aircraft Manufacturers Association, military representatives, and leading patent attorneys dragged on for months. By late April, with the U.S. at war, Wright-Martin and Curtiss tentatively agreed to a cross-licensing scheme drawn up by patent attorneys for the auto industry. NACA laid the scheme before the AMA, which had been sidelined during the negotiations but was needed to administer it. The AMA was torn, however, by a war of "labor piracy," primarily between Standard and Curtiss. When Mingle resigned in anger and a vice-president of Curtiss, Frank H. Russell, took his place as AMA president, Wright-Martin backpedaled on the agreement. The other members of the group preferred to keep themselves uncommitted until the much-discussed, but as yet unfunded, military aircraft program actually materialized. Waldon commented that "evidently the AMA is letting the matter die through lack of their own interest in its consummation."[25]

Coffin and his associates feared that the lack of mechanisms for cross-industry consensus and direction would inhibit mass production and generate doubts as to private industry's ability to deliver. The military might assume control of wartime production and perhaps permanent control of aeronautics by default. In the absence of a trade association, a clearing house between the industry and the military with quasi-official authority and dominated by civilian advisers seemed imperative. Coffin and NACA thus proposed an Aircraft Production Board (APB), which was established by the Council for National Defense on May 20, 1917. It included Coffin as chairman; three civilians, all at one dollar a day; and the commanders of the army and navy aviation sections, Gen. G. O. Squier, chief signal officer, and Adm. D. W. Taylor, chief of the Navy Bureau of Construction and Repair. The APB was to "assist and advise" the services and the manufacturers on ways to advance design and "quantity production," on the types of aircraft best suited for each plant, on the best allocation of facilities and priorities between the services, and on whatever new contracting arrangements were needed. Barred from making contracts and given no power to enforce its recommendations, the APB was limited to the powers of suggestion. The enthusiastic Coffin believed these would be effective, that the military would defer to his expert judgment in the same way Congress and the press did, and that with the rapid issue of contracts the manufacturers would forget their differences and rally around the board.[26]

Whatever confidence Coffin had in the board dissipated quickly as deference, contracts, and unity in industry were not forthcoming. Though the nation had been officially at war for nearly three months, the aviation branches of the army and navy guarded their plans carefully and were of course obliged to avoid commitments until Congress had appropriated funds. They largely ignored Coffin's pleas that the wheels of industrial harmony and mass production be started with contracts for simple engines, trainers, and reconnaissance planes. Given the attitudes toward aviation in the military establishment, the desire among Coffin and his associates to keep relations between manufacturers and the military as distant as possible becomes understandable as something more than a result of their ideals of the limited state and their visions of postwar commercial aviation. The military was unprepared intellectually and organizationally to deal with manufacturers on any extended and sophisticated level, and their attempts could well be expected to have only a negative effect.

The military aviation offices were denied the institutional identity that might have allowed them to operate consistently and effectively with industry. Lines of communication were confused by lack of a clear sense of where air power fit within the nation's military doctrines and establishment, a pattern that persisted through the interwar years.[27] Despite popular excitement over air power, the War and Navy departments kept their distances. The War Department reflected America's tradition of an amateur military called upon only in times of emergency. Debates on doctrine and organizational reform revolved around the problems of manpower, its mobilization, its proper use in battle, and the relative merits of a professional army versus the citizen militia. The problems of managing rapidly changing weaponry in an age of industrialized war were accordingly neglected.[28]

The air weapon did not call for the kind of centralized power the civilian planners would come to insist upon to enforce their goals of mass production, but it did call for professional management of technical information from the highest levels of command down to combat squadrons and aircraft plants and back again.[29] Coordination between the services was needed too. The civilian planners initially hoped the pressures for steady and intimate links between the users of aircraft and their suppliers could be lessened by the uniformity of mass production and processed through a civilian advisory board and trade association buffer. Yet rapid technical change and the unpredictabilities of manufacturing aircraft made sustained interaction between technical officers and particular company officials imperative. Aircraft contracting could offer only the roughest guidelines to both parties and became an endless process of revision and renegotiation. Military financing of company expansion as well as cost-plus percentage of cost-contracting made the joint public-private management of aircraft firms inevitable.

But the War and Navy Departments had been arranged by Congress precisely to avoid the kind of centralization required. At the outset, legal barriers to effective military-industrial relations existed, such as a law forbidding government officials from serving without congressional approval on boards with individuals representing private interests.[30] Advance payments and cost-plus contracts, essential for rapid aircraft production, were barred by law until late summer 1917.[31] In addition, career officers harbored a traditional mistrust of private industry that prevailed in their dealings with the aircraft industry throughout the war.[32]

The army was a politicized "hydra-headed holding company" of supply bureaus with separate statutory authority, contracting powers, and congressional funding.[33] Navy bureaus "were far too comfortable in their semi-autonomy to look with any but the most jaundiced eye at anything that suggested diminution of their authority." Control over naval aviation was thus split among the Bureaus of Construction and Repair, Steam Engineering, Navigation, and Ordnance.[34] For Congress, the peacetime military was a fount of federal patronage. It jealously guarded its control over the army and navy and reasserted its claims just as the air weapon was emerging. Theodore Roosevelt and his secretary of war, Elihu Root, had done much to advance hierarchical control and professional army reform, but the National Defense Act of 1916 amounted to a "congressional counteroffensive" on behalf of a "radical devolution of authority" within the services that kept control on Capitol Hill.[35]

The Wilson administration strove to preserve the limited state in its management of the war, but Congress still found much to criticize as unwarranted expansion and centralization of executive power at its expense and to the benefit of big business. The administration, partly out of commitment and partly out of necessary deference to Congress, held up voluntarism, promotion, education, cooperation, and patriotism, rather than central direction, as the moving forces for collective action. It sought to channel these noncoercive forces through public-private advisory committees, consulting boards, and the clearing houses of the associative state. But these proved weak before entrenched interests and bureaucracies in the military and the immense problems of industrial mobilization. Despite shared goals among most businessmen, civilian government advisers, and the military, without effective means for acting upon them in unison, their relations degenerated into conflict, blame, and suspicion. The seemingly ineluctable pressures toward a centrally orchestrated military-industrial complex, so apparent in the advent of military aeronautics, were allowed only minimal fulfillment.[36]

Congress abdicated the direct control over the aircraft program that would later be wielded unforgivingly over the postwar industry and permitted men who claimed to represent the industry and to understand its dynamics to set the program's agenda. But established bureaucratic patterns, career officers, and the two service secretaries were deeply imbued with the values and suspicions that reflected traditional congressional interests and perspectives. They accepted the progressive agenda of mass-produced air power, but their conservatism was reactivated by the patent pool and made itself felt upon the program just as large payments to manufacturers were needed. Coffin and his associates increasingly and mistakenly came to lay all blame on this conservatism for the program's demise and sought new powers to overcome it.

By June 1917 Coffin's patience with the military had worn thin. Displaying a political naivete that undoubtedly contributed to his increasing isolation from actual control over the aircraft program and the larger mobilization effort, he circulated proposals insisting that the direction of production be given entirely to him and that the APB be granted exclusive power to let contracts "without delay" to be funded retroactively by Congress. He argued that the services should concern themselves only with the "military use and maintenance" of aircraft, which civilians would supply. Waiting for Congress and the services to act, he warned, would force manufacturers who were holding facilities and staffs in anticipation of contracts "to disperse."[37]

The situation among aircraft manufacturers had become critical. On the basis of assurances and constant prodding from Coffin, who had led them to believe that he was their liaison to the army and navy, many had proceeded with financing, plant expansion, hiring, and acquisitions of raw material on the scale required for mass production. But still they had no contracts. Others watched helplessly as even some of the small contracts they held were rescinded for lack of funds. Some suspected that Coffin was an agent of the military, which planned to expropriate the industry once it had been built up. Coffin pleaded with them to reject such rumors and continue to prepare for mass production. Their unity and support were now his only hope for some role for the APB in limiting the military's influence over aeronautics. He tempted them with images of billions of dollars in contracts for 100,000 airplanes to be produced "within a couple of years . . . I tell you fellows that this whole situation is absolutely within our hands." He asked them to be patient and to trust the APB "to put more speed and punch and business management into the conduct of this war."[38]

Contracting delays persisted well after appropriation of the $640 million and the August 15 report of the War Department's technical mission to Europe under Raynal C. Bolling of United States Steel, which recommended specific models of aircraft to be built. The Signal Corps had to play its hand deftly as most army bureaus and line officers resented the new prestige of air power and the threats of its enormous and sudden expansion to existing institutional patterns and to their own industrial mobilization plans. Only in late August did the Signal Corps begin to reorganize itself for the staggering tasks it faced. It was responsible for the use and procurement not only of aircraft but also of a vast amount of equipment to fill the army's communication needs. Jealous of its new powers, it would rely on no one but its own offices to recommend contracts. An Equipment Division was created and staffed by newly commissioned figures from the business world. Its chief was Col. Edward Deeds who, along with Sydney Waldon, sensed that the real positions of power were where actual contracts would be made and so deserted Coffin's board.[39]

Panic among overextended manufacturers led them to agree to NACA's and the APB's terms on patents. These agencies had been authorized by the army and navy "to take whatever steps appear necessary to effect a solution to the patent questions." By now Curtiss would agree to "any new policy the government might desire," and Wright-Martin joined the trade association. On July 26, two days after President Wilson signed the "$640 Million Aero Bill," they acquiesced to a cross-licensing scheme managed by a new Manufacturers' Aircraft Association (MAA). To avoid patent suits, manufacturers were required to join and relinquish their patents to the MAA. They were to pay royalties of $200 per airplane delivered, to be forwarded to Wright-Martin and Curtiss until each had accumulated $2 million. The agreement released its subscribers from all pending litigation and gave them the right to unlimited use of airplane patents. To preserve competition each agreed to submit all new patents to the pool and not to license their use to anyone outside of it on more favorable terms. Members were free to accept production contracts for aircraft designed by other members and would be provided with complete drawings and specifications. The APB hailed the agreement as the end to "the virtual monopoly existing under the patent situation" and the "opening of the industry to free competition of all aircraft manufacturers." Since royalty payments were to be accepted as an element of cost in government contracts, the agreement removed patents as a potential barrier to entry into military aircraft manufacture, and over fifty firms joined the pool by war's end.[40]

Instead of harmony and increased production the patent agreement only created new troubles when it was broadly misinterpreted as a tool of aviation monopolists. Claiming to be the voice of small manufacturers and echoing the old populist critique of patent law as the servant of monopoly, the Aeronautical Society of America rekindled charges of an Aircraft Trust and denounced the agreement as spelling the "extinction of all other inventors' rights." Because NACA and the APB agreed that military contracts would include a clause stating that the government would "hold harmless" its contractors from any patent litigation, those contractors were free to use patents of designers outside the patent pool. The society charged that the APB and NACA were staffed by naive engineers and physicists and "guided by trust lawyers." It accurately predicted that military accountants would have great difficulty agreeing to such payments.[41]

In the following months Coffin was occupied primarily with countering charges of an Aircraft Trust rather than with directing aircraft production. Contracts and payments remained elusive, and suspicion among manufacturers, the military, and the government's advisers increased largely because of the patent agreement. Despite manufacturers' investments that expanded factory floor space from 740,000 square feet in July 1917 to 5.3 million in December, contracts were held up as the services tried to determine the types of aircraft they wanted. Delays were also produced by the lack of official approval for cost-plus-bogey contracts, which came from Attorney General T. W. Gregory only in late September, and by the extreme caution of army and navy accountants in all matters of contracting.[42]

Coffin continued to seek ways to enhance what little influence his board retained. He asked Secretary Baker to support a bill that would give him contracting powers; but Baker followed the advice of Navy Secretary Daniels, who regarded the APB as a minefield of conflicting interests and believed that the services could deal with manufacturers on their own. Instead, the board was even further weakened. In October 1917 it was renamed the Aircraft Board and jointly absorbed by the War and Navy Departments. For months Coffin vainly tried to get the secretaries to fill its civilian slots with influential businessmen. He interested Gerard Swope of General Electric, Cyrus McCormick of International Harvester, and Samuel Insull, the utilities magnate, but the secretaries declined to make the appointments. Coffin asked Daniels to appoint Assistant Secretary Roosevelt, but in Daniels's words, FDR "did not desire such responsibility."[43]

So shrill were antitrust attacks that Baker ordered contracting officers to reject royalty payments as elements of costs and recommended restraint in entering into any new aircraft contracts until the attorney general had ruled on the MAA. The attorney general found nothing in the patent pool that constituted restraint of trade. On the contrary he judged the agreement for what it was, an enhancement of competition, an opening of the patents' use to most anyone, but under organized conditions that would facilitate the industry's development.[44] Despite these assurances and Baker's willingness to cover royalties, officers in the Finance Branch of the Signal Corps effectively barred any new contracts or advance payments on existing contracts that included them. They were responsible for preparing contracts, monitoring performance, and making all disbursements and had been well schooled in procurement ethics of economy, accountability, and "the interests of the Government." Their diligence in assuring that estimates of cost in aircraft contracts matched figures presented to Congress caused delays of up to sixty days. They showed little tolerance for inflation, the costs of technical change, or the enormous start-up costs of mass production and placed manufacturers "in the position of having to continually demonstrate their integrity and good faith."[45]

The MAA and rumors of an Aircraft Trust increased old-line officers' natural mistrust of contractors and heightened the aura of suspicion and obstructionism in military-industrial relations, which became the focus of blame for the program's planners. The contracting officers could not see how payments to the MAA "could be explained to an unfriendly audience" and continued to block them. In their views the resulting likely collapse of the MAA was "something very much in the interests of taxpayers." A committee of patent attorneys appointed by the Signal Corps finally turned in its report on January 14, 1918, and concluded that both the Wright and Curtiss patents were "fundamental and controlling" and that the government should make the payments or face certain defeat in court. Coffin asked Baker and Daniels to act quickly and order the contracting officers to make the payments, but the stubborn Daniels held out until the end of March 1918 when the MAA at last agreed to his demand that the royalties be reduced to $100 and payments to Curtiss and Wright be limited to $1 million apiece.[46]

NUMBERS VERSUS PERFORMANCE

In the end, the patent disputes were resolved. But the attacks on the MAA contributed to an inertia among the aircraft program's managers. A sense of frustration emerged in the face of the apparent political futility of trying to direct and salvage the production program, a reluctance to take new approaches, outside mass-production thinking, to its endless complications. In the phrasing of one astonished War Department analyst, these complications "cannot be conceived or described."[47]

The first task was determining the types of aircraft to be produced. Yet decisions here were always second-guessed by rapid technical change, ongoing debates over the proper military role of aircraft, and poor intelligence on developments at a front thousands of miles away. In summer 1917 it was decided to mass-produce the best aircraft in the Allied fleets. Once models were finally chosen, samples had to be shipped across the ocean and broken down piece by piece as few blueprints existed and those that did were in metric units. When armies of draftsmen had produced blueprints (the French SPAD needed three thousand), design and production could begin on innumerable machine tools, jigs, and patterns and on plant arrangements for continuous-flow production. Tooling a plant for what the planners hoped would be mass production took at least four months. Factories had to be financed, built, and staffed by thousands of managers and workers inexperienced in aircraft. Hundreds of specialized parts and enormous quantities of unique, high-grade raw materials such as fabric, dope, and Pacific Northwest spruce had to be accumulated. A multitude of transactions and special contracting provisions to help "carry" contractors had to be arranged and constantly monitored by government auditors.

If all these challenges were somehow met and mass production was ready to begin, startled planners found that developments on the front had rendered the chosen design obsolete; hence planning the disposal of tons of scrap became the new order of the day. If airplanes were produced and had not become useless for combat because of obsolescence or the failure of high-quality standards to survive mass production, the problem of securing sufficient space for this bulky weapon on critically short Atlantic shipping would remain. Once in France, aircraft were grounded without a steady stream of fuel, oil, ordnance, spare parts, and trained mechanics. Bases, hangars, and barracks were also needed, and of course pilots and crew, who took months to train at flying fields that also had to be built.[48]

The aircraft program's logistics were bewildering and largely unanticipated. The key difficulty was the contradictory goal of mass-producing state of the art aircraft, which presented a dilemma under any arrangement of authority over the program. Particularly within the dispersed framework for decision making that defined mobilization in America, endless delays resulted as those wanting nothing but superior aircraft—the military—clashed with businessmen needing to produce.[49] The program's managers increasingly sought to reorganize such symptomatic clashes out of the program, rather than their source. For them, mass production was a matter of faith, an "orthodoxy," an "irresistible paradigm,"[50] the embodiment of progress, American society's crowning achievement. Their efforts had been heavily motivated by demonstrating its universal effectiveness to themselves and to the world. Their confidence in both mass air power and mass production fixed the two inseparably in their minds.

Even if the process could have been frozen in which "performances are bettered, now by the Allies, now by the Germans, from month to month, so that an airplane is generally considered obsolete after only a few months service," the inability of mass production to accommodate a product with the intricacy of wood, fabric, and wire biplanes would remain. Highly refined techniques of mass production could be applied to aircraft engines, as the relative success of the Liberty engine project suggests, but even here the sophistication of an engine's design and materials, as well as relentless changes to produce even the slightest increment in performance, caused continual delays. After incorporating 950 changes to the Liberty by March 1918, Henry Ford would permit no more on those he had contracted to build. "We are going to shut our eyes and produce as we stand equipped," he announced. High-performance aircraft engines also needed the flexibility of skilled-craft labor.[51]

Pioneer manufacturers heartily criticized the attempt of the "auto interests" to impose mass production. In Los Angeles, the young Glenn L. Martin, who with only ten years experience was a veteran in this new field, refused to reorganize for the production schedules insisted upon in Washington, D.C. For this he was blacklisted by the Aircraft Production Board and squeezed out of the Wright-Martin combine in summer 1917. He was denied contracts because he insisted that only three aircraft per day at the very most be expected of him. As a result, his skills and experience and those of other pioneers, were ignored until summer 1918. Then the army turned to him to build prototypes of a bomber which he, Donald W. Douglas, and Laurence D. Bell had prepared as early as summer 1917. It became the army standard and the world's best in the early 1920s. Putting aside questions of the military value of bombers, or of air power as a whole during the war—questions which would have plagued the aircraft program no matter how successful—Martin might well have produced 1,000 state of the art bombers by war's end. Similarly, the designs of Thomas-Morse Aircraft, Chance M. Vought, and Grover Loening, which later became first-class models, were ignored, as were their

Four young men who were already key figures in the American aircraft industry in 1918. From left to right, Laurence D. Bell (twenty-four years old); Thomas E. Springer, a test pilot (twenty-six); Glenn L. Martin (thirty-two); and Donald W. Douglas (twenty-six). They pose before an MB-1 bomber, which they designed together with James Kindleberger (twenty-three) in early 1917. The Martin bomber was ignored by the Air Service until March 1918 and it flew for the first time in August 1918. Powered by two 400-horsepower Liberty-12 engines, the MB-1 was capable of 105 miles per hour, carried a crew of three, and had a range of 390 miles.

calls for more flexible and less ambitious approaches to production. New but experienced smaller firms, such as Boeing Airplane, Witteman-Lewis, and Aeromarine were also largely passed over.[52]

The experiences of Curtiss Aeroplane, the largest contractor, illustrate the confusion, waste, and hostility among all concerned that developed when the aircraft industry was made to act as a vehicle for the ideology of mass production. In 1916 the Wall Street syndicate that bought out Glenn Curtiss borrowed heavily to expand capacity, acquire large stocks of material, and create a system of mass production for a series of British trainer and flying boat orders. By summer 1917, 2,200 Curtiss workers in Buffalo were assembling aircraft in a plant fed by adjacent woodworking

A panoramic view of the Fuselage Department of Curtiss Aeroplane Company in Buffalo, April 1917. In the foreground workers assemble the R-6 reconnaissance plane. In the rear are fuselage frames for JN-4 "Jenny" trainers.

and metalfitting plants, and another 540 workers assembled engines with parts made elsewhere. But auditors hired by the army to study the company in July 1917 reported that "changes in design were often made by customers after drawings and patterns had been prepared and the work gotten under way, which would upset the factory routine and cause delay and loss." They found unfilled orders, tons of wasted material, "absolute disarray in the company's accounts," no control over inventory, and "severe working capital problems." Still, they remained confident that with time and better management, mass production of aircraft at Curtiss would succeed.[53]

So did John N. Willys, president of Willys-Overland Company. Under Coffin's prodding and seduced by the vision of a boundless future for commercial aviation, he tried to rescue Curtiss in June 1917 with $2 million in cash, a new stock issue, and the techniques of mass production he had honed in his automobile works. He brought in new managers— Clement M. Keys, James E. Kepperly, and William A. Morgan—the latter "a business man of the new type, an idealist of the practical kind." On August 1, the aggressive Willys began construction of a $5.5 million plant in Buffalo. Again, Coffin encouraged this move and did nothing to dissuade Willys from his false impressions that Coffin and his APB were responsible for the program just signed into law and that the government would help finance the building. Severe cash-flow problems persisted at Curtiss as bottlenecks in production put delivery on the company's British contracts well behind schedule. As new army and navy contracts and money awaited decisions on types, an exasperated Clement Keys exclaimed, "Do you want us or don't you want us?"[54]

In September the Signal Corps decided on the SPAD, a French fighter

The French-built SPAD XIII fighter in 1918 with U.S. markings.

popular on the front. Gen. John J. Pershing requested 3,000 with a more powerful 200-horsepower Liberty engine, and on the eighteenth three sample SPADs arrived in Buffalo. After examining the planes, Sydney Waldon nervously warned Curtiss executives that the SPAD would not lend itself to mass production. For him, it demonstrated the need to "educate our workmen to entirely new standards," to "a degree of perfection that we know nothing about in this country." Nevertheless, a $30 million contract was signed and work was begun on redesigning the SPAD for mass production with the still undeveloped 8-cylinder Liberty. Tooling was begun, jigs built, tons of material and parts amassed. While the army deliberated week after week on an advance payment for the company, Willys was forced to negotiate a $4 million short-term loan in a very tight money-market. After two weeks of effort it was decided that the SPAD's design would be too greatly compromised by the Liberty and preparations were made at Wright-Martin to produce its original French Hispano-Suiza engine.[55]

By early October reports from the front described advances in German models that had made the SPAD "worse than useless" as was any combat aircraft not state of the art. Pershing advised that developments were moving too fast to settle on a combat design for production in the United States and that American efforts should focus on trainers while combat

This detail of the tail section of the SPAD, an array of wooden slats, metal fittings, and wire, suggests the intricacy of aircraft assembly and the challenges of quantity production during World War I.

planes were purchased in Europe. Still, Colonel Deeds ordered 1,500 SPADs on behalf of the Signal Corps. Army finance officers, irritated by the patent pool and mistrustful of the former manufacturer in charge of the Equipment Division, forced Willys to supply his personal note against a $1.5 million advance on the order. With Curtiss's general manager, William Morgan, "on verge of breakdown" [sic], Wright-Martin discovered it could not deliver the engines, and work on the SPAD was halted in mid-November. Without signing a contract, the army then told Curtiss to plan for mass-producing 2,000 two-seat British Bristol fighters undergoing redesign for the Liberty 12-cylinder. Curtiss was completely trapped. It could not even complain publicly because of secrecy restrictions. "The promises of the Board . . . the scores of men exercising more or less authority and more or less ability on behalf of the Government [are] fatal to the corporation . . . far from being able to crowd our great new plant to the doors with fighting machines [it] stands idle today and to all appearances will continue to stand idle for some time." Trainer and navy seaplane orders kept Curtiss at only 30 percent operating capacity. Its workers and managers were deserting, the company was almost bankrupt, and the Signal Corps Finance Division refused to compensate Curtiss for such outlays on the SPAD project as $300,000 worth of plywood.[56]

The responses of the military and the government's civilian advisers to the problems at Curtiss reveal their unwillingness to rethink the program's premise that high quality aircraft could be mass-produced. The minutes of a January meeting of the Aircraft Board, notable for the actual attendance of all its members, indicate how responsibility and accountability were lost among the program's dispersed centers of authority. They also suggest the planners' sensitivity to the political constraints upon a more centralized approach and their frustration as they came to think that such an approach would make mass production work. Coffin and the manufacturers blamed one another for broken promises and the services for allowing the desire for technically advanced aircraft to interfere with production. Army and navy representatives blamed each other for mutual interference and the manufacturers for incompetence and insufficient flexibility to accommodate technical change.[57]

Army and navy career officers scoffed at Curtiss's complaints and the need for any new approaches. They agreed the company was "the greatest problem we have got" but insisted its difficulties and failures to mass-produce were the results of poor management on the company's part that it could correct if only it found better people. The military's attitude toward Curtiss reflected its institutional conservatism and its intellectual resistance to the new challenges created by its desire for both technically advanced aircraft and a minimal role in the affairs of private enterprise, which it counted on to provide them. Summing up the attitude that largely guided the government through the war and beyond, Admiral Taylor simply stated that "the buyer is not responsible for production." In January 1918 as Curtiss's situation worsened, Coffin broached the suggestion of a military takeover of the company, but this was rejected by the army. He then proposed that the directors of the patent pool study the problems at Curtiss and make recommendations. But Colonel Deeds rejected even this as likely to produce "many prejudices" in the press and in Congress. They decided to satisfy themselves with the resignation of Curtiss's general manager, W. A. Morgan, the continuation of chaos in Buffalo, and the provision of large advance payments to stave off Curtiss's collapse.[58]

In December 1917 contracts worth $23 million were signed with Curtiss for the Bristol which was to replace the SPAD. Blueprints were finally completed by the end of January and production on the first twenty-five began. One government inspector described such "rotten" friction between army inspectors and company officials and between the company's production and engineering departments that they were not even consulting one another. A government auditor reported hundreds of workers standing about "loafing," the waste of material, and the "impossibility of making any kind of accounting." Another described millions of dollars in unexplainable invoices "scattered about among the offices and desks of the various plants." Meanwhile in Washington, the Signal Corps was immobilized by bureaucratic turmoil, "enormous red tape," and "demoralized" employees who "run rampant all over the building" and regarded their work as temporary and futile.[59]

Curtiss finished a Bristol on March 5 but its crash revealed the need for structural changes to bear the vibration of its overpowered Liberty 12-cylinder engine and the weight of more guns and accessories demanded by the army. By early May Curtiss owed the government $14 million in advances and was seeking another $5 million. A redesigned Bristol was ready to go to production in early June but its weight was still too great. A series of fatal crashes led the army to refuse further delivery. In late July the Bristol project was canceled, its prototypes and spare parts scrapped. Meanwhile Pershing and his staff had changed their mind on the SPAD, as improvements in the basic design by the French produced a formidable fighter. An order for 1,000 was placed in April but none were produced. In July Pershing's aviators were buying every French SPAD they could. By summer 1918 the government's policy was simply to keep advancing new money to Curtiss to help it pay off old advances. So great was the concern to maintain the impression of Curtiss's and the aircraft program's viability that the company was even permitted to distribute small dividends.[60]

Despite massive expenditures, as late as early March 1918 only 100 pilots had been trained and just 1,450 simple trainers produced. Only 5 percent of plant space available nationwide was being used for production of combat planes. Coffin's board at last began to fill a useful function for the military, serving as a clearinghouse for the waves of criticism that rose up in Congress and the press as these facts became more broadly known. In one analyst's words, "Neither the public, nor congressmen, who knew more than the public, could believe that American ingenuity was insufficient for the execution of the program."[61] Most did not believe it although others were delighted to have yet another way of attacking the Wilson administration. For them, the program's failures and the $200 million deficit run up by the Signal Corps by April 1918 could be explained only by graft and a conspiracy between an Aircraft Trust and its agents in the government. As the *New York Times* darkly put it: "These conditions plainly point to an organized conspiracy, bold, powerful, made up of numerous men able to formulate a great and definite plan."[62]

President Wilson was one of the first to accept the explanation of conspiracy for the aircraft program's demise. In mid-January 1918 he secretly authorized the sculptor Gutzon Borglum, who claimed to have evidence of malfeasance, to investigate the program's planners. Borglum's unsubstantiated attacks on Colonel Deeds were published in mid-March, and both Deeds and Coffin were forced to resign. Coffin secured a statement from the army's judge advocate general reaffirming the merely advisory powers of the board and the voluntary basis of the program to help him deny that it could have done all the corrupt things it was being charged with. The House, Senate, War Department, and Department of Justice launched investigations. The latter was directed by the jurist Charles Evans Hughes, Wilson's opponent for the presidency in 1916. Hughes's investigation, like the others, found much evidence of organizational confusion, evaporated funds, and insensitivity in matters of conflict of interest, especially on the part of Colonel Deeds, but nothing resembling corruption or conspiracy. However, their findings were not published until months later.[63]

Meanwhile the aircraft program provided an endless source for attacks on the Wilson administration's alleged capitulation to big business and restrained new initiatives by the program's planners. They were "unwilling to risk anything to improve production," complained John D. Ryan, the copper magnate appointed by Baker to replace Coffin on the Aircraft Board.[64] Passage of the Overman Act on May 20, 1918, gave the president new authority to reorganize the war agencies, and the Signal Corps lost control over army aviation. A new bureau, the Air Service, was created and divided between a Division of Military Aeronautics (DMA) under Gen. W. L. Kenly, which would select the army's aircraft and oversee their "military use," and a Bureau of Aircraft Production (BAP) under Ryan, which would manage production and supply. The separation of the operation and production of military aircraft was finally made, an organizational move long sought by Coffin and the manufacturers as a guarantor of private control of aircraft manufacture and as an end to friction and interference.

Still, interference was not eliminated by this change. Baker declined to appoint a chief of the Air Service, and delays and disputes continued not only between the two divisions but within them as well. At minimum, mass production of aircraft needed "frozen" designs, but the military could hardly be expected to commit itself to designs that it thought would embarrass it in battle. As Ryan put it to Senators, "If one department had the use and the real say so as to the types and another had production, and both were trying to play it safe, there would not be any production." On June 19 B. D. Gray, a Philadelphia industrialist, resigned as head of the BAP's effort to speed production because of "interference" by the military, which continued to demand design changes during production to such an extent "that there was no longer any hope of bringing about an improved condition of affairs."[65]

Because of continuing turmoil in the program despite reorganization, as well as ongoing attempts by congressmen to ferret out scandal, C. W. Nash, former president of General Motors, was reluctant to accept Ryan's request that he bring his mass-production skills to the BAP. It took Ryan two months to convince Nash that "he was not throwing away his reputation as a successful manufacturer and an upright citizen." Congress was suspicious but firm enough in its faith in aviation to appropriate another $840 million for army aviation. Only then, on July 17, 1918, did Nash finally accept appointment as assistant to the director of aircraft production at one dollar a day. His efforts were occupied with trying to formulate a coordinated system in which information on production problems and technical change could flow rapidly, decisions could be made quickly, and delays in production minimized. Yet as he admitted to senators in August, the BAP's plans to mass-produce 20,000 front-line aircraft by July 1919 were futile, as was most of the nearly $400 million so far expended on aircraft, since the "machine that is satisfactory to the Department of Military Aeronautics has yet to be built."[66]

Another attempt at salvaging the aircraft program through reorganization was made on August 31 when Secretary Baker unified command of army aviation under Ryan, who was appointed second assistant secretary of war and director of the Air Service. Ryan immediately left for a six-week European tour. By the time he returned, German forces were collapsing and the war came to an end before whatever success this reorganization might have had in realizing the aircraft program's conflicting goals could become apparent.

Much was made of the large numbers of the durable and legendary Jenny trainers Curtiss turned out but much less of its unchanging simplicity and the fact that 1,200 had to be destroyed as defectively produced at a loss of over $6 million. Many also pointed to the rapidly accelerating production of the DeHaviland observation plane, which increased from the approximately 1,800 in September 1918 to the incredible figure of 4,000 in

DeHaviland DH-4 fuselages lined up for a publicity photo outside the Dayton-Wright plant in Dayton, Ohio, July 1918. Only with this obsolete model did the planners of the World War I aircraft program approach their ideal of large-scale production in airframes.

November. However, this cumbersome craft only underscored the flawed approach taken by the Americans to providing themselves with air power. The DH-4, already obsolete in summer 1917, was built by Fisher Body and Dayton-Wright Corporation, which had been organized to mass-produce aircraft for the war. The great resources poured into it were clearly driven more by the desires to get something—anything—to the front and to salvage as much of the program and various reputations as possible. So strong were these pressures that Dayton-Wright shipped DH-4s to the front after randomly testing one in six. There the aircraft was reviled by aviators as the "flying coffin" and at home by congressmen as "more than ordinarily dangerous." Then, too, the mass-produced Liberty engine was criticized for encouraging a false sense of the possibilities of standardizing aircraft for mass production. Aircraft were designed or redesigned to conform to that single engine well into the postwar years when a range of different aircraft types, each evolving rapidly, required a reverse of that approach.[67]

The World War I aircraft program represented America's first taste of the seemingly inherent wastefulness and uncontrollable costs of military aircraft production, and it left a bad aftertaste for a long time. When unexpended funds were returned to the Treasury, the final tally for wartime army aviation was $720 million. After the Air Service's operational costs were deducted, a figure of about $600 million remained to be accounted for by aircraft and engines. Nearly $80 million was spent trying to develop new supplies of spruce, dope, fabric, and castor oil, a figure that can be included in production costs. During the war the average price of both aircraft and engines was about $6,000 apiece, and the army received 41,000 engines and 19,000 airplanes. Thus it paid $600 million for engines and aircraft worth $384 million. In terms of value received this figure is still too generous, for while the figure of 19,000 aircraft included 5,500 advanced aircraft purchased from the Allies, it also included 8,600 simple trainers worth much less than $6,000 each. Although impossible to compute, military value received by the taxpayer must be further reduced because of the 4,900 remaining service aircraft built by the Americans; the bulk was represented by the DH-4. Most of the waste can be attributed to the priorities of the program's planners, but some must also be credited to the rapid rates of obsolescence and deterioration of early aircraft. The great postwar bonfires in Europe in which thousands of surplus aircraft were disposed of testified to these dynamics but were widely viewed as confirmation that the American people had been systematically swindled.[68]

Historians have found much evidence that, for better or worse, many of the corporatist experiments in the management of wartime mobilization left enduring legacies for peacetime social and economic management and that the ideology and methods of corporatism American style—organized private elites directing positive but limited state intervention to regulate change and foster growth in accord with scientific principles—were generally legitimized.[69] Still, it was in the aircraft industry where engineers, scientists, and technological change were so prominent and where partnerships between industry and government so necessary that the wartime experiments in political economic reform were most thoroughly rejected. Aviation continued to generate futuristic fantasies, including that of an independent, mass-production, commercial aircraft industry managed by enlightened elites; but the industry's bread and butter remained military aircraft, leaving it open to the whims of an angry Congress. Despite the hopes of corporatist reformers, aircraft manufacture did not help resolve the tensions of a modern, industrial political economy committed to traditional, democratic ideals. In their hands it preserved and heightened the pressures.

CHAPTER THREE

Congress's Business:
A Peacetime Industry at War

PUNITIVE PRICE COMPETITION

If the wartime aircraft program was a failure for the American version of technology-based corporatism and for the "ethos of mass production,"[1] it was also a disaster for America's new aircraft industry, and its effects were felt throughout the interwar years. On the level of industry structure, the wartime expansion left a large reservoir of expertise and skills that fed the natural competitiveness of the industry during its early "stick-and-wire" years. Yet the war's legacy was most critical on the political level since in the end the industry's structure was a matter of national politics. Its dependence on military spending allowed Congress to punish the industry for its wartime performance and prevent it from establishing regulatory mechanisms that could have helped it maintain a stable and healthier business environment for the development of aeronautics.

The suspicion that only conspiracy, graft, and fraud could explain a failure on such a scale lingered through the interwar years and was fundamental in the industry's development, along with desires in Congress to preserve decentralized principles of governance and market capitalism. Although they saw little more than what they wanted to see, congressmen kept the industry under constant scrutiny, investigating and reinvestigating it numerous times. During the war, its government overseers had tried to make the industry vindicate a corporatist vision of reformed capitalism and might have achieved a significant part of that goal had they not so thoroughly linked mass production and air power. Until World War II, the congressional overseers tried to make the industry a model of traditional, laissez-faire capitalism, an ideology for which it was equally unsuited. Most congressmen concluded that the wartime deficiency resulted from a failure to give free enterprise sufficient reign. Manufacturers in league with "dollar-a-year" men in the government had hoarded the business and then not performed. Despite no evidence of the "Aircraft Trust" so earnestly sought by "these little narrow committees," as they were contemptuously called by Clement Keys, president of Curtiss Aeroplane, congressmen used their powers over military contracting to preserve a destructive, competitive regulatory environment for aircraft manufacture. They hoped to cleanse the industry through the supposedly purifying forces of stiff price competition.[2]

Congress's competitive approach was encouraged by the war's other major legacy to the industry, a vast reserve of the essential elements of aircraft manufacture—aeronautic engineers, skilled aircraft workers, and entrepreneurs whose enthusiasm for aeronautics was much stronger than their business acumen. While investment in the industry contracted by about 90 percent to a mere $5 million in 1919–1920 and production shrank from 14,000 aircraft in 1918 to 263 in 1922,[3] more than 100,000 workers, engineers, and managers remained who had been involved with aircraft manufacture during the war, along with 20,000 pilots and thousands more administrative officers, mechanics, and the like mustered out of the military after the Armistice. For them, "aviation is a new lure." They "are coming back with a craving for space," especially "those men who have been up in the air, who have been flying."[4]

This reserve of "air-minded" men was the only true measure of value received for the hundreds of millions of wartime tax dollars. In the broadest sense it provided the foundation of experience for what became the heart of American global power during and after World War II. In the short term it meant an inexhaustible private base of designers, workers, managers, and investors whom Congress exploited with ease for two decades, thereby recouping some of its wartime losses. The builders of aircraft—manufacturers and workers—effectively subsidized military aviation as too many companies eagerly competed to supply the few aircraft that Congress was willing to fund and drove the value of military contracts below the costs of development and production.

Data on the profitability of early aircraft firms is scarce. It does not seem possible to determine how the various firms fared during the war, so poorly kept and thoroughly scattered by the numerous investigations of the industry were the records of the wartime procurement agencies. It can be assumed that had large profits been made, they would have received greater prominence in these investigations; the firms themselves apparently left no records. But if the way in which accounting practice was overwhelmed at Curtiss can be taken as the norm for the industry, then it is likely that few aircraft manufacturers or anyone else ever had a clear sense of where they stood. Despite cost-plus contracts, some of the larger firms such as Curtiss and Standard Aircraft finished the war with heavy debt, most of it to the Treasury.[5]

Profitability data remains scarce until most aircraft firms went public in the late 1920s. Even then it is difficult to use because of the standard practice of deferring large development charges against future earnings on expected production contracts that usually did not materialize.[6] This practice, along with arbitrary valuations of such intangible assets as patents and "goodwill"—a company's name—gave manufacturers much leeway in presenting the health or weakness of their firms. Their figures are not entirely reliable. However, numerous bankruptcies, the manufacturers' business strategies, and their constant complaints under oath of losses and inability to draw outside investors make it plain that Congress successfully exploited and punished the industry. Firms such as Standard, Gallaudet, Thomas-Morse, L.W.F. Engineering, and Aeromarine lost heavily on postwar government contracts and folded early. John J. Raskob and Alfred P. Sloan, hard-headed vice-presidents at General Motors, decided to withdraw GM from the aircraft field and liquidated Dayton-Wright at the end of 1922 when its postwar losses amounted to $400,000. "The present market," wrote Raskob, "is entirely Army and Navy and so much difficulty has been found in dealing with the Government that it is considered useless to carry on."[7]

Other firms, never employing more than two to three hundred workers, survived but generally operated with losses or unhealthy profits. Curtiss lost heavily on military sales of $8.2 million from 1919 to 1924. From May 1923 to the end of 1927, Consolidated Aircraft lost 10 percent on its $3.2 million in military sales. From 1920 to 1923, Glenn L. Martin Company returned 4 percent on $3.5 million. After absorbing losses in its first two years of operation, Douglas Aircraft, founded in 1922, became an important exception to the pattern of unprofitability until losses began to accumulate in the late 1920s and through most of the 1930s. In the years 1924–1927, Douglas showed profits on sales of 2.1 percent, 13 percent, 22 percent, and 18 percent. Returns on sales, however, could not be viewed as conventional profits as the manufacturers continually pointed out. To stay in the business and to satisfy their desires to build better aircraft, manufacturers were compelled to reinvest any earnings in new designs. Douglas's profits were all "plowed back" into the business.[8]

A highly competitive aircraft industry was the outcome of its relative simplicity during the 1920s but more directly of congressional policy, which prevented the leading firms and the army and navy from managing competition. Negative attitudes in Congress toward military spending severely limited the aircraft market's size. The Army Air Service distributed only $19 million in major aircraft contracts among fifteen contractors during 1919–1924 (see Appendix 1). More critical were the rules that Congress insisted the military follow as it went about the business of buying aircraft. As a virtual monopoly client, the government wielded de facto regulatory power over the industry. But Congress refused to allow the military to use that power to rationalize aircraft manufacture, limit competition, allow long-range business and technical planning, and encourage military aeronautics. Congress insisted that the military contract for aircraft as if a free market prevailed.

To observe Congress's wish for the preservation of free enterprise, the lowest bid, and equal access to federal contracts, values at the heart of "the statutory tradition"[9] of regulations governing procurement practice, the army and navy were forced to ignore the manufacturers' proprietary rights to their designs. Only if aircraft designs were considered public property could there be open price competition for production contracts. Firms that maintained costly design staffs and lost money on producing new aircraft prototypes could do nothing to suppress the industry's natural competitive forces. These included the strong noneconomic appeals of aircraft manufacture to entrepreneurs, the rapidly evolving nature of the industry's product, which provided many windows for new entry, and the industry's high labor intensity, which kept the costs of entry low. Manufacturers might have contained this competitive turmoil had the government recognized and not expropriated their design rights. Had manufacturers' design rights been observed, concentration and rationalization of the industry would likely have been quickly achieved, most particularly when the costs of new development ballooned during the transition to metal aircraft in the late 1920s and early 1930s.

Congress imposed a "dog eat dog era of destructive competition."[10] Manufacturers were forced to compete in two markets kept artificially distinct. First they competed for "experimental contracts." The services circulated specifications and performance requirements, and manufacturers responded with design proposals on paper along with their prices to build prototypes. Two to four of these proposals were accepted and "experimental contracts" were issued. Whether out of ignorance or in an attempt to assure themselves positions in the running, manufacturers almost invariably underestimated the costs of building their prototypes and accumulated substantial overruns. The completed prototypes were paid for by the military at prices well below cost and became public property. Manufacturers then squared off in performance competitions, which determined the services' final choice for production. The next stage of competition came when the production contracts for selected designs were opened to bidding. At this stage competition hinged almost solely on price, and designers who needed to amortize their development costs were at a great disadvantage. Manufacturers such as Clement Keys complained about the delays of competitive contracting for production and the fact that "the designer can never be the lowest bidder on production work."[11]

Essential to Congress's success through the interwar years in extracting from private industry a good share of the costs of military aircraft was the seemingly unending willingness of entrepreneurs to stay in the business despite congressional abuse. In 1919 Secretary of War Baker called for a long-term procurement program for military aircraft and warned Congress that "it cannot be expected that industry will long engage in an unremunerative line," but he underestimated aircraft manufacturers for whom the industry's appeals defied rational calculation. For some, apart from such conservatives as Raskob and Sloan at General Motors, the glamour and prestige of a "progressive" industry were irresistible. For others, personal commitments to rapid progress in aeronautics and the development of the nation's air power made aircraft manufacture more a calling than a business. "Achievement in engineering and airplane performance was the motivation rather than the profit, which was as tempting and as elusive as the pot of gold at the end of the rainbow."[12] Windows of opportunity abounded for those seeking to follow their callings, provided in part by the sheer diversity of aeronautic technology, its reliance on numerous separate technical spheres—aerodynamics, propulsion, structural engineering, materials, and so on—the rapid pace of change, and the fact that basic developments, often made outside the industry in agencies like the National Advisory Committee for Aeronautics, were available to all.

Noneconomic reward as a prime motive of entrepreneurship and the development of science and technology as largely independent of market variables are classic perceptions of these forces supported by the early aircraft industry's experiences. Instead of the "typical" capitalist who sought to protect markets and maintain economic security, the entrepreneur had other goals.[13] William McNeill has pointed out the noneconomic motives of high-technology military entrepreneurs—patriotism, problem solving, and a desire to be on the edge of technical change. Illustrative of these qualities was one of the loudest and most articulate critics of Congress's policies, Clement Keys, who controlled Curtiss Aeroplane. In response to suspicious congressmen's questioning on why he remained in the business if it were so unprofitable, he answered that he was willing to subsidize the development and production of military aircraft in the vague hope that he might "earn money in the future." Although a Canadian, Keys was driven by a patriotic concern that "this country would remain a second rate power in the air and would be a laggard behind Europe for many years." He had been irked by "the comments of the British and the French and the Italians who came over here and talked about the superiority of their staffs, when I knew very well that we had in the Curtiss Co. . . . plenty of ability to hold our own with Europe, in fact, to beat them in the air." When Willys-Overland, in the midst of an auto-industry recession, put Curtiss into receivership in August 1920, Keys, who owned a lucrative Wall Street bond business, borrowed $650,000 to buy its worthless stock and pay off some of its debts. The reasons "that I did that foolish thing . . . and I have often been sorry since" were "regaining some prestige in the air . . . giving the United States an aircraft industry," and doing "what we could to keep the flag flying." From 1920 to 1928, he drew no salary as president of Curtiss and paid his own expenses. Secretary of War Baker reportedly had bet Keys five dollars that he could not compete with the Europeans for speed records. Baker lost the bet when Curtiss aircraft, largely at Keys's expense, set numerous world records during the first half of the 1920s.[14]

These sentiments rather than the profit motive explain the persistence of other wartime manufacturers such as William E. Boeing, who was also independently wealthy. Boeing owned real estate in Seattle and vast tracts of Pacific Northwest timber and Mesabi Range iron ore. He viewed the aircraft business more or less as a hobby. Noneconomic sentiments also explain entry into the business during its least promising postwar years by Donald W. Douglas, Chance M. Vought, Reuben H. Fleet, who established Consolidated Aircraft in Buffalo, and Henry Ford, who bought Stout Metal Airplane in 1925 and was able to absorb losses on the Ford Tri-Motor transport that reportedly approached $3 million.[15]

If noneconomic motives to participation in the industry were strong, economic barriers were weak, acting as further inducements to enter and

Table 3.1. Current Assets and Property and Equipment as Percentages
of Total Capital in Aircraft Manufacture, 1921–1930

	1921	1922	1923	1924	1925	1926	1927	1928	1929	1930
Current assets	61	40	59	58	61	45	45	62	70	71
Property and equipment	24	16	32	31	28	22	23	33	22	28

Current assets include cash, raw materials, parts, and inventory. Total capital equals net
worth plus total debt.

Source: Paul A. Dodd, Financial Policies in the Aviation Industry (Philadelphia: University of
Pennsylvania, 1933), 93.

stay in the business. Participation was at least a manageable risk since
capital was mostly liquid (see Table 3.1). Still, although they did not have
to be tied up in machinery and other fixed assets, aircraft manufacture
did require financial resources. Most of a firm's capital was in designs,
which, according to their main client on Capitol Hill, were not worth anything beyond the undervalued first prototype. The risks for manufacturers who wanted to create new aircraft increased rapidly as aircraft became more sophisticated and as a monopoly client continued to pay less
than full value for the products it desired. Manufacturers had to be able to
absorb the costs of development and to view rare profits on production
contracts as "surplus," only to be reinvested in new designs.[16]

Moreover, to win military contracts manufacturers had to post performance bonds; and since advance payments were barred by law[17] and
most contracts took months, sometimes years to complete, day-to-day
cash flow had to be financed. Nevertheless, the primitive state and low
value of aircraft in the early years meant that many could shoulder these
costs. The length of time required to complete contracts also meant that
actual costs were not perceived until work was well advanced. Even then
manufacturers continued with supreme confidence in their products, in
the hope that a "responsible" government would see the desirability of
their financial health and help them amortize cost overruns through
"follow-on" orders. If in rare cases those orders came, it was only because
contracting officers were willing to stretch the law.

Aircraft manufacture was labor-intensive, an industry of expertise dependent upon the careful orchestration of engineering talent and many
traditional craft skills.[18] Wages and salaries figured as the major elements by far among the costs of producing aircraft. Table 3.2 shows the
heavy proportion of costs absorbed by wages to which must be added the
costs of a high concentration of salaried employees. In those years for

Table 3.2. Wages as a Percentage of Value-Added to Aircraft and
Aircraft Parts Manufacture, 1919–1939

	Wage Earners	Wages (in $Thousands)	Value of Products	Value-Added by Manufacture	Wages as a % of Value-Added by Manufacture
1919	3,638	4,907	14,373	7,246	67.7
1921	1,395	2,202	6,642	4,235	51.9
1923	2,901	4,522	12,945	9,155	46.8
1925	2,701	4,222	12,525	9,655	43.7
1927	4,422	6,875	21,162	13,645	50.3
1929	14,710	21,924	71,153	43,785	50.0
1931	9,870	15,481	40,278	27,177	56.9
1933	7,816	10,308	26,460	18,503	55.7
1935	11,384	14,893	45,347	31,050	47.9
1937	30,384	43,827	149,700	93,144	47.0
1939	48,638	77,488	279,497	183,247	42.2

Value-added is the difference between the final value of output and the cost of materials used in production. Figures for 1935, 1937, and 1939 include more capital-intensive engine manufacture.

Source: Compiled from Statistical Abstract of the United States, Department of Commerce, Washington, D.C. (1924), 749; (1928), 773; (1929), 809; (1933), 715; (1942), 917.

which complete figures are available, there was one salaried officer or employee (engineer, draftsman, shop superviser, and so on) for every three wage earners (see Table 3.3).

The major requirement for participation in the industry was access to a group of trained and committed men and women, widely available thanks to wartime expansion, along with adequate hand tools and a reasonably large building that could be located where runways could be built. Skilled handwork and little special machinery were needed. Small orders, technical change, and the complexity òf the product made low-unit volume inevitable, the techniques of mechanized production inapplicable, and their capital costs unnecessary.[19]

The transition to metal in aircraft construction during the late 1920s and early 1930s did not alter these basic features of the industry. A metal airframe was a complicated structure made up of tens of thousands of parts fabricated from chrome molybdenum and aluminum sheet and extrusions. Aircraft assembly had to conform to the tightest of tolerances and was quite unlike the assembly of products such as automobiles or electrical appliances, which were comprised of rigid machined parts with large mating surfaces. Aircraft parts—spars, ribs, bulkheads, and so

Chance Vought woodworkers, mostly boys and some women, make wing ribs by
hand for the Vought O2U Corsair navy observation plane at Long Island City,
probably in 1927. The O2U saw action with the marines in Nicaragua against
Sandino's rebels in 1928.

on—could not usually be completed in advance of assembly as inter-
changeable parts of aircraft in a production series. This was so not only
because so many changes had to be made to accommodate continual technical advances, even within the same production series, but also because
of the large size of aircraft parts, their variegated, twisting contours, and
the flexibility of the material used.[20] Metal aircraft called for much
greater use of machinery and tooling. However, until the large exports of
the 1930s, product differentiation and intricacy meant that whatever new
manufacturing technologies were applied tended to augment rather than
eliminate the need for the skills of aircraft workers.

Its craft base and technical dynamics suggest the industry's suitability
for "flexible specialization," an organization of manufacture recently described by M. J. Piore and C. F. Sabel as a historical alternative to mass
production, one much better able to accommodate rapid technical change.
Their more general arguments about how modes of production and tech-

Table 3.3. Employment in the Aircraft Industry, 1914–1939

	Wage Earners, Average for Year	Salaried Officers and Employees	Total
1914	168	54	222
1919	3,638	659	4,202
1921	1,395	557	1,952
1925	2,701	N.A.	N.A.
1927	4,422	1,064	5,486
1929	14,710	3,910	18,620
1931	9,870	N.A.	N.A.
1933	7,816	1,810	9,626
1935	11,384	3,547	14,931
1937[1]	24,003	7,917	31,920
1937	30,384	N.A.	N.A.
1939[1]	48,638	15,233	63,994

[1]Includes aircraft, parts, and engine manufacture. Engines not included in other figures.

Source: H. O. Stekler, The Structure and Performance of the Aerospace Industry (Berkeley: University of California Press, 1965), 8.

Fabric workers prepare wings for the Vought O2U Corsair.

Wallpaperers and painters apply their skills to control surfaces for the 02U Corsair.

nical change are largely determined and given institutional momentum by political choices and state intervention also fit the aircraft industry's experiences during the interwar years. Its leading spokesmen advocated a system similar to Piore and Sabel's model but repeatedly failed to persuade Congress to alter its regulatory framework in ways that would have allowed them to realize flexible specialization. In this system skilled workers in close collaboration with managers of small- and medium-sized firms make sophisticated and ever-changing products. Sharing emotional commitments to a product or technology and to the stability of a community of workers, designers, and employers, these firms compete on the basis of quality and performance of products rather than on price. At the same time different firms cooperate to encourage "permanent innovation" in the product and in manufacturing techniques, both on behalf of technical advance and industry stability in a competitive international market. Given that aircraft manufacturers were more interested in technical advance and prestige than in profits and given the technical scope and dynamism of aircraft manufacture and the range of different types of aircraft needed, such a competitive-cooperative arrangement seemed ideal. As Keys put it in 1923 in his plea for continued commitment to the industry by General Motors, "[there is] plenty of room for everybody . . . we might as well dabble, it seems to me, in separate branches, so as to gain as much in the aggregate as possible."[21]

But flexible specialization and permanent innovation in a craft industry depend on the ability of separate firms to generate mutual trust and on industry organizations for cooperation and planning and for the prevention of price competition through new entry and wage reductions. Sabel and Piore cite communal pressures for cooperation in industries concentrated in "industrial districts." Aircraft manufacture, however, was geographically dispersed, largely for random reasons,[22] although industrial location would increasingly tilt toward low-wage areas, especially Southern California. The initial dispersal might have been overcome if the manufacturers' primary market had been managed by the military to permit associationalism, a shared sense of industrial identity and cooperation. But Congress said no, insisting on the competitive low bid, a contracting approach more suitable for slow-changing and generic items.

Congress's regulatory framework for aircraft manufacture was based on old connections among price competition, individualism, and technical advance and on fears of the power of large industrial firms. These were buttressed on one side by an enduring sense of air power as the best way American mass-production industry made itself felt in war and on the other by the idea that aeronautics was in a preliminary experimental stage about to culminate in the standard aircraft, which, like automobiles, would be widely owned and mass-produced by machines, unskilled workers, and giant firms. The failure to perceive aeronautics as high-technology—always reaching for higher levels of sophistication and always dependent upon many specialized personnel—was widely shared, even in the branches of military aviation and among many in the industry through the interwar years. Congress hoped that its regulations for military contracting would prevent any one group of firms from monopolizing the experimental process or the standard aircraft when it finally emerged.

The result was an industry dysfunctionally geared for repetitive, quantity output, even if large contracts for single, unchanging models were not let until World War II. Their business environment forced manufacturers to avoid associationalist ties, restrain their costs and innovative inclinations, and strive for relatively static designs that lent themselves to production contracts where profits might be made to cover development costs. Manufacturers were unable to influence the regulatory framework that repressed them. In 1921 Keys described the situation that he and his colleagues nevertheless endured through the interwar years:

> It is fairly obvious that no company can spend that amount of money and suffer the grief and disappointment of experimental labor—which is so often lost labor—only to have the product of that labor taken up by the Government and thrown open to competitive bidding. It is fair to say that because of these conditions over which the industry has no control, not only the Curtiss Company, but all other forward looking institutions in this art, have curtailed their efforts, economized their resources and foregone their ambitions for the art in order to adapt themselves to the policies of their Government.[23]

Nor could aircraft workers, the key contributors to aircraft manufacture, shape the industry's regulatory environment. They lacked effective unions and the power to prevent their employers from forcing upon them the costs of their industry's labor intensity and of Congress's maintenance of artificial competition through nonrecognition of design rights. With few ways to utilize cost-cutting machinery, manufacturers had few alternatives but to impose upon their workers much of the costs of price competition. In 1921 Keys set a tactical pattern for survival in the aircraft business that prevailed through the interwar years when he ordered his factory managers in Buffalo and Garden City, New York, to "downgrade labor." He gave the order reluctantly since "the great majority of the workmen are capable of being foremen" and because of the "necessity of enlisting the absolute loyalty of personnel and foremen to the corporation" to ensure promising new designs, quality workmanship, and "the success of the Curtiss Company."[24]

The strategic position of workers in aircraft engine manufacture was similar despite the much greater capital intensity of this branch of the industry. Engine technology was less complex and developed at a slower, more even pace. Longer production runs and the more extensive use of tooling common to the metalcutting industries were possible, although high-precision requirements, steady change, and limited volume still inhibited techniques of mass production. Unlike auto engines, aircraft engines were designed for maximum horsepower at minimum weight and were constructed of alloyed steel and aluminum, requiring much greater care in machining. Parts were ground and honed right up to final assembly; skilled machinists were needed throughout. Still, the successful engine manufacturer who had invested in the many jigs, dies, and fixtures necessary acquired a "natural monopoly" in a highly restricted market.[25] The critical difference, however, was that Congress tolerated the military's recognition of proprietary rights to engine designs. Nevertheless, the military dominated the market and contracting officers felt compelled to promote competition among engine manufacturers on the basis of price, successfully doing so by specifying particular engines in various aircraft designs.[26]

In these ways ideology applied through a congressionally enforced business environment, stamped the technical evolution of military aircraft. Apart from how it led to waste, secrecy, and technical conservatism, the premium placed on contracts for large bombers rather than smaller, more sophisticated fighters and ground-support craft is suggestive of how the development of military aircraft was shaped by an aircraft industrial base built in accord with old intuitions of the rigors of price competition. Like advocates of strategic air power and independent bureaucratic status for an air force, Keys shared a sense of the large bomber as the "plane of the future." But financial pressures were as important for him as the potential military utility of the long-range bomber. The irregularity of military contracting meant that usually "we only use 50% of our floor capacity at best." Bomber contracts were worth much more per unit, used more plant space, and made the company look stronger to investors. "I am especially anxious to get back into these big ships," Keys wrote his Washington agent, instructing him to promote the big bomber.[27]

The war left other legacies that contributed to a competitive environment for aircraft manufacturers during the interwar years. Not the least of these were the separate aircraft-procurement activities of the army and navy and the weakness of the new aviation branches within the military establishment. Military aeronautics was still primitive, and both services downplayed its worth and subordinated it to minor roles auxiliary to the infantry and fleet. Postwar navy doctrine reflected the forward tasks prescribed for American sea power by Alfred Mahan—the protection of foreign markets, sources of raw materials, and international shipping routes. In the 1920s the sea lanes of the western Pacific and an offensive war with capital ships against Japan preoccupied the navy. The Army War Plans Division shared this Far Eastern orientation. Only later would the navy concede room to air power in its global plans, and the army resisted military aviation through the interwar years.[28] Thus the embryonic aviation bureaus were left to prove themselves constantly. They insisted on the most from the limited funds they were provided to buy aircraft, compelling manufacturers to participate in their rivalry for funds, prestige, and missions.[29]

The Naval Aircraft Factory (NAF) at Philadelphia, a government-owned and -operated aircraft plant established in July 1917 by Secretary of the Navy Josephus Daniels and his assistant, Franklin D. Roosevelt, was another survivor of the war. It was also a source of competition for the industry but not of the organized variety envisioned by corporatists who wanted businessmen to formulate common approaches to their shared market problems. Daniels, a vocal defender of small enterprise and the "New Freedom" in the Wilson cabinet, hoped the NAF would provide the government with a "yardstick" for the prices, costs, and performances of private contractors, thus preserving the free market. In his view the "New Competition" of the business progressives was a code for collusion, and he had had a taste of it in his dealings with producers of armor plate and steel for large guns. Before his tenure began, the navy had worked out a cartel arrangement with steel companies in which prices were set and contracts allocated by the firms themselves. The navy hoped these firms would continue to produce and maintain expensive capacity for products with little commercial value. When the steelmakers insisted the New Competition be continued, Daniels turned to the price-competitive pressure of a government plant. Daniels did not want a nationalized steel armament industry, only a stimulus to private enterprise, a way to disrupt any system limiting the "market." These were also the goals behind the Naval Aircraft Factory and justified in the minds of congressmen its continued activity through the interwar years. Rightly, but to no avail, manufacturers condemned the NAF, along with other government production and design facilities, for establishing standards of contract performance and costs that were not comparable to the private sector. At the end of 1924 more civilian workers were at the NAF, the Pensacola Naval Air Station, and at McCook Field in Dayton than were in the entire private industry.[30]

BITTER RELATIONSHIPS

During the 1920s few manufacturers had illusions about the nature of their market and its control by Congress and the military. In the immediate postwar years some tried to escape this control and, sustaining the hopes of the wartime aircraft program's planners, made elaborate preparations for "peace aeronautics" and a widely expected commercial aircraft market.[31] But as Inglis M. Uppercu, president of Aeromarine Plane and Motor Company and Aeromarine Airways discovered early on, this market was not likely to emerge from a state of "hope deferred"[32] until air transport overcame the dilemma of proving its viability to patrons and investors before the fact. That difficulty could be eased only by significant advances in aircraft design and by extensive government subsidy and regulation. These were slow in coming. But even when they did—with the development of such commercial aircraft as the Ford and Fokker Tri-Motors and the Boeing B-40, with the Air Mail Act of 1925, and with the federal navigational aids and licensing powers authorized by the Air Commerce Act of 1926—commercial demand was not sufficient to allow most manufacturers to abandon their primary market and interest in military aircraft.

"We are dealing purely and simply with a thing that is at the present time altogether military," Keys declared in 1926. After the war and still under the control of John Willys, Curtiss Aeroplane established a sales network throughout the United States, South America, and the Far East. The company built airplanes in anticipation of the market, but as Keys sadly reported, "it cost us $1.5 million to find out the commercial era had not arrived." Acquiring Curtiss in 1920, Keys redirected it to the military market. In that year the firm lost another $1.75 million, and Moody's rated its preferred stock as "highly speculative" and its common stock "hopeless as an investment value." In 1926 Keys accurately predicted that "it will be ten to fifteen years before commercial aviation can support even one single first class factory" and that the military would continue to generate at least 80 percent of the industry's business.[33]

The military dominated the industry (see Table 3.4). Similar figures for the early 1920s are not available but with no significant commercial activity during these years before the commercial air acts, they would reveal even greater military dominance. Keys and the other major manufacturers were not at all uncomfortable that the bulk of their efforts were toward military ends. Aircraft industrialists were dedicated to the rapid advancement of aeronautics, and their goals merged with the military's desire for high-performance aircraft. They were proud of their work and its assumed contribution to the nation's prestige and security and were happy to concentrate on military aircraft. Although they accepted the military's dominance of their industry, they complained bitterly about how their exclusive clients administered its dominance.

Table 3.4. Military and Commercial Business of Eleven Major
Aircraft Manufacturers, 1927–1933 (in $millions)

	Military Aircraft Sales[1]	Commercial Aircraft Sales[2]	Military Sales as % of Total Sales
Douglas	$14.42	1.41	91
Boeing	10.32	7.03	59
Martin	9.88	0	100
Curtiss	7.27	2.60	74
Chance Vought	6.46	2.18	75
Keystone	5.95	1.77	77
Consolidated	4.29	1.11	79
Great Lakes	2.44	.90	73
Grumman	.44	.15	75
Subtotal	61.47	17.15	78
Wright	30.57[3]	22.43	58
Pratt & Whitney	33.37[3]	18.83	64
Total	125.41	58.41	68

[1]Army and navy production and design contracts
[2]Includes exports, most of which were military
[3]Engines

Source: Compiled from data in Hearings before the Subcommittee on Aeronautics Making Investigation into Certain Phases of the Manufacture of Aircraft and Aeronautical Accessories as They Refer to the Navy Department, 73rd Cong., 1st sess., 1934 (Delaney Hearings), 502.

Reuben Fleet, president of Consolidated Aircraft, was well versed in the problems of military aircraft procurement. Before founding his firm he had served as contracting officer and business manager for the Army Air Service. In 1922 he resigned his commission and, just in time for its demise, joined the Gallaudet Aircraft Company in East Greenwich, Rhode Island, formed during the war by a group of young investors, including William Averell Harriman. Fleet bought the bankrupt firm in 1923 and also acquired engineers, designs, and a contract for military trainers from the Dayton-Wright Company which General Motors had liquidated. He moved his new firm to Buffalo and produced the PT-1, the military's standard trainer during the 1920s. For Fleet, the sustenance of a healthy aircraft industry was clearly a "military problem," but Congress was too parsimonious and would not assume its "responsibility" for providing for the national defense. It would not allow the military to help the manufacturers manage their industry cooperatively and cope with a restricted market while encouraging technical advance.[34]

Nonrecognition of property rights to aircraft designs was at the heart of the competitive "strangle hold maintained by the Government" and the focus of the manufacturers "pitched battle" with it.[35] Emotionally attached to their work, they deeply resented the letting of production contracts for their designs to competing firms yet had no practical way to protect these designs. Army aircraft contracts included a proviso similar to the navy clause: "The contractor shall indemnify the United States and all officers and agents thereof, for all liability incurred of any nature or kind on account of the infringement of any copyright or patent rights." Those seeking redress from the military's arbitrary use of aircraft designs could only sue the government in long and costly proceedings in the Courts of Claim. In 1925 even this option was closed when the comptroller general, Congress's "watchdog" on federal spending, decreed that no proprietary right existed in an aircraft design. Thus the army and navy could pay for the services that produced a design but could not pay for the design itself since it could not be owned.[36]

The manufacturers demanded laws that would authorize the services to let production contracts as if proprietary rights to designs existed. They put forth a range of persuasive arguments to show how competitive contracting for production work handicapped the industry and worked to the disadvantage of military aviation. They insisted that for financial and technical reasons the design staff and factory were integral to one another. Only the profits from production contracts could finance the unpredictable costs of aircraft design. Competition for production contracts stifled the development of aeronautics by discouraging firms that maintained expensive design staffs and facilities. It also interrupted the flow of innovation, manufacturers argued. They insisted that an airplane's design was never complete, that it should be allowed to evolve throughout the production stage, and that each airplane produced should be a technical advance upon the one that preceded it. They maintained that it was impossible to transfer design data from one group of designers to a separate group of constructors. When an airplane was simply copied in quantity production—"China copy" was their term—its design was "frozen" or "stillborn," its designers unable to "follow through." Complexity and the dependence of aircraft manufacture on handwork made the knowledge of particular airplanes intuitive for its designers and builders and the blueprints and data of one design group incomprehensible to another.[37]

A winning contractor for the quantity production of another firm's design was never sure of what it was he had contracted to build or what it would cost. The prototype, not the blueprints, was delivered to his factory; the first task was the costly one of dismantling it and drawing up hundreds of blueprints for his workmen. Inferior aircraft were usually produced. Firms that underestimated production costs cut corners and ignored the technical advances of others that could not be easily understood or duplicated. Even worse for military aviation, companies ceased to develop the type of aircraft for which they had attained an expertise but whose production contracts they had lost to competitors.[38]

A number of production contracts stood out in the minds of manufacturers as examples of military aircraft procurement at its worst and as evidence that private industry subsidized military aviation. In 1917 engineers at the Glenn L. Martin Company, including the young Donald Douglas, Laurence Bell, and James Kindleberger, designed a promising bomber. Martin sold the prototype to the army at a loss and in 1919 was underbid by three contractors on the bomber's production. Martin was given twenty to build anyway but lost money on the reduced volume, suspended the bomber's development, and in disgust, declined to deal with the army until 1931. L.W.F. Engineering built fifty, Aeromarine built twenty-five, and both firms showed large losses. Curtiss built fifty Martin bombers, only because, as Keys admitted, "we purposefully bid 20% below costs" since "all the production orders of the War Department for eighteen months past have been placed with companies whose engineering divisions are practically production engineering . . . we cannot bid within 25% of these firms." Curtiss lost $250,000 on the bombers. Produced by different factories, the bombers in the field proved to be completely different airplanes and of widely varying quality.[39]

Also in 1919 the Ordnance Engineering Company developed the "best pursuit in that day." At $725,000 Curtiss was the low bidder in a production competition for fifty Orenco-D pursuits. Ordnance Engineering liquidated; and the fifty planes built by Curtiss, which Keys acknowledged "were way below standard," had to be destroyed as unsafe.[40] In 1922 Donald Douglas sold his first airplane to the navy. His DT-2 torpedo plane was a great success, but he had spent heavily on its development. When the navy split the DT-2's production among Douglas, the Naval Aircraft Factory, and L.W.F., Douglas dropped the design and L.W.F. went bankrupt.[41]

The Boeing Company's successful bid for the production of another's design in 1921 provides an exception to the rule that contracts granted to firms for the production of another's aircraft design resulted in inferior aircraft and losses for the producing firm but not to the rule that it resulted in liquidation for the designer. In 1920 Boeing lost $300,000, but in 1921 the company won the largest contract for military aircraft since the

This Boeing XPW-9 (Experimental Pursuit Watercooled) was delivered to the Army Air Service in May 1924 and led to a series of production orders for Boeing into 1928. The PW-9 was capable of 155 miles per hour and 18,000 feet. Boeing tried unsuccessfully in the Courts of Claim to win proprietary rights to this design.

war. The Seattle firm's bid for the production of 200 Thomas-Morse MB-3 pursuit planes, capable of 177 miles per hour, was so low that others were only in the running as long as Secretary of War J. J. Weeks considered splitting the contract among the firms to keep them operating. The politics of this option were too much for the secretary, and the full contract went to Boeing, precipitating an ongoing industry-wide resentment of the firm. But the MB-3 proved a successful plane and served as the basis for Boeing's continuous development of the type within the technical constraints imposed by the need to recoup development costs through profits on regular quantity production. Thomas-Morse subsequently declined and was absorbed by Reuben Fleet's Consolidated Aircraft.[42]

A sense of the manufacturers' situation can be gleaned from the payroll variations at the Curtiss plants. In 1919 it stood at $100,000 per month; in July 1920 it was down to $17,000. A year later it had climbed to $33,000. By July 1923 it had risen to $110,000, but by November 1924 had fallen to

$20,000.[43] Few firms could sustain such conditions for long. Competitive contracting practices were obviously destructive for the industry and wasteful of what limited funds could be coaxed from Congress. Consequently, the conservatism of contracting officers, induced by a traditional mistrust of private industry, by fears of Congress, and by lingering allegations of wartime fraud, gave way to a greater appreciation for the manufacturers' plight and to a growing willingness to negotiate production contracts with the designers of aircraft.

By the mid-1920s the negotiated contract was common in military aircraft procurement, but the circumstances surrounding its use offset the value it might have had for manufacturers and for the development of aeronautics. Although the negotiated contract spared the government the waste that resulted from contracting for an aircraft's production with firms other than its designer, the industry was maintained in an atmosphere of potential competition because of the negotiated contract's informality. The contracting officer's authority to engage in it was extremely vague and involved the circumvention of the basic thrust of procurement law. If in his judgment the government's best interests were served by a negotiated contract with a select firm, he could find defensible legal grounding in the sometimes ambivalent wording of the many statutes that governed army and navy purchasing. For example, by defining aircraft as ordnance, navy officers could cite an 1843 regulation that authorized the disregard of advertisement and lowest-bid standards when no other supplier was available for the purchase of ordnance, gunpowder, and medicines.[44]

This law and similar provisions used by the army were drastically stretched to apply to aircraft. The use of ancient regulations to negotiate contracts could easily open contracting officers to charges of favoritism, if not collusion, and were therefore turned to only with reluctance and if concessions on price or performance could be extracted from the contractors. Their use meant the time-consuming review of each contract by the services' legal bureaus and by the comptroller general, who, in the words of Adm. William A. Moffett, chief of the Navy Bureau of Aeronautics, "is always hanging over our heads."[45]

If negotiated production contracts were to protect aircraft firms from competition and ease the financial burdens of the private development of military aeronautics, they needed to be used on a consistent and systematic basis. But negotiated contracts were used only partially and in an atmosphere of potential competition. The value of major contracts during the first half of the 1920s let through negotiation was $5.7 million, and

$4.3 million in contracts were let through open-price competition (see Appendix 2). When negotiating with their budget-conscious military opposites, manufacturers were fully aware that they were doing so at the services' pleasure and that if they bargained too hard the contracts could be opened to competitive bidding at any time.

In late 1923 when it appeared to manufacturers and some contracting officers that trends in aircraft procurement might be toward the more consistent and generous use of negotiated contracts, the Curtiss Scout (CS) incident rudely reminded them that low-bid competition for production contracts was a matter of policy rather than a mere consequence of inexperience with a new high-technology military industry. Committed to developing military aeronautics, Keys had greatly expanded his engineering force in 1922 despite the risk. Curtiss lost $182,000 on a $175,000 development contract for the successful navy CS. Keys described it as "an enormous job," requiring the "same work over and over." There was "no way to predict" the costs and complications that arose from some major new steps in the use of metal in the airplane's construction. Admiral Moffett wanted to take advantage of Curtiss's laboriously acquired expertise and give the company the CS production contract, but he could not demonstrate to the satisfaction of the navy's judge advocate general that no other supplier was available. When Keys realized that the navy was opening CS production to competitive bidding he angrily ordered the development of that type stopped and began liquidating his design staff. In the competition to build forty Scouts, he submitted a bid of $32,000 per plane, but Glenn Martin won the contract at $23,000 apiece. Martin complained that the plane came with no blueprints but admitted that they would have been useless in his shop anyway. His staff drew up new blueprints and in the process produced an entirely new plane inferior in performance to the Curtiss design. Keys complained to congressmen that he had paid for the development of the nation's air defenses. "If you want an industry that can create a design, that certainly has to be paid by someone. Well we paid it . . . our job in the aviation game seems to be to contribute quite a little bit of money year by year to the Army and Navy for aviation."[46]

THE FAILURE OF ASSOCIATIONALISM

The Curtiss Scout incident helped spur one of the rare occasions during the interwar years when the manufacturers banded together in an attempt to rectify the mismanagement of their industry by the government. Aside from this episode and two repeat performances of collective action in response to the National Recovery Administration and New Deal labor laws, aircraft manufacturers had little choice but to resolutely pursue independent, secretive business and technical strategies. They were almost solely dependent on the military aircraft market, whose size and artificial competitiveness were politically maintained, a process in which they held little sway. With no influence over their only real market, they had few options other than to reduce their costs, which largely meant engineers' salaries and workers' wages. Cautious and private, their efforts fragmented and dispersed, manufacturers sought only incremental technical advantages in competitions for military contracts. They strove to cultivate informal ties with and concessions from individual contracting officers at the procurement centers at Dayton and Pensacola. They largely avoided Washington, D.C., political activity, and the collective organizations it required. Manufacturers rejected business associationalism, despite the persistent arguments of many that their industry was made to order for it.

In general, businessmen had had negative experiences with wartime corporatist experiments. These had been obstructed by military bureaucracies, by Congress, or in the case of aircraft by the inappropriate application of a corporatist vision tied to mass production. A broad, postwar resurgence of economic individualism and antistatism resulted. Yet the search for new ways to accommodate the organizational needs of advanced capitalism without violating traditional values—the search for a "new individualism"—continued under the skilled leadership of Herbert Hoover, secretary of commerce in the Harding and Coolidge administrations.[47] Like the business progressives who managed the wartime aircraft program, many continued to view aircraft manufacture as an ideal forum for Hoover's vision of associationalism. In its technical dynamism and complexity and its dependency on the state, it still seemed perfectly suited for a framework of social and economic management that relied on an elite of enlightened public and private experts to produce solutions to the problems experienced by a market society undergoing rapid technological adjustment.

Aircraft manufacturers gave this vision short shrift. They knew the problems of their market were beyond the scope of integration, voluntary agreements, industrial self-regulation, and trade associations. From the associationalist perspective, it was through such arrangements that consensus could be built within industry, supportive links with federal agencies pursued, and solutions implemented that did not violate basic values of republican individualism, antistatism, voluntarism, and free enterprise. Thus could government be a facilitator rather than a coercive force, a partner rather than a dictator.

Yet aircraft manufacturers rejected trade associations. The Manufacturers' Aircraft Association, the patent pool imposed upon the industry by the government during the war, was of little use to manufacturers outside the tiny area of commercial aircraft since patents for military aircraft were allowed no legal standing. Manufacturers also displayed indifference and frequent hostility to the Aeronautical Chamber of Commerce (ACC), a New York-based trade association established in 1922 and managed by men who, under the direct encouragement of Hoover, professed the associationalist ethic. The experiences of this association during most of the interwar years suggest the dangers of assuming, as historians of associationalist political economy often do, that trade associations, merely by their existence, reflected the successful suppression of intraindustry discord and that they actually represented the industries their promoters claimed.[48]

The ACC was a promotional agency for commercial aviation, which aircraft manufacturers for the most part either ignored or tolerated apathetically. Only when it seemed immediately possible that associationalist activity might result in procurement-law reform and during the late 1930s when the Department of Labor sought to impose wage increases upon the industry did manufacturers display genuine interest in the chamber. Conceived by visionaries of air commerce who hoped to end the military's dominance of aeronautics, the ACC was founded from a perspective at odds with the views of most aircraft manufacturers, who recognized and preferred their dependency upon military aeronautics. Its founders believed that aeronautics needed "a broad vision," an end to the military "parochialism" that forced manufacturers to produce designs unsuitable for commercial use.[49]

Grover Loening, Samuel Bradley, and Inglis Uppercu, a hopeful airline operator and the chamber's first president, began their campaign for a trade association as early as 1919, but "disruption in the industry suggested postponement" until 1921. Then, against much resistance, they called upon manufacturers to recognize the potential of commercial aviation and the need for an initial stimulating stage of government aid. In tandem with federal agencies, an industry association could promote commercial aeronautics and mobilize a constituency for congressional funding of start-up subsidization, airway maintenance, and "competent national regulation." With its stamp of legitimacy, federal regulation would foster air transport, allay concerns about public safety, expand the market, and help manufacturers attract private capital and insurers. Cooperative and assertive action among all elements of the aviation industry was immediately necessary to ensure a dominant role for private interests in the formation and management of federal air regulation and to avoid more statist approaches, perhaps even under military control. For these reasons Loening insisted that an "industrial representative body of the aircraft constructors" was an "essential burden to carry."[50]

The chamber's promoters succeeded in attracting to its founding subscription a widely assorted group of "manufacturers, dealers, distributors, operators and owners, associations, corporations, firms and individuals," most of whom were prospective rather than active members of the aviation industry. Unlike the active manufacturers, these had been seduced by the bandwagon effect created by the chamber's promoters and by its success in attracting big names but minimal participants in aviation such as RCA, B. F. Goodrich, Eastman-Kodak, Goodyear, and Standard Oil. Many subscribers gambled on immediate results in the form of federal support for commercial aviation and could not afford to continue paying dues to the chamber while its financially strapped staff went about the time-consuming tasks of educating the public on commercial aviation and building support in Congress for their legislative package.

The chamber's staff promoted commercial aviation primarily through the preparation of an annual *Aircraft Yearbook* that stressed the theme of "Putting Aircraft to Work." It organized air shows and flying meets and worked closely with Hoover in an attempt to drive air mail and air commerce laws through an indifferent Congress. It sought to "straighten out public thought" on the matter of wartime profits. Venturing in a small way into the more conventional roles of a manufacturers' trade association, it provided members with information on credit, stock promotions, and sales opportunities in the United States and abroad. It persuaded the Interstate Commerce Commission to reduce railroad charges on the shipment of bulky aircraft and parts. Without success, it promoted a labor pool and the joint purchase of spruce and other supplies.[51]

Aircraft manufacturers were unimpressed. Despite vigorous efforts to recruit them, the major manufacturers rejected the ACC, forcing upon it frequent financial crises that it survived only by "compromising our activities." Martin, Boeing, Chance Vought, Douglas, Dayton-Wright, and Consolidated spurned the chamber's overtures. Frank H. Russell, a Curtiss executive, campaigned for the chamber and persuaded Curtiss to join, but the company's president, Clement Keys, doubted commercial aviation's prospects and largely ignored the chamber except when procurement reform seemed in the offing.

Glenn Martin, building bombers in Cleveland, was opposed to a trade association for fear that it would only encourage new entries to an already crowded industry. He declined to join the ACC and pay its $600 annual fee, stating that he was "unable to be of very great assistance to others than to the Glenn L. Martin Company, as it seems to keep me fairly busy with my time and credit." Martin, who snubbed the chamber until World War II even when other manufacturers later found temporary cause to support it, was "more interested in self-preservation, avoiding the sheriff's padlock for the next twelve months, than in missionary work on [commercial] futures. . . . What is most important to me," he added, summing up the position of most manufacturers, "is making a success of my own business."[52]

The trade association was the wave of the future, Luther K. Bell, the chamber's secretary, wrote the skeptical Jesse Vincent, codesigner of the Liberty engine and chief aircraft engineer at Packard. "You are doubtless familiar with what Bernard Baruch had to say of them as assisting in the war. And doubtless you know that one of Secretary Hoover's first steps upon entering the Cabinet was to let it be known that he would look first of all to the trade associations, for cooperation and information." But Vincent felt that "this country as a whole has become very largely overorganized. . . . My undivided attention must be given to the work of Packard," he wrote, adding that other manufacturers should strive to improve their own businesses rather than concern themselves with "side issues." Similarly, G. M. Williams of General Motors' Dayton-Wright opposed the chamber as a "project the results of which are not entirely tangible." "A baby industry should not start boasting until it has something to yell about," wrote Reuben Fleet, president of Consolidated Aircraft. Throughout the 1920s and 1930s Fleet generally ignored the chamber and refused to contribute to its *Yearbook* since he saw only a distant future for commercial aviation and did not regard his trainers as "worthwhile advertising."[53]

With 300 employees and a contract for 200 army pursuits in 1921–1922, Boeing Airplane was the nation's busiest aircraft firm. Bradley canvassed Boeing, arguing that since it was destined to hold a "salient position" in the industry's future, it should be a leader in the chamber, which otherwise would be "seriously embarrassed" by its nonparticipation. On behalf of William Boeing, Edgar N. Gott, his vice president and cousin, scoffed at the "so-called commercial activities" the chamber sought to promote. Boeing rightly felt that his Seattle firm had been discriminated against during the war because of its location on the West Coast and distrusted what he considered to be a New York aviation establishment now supposedly behind the chamber. He insisted that an aircraft-industry trade association be based not in New York but in Washington, D.C., where it might be of some use to military contractors, or somewhere in the Midwest, where West Coast manufacturers would not have to travel so far to attend its meetings. In the end, Boeing saw nothing in a trade association but encouragements for new competitors.[54]

One of the many new entrants to the depressed industry in the early twenties, Douglas Aircraft was too busy to respond to the chamber's solicitations. Douglas had worked with Glenn Martin at Los Angeles and Cleveland and in 1920 returned to Los Angeles under the encouragement of Harry Chandler, the powerful publisher of the *Los Angeles Times*. Douglas's first company quickly failed, but on the strength of navy orders for his torpedo planes and with financing and factory space provided by local businessmen led by Chandler, Douglas Aircraft was formed in 1922 and began its life as a major supplier to the army and navy and as a leading force in air transport development. As one of few aircraft manufacturers with significant orders, Douglas's nonparticipation in the chamber particularly rankled its staff.[55]

Embodied in the air mail acts of 1925 and 1930 and the Air Commerce Act of 1926 and eventually entrenched in the Civil Aeronautics Act of 1938, the principles and practices of associationalist political economy proved workable for air transport, at least to the extent that the industry's much wider commercial base gave it and its advocates in federal agencies greater autonomy from congressional scrutiny and interference.[56] Yet even here the process toward associationalist solutions was never even or automatic. That is suggested most notably by the politics and protracted legislative process that produced the mid-1920s aviation acts[57] and by the 1934 legislation that sharply circumscribed the associationalists' programs for commercial aviation after Senator Hugo Black's sensational investigation of air-mail contracting. Some authors have conflated the air transport and aircraft manufacturing industries and assumed that the corporatist principles that shaped one guided the other as well.[58]

The records of the industry trade association reveal that apart from its limited application during the 1930s to promote exports, associationalism held out little for a manufacturing industry characterized by overwhelming dependency on the military, rapid technical change, high variable costs, ease of entry, and most especially the specific attention of congressmen who thwarted all attempts to limit competition. Like the other competitive, overbuilt "sick industries" of the 1920s, aircraft manufacture provides a case study in the limitations of Hooverian associationalism.[59] In aircraft, the value of the associationalist model, like Piore and Sabel's model of flexible specialization, serves as a plausible alternative to what actually happened, thus underscoring what actually did happen and the importance of political culture, the decision-making process, and human agency in organizational and technological change.

Even if the manufacturers had been eager associationalists, they would have found few officials in the military bureaus with influence, organizations, or views of political economy that were as developed as those among Commerce Department or Post Office civilians. Even those officers charged under the Defense Act of 1920 with planning industrial mobilization, with "keeping memories of the tremendous logistical problems of World War I alive,"[60] displayed little understanding of the need for ongoing and systematic links with makers of advanced weapons. Nowhere was the displacement of the problems of military strategy and tactics by the logistical problems of producing and supplying complex weaponry more obvious than in military aeronautics. In the words of Maj. B. D. Foulois, who later became chief of the Army Air Corps, "the operation of the Air Service of the Army ever since its birth has involved duties approximately 90 percent of which are technical, mechanical, and industrial, and only 10 percent of which can be classed as strictly military. This classification of duties will always remain the same."[61]

But the new ascendancy of logistics was only minimally reflected in military planning, doctrine, and organization during the interwar years. When some officers tried to rectify this deficiency through the reform of procurement law and through the provision of greater autonomy for the air forces, bureaucratic inertia in the military establishment and congressional opposition blocked the way. In the case of air power, the emerging outlines of a cohesive warfare state or military-industrial complex, which some historians have strained to find during this period, are not readily apparent.[62] In the Defense Act of 1920, Congress voted to contain the drift toward a more centralized, professionally directed defense establishment and reassert its control over all things military. It maintained the various military bureaus within a "maze of authoritative confusion," each on a separate line of budgetary control leading to Capitol Hill, where a good part of the time and energies of the Bureaus was spent dealing with Congress. Thus Congress reserved for itself the gulf between military bureaus and contractors as a place where it could make the military and its spending serve its political and ideological goals.[63]

Still, an Industrial War Plans Division (IWPD) was created in the Army Air Service as part of the assistant secretary of war's attempts to plan for industrial mobilization and avoid future disasters on the scale of the wartime aircraft program. But the attitudes of those who staffed this new planning bureau, as well as the meager levels of funding and personnel provided for it, reflected a lingering perception of warfare as intermittent emergency, something the nation mobilized for and then demobilized from. Weapons technologies that evolve continually during war and peace had yet to be accounted for.[64]

The planners' surveys of the aircraft industry sought only to anticipate problems that might be encountered during war mobilization, not those that actually existed for manufacturers. To avoid the "confusion" in a future war which had characterized the "late emergency," the chief of the IWPD, Maj. J. A. Mars, inquired after the manufacturers' labor and material needs, their possible production curves in case of war, and the legislation they would like to see passed under war conditions. He suggested that they limit technological changes to once per year to help facilitate quantity production. Manufacturers ignored him, his surveys, and the ACC, which assisted him. They resented the "war games" of planners, the tours of their plants, and the detailed paperwork they were expected to complete without compensation. Instead they concentrated on the immediate problems of business survival, technical change, and maintaining positive individual relations with those officers who controlled contracts in the present.[65]

Aircraft manufacturers engaged in collective action only when there was some immediate possibility that they might sway the de facto regulation which Congress, acting through its agents in the military, wielded over their industry. During 1924–1926 this possibility seemed real to Charles L. Lawrence, vice-president of Wright Aeronautical and pioneer developer of the air-cooled radial engine. Lawrence wrested the chamber's presidency from Uppercu, redirected its priorities on behalf of military contractors, opened an office in Washington, D.C, and launched a campaign to change the procurement laws and to increase funding for military aircraft. His efforts were aided by the sense of crisis among manufacturers in the wake of the Curtiss Scout competition and by the weakness of the commercial aviation advocates who, because of delays and defeats of laws regulating commercial aviation, were "disappointed in the complete realization of their plans."[66]

Before the strength of the political resistance to Lawrence's program became apparent it was actively supported by the manufacturers. Those who had resisted the ACC gave Lawrence their temporary support. Clement Keys was on a five-month vacation and feeling optimistic. He had told Curtiss stockholders only one month earlier that the company was on the brink because it was the government's "settled policy . . . to buy aeroplanes below the cost of production" as if they were "articles of a standard type for which there is a constant demand." But Lawrence's efforts helped persuade him that "constructive forces are at work for the first time since 1918 and that before long the entire policy of the Army and Navy will be dictated by Congress to be that those factors in the industry which have been constructive from the beginning will get the jobs."[67]

Boeing, who sought to reverse an August 1924 decision by the comptroller general denying his proprietary claim to the MB-3, supported the chamber's legislative program. Still, he refused to enlist his company as a member, taking out membership only for himself and his executives "as individuals interested in aviation." The company saw no direct benefit in joining, Gott wrote, but did not "want to be looked upon as hindrances." Chance Vought also joined in 1924, but Martin remained a holdout, though he conferred with the chamber and worked for procurement reform as a member of the platform committee of the 1924 GOP convention in Cleveland. Douglas began paying dues in 1924 and sent a representative to cooperate with Lawrence. To him, too, it seemed "that engineering accomplishments are being credited, at last, to the organizations responsible for them."[68]

The manufacturers had no difficulty supporting Lawrence's calls for rejection of the notion that the best aircraft were generated by price competition and for more and larger military contracts and protection from the unpredictable costs of development. In the initial enthusiasm of the campaign for procurement reform, they also backed his associationalist proposals for preserving competition, but limiting it to technical innovation and managing it through collective self-regulation and cooperation with the military. Lawrence demanded an end to the arbitrary and ineffective use of nineteenth-century regulations for negotiating contracts. He wanted the war and navy secretaries empowered to use "discretion" in their procurement of aircraft. He called for a system of contracting among only those firms on an "approved list," which "have a completely balanced organization of creative engineers with their laboratories, manufacturing personnel with their factories." Such a list of bidders was needed "so that fly-by-night concerns with no capital, cannot jump in and obtain contracts at absurd prices," demoralize designers, and discourage the development of military aeronautics. Product performance rather than price would be the basis of competition. Contracts would be negotiated with winning firms by officers who would use audits to protect the government's interest and guard against excessive profits.[69]

A winning aircraft's designer would be assured the contract for its production and would automatically receive a development contract for a more advanced version of the design. The designer's development costs would thus be amortized, the specialization of firms by aircraft type would be encouraged, and limited federal funding would no longer be dispersed. Aircraft firms would enjoy profitable cycles of "continuous production" and become manufacturers in the conventional sense rather than "feast-and-famine" contractors. Military aviation would make rapid strides, and healthy competition would be preserved but restricted among only two or three firms at the design stage. Government facilities such as the Naval Aircraft Factory would be limited to the design and production of specialized equipment—bomb racks, catapults, armor, and so forth. In case the discretion of secretaries could not always be counted on to be applied in the interests of aircraft designers, their contracting options would be limited by the full legal recognition of proprietary rights to military aircraft designs.[70]

Such proposals involved fairly radical departures in procurement law and military-industrial relations. If implemented, they would have generated a developmental pattern for the industry and its technology entirely different from the one that actually emerged. Lawrence's program also involved a significant increase in the power of the bureaus of military aviation. However, its slow progress in Washington was not due to any interest group or institutional opposition; no group of aircraft manufacturers lobbied for the status quo. And most everyone in the GOP administrations, military and civilian, agreed that a viable aircraft industry was under siege and that new practices of procurement were needed.

Admiral Moffett, a vocal advocate of advanced naval aviation, always supported the industry's position. He wanted the old laws he was using to negotiate contracts replaced by new ones applying specifically to aircraft. Such laws, he thought, could end the uncertainty that pervaded his dealings with manufacturers and staunch the dispersal of his limited funds by encouraging just two dependable sources of supply per aircraft type. Both he and Gen. Mason Patrick of the Army Air Service accepted the

Charles L. Lawrence, pioneer of the radial air-cooled engine, vice-president of Wright Aeronautical Company, poses with a 200-horsepower Wright J-5 Whirlwind in June 1927. Lawrence was the leading voice for organized competition, or "associationalism," in the New Era aircraft industry.

need for an approved list of bidders and the recognition of proprietary rights to design. E. H. Campbell, judge advocate general of the navy, also appealed to congressmen to recognize that "aircraft stands in a class by itself." Writing to the House Military Affairs Committee, Secretary Hoover argued that on behalf of both national defense and commercial aviation, "it would be of great value if in the legislation you are now considering a provision could be inserted removing the restrictions imposed by law upon government purchase so that competitive bidding may not be required [and] design rights might be observed."[71]

Many in Congress, particularly in the Senate, were sympathetic to the industry's plight, and were willing to grant the bureaus of military aviation greater funding, autonomy, and the formal regulatory power over the aircraft industry that they and the manufacturers sought.[72] Still, the problems of aircraft procurement were never made priorities by the industry's sympathizers. Although he stated the need for special consideration of the aircraft industry's problems in his December 1924 budget message to Congress, President Coolidge, a champion of limited government, was loathe to make a priority of any matter and always deferred to Congress's legislative prerogatives.[73]

Ongoing uncertainty over the military importance of air power also limited advocacy for procurement reform. The military establishment resented aviation's growing shares of both military funding and debate on military affairs at the expense of its traditional branches. In the hands of Gen. William Mitchell, military aviation was the main thrust behind a threatening argument for the radical reorganization of the military into a Department of Defense. In addition military spending and reform were checked during the 1920s by a popular indifference for military matters, by a broadly based peace movement, and by a common distaste for standing armies and a "Big Navy." Most Americans and their congressmen agreed with the fiscally conservative Coolidge, who argued that "a country loaded with debt is a country devoid of the first line of defense . . . economy is the handmaid of preparedness."[74]

Prompted by these popular attitudes and by their own preferences, the makers of national security policy stressed disarmament and reliance on economic might rather than military and political power to advance America's interests abroad and to prevent war.[75] During the New Era the seemingly greater cost effectiveness of air power had its appeal among the efficiency-minded and anti-imperialists such as Sen. William E. Borah, who wanted an inexpensive military restricted to continental defense. But the argument that air power had made armies and navies obsolete persuaded few beyond a handful of zealous followers of Billy Mitchell.[76] Many hoped the successes of the 1921–1922 Washington treaties on naval disarmament could be duplicated for air power. Yet even the failure of talks on aerial disarmament and the consequent encouragement for the navy to pursue its global ambitions through aircraft carriers produced no rush in Washington to address the problems of military aviation. Although they gave the aircraft industry their verbal support, government officials such as Hoover hoped its problems could be ignored until they were offset by the always-anticipated mass commercial market for aircraft.[77]

Lukewarm efforts on the part of the New Era administrations, the political weakness of the aircraft industry, and the subordination of the military to Congress left procurement reform to its fate in the hands of traditionalists on Capitol Hill who remained suspicious of the Aircraft Trust and opposed on ideological grounds any attempt to skirt the tenets of free access to government contracts based on price competition. The industry's behavior played into the hands of the advocates of competition. The independent-mindedness and desire among manufacturers to enter and remain in the business was so strong that it gave a competitive industry the appearance of viability; they seemed perfectly willing to sustain abuse at the hands of their government patrons. In answer to congressmen's persistent questioning on why they stayed in the business if it were as onerous as they claimed, Lawrence admitted that those who were "foolish enough to engage in the business when there isn't any profit" were difficult to account for.[78]

As Lawrence's proposals for reform made little headway, manufacturers began to break ranks with the chamber, helping confirm impressions of a viably competitive industry. A code of industry ethics prepared by Lawrence and calling for agreement that no manufacturer would bid to produce another's design was only winked at by the industry's members. Bitter disputes erupted among the manufacturers over who was best suited to compete for particular aircraft types and who had encouraged the military's practices by "buying" contracts. "Today, the aircraft industry is composed of all kinds of units, all of which are working for their individual advantage and not for the common welfare at all," Lawrence complained. "The idea of an approved list of responsible manufacturers has been suggested but no single manufacturer can be expected to approve qualifications that do not fit his particular case." To his disgust, manufacturers were quarreling on matters "of primary business integrity and honesty."[79] They increasingly blamed one another but reserved especially bitter criticisms for the army and navy, which they accused of using the enthusiasm of aircraft builders to foster an ever-expanding list of manufacturers. The military's strategy of "divide and conquer" was designed, some manufacturers believed, to reserve credit for new developments to "ambitious" military engineers with eyes on their own futures as "potential captains of industry."[80]

By late 1924 Lawrence and Bradley had given up on consensus in industry and self-government generated by firms themselves, as was supposed to occur among enlightened, associationalist businessmen. Afraid that new production orders under a program of expansion for military aviation then being discussed in Congress would find the industry in such a chaotic state that the government would be forced to seek alternatives of the Naval Aircraft Factory variety, they turned to "emergency" tactics. Ignoring the peculiar structures and mechanisms of control within these industries, the chamber's leaders cited "the experience of organized baseball and the moving picture industry" and proposed the appointment of a "dictator . . . with a broad point of view" who would direct the aircraft industry and override particular interests, "competitive backbiting," and geographic dispersal. With no interests in the industry, such an autocrat could transcend the taint of the "lobby" and act as a mediator with Washington. Believing that the disputatious manufacturers would be awed by his stature, they appointed as "dictator" William H. Hays, the famous Washington insider, former GOP national chairman and postmaster general, and current president of the Motion Picture Producers and Distributors of America.[81]

"Secret" meetings were held, attended by Hays and representatives of select firms. A Special Committee of the Aircraft Industry was struck, consisting of Lawrence, C. B. Fritsche of the Detroit-based Aircraft Development Corporation, Loening, Martin, Russell, Vought, and Bradley. It seemed that the "dictatorship plan" might succeed. "Upon learning of Mr. Hays' active interest in the subject, President Coolidge at once arranged a conference with the Secretary of War and the Secretary of the Navy with Mr. Hays."[82] After these developments, it occurred to other manufacturers that the chamber's proposals might well be implemented. If they desired enrollment on any forthcoming "approved list" and participation in the rumored long-term military aircraft program, they had best display considerable backing for the chamber's program. At an early 1925 meeting with Hays, a large contingent of manufacturers proved responsive to his platitudes on cooperation, the mutual interests of the industry and government, and the unselfish patriotism of the manufacturers. He voiced the need to avoid the detail of the industry's problems, which he had little time for, and his hope that encouragement would be found, not in the "length of the steps" taken but in their "direction."[83]

Hays's genial boosterism also seduced government officials, who agreed on matters over which they had no authority. In January 1925 Hays and the Special Committee met in Secretary of War Weeks's office with Navy Secretary Wilbur and the air bureau chiefs. "We were assured," the committee reported, "that it was the present policy of the Government to encourage specialization among the manufacturers and to recognize the principle of proprietary rights." The group and its proposals were favorably received at the White House and even President Coolidge gave vague promises that the details would be worked out.[84] But late January found the movement for procurement reform slowing as military lawyers balked at Lawrence's suggestion that new contracts immediately include a clause restricting the military's use of drawings and specifications of aircraft to maintenance purposes only. Conferences intended to bring the manufacturers' proposals down from the realm of abstractions to the details of concrete measures were postponed, and the manufacturers again broke ranks. Bradley warned that "delays are frequently said to be dangerous. It seems to me they may prove to be very dangerous to this movement."[85]

Cordiality between the manufacturers and the services dissipated as it became clear that the military's endorsements of such radical changes in procurement rules were worth little without changes in the laws, which only Congress could make. Keys, who had lost $400,000 on naval aviation since the war, was "tired of paying subsidies" for warplanes. He seethed that the military was only leading the manufacturers on. In his mind, Admiral Moffet "was saying whatever will please his listeners at the time." Privately to a congressman on the Lampert Committee he attacked "the complete incompetence of the present Secretaries" who had "not the slightest idea of aviation matters . . . Naval aviation under the present control is more or less of a joke." He warned the secretary of the navy that he would take his business to the Japanese.[86]

The law gave the services no choice but to continue contracting without recognizing design rights and thus to sustain the false atmosphere of competition among manufacturers of military aircraft. The chamber fell short in overcoming congressional resistance to procurement reform, despite its success in keeping the aircraft industry's needs on official agendas and in cultivating the support of high administration officials and congressmen such as Carl Vinson of the House Naval Affairs Committee and his cousin Fred Vinson of the House Military Affairs Committee. The chamber's failure came during a period when Congress for the first time since the war was not hamstrung by factions, particularly within the GOP majority. The Republican Insurgents, agrarians who were least sympathetic to the aircraft manufacturers, had supported Senator Robert M. LaFollette's 1924 bid for the presidency under the Progressive banner. For them there was one "great issue . . . the control of government and industry by private monopoly," which had "crushed competition, stifled private initiative and independent enterprise." Their fractious presence in Congress was swamped by the Coolidge and GOP mainstream regular landslide, but the aircraft industry did not benefit from the new political tide.[87]

THE AIR CORPS ACT

Congress's resistance to procurement reform was codified in the Air Corps Act of July 1926, for the most part a conservative response to the debate over the proper status of military aviation within the defense establishment. Congress withstood the views of Billy Mitchell and his followers, who insisted that military aviation be given not just organizational unity and autonomy from the Navy and War Departments but that it form the center of a new Department of Defense. Instead Congress heeded warnings, first made by Newton D. Baker, that independent military aviation closely linked with its industrial base might evolve into a powerful, expensive, and dynamic bureaucratic threat and undermine the military's subordination to Congress. In the Air Corps Act Congress renamed the Air Service and granted slight personnel expansions but basically reasserted the organizational status quo that persisted into the 1940s, confining military aviation within separate and subordinate bureaus in the army and navy, each competing and individually dependent upon Congress for funding on a year-by-year basis.[88] The Air Corps Act was also Congress's conservative response to the calls for reform in aircraft procurement. Congress made some gestures toward lightening the industry's burdens; but it also ensured that laissez-faire traditions would continue to shape its relations with the government, that an atmosphere of open competition would be maintained in aircraft contracting, and that private industry would continue to bear the financial risks of providing military aircraft.

In a nod to those who insisted that the steady development of military aviation and the industry's health depended upon continuity in orders, Congress approved a five-year program of equipment expansion for the air wings. Still, a policy of more planes for army and naval aviation did not solve the problems of aircraft firms unless it was matched by actual appropriations and by a contracting policy that guaranteed the regular and profitable patronage of the same firms. Orders along the lines proposed in the act were forthcoming and led to a brief but solid expansion of production beginning in 1928. However, they were distributed on the basis of price competition and always depended upon the annual politics of the budget and Congress's willingness to spend on the military. The Air Corps Act's annual increments in aircraft strength proved to be mere suggestions, and the five-year program immediately fell behind its schedules.[89] For aircraft manufacturers, budgetary politics meant that continuity in orders from their only dependable client for aircraft was never anything more than a possibility.

Like the manufacturers, congressional opponents of selective contracting were also concerned about the impending demise of the private industrial base for military aircraft. They too wanted "to obviate the necessity of the Government's entering the business of building aircraft for military purposes,"[90] but they insisted that the solution lay in an even greater reliance on competition. Unlike some in Congress who advocated the industry's position—limited competition, regular negotiated contracts with firms on an approved list, and recognition of proprietary design rights—the traditionalists were unable to suspend their qualms about possible profiteering and collusion between manufacturers and contracting officers. They could not accept that the public would be protected by government inspectors, auditors, and regular reports to Congress.

While partially made up of those who sustained the tired accusations of wartime graft and an Aircraft Trust,[91] the industry's opponents in Congress were motivated more by a deeply felt apprehension about the meaning of the industry's proposals for what they perceived as the traditions of business-government relations and technical innovation in America. They denied the assumptions of the associative state, particularly the claim that the public interest could be entrusted to an enlightened elite freed from the discipline of the market. For them a primary function of government was the maintenance of market discipline. They also continued to believe that technological advances derived from the efforts of independent inventors, such as Thomas Edison, George Westinghouse, and Alexander Graham Bell, and refused to accept that technological development had largely become the business of formal organizations and experts with specialized training. Insisting that "competitive bidding is the American way of doing business," they would not accede to the chamber's demand that an aircraft's production contract be assigned to its designing firm.[92]

The traditionalists were led by Cong. John J. McSwain, a South Carolina Democrat and member of the Military Affairs Committee who sympathized with the Insurgents and described himself as a legatee of Woodrow Wilson's New Freedom, a champion of the Jeffersonian Garden, the invisible hand, and of rural America against big business.[93] McSwain was sure that aeronautics was in the grip of an Aircraft Trust with agents in the military. He hoped to democratize this technology and allow it to fulfill the widely held vision of aeronautics as technology for the people. Opposing federal aid for business, he denied that large firms engaged in both designing and manufacturing aircraft were required to preserve a private industrial base for military aviation.

> I insist that the only way to develop this industry, as to develop any industry, is not by governmental action but by private enterprise and that in order to do that the maximum of initiative must be invoked in some way and I believe that the history of civilization will show that only the sharp clash of competition will bring about genuine and permanent progress.

He proposed the national advertisement of broad military aircraft requirements and rewards of $100,000 for winning designs. The government would control these designs and competitively let contracts for production to newcomers who would use the prize money to finance production. In this way, McSwain argued, everyone could participate and the real source of "inventive genius"—rural America—could be tapped. The best airplanes would be designed by "some fellow in the back woods, like Henry Ford was 20 years ago."[94]

The manufacturers and aviation officers scoffed at McSwain's scheme. "We are not playing with toys; we are developing engines of war . . . that have really gotten beyond the invention stage," exclaimed Keys, who tried to educate McSwain on the difference between invention and engineering and on technical advance as a bureaucratic process. The excitement and promise that pervaded the breakthrough by the Wrights no longer applied to aeronautics. "It is a matter of weights and measures and arithmetical calculation," he insisted. In all the nation only "two or three firms . . . can possibly be taken seriously" as builders of various types of advanced aircraft, yet they were made to compete with one another as if many more existed.[95]

For most congressmen, few of whom had time for the aggravating complications of the problems at hand, it was not the practicality of McSwain's scheme but the simple sentiment behind it that commended it to them. The opponents of reform were inspired solely by such feelings. Neither McSwain's proposal nor the sense that a competitive aircraft industry was desirable reflected the aspirations of any organized interest bringing pressure to bear upon Congress.[96] In the House a predilection for democratized technology and traditional perceptions of proper relations between the state and the private sector blocked proposals for procurement reform supported by the industry and the administration.

McSwain's scheme was lost in bargaining within the Military and Naval Affairs committees, but its spirit survived these negotiations and guided the procurement provisions of the Air Corps Act. As the bill's provisions materialized, the manufacturers, their program, and their lobbyists were increasingly sidelined. The chamber's staff expressed bewilderment, exasperation, and panic before the plethora of aviation bills of 1926. Most disturbing was that despite the efforts of Hays, Hoover, the secretaries of War and Navy, and the chambers' supply of lawyers to Carl Vinson to help draft a favorable law, "nobody appears to be taking the initiative on the industrial recommendations. . . . Unless the industry gets the treatment from Congress now, when everything is arranged," warned a chamber representative, "all the bad practices of the past—Government plants, competitive bidding, disregard of design rights, etc.—will become more firmly entrenched."[97]

The chamber's managers were mystified by the attitudes of the traditionalists, reflected in such comments as McSwain's:

Gentlemen, I think that something can be done along the line of stimulating inventive genius, along the lines of encouraging the men of this country, young, old, rich and poor, to devote their talents and their thought to the development of aircraft . . . restricted competition [is] the camel [which] will be in bed with us again, as he was during the great emergency, when we wasted practically $900,000,000.[98]

The views of Cong. Clyde L. Garret of Eastland, Texas, were prophetic but sadly irrelevant to the issues of supplying advanced military aircraft, given the agreement that they were needed and that private industry should produce them.

> Should we depart from old customs? . . . 150 years of practice got us this far through the big war and in a position where everybody owes us. Under this system [negotiated contracts] there will be no way of stopping . . . because it will become a fixed part of the national defense system and the Army and Navy will be so interwoven with private industry in the production of national defense materiel that there will be no way to separate without disaster to somebody.[99]

The ACC could not believe such views were genuinely held. Its managers thought the industry had become a "political football" in the hands of those seeking an independent air force. Insistence in the House upon competitive contracting, it seemed to the ACC, was a cover for the efforts of Mitchell's followers, who hoped to achieve their goals by creating a disastrous situation in aircraft design and production, which they would then be called on to remedy. Whatever the motivations or the outcome of deliberations on Capitol Hill, the chamber was resigned to the reality that having made their pitch, the manufacturers could only wait for government policy to be laid down by Congress, to which they "will necessarily have to adapt all their operations."[100]

In the conference to settle differences between House and Senate versions of procurement-reform bills, bows to radical changes had to be made since so many government officials and congressmen had insisted that aircraft posed a special case in procurement, and since all government studies had recommended reform along the lines sought by the manufacturers.[101] But for aircraft manufacturers, bows were not enough. Applying to both services, the act's Section 10 on procurement was a compromise between advocates and opponents of procurement reform. Settling none of the differences between them, its wording both restrained and encouraged price competition but in effect preserved the status quo.

The principles of competitive bidding and equal access to military contracts were upheld in Sections 10a to 10e of the act. But Section 10k authorized the secretaries to use discretion when negotiating for new designs and prototypes, to "purchase . . . with or without competition, by contract, or otherwise, such designs, aircraft, aircraft parts, or aeronautical accessories as may be necessary in his judgement. . . ." In regard to production contracts, Section 10k further stated that if a superior product resulted from designs or samples procured through negotiation, the secretaries "may enter into a contract . . . for the procurement in quantity of such aircraft, aircraft parts, or aeronautical accessories without regard to the provisions of paragraphs (a) to (e). . . ." Whatever steps taken here toward the power to negotiate contracts were offset by the act's ambivalent Section 10t. It gave the secretaries full discretion in aircraft procurement, granting contracting powers beyond the review of all but the president and the federal courts, but then reaffirmed the basis of contracting in price competition: "said Secretary is hereby authorized to award such contract to the bidder that said Secretary shall find to be the lowest responsible bidder. . . ." Vagaries in the act's wording also prevented the manufacturers from winning crucial recognition of their proprietary rights to their designs. While authorizing production contracts for aircraft designed prior to the act's passage with the aircraft's designers, the act failed to make such provision for aircraft designed after the act.[102]

For manufacturers the act resulted in ongoing uncertainty about how its congressional-military client would apply its regulatory powers over their affairs. Congress left it up to contracting officers to risk interpreting the laws in ways that might assist the industry, just as they had done previously under the nineteenth-century regulations. For a secretary to allow production contracting to go beyond the simple criteria of lowest price would require "an extraordinary amount of courage" in the face of close congressional scrutiny.[103] Whether the act intended contracting for military aircraft to be based upon principles of competition or negotiation "came down to a hopelessly moot question."[104] This unresolved problem preserved competition by default, as well as resentment and mistrust among all involved with the industry. Despite the relative insignificance of the aircraft industry at the time, the Air Corps Act was one of the most important events in contemporary American political economy. Supplemented by the Vinson-Trammell Act of 1934, it defined the aircraft industry's business environment until the eve of World War II, and thus the institutional foundation for the nation's vast air power arsenal during that conflict.

Carrying Congress's Business: The Commercial Aviation Bubble, Exports, and Wage Cuts

COMPETITIVE PROCUREMENT

The Air Corps Act encouraged greater spending for aircraft in quantity, which for some firms contributed to a brief period of profitability. However, the act did not alter the basic business parameters within which aircraft entrepreneurs and innovators had to operate. It included phrases that vaguely authorized the war and navy secretaries to use their discretion in negotiating aircraft contracts, but as the secretaries knew, its thrust was clearly behind contracting on the basis of price competition as if the commodity in question were generic items—uniforms, medical supplies, or trucks.

Nor did the act, despite its gestures in this direction, grant the manufacturers proprietary rights to their designs, essential to the competition imposed by Congress and managed by the military. In 1934 Comdr. R. D. Weyerbacher of the Navy Bureau of Aeronautics bluntly explained the rationale from the government's perspective: "In order to have price competition in aircraft you must have the right to construct those aircraft." Rather than give up on the business, however, manufacturers continued to risk losses or marginal profits on military work. One contractor described nonrecognition of design rights as "absolute robbery by the Government" but when asked by congressmen why he signed contracts with nonrecognition stipulated, which on average returned only 60 percent of the cost of designs, he could only respond that "my competitors sign them and therefore that forces me to sign."[1]

It seemed that there were always those whom the government could count on both to prod and to chase the dynamics of aeronautics, who would design and build military aircraft under any terms. Yet it is doubtful if many aircraft firms or military aeronautics could have long survived Congress's abuse had it not been for the frenzy of investment in aviation in the late 1920s, a developing export market that provided firms a profitable outlet for reproduced obsolescent designs, and as the depression took hold and wore on, an unorganized and unprotected work force to absorb wage cuts.

As the complexity and costs of military aircraft grew and as firms increasingly concentrated on particular aircraft types, seeking price competition and equal access in contracting became even more of an obstacle to military aviation. From 1927 to 1933, because of the persistence of innovators faced with still relatively minor costs, aeronautics leapt forward, or rather the various technologies that comprised aeronautics underwent simultaneous revolutions. High-horsepower, air-cooled engines developed by Wright Aeronautical and Pratt & Whitney under navy contracts in the mid-1920s were matched by radical advances in airframe construction, initially introduced by the German engineer A. K. Rohrbach and developed in the United States chiefly by private industry. Aluminum alloy monocoque frames, cantilevered wings, and smooth, stressed-metal skin significantly increased strength and lift while reducing air drag. Other key developments that coalesced during this period were high-octane fuels, retractable landing gear, streamlined engine cowlings, and variable pitch propellors. The problem of slowing down the speedy new craft and bringing them to a safe landing was solved by the development of wing flaps or air brakes.[2]

Since manufacturers bore the costs of technical development, it worked to limit the numbers of firms that could seriously compete to produce new designs for the military. Though basic innovations were freely available, the costs of design and development associated with the technical leap during the late 1920s and early 1930s grew by 200 percent while prototype costs rose from about $10,000 in the early 1920s to nearly $600,000 in 1939.[3] These cost factors were especially strong in army work, where to stay in the running for contracts manufacturers had to offer paper designs with a fixed price for the final product, finance and produce complete prototypes ready to fly in all-or-nothing performance competitions, turn the prototype over to the Air Corps if it won, and hope for favorable consideration in the competition for the production contract.

Navy procedure on competition for new designs was similar to its practice before the Air Corps Act. It selected three competitive paper proposals for whatever type it required and let "experimental contracts" for their development to the prototype stage. The prototypes would then compete to become the navy's final choice for production. Although the risks of developmental work were reduced somewhat, navy methods also encouraged a greater number of participants. As is demonstrated by the appearance during this period of new competitors such as the rebuilt Lockheed Aircraft, Grumman Aircraft, and Seversky Aviation, technical change cut both ways with competition. It was limited on one side by increasing prototype costs, a constant pressure toward concentration in the industry. Yet, without countering regulatory mechanisms, technical change and the sheer diversity of aeronautics expanded competition by providing opportunities for entry to those who could finance development or a competitive position for production contracts—not a difficult undertaking in the securities boom of the late New Era. Design costs escalated but had not attained prohibitive levels, thanks in part to the brake on innovation imposed by congressional regulation. Costs were still within reach of the dedicated small- to medium-sized firm, and innumerable real and prospective competitors emerged, keeping the organization of this industry at constant odds with its technology and mainly military market.[4] Small firms that built a handful of simple private planes or specialized sports planes considered themselves prospective military contractors and solicited government work. The military was obliged to consider them.

Table 4.1 suggests a heavy degree of concentration in the military market and it certainly did to suspicious congressmen. Between 1927 and 1933 two companies received the bulk of federal money spent on military aircraft. But this table, widely cited in Congress and the press, obscures the fact that about half the military aircraft dollar was spent on engines. United and Curtiss-Wright were holding companies that respectively controlled Boeing and Curtiss Aeroplane, as well as Pratt & Whitney and Wright Aeronautical, the two halves of a competitive duopoly in high-powered engines. The five other airframe firms were more than enough to maintain both actual competition in prototypes and potential competition in production.

In Admiral Moffett's view, competition was becoming more of a hindrance to his responsible use of the limited funds provided him and to the achievement of his bureau's goal of developing aeronautics so that the value of carrier-based air power could no longer be doubted. Possessing a clear and uncommon sense of aeronautics as high technology, Moffett viewed aircraft procurement as a process in "continuous experimental

Table 4.1. Concentration of Major Military Aircraft and
Engine Contracts, 1927–1933 (in $millions)

	Sales and Percentage of Total	
United Aircraft	$50.1	39.7%
Curtiss-Wright	44.7	35.4
Totals	94.8	75.1
Douglas	14.4	11.4
Glenn Martin	9.8	7.8
Consolidated	4.3	3.4
Great Lakes	2.4	1.9
Grumman	.5	.4
Totals	$126.5	100.0

Source: Compiled from data in Hearings before the Subcommittee on Aeronautics Making Investigation into Certain Phases of the Manufacture of Aircraft and Aeronautical Accessories as They Refer to the Navy Department, 73rd Cong., 1st sess., 1934 (Delaney Hearings), 503.

procurement." For him the distinction between aircraft design and production was meaningless and an obstacle to procurement. By the time manufacturers could present competing bids for production contracts, new advances and requirements had changed the product significantly. Ascertaining that various bidders were responsible and that they knew what they were competing to build was time-consuming and often impossible. Still worse for naval aviation in Moffett's view was the tendency of price competition to deter aggressive innovation. Moffett realized that to fill its needs, the navy was wholly dependent upon the specialized design staffs and production workers of a handful of companies. He felt procurement laws dishonored the government and did his best to discourage the disruption of private expertise by new competition and "to recognize design rights to the extent of existing law."[5]

Even after suffering the delays of advertising, Moffett was still nervous about negotiating contracts and continuously sought stronger authority to engage in them. Yet Cong. Carl Vinson's efforts to change the law were unsuccessful and, like the chief of the Air Corps and his respective successors until World War II, Moffett was always wary of pushing the issue too hard and provoking Congress into measures even more restrictive than the Air Corps Act.[6]

No amount of contempt for the system could persuade officers to violate the law and systematically deploy their contracting powers to stabilize the industry, help manufacturers offset the costs of design and

Adm. William A. Moffett, chief of the Navy Bureau of Aeronautics, with Henry Ford at the Detroit air races on a frigid day in 1922. Behind them is the navy's entry, the UO-2, built by the Naval Aircraft Factory. Mounted beneath is a Lamblin radiator.

development, facilitate the specialization of firms by aircraft type, and get the most from their funds. In an attempt to bypass the Air Corps Act's ambiguities, the army turned, as it had before the act, to an equally dubious old regulation for negotiating contracts;[7] but the effects of potential competition were sustained. As early as December 1926 the new Army Air Corps issued circulars of requirements to manufacturers stipulating that all new designs would be surrendered to the government with no compensation beyond the prototype price arranged before it was built. In May 1929 the army's judge advocate general decided that the Air Corps Act gave no power to let production contracts until after advertising and competitive bidding. In January 1931 the navy's judge advocate general agreed.[8] The bulk of navy production contracts were negotiated but only after advertisement had brought what Moffett called a "base price" (see Appendix 3). Manufacturers were required to submit quotations for aircraft based on a production volume of twenty-seven planes and were not permitted to seek higher prices if smaller production runs were finally contracted for.[9]

Just as before the Air Corps Act, competitive pricing was also effectively maintained by the awareness among manufacturers that negotiations took place only at the contracting officer's pleasure. Thomas A. Morgan, president of Curtiss-Wright and Sperry Gyroscope, complained in 1934, "whether you have active competition in that model or not you have the threat of competition," or as Admiral King put it, "we have very keen competition . . . it just does not happen always to be handled by sealed bids."[10] Reuben Fleet pointed out that even to term such dealings as negotiated contracting was to create a

> gross misconception . . . namely, that they are handouts and perhaps involve collusion, whereas they are awarded only after the severest competition. Performance and suitability of all competitive models are carefully checked, and then Government audited costs and accumulated cost data from the entire industry, together with delivery records, are weighed as to each competitive model. Government officers have then used every conceivable means of chiselling prices, including threats to buy an admittedly inferior product, or to appropriate the creator's design and invite formal competitive bids from other manufacturers, or to have Government plants build them, or let the funds revert to the Treasury. Particularly unfair has been the Government practice to try to force successful design creators to meet the prices of competitors who have reduced their prices under cost for their inferior products in a deliberate attempt to obtain a foothold.[11]

Fleet had lost $500,000 on the design of a navy flying boat in 1929 and had bought materials in anticipation of its production contract only to see it go to an underbidding Glenn Martin, who had no development costs to cover but nonetheless lost on the contract.[12]

Also unchanged by the Air Corps Act was the ad hoc and adversarial relationship between the military aviation bureaus and their industrial base. Manufacturers needed to know where and at what levels to invest time and resources in new designs. They continually urged the military to develop long-range plans, laying out spending goals as well as likely trends in official doctrine on the uses of air power. Hoping to contribute, they also sought access to the planning process.[13] In 1928 Curtiss Aeroplane reasonably inquired of the chief of the Air Corps "whether it is not possible . . . to ascertain your attitude on the subject of performance and cost . . . you appreciate that as we have in the past, it is possible for this Company to mistake the desires of the Government." Specifically, Curtiss wanted to know whether its engineers should continue their focus on incremental developments of the 1923 Curtiss Hawk, designed for a 400-horsepower engine. With the development of 600-horsepower engines, the company could now either produce a new pursuit plane "of unsurpassed performance" at an estimated cost of $75,000 or revise the old design for the new engine for only $15,000. Curtiss wanted to pursue the new design but was afraid it could outrun the Air Corps' desire and ability to pay for better performance. It could also find itself in a noncompetitive position in production contracting if existing designs were continued. "Would it not be possible," the company asked, "to arrange conferences between your Procurement Board and representatives of the Company from time to time" to discuss matters of types, performance, and costs, and to "intelligently guide the Company in selecting that line of development most nearly meeting the Government's requirements?"[14]

The suggestion was rejected by the Air Corps as likely to produce "competition of high-powered salesmanship, misunderstandings, and would make public a proceeding that must be kept confidential." Such concern with public suspicion of military-industrial conferences indicates the conservative effect of politics on technical change, limiting the institutional environment in which it could be pursued. More striking was the Air Corps' argument that manufacturers could acquire a "reasonably correct idea of our requirements" from past trends, from "previous estimates and appropriations already approved [by Congress] which set forth and limit types, quantities and prices." The Air Corps "has only a limited option in changing and modifying what has previously been decided upon and approved."[15] Thus, to look forward, the aircraft industry and its technology were told to look backward.

A wasteful and hostile pattern of military-industrial relations was the outcome of a contradictory political economy of high-technology weapons supply. On the one hand there was no question that private industry must supply these weapons. Dabbling in nationalization went no further than the Naval Aircraft Factory, intended only to provide a yardstick to measure private costs and performance and to keep private industry "honest." On the other hand were the ideological needs to keep relations between industry and the military as distant as possible—to resist the consultative links that both parties required—and to preserve a market discipline as if sophisticated weapons production was a commercial enterprise. The entire framework was shot through with mistrust, misunderstanding, and resentment.

In 1934 Claire L. Egtvedt aired his frustration on Capitol Hill. The usually cool Boeing president, speaking off the record, was outraged by the intimations of the constant queries from congressmen on his contacts with officers and by growing criticism of what later became known as the "revolving door" between industry and the services. Without the formal, consultative links Congress would not tolerate, how else was he to follow trends in his primary market except by personal contacts with officers? And under the artificial business environment maintained by Congress, how else was he to pursue those contacts but in secrecy, not so much from public scrutiny but from other manufacturers?

> Will we just go home and not try to find out what is coming up or do we go around [Washington and Dayton] and try to find out what possible business is coming; if they are going to let business on bombers, or if there is going to be business in pursuits, or attacks, or corps observation, or whatever it is? Or will we be notified as to when there is business, or the possibility of getting business, or just what procedure is going to take place? That is something that is of some importance to us, because we need business and need it bad.[16]

THE AVIATION INDUSTRY
ON MAIN STREET AND WALL STREET

Despite ongoing problems with military contracting during the period from the passage of the Air Corps Act to the beginning of the depression, manufacturers, aside from occasional grumblings, were notably restrained in their criticisms of the government. Some perceived the act as a victory for the industry, believing that its ambivalent procurement provisions would be either interpreted by "responsible" contracting officers in the industry's favor or amended by Congress when its "errors" became clearer.[17] Although actual appropriations did not materialize until fiscal year 1928, others were content with the upsurge in demand for quantity aircraft under the act's provisions for equipment expansion. The major manufacturers snubbed the Aeronautical Chamber of Commerce and collective political action again, sensing that associationalist efforts were wasted and likely only to encourage new competitors. After the failure to win procurement reform in the Air Corps Act, Douglas, Boeing, Fleet, Vought, and Martin ignored the chamber.

More importantly the nation was once more gripped by aviation fever, driven this time by fantastic visions of private and commercial aeronautics. Many manufacturers began to regard military contracting as a sideline, a duty to national security, and to believe that aeronautical progress, profits, and prestige were best pursued in the commercial realm, a market they could shape themselves relatively free of government interference.

During the years 1926 to 1929 a number of developments combined to drive the euphoria that by the time of the Great Crash had flooded the aviation industry with hundreds of millions in new capital. Most critical were technical advances that in the public mind delivered aeronautics from its primitive "stick-and-wire" stage. Further assurances were given by the legislation for commercial aviation of the mid-1920s, which provided federal safety regulation, navigational aids, and air-mail subsidies to new airlines. The persona of Henry Ford and his participation in aircraft manufacture also contributed. The Flivver King's subsidization of the famous Tri-Motor, which first appeared in 1926, helped reinvigorate the wartime fantasy of an aircraft industry soon to rival automobile manufacture by mass-producing thousands of passenger airliners to crisscross the globe and millions of "automobiles with wings" to fill everyman's garage.[18]

The catalyst for the frenzy of financial commitment by investors small and large was Charles Lindbergh's epochal New York-to-Paris flight in 1927. The soft-spoken, coverall-clad Lone Eagle from small-town Minnesota struck a deep chord within American culture, prompting an outpouring of public adulation and hero worship. Lindbergh reassured Americans that their values and myths of independence, initiative, defiance of nature, and social mobility were alive and well despite ample evidence to the contrary in a bureaucratized, urbanized, industrial society.[19] Lindbergh tempered insecurity over technological change by underscoring the ambiguity of the impact of aeronautics, the fact that despite its complexity and disruptions of tradition, an airplane was an inanimate object until brought to life by the skills of a single pilot. Aeronautics both disciplined human control and expanded its scope. Through Lindbergh, Americans again found consolation in aeronautics as they gazed into the future. The unpredictability of this technology, which revolutionized perceptions of space, time, and limits, lent itself to whatever ideal future one hoped for—a new era of endless invention and technical progress, of technology for everyman, of business enterprise with global reach, of a world made free from warfare by the preventative, omnipotent might of air power.

Also essential to the boom in aviation securities was a voracious investing-public, awash with cash and eager to celebrate an apparently triumphant New Era capitalism through a frenzy of speculation in an industry that seemed to be one of its most promising sectors. Aviation stocks were bought at a phenomenal rate during 1928 and 1929. In 1927 the aircraft industry had generated barely $500,000 through public securities. By March 1929 aircraft, air transport, and related stocks generated a new securities subindustry that raised $175 million, representing 11.2 percent of all new corporate issues to that point in the Wall Street boom. Three hundred million had been raised by October when the crash sent stock values through the basement floor and the flow of investment dried up. Only $1.8 million in new aviation stocks were issued in 1930.[20]

Such a mass infusion of new capital had profound effects on the aircraft industry. Since virtually all of it came via common stock with no par value, the industry was free to invest or squander it as it saw fit. A post-crash ad hoc industry committee struck by Clement Keys and Robert Lehman in an attempt to put the preceding years into perspective agreed that the collapse in aviation stocks should have "been followed in the usual course of events by a long list of receiverships and bankruptcies." "No such thing occurred," however, because of the enormous reserves of free working capital available to aviation firms. "Companies have had room to weather the storms and keep engineering and plants active."[21] Spirited efforts were made to use up these funds in the creation and acquisition of aviation firms, in research and development projects, in building aircraft for inventory, and in huge managerial staffs and bloated salaries. But most firms were left with much more cash than they could use, allowing them to absorb heavy losses through the early years of the depression as the expected mass market for commercial aviation failed to emerge.

This "free" capital provided mostly by small investors helped Congress maintain a competitive industry. Some manufacturers and promoters tried to use their new funds to rationalize the industry through vertical and horizontal acquisitions, which they hoped could produce economies in design, production, sales, and service. But they were only partly successful. Key manufacturers used their funds to protect their independence while others used theirs to create new firms and significantly expand capacity. As it became clear that the manufacturers' primary business was still in the military market with its unchanged competitive dynamics it also became obvious that the industry as a whole had benefited little from the investment boom. There was little change in terms of industrial order, predictability, or in the mechanisms for encouraging and managing technical change free from the debilitating fiscal need to produce aircraft in quantity—the outcome of procurement law.

Aside from those designers who took the opportunity to recoup the sacrifices of the previous decade by selling out at high prices, retiring to their drawing boards, and leaving to promoters the aggravations of finance and management, or those remaining manufacturers who inflated their salaries, accumulated profits in stock dealings, and lived the high life so vividly described by John Dos Passos, perhaps the only real beneficiary of the investment boom was the United States taxpayer. The new appearance and improved financial strength of numerous competitors kept downward pressure on prices for military aircraft. Otherwise the government would have had to finance the costly technical strides that some of these cash-choked companies took despite the risks—strides that made possible both modern air transport and air power.

The details of the corporate maneuvers in aviation during this period are as bewildering to the historian as they probably were even to those most directly involved in them. Hundreds of companies were formed in the industry's numerous subfields, primarily with a view of "getting in on the ground floor" of commercial aviation's future, of staking a claim in what was widely perceived as the "gold rush" of the 1920s. New manufacturers of aircraft, engines, parts, and accessories emerged along with operators of advertising, consultancy, insurance, finance, and engineering firms, airports, flight schools, and airlines. A semblance of order to this blur of activity was provided by three new holding companies— United Aircraft and Transport Corporation (UATC), North American Aviation–Curtiss-Wright, and the Aviation Corporation (AVCO); together they controlled 48 percent of the industry's assets by August 1929.[22] However, the latter two consolidations—NAA–Curtiss-Wright and AVCO—tended to reflect the industry's centrifugal forces rather than any ordering of them. These were guided by men much more heavily seduced by the visions of commercial and private aviation than were the directors of UATC, who conservatively focused upon firms tied closely to the government—manufacturers with strong presences in the relatively more stable military market and airlines with choice mail contracts.

The strength of the commercial vision is best gauged by its conquest of

Clement Keys, long one of the better analysts of his industry's dynamics and a pessimist about commercial aviation's prospects. The same Keys was the moving force behind the disastrous Curtiss-Wright combine, which in turn became the impetus in the decline of Keys's health, his business reputation, and his role in the industry. His change of heart began after the passage of the 1925 Air Mail Act when he, along with Howard Coffin, Henry Ford, William Averell Harriman, William Rockefeller, and Owen D. Young, among others, formed National Air Transport (NAT) to carry mail between New York, Chicago, and Dallas. NAT and eight of the other ten new air-mail carriers consistently lost money.[23] Nevertheless in 1928 Keys's confidence was buoyed by a full year of solid returns at Curtiss, thanks mainly to private sales. He took special pleasure in informing the Air Corps that he had

> instructed the Curtiss officers to prepare a plan for the expansion of Curtiss plant facilities and working capital to take care of our proper share in the growth of commercial aviation. [It] will of course inevitably surpass the production of both military services in volume and will also of course, carry a better margin of profit than the Army and Navy contracts, because of the very large engineering costs that the Curtiss Company has always carried in pushing forward design work for advanced types.[24]

In 1928 Keys financed a major expansion of the Curtiss plant in Buffalo and a branch plant in St. Louis in anticipation of the commercial boom.[25] With common stock issues arranged by Hayden, Stone and Banc-America Blair, he incorporated North American Aviation as part of a long series of convoluted dealings aimed at building a dominant presence in commercial aviation. Keys amassed a portfolio in over twenty engineering, manufacturing, sales, service, financing, transport, and training firms, including Sperry Gyroscope and Ford Instrument. In March 1929 he arranged a $31 million stock issue in Curtiss Airports.[26] Telling the press that "there is nothing to criticize our government for,"[27] in June 1929 he joined with Richard F. Hoyt and formed a merger within a merger, the Curtiss-Wright Corporation, consolidating assets with a paper value of $70 million.[28] Hoyt was chairman of Wright Aeronautical, the Paterson, New Jersey, engine manufacturer, and had acquired such small private-plane builders as Travel Air, Walter Beech's first company in Wichita. Together Keys and Hoyt greatly overextended NAA–Curtiss-Wright in poorly integrated, primarily commercial acquisitions. The only direction to these combinations seemed to be the misguided faith in the boundless prospects of the commercial, particularly private, aircraft market.[29]

The optimism of Keys, Hoyt, and their associates rebounded with devastating force when the market for private aircraft collapsed even before the crash and when airlines such as NAT, Keys's failed China Airways venture, and the new Transcontinental Air Transport—"The Lindbergh Line"— generated huge losses.[30] Curtiss-Wright alone posted losses that reached $15 million. Keys suffered a nervous collapse in 1931 after prolonged battles with the United group for control of NAT and with General Motors for control of North American. GM had reentered the field with the purchase of a 40 percent share of Fokker Aircraft and 25 percent of the parts manufacturer, Bendix Aviation, moves widely hailed as proof that the aviation boom was no bubble.[31] In 1930 GM established General Aviation, concentrating its aircraft manufacturing interests in Baltimore and divesting itself of the Fokker name, tarnished by a crash that killed the famed football coach Knute Rockne. The new firm lost $750,000 in its first year.[32] At fire-sale prices, GM also began accumulating shares of NAA, the umbrella for promising but losing firms such as Eastern Air Lines, the new Transcontinental and Western Air, and the Berliner/Joyce Aircraft Company of Baltimore, a new manufacturer of army pursuit planes.[33]

Keys's replacement as president by Thomas A. Morgan, president of Sperry Gyroscope; liquidations of airport, flying school, and private airplane subsidiaries; a refocus on the relative strength of its military contractors—Curtiss Aeroplane and Wright Aeronautical; and a surging export market for American warplanes together helped Curtiss-Wright staunch its losses in subsequent years.[34] Millions more were lost in 1931, but in 1932 and 1933, after huge write-downs and with the help of highly flexible accounting measures, nominal profits were returned. In 1933 Curtiss-Wright's first profit was 2.5 percent on sales of $9.2 million, $3.5 million of which were military exports.

Richard Hoyt was also party to the creation of the Aviation Corporation, capitalized in March 1929 with $35 million in no par value stock, which had been issued with the fair warning to investors that it "must be regarded in the light of speculation." Its holdings centered upon Pan American Airways and the Fairchild Corporation, a builder of small cabin-planes worth $2.6 million in sales in 1928. AVCO's list of directors featured a who's who of prominent bankers, aircraft builders, railroad and steamship men who shared in the vision, fantasies, or avarice prompted by aviation. The board was chaired by W. A. Harriman and

included Hoyt, Juan Trippe of Pan Am, Robert Dollar, the West Coast
shipper Charles Hayden, Robert Lehman, R. K. Mellon, William Rockefeller, William Vanderbilt, Cornelius Whitney, and Robert Woodruff,
president of Coca-Cola.[35]

AVCO absorbed small manufacturers, parts suppliers, and airports
and acquired various airlines, which together formed the nucleus of
American Airlines. By the end of 1929 AVCO had about eighty subsidiaries and 9,100 miles of poorly coordinated transport routes, often
competing directly with one another. A common accounting system to
help the company trace its huge losses was not set up until 1930.[36] In 1931
AVCO lost control of the Fairchild manufacturing works when Sherman
Fairchild deserted the company and established a new independent firm
on Long Island. In the same year the corporation developed links with
the young automobile racer Errett Lobban Cord, whose aggressive
speculations and attacks on the company's management compounded the
turmoil of ongoing losses, which totaled $38 million in its first three
years.[37] Cord controlled the Auburn and Duesenberg auto companies
along with a number of aircraft firms serving the deadened private market, including Stinson Aircraft of Detroit and the Lycoming Company of
Williamsport, Pennsylvania, manufacturer of small aircraft engines.[38] By
March 1933 Cord had gained control of AVCO and ousted Harriman and
Hoyt, but losses continued. In 1934 Cord was in England ducking the new
Securities and Exchange Commission.[39] The company was placed under
trusteeship and bought in 1935 by the young financier Victor Emanuel, who
rationalized its manufacturing holdings and such new firms as Vultee Aircraft of Downey, California. In 1942 AVCO bought Reuben Fleet's Consolidated, which in combination with Vultee would later form a building
block of General Dynamics, the military conglomerate.

United Aircraft and Transport Corporation was much more successful
than the other holding companies but nevertheless revealed the limits of
even the most careful strategies of corporate integration within an industry ultimately determined by congressional politics. UATC evolved from
the Boeing Aircraft and Transport Corporation (BATC), an October 1928
consolidation of William Boeing's Seattle operations and his new airline
that flew the mail between Chicago and San Francisco. The Rockefeller-
controlled National City Company financed BATC. In a move typical of
the manipulations of stock issues during this period, which later so an-
noyed congressmen and produced even more political obstacles to rationalization of the industry, National City withheld public issue of the stock
until it had been distributed in units to individuals on a "preferred list." A

few days later, once public expectation had been raised to a sufficient pitch, these individuals realized large profits when the stock was listed on the Curb well above the unit price.[40]

To expand upon BATC and to raise even more "adequate capital upon a conservative and business-like basis,"[41] Boeing and National City formed UATC, capitalized at $25 million in January 1929. UATC stock was also issued in a manner contrived to take advantage of the public euphoria over aviation and to reap big profits for those on a preferred list, which included most of the directors of UATC, National City Bank, and its affiliates. But UATC, like its predecessor, was intended to do more than simply produce windfalls for insiders. Cautiously and with careful planning, the new holding company aimed to secure its position in aviation through a union of some of the disparate yet interdependent elements that comprised the industry. UATC's strategies of integration and diversification never wavered from a primary focus on government work. Its directors remained skeptical of the presumed mass market in private flying and passenger traffic that drove the other combines. It obtained only a small holding in private aircraft production with its purchase of the Stearman Company of Wichita and a minor presence in passenger air-transport production through Sikorsky Aviation. Building on Boeing Air Transport, UATC also restricted its airline acquisitions to firms with strong federal subsidies in the form of air-mail contracts. UATC airline acquisitions evolved into United Airlines, which nearly had a monopoly on transcontinental air mail.[42]

UATC also acquired outright some of the strongest and most specialized military aircraft producers, including the Chance Vought Corporation; the Avion Corporation, an experimental firm established by the brilliant designer John K. Northrop; and Hamilton-Standard Propeller, which wielded a virtual monopoly in the manufacture of metal propellers. Although these firms were left to operate separately within the multidivisional form, UATC moved Chance Vought from Long Island City and Hamilton-Standard from Pittsburgh and concentrated them in a new East Hartford, Connecticut, plant which they shared with another UATC subsidiary, Pratt & Whitney Corporation, a highly successful engine builder.[43]

Pratt & Whitney was guided by Frederick B. Rentschler, a close associate of Boeing and brother of National City Bank's president, Gordon Rentschler. Established in 1925, Pratt & Whitney proved to be an "Aladdin's lamp" for its three original investors, much to the later indignation of congressmen.[44] Its Hornet and Wasp air-cooled radial engines were the world's best and generated 60 percent of $8 million in 1929 UATC profits. UATC lost heavily in Sikorsky because of bad deals made between Igor Sikorsky and Pan Am's Juan Trippe on flying boats prior to its acquisition. It only broke even on Chance Vought's navy Corsair, and throughout most of the 1930s UATC's airline holdings operated at losses or barely broke even.[45] The remainder of UATC's profits were produced by stock dealings, by Hamilton-Standard, and by Boeing Airplane, which remained in Seattle and manufactured almost entirely for the government. In 1927–1933 Boeing turned in an average annual profit on sales of 12.5 percent.[46] In the depths of the depression, it operated at full capacity, employing 1,100 workers in 1931–1932 to build 200 army P-12 pursuits, 121 navy F-4B fighters, 5 monoplane bombers, 12 mail planes, and the first two 247-transports. UATC earned more than $3 million in 1930; in 1931 it earned $2.7 million, a respectable profit on $30 million in sales. Throughout these years UATC operated with great restraint, never paying dividends and annually writing off 20 percent for depreciation of plant and equipment.[47]

Still, the most conservative management was not enough to keep UATC prosperous. Profits were firm in 1932 but declined rapidly when Boeing lost an important bomber contract to Martin, as cutbacks in military spending took their toll, and as procurement law kept pressure on prices. Management could do little to combat a political atmosphere that was growing more hostile to military contractors and airline operators (see chapter 5). Nineteen thirty-four was a trying year for UATC: The company showed a deficit of $3.1 million, thanks to a halt in Boeing's production of its P-26 pursuit after a fatal crash; the eclipse of its revolutionary new 247-transport by the still-superior Douglas Commercial-2; a six-week strike at its Connecticut holdings; and the loss of revenue for the period from February to May, when its air-mail contracts were suddenly cancelled by President Roosevelt. Along with the other holding companies, UATC was forced by the Air Mail Act of 1934 to separate its air transport from its manufacturing units to be able to bid for air-mail contracts. The United Aircraft Corporation became the new parent of Pratt & Whitney, Chance Vought, Sikorsky, and Hamilton-Standard. United Airlines was spun off, and Boeing separately absorbed the Stearman works in Wichita, converting it to military work, primarily trainers.[48]

Corporate integration and the intraindustry linkages created by a kaleidoscopic network of interlocking directorships failed to contain competition in aircraft manufacture, despite the subsequent charges of congressmen.[49] Indeed, apart from the United group, containing competition seems to have been only a minor goal among those who directed the new holding companies, one well behind immediate paper gains and preparation for the imagined new era of commercial aviation. Even had all the new combines emulated UATC's restraint, greater success in limiting competition in aircraft manufacture was unlikely, given the still relative ease of entry for new firms. And, limited as they were, these new consolidations only encouraged a New Deal Congress to insist even more rigidly on a competitive, antitrust approach by the military in its dealings with the aircraft industry.

The failure of integration and the persistence of competitive pressure is best measured by the industry's massive overcapacity. In 1929, the industry's best year until pre–World War II expansion, 286 manufacturing firms could produce 20,000 planes. Only half of the 6,193 mostly commercial planes actually built during that year were sold. The rest languished in inventory, where they drove prices below cost until overcome by deterioration or obsolescence.[50]

Many firms and their capital disappeared, but others survived to remain competitors as the costs of new development, mismanagement, and overcapacity were absorbed by the reservoirs of working capital provided by hapless investors. Douglas Aircraft successfully spurned its many suitors. It made its first public offering of no par value common stock in 1928, and although NAA acquired a share in it and Keys briefly served on its board, the company remained independent. From 1925 to 1931 Douglas's engineering staff, low wages, and concentration on government manufacture produced healthy profits, almost all of which were reinvested in new designs. During those years Douglas sold 814 airplanes— 635 to the army, 78 to the navy, 51 to the Post Office, 34 to the Chinese, Mexican, and Peruvian armies, and only 14 in the commercial market. In 1933 Douglas absorbed Northrop as a subsidiary and with the success of its DC-2 began a shift to commercial production that by 1934 relegated military work to only 15 percent of its output. Despite their domination of the air transport market, the sleek new DC-2s and DC-3s generated losses for Douglas that prevailed until the war. Even if Douglas was temporarily absorbed by commercial work, he continued to exert pressure on Boeing and Martin in the bomber business, outlining to the military the bomber potential of the DC-2 design, which was faster than Martin's bomber then in service and which outranged it, 2200 to 700 miles.[51]

Reuben Fleet of Consolidated Aircraft proudly declared to suspicious congressmen the independence of his firm from "the big companies . . . no holding company owns or controls us . . . the corporate structure of Consolidated Aircraft is clean cut." The mainstay of Consolidated's production was military trainers. Their relative simplicity and high unit-volume helped Consolidated turn its first and quite substantial profits of 36 percent on sales of $3.1 million in 1928 and 24 percent on $2.6 million in 1929. However, profits declined rapidly in 1930 to 4 percent on $4.3 million and .4 percent on $2.3 million in 1933, mainly because of large losses on new army business and the loss of production contracts for a navy flying boat, developed at great expense by the company. Had it not been for the working capital provided by stock issues and the strength of foreign demand for its military trainers, Consolidated's position would have been untenable.[52]

The individualistic Glenn L. Martin was also untouched by the merger mania. Nevertheless, the same enthusiasm for aviation's prospects that drove the boom seduced him as well. In early 1929 he moved his company from Cleveland to a 1,200-acre tract on Chesapeake Bay near Baltimore. There he built, just in time for the depression, a giant plant in anticipation of mainly private and commercial work requiring 10,000 employees. Martin's individualism almost cost him his company, one of the strongest innovators in military aircraft designs. He would not tolerate the dilution of his and his mother's control through equity financing and turned instead to funded debt. In 1929 he borrowed $2.8 million in 6 percent five-year gold notes. When they came due in 1934 Martin could not honor them, despite a prime $2.5 million bomber contract in early 1933 and another in 1934. Unable to deflect losses onto stockholders as his competitors could, Martin went through Section 77(B) of the Bankruptcy Act. With the help of a $500,000 Reconstruction Finance Corporation loan, the notes were renegotiated; but Martin did not recover until the war.[53]

Another important firm that remained free from the consolidations was Lockheed Aircraft. Killed by the merger movement, Lockheed was later revived by a group of aggressive and capable managers and designers who carved out a new foothold in the aircraft market. The company was incorporated in late 1926 by the Loughead brothers, Malcolm and Alan, who had built aircraft in Southern California since the war and had changed their name because it was so often mispronounced. With John Northrop they produced the Vega, a highly advanced, small air-transport of wooden monocoque design and single cantilevered wing. In 1929 Lockheed attracted the attention of the Detroit Aircraft Corporation (DAC), a holding company directed by auto industry leaders Charles F. Kettering, Charles S. Mott, William B. Mayo, and Ransom E. Olds. In a hostile takeover DAC acquired 87 percent of Lockheed. The Lockheed brothers resigned in anger and by 1931 DAC was bankrupt, pulling down its only strong subsidiary.[54]

The bankrupt Lockheed appealed to two brothers from Boston, Robert E. and Courtland S. Gross, who, with others, were willing to gamble on the company and bought its assets from the receiver for $40,000 in June 1932. On the strength of its commercial products, the Vega and the Orion, and the willingness of its management and employees to bear heavy sacrifices, Lockheed was operating at capacity and began to turn slim profits by September 1933. With the help of a Reconstruction Finance Corporation loan and a thinly subscribed public offering, the company also began development of the spectacular Electra, the most successful small transport of the 1930s. Beginning in 1934 Lockheed's offerings of the Electra to the Air Corps as a light bomber and attack plane remained in the blueprint stage, but even there they served as a competitive spur to military contractors. Lockheed operated marginally, doggedly pursuing any sales opportunity for the Electra whether at home or abroad, until 1938 when a $25 million British order for the Hudson, a light bomber version of the Electra, secured the company's future.[55]

As president of Lockheed, Robert Gross left an assessment of the relations among the holding companies during 1933 that suggests the competitive pressures not only from those outside their control but also from the combines. He described the

aircraft field narrowing down now to a very interesting struggle between two or three groups. The United group, whose Pratt & Whitney engine is still the best product, are on one side of the fence; and the GM–NAA–Wright Aero. group are lined up against them with Cord [AVCO] sitting in the middle not knowing which way he is going to jump.

Gross foresaw competitive "fireworks" in a stagnant market as each scrambled for aircraft and engine orders from independent airlines, manufacturers, and the military. Even as strong a manufacturer as Boeing Airplane felt compelled to launch a claim in the industry's commercial patent pool against Lockheed and Douglas for the development of the Electra and the DC-2. Boeing charged that these infringed upon its patented low-wing, twin-engined transport, the 247.[56]

Old competitors survived the depression and new ones appeared, also outside the orbit of the combines. In December 1929 Leroy R. Grumman, a gifted designer and former engineer at the Naval Aircraft Factory, established Grumman Aircraft Engineering Corporation at Farmingdale, Long Island, which quickly emerged as an important competitor, particularly for navy contracts. Grumman was pleased to tell congressmen about his minimal overhead in contrast to the managerially top-heavy holding companies. He told them he was "proud to be outside the trust," which he was well aware did not exist in the way many congressmen thought it did.[57] Grumman shared his Farmingdale plant with newly independent Sherman Fairchild and another new entry to the industry, Seversky Aircraft Corporation, founded in 1931 by Alexander P. deSeversky, a Russian expatriate engineer who in later years developed an army trainer and the P-35, the first American fighter to reach 320 miles per hour and 30,000 feet. In 1939 Seversky was reorganized as Republic Aviation.

Other important firms that appeared or remained independent were Bellanca Aircraft of Wilmington, Delaware, named after an Italian engineer, Giuseppe M. Bellanca, and controlled by bankers led by Otto Kahn; the Great Lakes Aircraft Corporation, which continued to operate Martin's facilities in Cleveland and was willing to absorb continuous losses on its military work until finally liquidated in 1935; the Airplane Division of the Ford Motor Company, which built air transports; and smaller firms such as Clyde Cessna Aircraft and Swallow Airplane, both of Wichita, and Waco Aircraft of Troy, Ohio, all of which had the developed expertise to construct, if not design, most any aircraft.

THE AERONAUTICAL CHAMBER OF COMMERCE: IN SEARCH OF A NEW DEAL

During the late 1920s the ACC embodied the diversity, the competitiveness, and the explosive expansion of the aviation industry rather than any significant success in containing them. Coping with these dynamics was difficult enough even during the brief prosperity. The chamber's problems were compounded as the boom cooled and the industry's various units rediscovered their conflicting interests. Many of the new firms that optimistically entered aviation in a wave during 1927–1929 eagerly took up membership in the ACC. As their predecessors had during the postwar years, they saw in the chamber the best means of pursuing the national promotion of aviation. The ACC organized annual air shows and planned joint publicity campaigns. It also offered newcomers valuable information on technical and legislative developments and provided a sense of collective identity to an energetic and diverse group of mainly small businesses that considered themselves part of a revolutionary development in commerce. Initially it seemed again that with divisiveness subsumed by unlimited growth, the industry could serve as a new model of Herbert Hoover's associationalism. Faced with widening and increasingly detailed federal regulation of their affairs, commercial aviation entrepreneurs hoped the chamber might arrange industrial self-regulation, "the idea and policy for the operations of the Aeronautical Branch of the Commerce Department as laid down by Mr. Hoover."[58]

The ACC responded to the sudden expansion by decentralizing and diversifying. It established geographical divisions to accommodate membership in thirty-three states and a separate department each for the industry's numerous units—commercial and military aircraft builders; manufacturers of engines, parts, and accessories; producers of fuel and lubricants; suppliers of material and equipment; operators of airlines, flying schools, and airports; distributors and dealers; financiers and insurers; and so forth. Frederick Rentschler, president of UATC, was the chamber's president in 1929–1930. But apart from UATC, which perceived the trade association as part of its integrative strategy, the holding companies treated the ACC with indifference. Major manufacturers—Martin, Grumman, Douglas, Lockheed, and Consolidated among them—also continued to reject the chamber's invitations to join.[59]

Because of their numbers, small manufacturers of commercial airplanes became a presence in the chamber out of proportion to their importance in the industry as a whole. Despite the boom, aircraft sales were still dominated by military contractors. In 1928, 3,542 of the 4,761 aircraft built were for the commercial market; but at a collective value of $17 million, they were worth $2 million less than the 1,219 military planes manufactured during that year by a handful of contractors.[60] Among the small commercial builders, Clyde V. Cessna was a particularly strong advocate of collective action. To cut costs and to assure the industry's effective influence as regulations were formulated in Washington, Cessna unsuccessfully tried to persuade the industry to duplicate on a national scale the cooperative arrangements he had initiated in Wichita. He described a joint corporation through which he, Walter Beech of Travel Air, Lloyd Stearman, and the Swallow Airplane Company purchased raw materials and accessories; promoted standardized manufacture, design and accounting; promised not to "pirate" each other's workers; and stood by one another as the Department of Commerce set standards for airworthiness under the powers of the Air Commerce Act. "We should make our own regulations and have the Department enforce the regulations," Cessna insisted, arguing that only a united industry could aspire to this ideal.[61]

As flying regulations and aircraft manufacturing standards evolved, however, the fact that manufacturers significantly shaped both their substance and details was due less to any united front of businessmen in aviation than to the predispositions of the Department of Commerce, its sympathetic secretary, R. P. Lamont, and its assistant secretaries for air, Clarence M. Young and William P. McCracken, both of whom had close ties with the industry and the ACC. United fronts among entrepreneurs in aviation proved even more difficult to achieve as the expansion in manufacturing capacity and inventory evolved into flooded markets, depressed prices, and large losses. New ACC members discovered basic conflicts of interest both among and within aviation's various branches. Except for a broad agreement on the need to promote aviation, a role which the chamber tried to play, operators found that their interests clashed with those of the manufacturers, and manufacturers with suppliers, and so on.

In the summer of 1929, for example, commercial aircraft builders wrangled with engine manufacturers. The builders felt that the more profitable engine manufacturers were getting a free ride from the airplane manufacturers, who in effect advertised, sold, and distributed engines along with their airplanes. The engine manufacturers were asked to extend discounts to the builders to help cover the discounts they were forced to offer in an attempt to rid themselves of growing inventories. B. G. Leighton of Wright Aeronautical sympathized with the builders and denounced the emerging "you and me idea, rather than the we idea," but he offered no discounts.[62]

As their inventories grew, the commercial builders remained just as convinced as had been postwar proponents of commercial aviation that only "public education" stood between them and a vast market for private aircraft. Advertisment was perceived as the key for unlocking this market, and the builders proposed that all the industry's units participate in a collective marketing campaign. They alone among the industry's groups responded positively, and the marketing consulting firm hired by the chamber in April 1929 could make no suggestions as to how the industry might profit in an immediate way from the growing public interest in aviation. No common message that all the industry's units would support in a national advertising program capable of immediate returns was apparent to these experts.[63]

Well before the Great Crash, the chamber tried to dampen the investment mania fueling the industry's explosive expansion. Rentschler sensed the potential damage in denied expectations among investors and in false perceptions of the industry's strength among the public, congressmen, and government officials. The chamber publicized Rentschler's corrections to "a few erroneous ideas concerning the aircraft industry," including the beliefs that investments were ensured enormous returns, that demand for aircraft far exceeded supply, and that the industry no longer cared for military orders. The industry may have been "rolling in capital" but "not in wealth" since most of the new capital was not producing returns. It had been foolishly invested, based on the "imagination of an existing market," on "thoughtless enthusiasm . . . inspired by one great flight after another." The results were "a substantial surplus of civilian aircraft" and the realization that "military production . . . must continue to be the backlog of the aircraft manufacturing industry."[64]

After the crash, with aviation stocks plummeting and the extent of the unjustified hopes for commercial aviation becoming clear to all, the chamber used the business survey undertaken by the United States Chamber of Commerce in December 1929 to advise President Hoover on the state of the collapsing economy. It reminded the president of the industry's "fundamental needs," which it equated with the nation's defense. Such emphasis was necessary not only because its recent profligacy might impede any special consideration from a government facing a massive contraction in the business cycle but also because in output value the industry still ranked only 144th among American industries.[65]

Military contracts were the industry's bread and butter, the chamber repeatedly stressed. It warned the government not to be lulled into thinking that because of the growth of commercial aviation "the necessity for intensive military development had decreased." The government's responsibilities in preserving the industry through generous appropriations for military aircraft and more liberal contracting provisions had not been relieved by the recent burst of new investment capital. "Commercial aviation offers no substitution nor even a dependable reserve for our air defense," declared Rentschler.[66] Despite such entreaties relations between the manufacturers and the government steadily worsened during the Hoover administration and into the New Deal. The industry's behavior on Wall Street left it with fewer sympathizers in the White House, in Congress, and, increasingly, within the bureaus of military aviation.

For the most part navy contracting officers came to share the hostility toward the industry that underlay the Air Corps Act and its various official interpretations even though many of their negotiating opposites were former fellow officers. They came to believe that the navy had best assume the worst in manufacturers and that price competition be used to discipline the industry after its recent excesses, "inordinately high salaries," and "spendthrift habits."[67] Against this tide of negative sentiment, Admiral Moffett continued to believe that the rules he was obliged to follow in procuring aircraft dishonored the government. Adm. Ernest J. King, who became chief of the Bureau of Aeronautics after Moffett's death in the 1933 crash of the navy dirigible *Akron*, showed less remorse for the military's exploitation of the industry. He proudly reported to congressmen that navy audits revealed many of its contractors operating at substantial losses. He provided statistics showing an average profit of 8 percent on the costs of naval aircraft production and a loss of 34 percent on design and development work, for a before-taxes average profit of a mere 4.3 percent on total navy business since 1927. In response to suggestions that the government fill more of its needs at the Naval Aircraft Factory, King argued that the government was better off to continue taking advantage of the "talent" of private industry and the fact that "contractors always bear the losses."[68]

The ACC could do little to alter procurement law in this atmosphere. The limits of the trade association approach in instituting a new regulatory framework in the face of congressional resistance were clear even in 1924–1926 when the industry had the military's support. Military contractors ignored the chamber, and as the industry's fortunes declined, membership in the ACC fell off steeply. The number of member businesses dropped from 419 in 1929 to 120 in 1933. During the same period its operating budget shrank from $188,000 to $68,000.[69] Those firms that remained displayed only fleeting interest, rarely showing up for chamber meetings, voting by proxy, and resisting its staff's attempts to increase assessments from a shrinking membership to cover operating costs. The ACC was obliged to limit its activities in 1930–1931 to facilitating the manufacturers' input into Department of Commerce regulations on airworthiness, to issuing a code of 40,000 terms and phrases for aircraft parts, and to lobbying for increases in appropriations for air mail. It discontinued its annual air show, a central and usually profitable event for the chamber. Member manufacturers reluctantly came to the conclusion that speed and aerobatic demonstrations did not help them promote an image of a safe, conservative commercial enterprise.[70]

Despite Rentschler's insistence in his submissions to the Hoover/U.S. Chamber of Commerce Business Survey that the problems of military aircraft producers were at the heart of the aircraft industry's dilemmas, under his guidance the chamber's effort on behalf of military contractors was notably restrained. Like Admiral Moffett, the ACC deemed a more aggressive posture impolitic at a time of retrenchment in federal spending, at least until Charles L. Lawrence, now with Curtiss-Wright, reassumed the ACC's presidency in January 1931. As the depression wore on, as the expiration of the Air Corps Act's five-year equipment expansion program loomed, and as the costs of Congress's regulation of the military market ate away at company treasuries, Lawrence insisted that "more definite leadership" for the industry and a new "National Aviation Policy" were needed. Reviving the political strategy he had pursued as chamber president in 1924–1926, he again focused the chamber's waning energies on the expansion of appropriations for military aviation, the reform of procurement practice, and the "responsible" implementation of the military's de facto regulatory control over the industry. Lawrence would have been satisfied with a repeat of the multiyear authorizations for aircraft purchasing but at the end of his tenure was disappointed even in that limited goal.

He began his campaign by "enlarging" the chamber's "legal and legislative work," addressing a blunt statement of the military contractor's needs to President Hoover:

> It is our desire to develop aircraft primarily as a vehicle of peace [but] commercial aviation has yet a long way to go. . . . The military contractors as a class are losing money . . . the industry is now almost back to where it was in 1926. . . . In invested capital, experience and resources, the military contractors represent the substance of the industry. It is to aid us in preserving this substance that we ask your help and guidance.

As part of his proposed national aviation policy, Lawrence repeated the associationalist formula he had pushed for in 1924, insisting that freedom from price competition form the heart of a clearly stated and consistently followed federal policy for procuring military aircraft, a policy that would be implemented by the industry's representatives in the chamber working closely with military experts free from congressional scrutiny. He did not revive the term "approved list" but argued that experimental and production contracts must be negotiated exclusively with "specialized organizations" that would cooperatively compete on the level of performance only. Once again Lawrence called for the elimination of the government's system of maintaining competitive aircraft manufacture through "undeviating recognition of the design ownership principle." Assistant Secretary of War F. H. Payne, whose official responsibility was the "encouragement of mobilizable industries" for war, sympathized with Lawrence's proposals but could only reiterate the cardinal point that the "powers and duties of the War Department in the procurement of government supplies are prescribed and limited by Acts of Congress."[71]

On a less ambitious but still noteworthy level, Lawrence proposed the formulation of standardized accounting practices among manufacturers and the services' contracting officers and auditors, an anticompetitive mechanism that did not require legislation. Firms in price-competitive industries frequently "bought" work during downturns to ensure at least some return on fixed capital. Essentially, the aircraft industry had always been defined by this practice, not so much to protect capital investment, which though increasing was still relatively low, but to satisfy the personal desires of manufacturers to be in the business. Some firms submitted bids with no real idea of actual costs; others bid well below costs for development contracts in the hope of recouping losses in production contracts. As Temple Joyce of GM's General Aviation told congressmen, "we knew when we took the contract that we would lose money, hoping that when we got a production order that the losses on that experimental contract would be amortized. That has been the policy of all aircraft manufacturers." Lawrence complained that regular policy was also to hide the costs of mismanagement and the "many contingencies that arise," through large "deferred development charges." He insisted that the "manufacturer remaining liquid on the basis of delayed and transposed costs does not constitute a source of supply as contemplated by our National Aviation Policy." The chiefs of the air bureaus agreed. Firms resisted the chamber's "Chart of Accounts for Manufacturers of Airplanes for the U.S. Government," which established cost standards, but the services adopted it in early 1933. Nevertheless, obfuscation of costs, especially those connected with new development, remained an important tactic for aircraft firms seeking new investment.[72]

Standardization of accounting was about all the chamber accomplished for the industry during Lawrence's second tenure as president. On the industry's "most serious concern"—the crucial matter of design rights—no progress was made. Admiral Moffett and General Foulois jointly informed the Chamber that because of the Air Corps Act it was "not possible . . . to acknowledge . . . the principle of proprietary right of design." Also of major concern to Lawrence at the end of 1932 was that while indignation over big business, widely symbolized by aviation, increased as the depression unfolded, the industry's members continued in their indifference toward the chamber and collective action.

Unless greater and more sincere support is given to the Chamber the attacks on the industry in Congress . . . will become more severe and certainly more effective . . . [it] is not a question as to which manufacturer shall obtain contracts from the War and Navy Departments; it is, rather, a question as to what we can do to make sure there is business at all in the face of declining appropriations and increasing disfavor for munitions establishments.[73]

SAFETY VALVES: EXPORTS AND WAGE CUTS

As conditions worsened for manufacturers after the crash, Guy W. Vaughan, president of Wright Aeronautical, reiterated their old complaint that rapid strides in the development of aeronautics and the supply of aircraft to the military were not being paid for by Congress, whose responsibility it was to provide for the national defense. Instead these were being subsidized by unprofitable manufacturers, "plus contributions by optimistic stockholders."[74] Vaughan might have mentioned the contributions of aircraft workers, too, who were being forced at his own plant to bear a growing share of the costs of Congress's procurement policies. Also neglected by Vaughan were the contributions of foreigners, who provided a surging export market that during the the first half of the 1930s absorbed up to 41 percent of the industry's output (see Table 4.2).

The manufacturers' complaints that private capital was subsidizing military aviation should have been qualified as well by the fact that this foreign market relied upon the promotional efforts of the federal government through the Bureau of Foreign and Domestic Commerce (BFDC), a branch of the Commerce Department, and the State Department. Exports were, of course, dependent in the first place on the desirability of the American product, particularly the engines of Pratt & Whitney and Wright Aeronautical. Curtiss-Wright Exports and UATC Exports also acted as private consortiums of aircraft exporters under authority of the Webb-Pomerene Act (1918), which suspended the Sherman Act for foreign trade.[75] But the complications and political intrigue involved with selling mainly military aircraft to widely scattered foreign governments in stiff competition with subsidized European producers required re-

Table 4.2. American Exports of Aircraft, Engines, and Parts, 1929–1935

	Total Production in $Millions	Total Exports in $Millions	Percentage of Total
1929	70.9	N.A.	N.A.
1930	51.7	8.8	17%
1931	47.1	4.9	10%
1932	32.0	7.9	24%
1933	33.5	9.2	27%
1934	42.8	17.7	41%
1935	45.2	14.3	32%

Source: W. B. Harding, The Aviation Industry (New York: C. D. Barney & Co., 1937), 33, and R. Modley and T. J. Cawley, Aviation Facts and Figures 1953 (New York: Aircraft Industries Association, 1953), 158.

sources, tact, and connections that American aircraft manufacturers did not command.

Much to the chagrin of Secretary of Commerce Hoover, BFDC operatives, and the promoters of the Aeronautical Chamber of Commerce, manufacturers displayed little interest in the foreign market until the late 1920s. Under the "helpful Hoover," as the ACC's manager described the secretary, the BFDC early accepted the task of promoting American aeronautical exports throughout the world. It existed to provide information, advice, and promotion for private business, which in the Hooverian view was "the main instrument of economic expansion."[76] For BFDC operatives aircraft, although amounting to an insignificant part of American industry, was high profile, far more exciting than the usual fare of industrial exports. Aircraft could enhance impressions abroad of American manufacturing and technology. Since the future of military power and transportation lay with aircraft, American manufacturers had a duty, they argued, to compete with European powers that were actively pursuing exports as a way of shifting the cost of aircraft development onto the backs of "less ambitious and farsighted governments." Without discussing who would shoulder the costs of international sales and service, the BFDC continually pleaded with the manufacturers to consult with it "in order to assure ourselves that we are working completely in line with the requirements of the various branches of your industry, which we serve." Through most of the 1920s the manufacturers ignored such overtures. They were already subsidizing American military aviation and saw no easy returns helping the BFDC compete for markets abroad. The chamber tried to assist the BFDC but found itself apologizing repeatedly for the manufacturers' apathy in this one aspect of the aircraft business in which the principles of the associative state seemed active.[77]

The investment boom resulted in the capital manufacturers' needing to organize foreign sales as well as the overproduction of aircraft that encouraged an overseas outlook. Central to their success were the efforts of the indefatigable Leighton W. Rogers, director of the BFDC Aeronautics Trade Division during the Hoover administration, who later became executive director and president of the ACC. He enlisted the aid of military and commercial attaches in American embassies to cultivate the foreign market and apply pressure on governments to win military sales. Aeronautics trade commissioners were appointed for Latin America and China, areas that drew the bulk of American aircraft exports. In 1928 the BFDC funded an American presence at the prestigious Paris Air Show despite the lack of interest among aircraft firms.[78] It also lobbied the military to relax restrictions on military exports, using arguments that became standard in the 1930s as military tensions and export opportunities mounted in tandem. If America did not sell military aircraft abroad, the arguments went, other nations would. America's industrial base would suffer in relation to other nations', thereby undermining American national security. Fears about providing sophisticated weapons to potential enemies were unfounded since the pace of technical change rapidly made them obsolete. Furthermore, military aircraft exports enhanced world peace by bringig wars to quick conclusions or by making them too horrible to even begin.

The BFDC's efforts resulted in firms such as Curtiss-Wright selling large numbers of aircraft abroad. Hawk, Falcon, and Osprey fighters from Buffalo went to Latin America and China, a significant relief for Curtiss Aeroplane, which lost $378,000 on $10 million in army work for the period 1928–1933. Wright engines went to China, Latin America, and the Soviet Union. As one grateful aircraft manufacturer put it, "the Bureau of Foreign and Domestic Commerce is the greatest single influence at the service of the American manufacturer and exporter in developing and maintaining a flow of free foreign trade, I'm sure you will agree."[79] Like the stock boom and the industry's willingnesses to subsidize military aviation, if exports helped stave off the crisis that Congress's price-competitive regulatory framework would otherwise have generated, they also helped entrench an industry structure geared by procurement law to repetitive quantity-production since the bulk of foreign sales consisted of obsolete, easily reproduced aircraft and engines.

The postcrash hostility toward aircraft manufacturers augmented the fundamental mistrust of the industry within Congress and increasingly within the executive branch. Edward P. Warner, aeronautical engineer, assistant secretary of the navy for air under President Coolidge, and editor of *Aviation*, unsuccessfully took up the industry's case in the pages of his journal and in correspondence with the assistant secretary of war for air, F. Trubee Davison. Somehow, Warner argued, the process of aircraft procurement had to be relieved "from the despotic sway of the Controller General," Congress's watchdog. Warner asked Davison to confront the industry's present realities, to "take the companies as they now stand . . . sweep away the memory of past errors, and abandon any consideration of the year 1929 in determining the industry's relation with the government." To ensure the quality of military aircraft, to permit firms to amortize design costs, and to eliminate an artificial atmosphere of potential competition, design rights had to be recognized without qualification. Production contracts for aircraft designed by another "fortunately . . . are quite rare, but they still occur on occasion, and every recurrence is fearfully upsetting to the stability of the industry." The services "have it in their power . . . to force manufacturers to take almost every order at cost or below."[80]

As Warner realized, to produce a high-technology, labor-intensive product yet remain contenders in a price-competitive business environment, aircraft manufacturers had to minimize the costs and risks of research and development and more importantly reduce their wage bills. As one expert on aircraft production put it: "In the last analysis, material reductions in production costs are dependent on the workmen."[81] After the aviation bubble burst, manufacturers increasingly acted upon this basic fact of their industry. Since the volume of production was much too low and the always-changing complexity of the product far too great to allow significant savings in labor costs through the replacement of craftsmen with machinery and unskilled workers, manufacturers simply cut wages. During the early 1930s wages were cut by up to 40 percent in aircraft plants from Buffalo to Seattle and from Baltimore to Santa Monica.

Warner hoped to use these cuts to embarrass the War Department into a new procurement policy. The center of the Hoover administration's minimalist strategy for industrial recovery was to win promises from business that wages would not be reduced. "The preservation of wage scales has been the first plank in the official platform throughout the depression," Warner pointed out. "It would be well for the administration's

Executives of Curtiss Aeroplane pose in July 1932 with a "Turkey Hawk," one of nineteen Curtiss Hawk II fighters exported to Turkey in that year. At left is Theodore P. Wright, vice-president and general manager, and with him, Burdette S. Wright, vice-president and sales manager.

right hand to inquire into what its left hand is doing." The manufacturers' "practices [are] absolutely dictated by the terms upon which the government purchases [aircraft and by] the prices that the government will pay." But the assistant secretary's authority was nominal, not only in relation to Congress but also to the contracting bureaucracy at Wright Field. His answer to *Aviation*'s editor could only be a softening of a hostile response prepared by officers at Wright Field, who felt that the government was more than fair with a profligate industry and that wage cuts were the result of mismanagement by the firms.[82]

The manufacturers also hoped their wage cuts might prompt new procurement policies. At Curtiss-Wright this strategy was explicit. Nineteen thirty was disastrous for the holding company; it lost $9.4 million and was forced to set up a $6 million reserve against future losses. At the end of 1930 its surplus account was at an $18 million deficit. Curtiss-Wright's directors decided to cut costs, liquidate unprofitable commercial aviation holdings, and refocus on military work. They pushed for an increase in the volume of military business at the company's Wright Aeronautical in Paterson, New Jersey, and for a reversal of downward pressures on prices for the company's engines, driven by stiff competition with Pratt & Whitney. Wright was Curtiss-Wright's strongest subsidiary even though it was carrying a large inventory of cancelled commercial orders from 1929, was operating at only 25 percent capacity, had taken its contracts well below cost, and was turning a 1930 loss of $2 million.[83]

The central role in Curtiss-Wright's retrenchment strategy was assigned to Guy W. Vaughan, president at Wright, who ruthlessly cut wages and introduced his workers to the group and bonus systems. The moves were radical since the company knew that its main asset was its work force of machinists, built up over fifteen years and dedicated to the firm's specialized products, the mighty Whirlwind, Cyclone, and Conqueror air-cooled engines. The company had been a leader in welfare capitalism in the aircraft industry, shunning wage-incentive systems; maintaining a cafeteria, sports teams, employee journals that nurtured camaraderie, pride, and commitment to the firm; and a Mutual Benefit Association that provided loans, medical service, and pensions to the workers.[84] Vaughan trusted that his new draconian measures would be only temporarily necessary, hoping they would produce conflict with his workers and that the ensuing publicity would produce a softening of the government's approach to the industry. Summing up the situation that aircraft manufacturers faced because of Congress's price-competitive system, Vaughan explained to the Department of Labor:

> It is impossible for this company to continue on government contracts without effecting some important economies . . . the method now employed by the government in awarding contracts . . . forces prices downward to the point where actual losses on the transaction are effected . . . yet we must take this work at losses in order to keep the plant in operation . . . commercial business is insufficient . . . a general reduction in wages is one of the economies effected.

Vaughan offered access to the company's books and expressed his hope that the workers' plight would be properly understood in the context of the industry's dilemma at the hands of Congress.[85]

The outcome of the company's strategy was not a changed business environment for aircraft manufacture but a violent and lengthy winter strike. The 1,200 workers at Wright deeply resented Vaughan's "group incentive system," which denied them many of their prerogatives on the shop floor and, combined with a 10 percent wage reduction, amounted to a 40 percent pay cut. New rules forbade the men from eating or speaking while working. They were fingerprinted and required to pay for any scrap resulting from errors. On December 11, 1930, all but seventy-five Wright workers struck, asking the public "to imagine," in light of massive unemployment in the Paterson area, "what must the working conditions be in a manufacturing concern that would cause its employees to quit their jobs under such outside conditions." They had reached "the limit of physical endurance . . . the company through its so called efficiency engineers demanded more and more until there was nothing more to give. In order to preserve the little sanity left in us we were forced to suspend work." They demanded the restoration of wages, the suspension of the speed-up systems, and the rehiring of the strikers without discrimination.[86]

The strike continued into 1931 as workers picketed in subzero temperatures and fought stone-throwing battles with private police and as the mayor of Paterson held hearings into why one of the few manufacturing establishments in the area with a backlog of orders was shut down. Hopes that the strike would end when the unyielding Vaughan took a Caribbean vacation were dashed when negotiations with his replacements, Charles Lawrence, president of the ACC, and Richard Hoyt, chairman of the board at Curtiss-Wright, only confirmed that a prolonged strike to pressure the government for better contracting terms was the company's plan. Finally on April 17 the eighteen-week strike was called off as the exhausted workers, denied aid from the American Federation of Labor and International Association of Machinists, conceded defeat. It was estimated that it would take the workers a month to undo damage to equipment caused by strike breakers hired to complete engines for the army, which was complaining about delays. Still, the company would agree to nothing more than an offer to rehire them. It reserved the right to place them in any position and at any wage. All the old rules were retained and the "stop watch speed up system" was "forced to the limit."[87]

The strike was a defeat for the workers, but it was no victory for Wright, whose actions offended influential congressmen such as LaGuardia who blamed mismanagement at Wright and thenceforth became "very anxious to embarrass the Wright company." Rather than altering the evils of the government's contracting methods, the strike only irritated the Air Corps, which in no sense sympathized with the company or its workers even after a full audit of the company's books ordered by Assistant Secretary Davison amply documented its financial troubles.[88] Yet if the Air Corps and its congressional overseers gained in the short term, acquiring aircraft engines at costs subsidized by Curtiss-Wright and its workers, it lost over the long term as labor relations at Wright and in the aircraft industry as a whole were poisoned through the 1930s and as Wright became even more reluctant to take costly new steps in engine development. The defeat of the Wright workers left little doubt in the minds of manufacturers that wage suppression and the reorganization of production to minimize labor costs were the few options still available to them in this congressionally controlled industry.

During the 1930s, however, the steps manufacturers could take in this direction, apart from wage cuts, were limited by the complexity of aircraft, by small-batch orders, by constant technical change, and by the continued overwhelming need for the dedicated skills of craftsmen. Thus the industry was fundamentally at odds with itself, always searching for ways to emulate the shop-floor practices of assembly-line mass production and apologizing in the trade journals for its "primitive" state. Techniques of mass production were essential it seemed, not only because of the price-competitive pressures of military procurement and the growing resentment of skilled workers but also because of the power of the idea of mass production in America and the sense that air power was a weapon to be applied in mass numbers. An increasingly inflexible and unsophisticated industry that hampered the development of military aeronautics resulted. The United States was saddled with a production base in air power that gave it little credibility as a military power and that when pressed compelled it to develop its air forces according to the costly and destructive precepts of numbers over performance.

CHAPTER FIVE

The National Recovery Administration, the Aircraft Industry, and Congress

"THE WONDERFUL WORK OF THE NRA"

Franklin D. Roosevelt and the New Deal were heartily welcomed by aircraft manufacturers. Charles Lawrence, outgoing president of the Aeronautical Chamber of Commerce, sent his appreciation to the new president: "I have been a pretty loyal Republican all my life but more power to you . . . at last a real leader at the helm of the nation."[1] During spring 1933 as the Army Air Corps and Navy Bureau of Aeronautics proposed that $79 million in money from the Public Works Administration be earmarked for new military aircraft, manufacturers had good reason to believe that their troubled industry would be a major beneficiary of federal efforts to "prime the pump" of recovery from the Great Depression.[2] Of even greater appeal was Title I of the National Industrial Recovery Act (NIRA) signed by FDR on June 13, 1933, which authorized businessmen to draw up "codes of fair competition" for their industries that would supposedly provide them with new powers to regulate and plan their affairs. To aircraft manufacturers it appeared that at last they were to have a voice in how their industry and technology were organized. Their industry was less than two decades old, but it seemed a lifetime of standing by helplessly as their virtually exclusive client on Capitol Hill used its powers of appropriation and rule making for military procurement to maintain wasteful competitive patterns that impeded the development of military aeronautics. Finally, it seemed, their industry was to be adequately funded, depoliticized, and left to the direction of men in business who knew its needs best.

They were disappointed on all three counts. As matters transpired, Washington under the early Roosevelt administration provided them little in the way of a new deal. Make-work spending on military aircraft was limited to only $15 million, and the manufacturers could not come up with an industry code that the National Recovery Administration (NRA) would approve. Indeed the early New Deal added to the industry's woes as congressmen, with FDR's blessing, made it a central focus of renewed antitrust hostility and intruded even further into its affairs. Forced to continue operating in an artificial price-competitive market, manufacturers also found their options newly limited as aircraft workers won new rights to assert their interests. The manufacturers' experiences during the early New Deal only reconfirmed the determining role of national politics in the organizational and technological evolution of military industries.

Their experiences also provide a fresh perspective on the NRA, pointing out the strength of traditional constraints on the development of the American state. The NRA represented a telescoping of the historical trend in which the breadth of legislative and judicial power was continually widened and delegated more and more to new federal agencies. But studies of its workings on an industry-by-industry basis reveal that the NRA also represented an intensification of the difficulties that had made the evolution of the regulatory state an episodic and uneven process in the past. It reshaped both business-government and labor relations but in ways limited by its simultaneous reassertion of old principles and practices. It temporarily shifted to a higher plane of negotiation old battles among conflicting interests within specific industries and among old perspectives on how the state-society relation ought to be reformed in response to mature industrial capitalism. It provided a new national forum for conflict and debate and vague new legitimacy for organized labor, an ephemeral public interest, and theories of national planning. Yet it did little to alter the balance of power among clashing interests and ideologies that had always determined the policy-making process. The NRA highlights state development as a social movement, a dialectic between the forces that compel turning to the state and those forces—cultural, legal, political, institutional—that restrain the state by demanding that it conform to prior patterns of legitimacy and power.[3]

The irregular patterns of American state development emerge from the experiences of aircraft manufacturers and workers, not only with the NRA, but also with the federal government through the 1930s and into the 1940s. Both groups hoped the NRA would mean a reshuffling of control and direction over their industry but found instead that traditional arrangements and attitudes were most often merely confirmed. It seems paradoxical that the aircraft industry, directly dependent on the state, could underscore the limitations of the NRA and the obstacles to radical departures in political economy. Yet because the industry was so close to the state it reflected the politics and turbulence of state development. During the early New Deal the industry became the focus of intense hostility toward big business and the "trusts," which many blamed for the nation's economic woes. The industry also shared in a surge of opprobrium for munitions manufacturers, naval shipbuilders, and other "merchants of death." On a deeper level, it acted as a receptacle for the frustrations of a society turning to, yet deeply ambivalent about, state power. The industry's dealings with the NRA may seem to say less about the NRA than about its own unique problems, but its experiences were only an extreme version of the politicization of most of the NRA's activities.[4]

The Recovery Act itself reflected the need to accommodate a diversity of well-established interests, advocating a range of competing proposals that agreed on the need for expanded federal power but disagreed on how best to deploy it to combat the nearly four-year-old depression.[5] At the act's heart were modifications of associationalism, the vision of self-regulating industry in cooperative partnership with a limited state, which underlay the reforms proposed by Charles Lawrence and the ACC through the 1920s to the New Deal. The new associationalism, or the "business commonwealth," advocated by such corporate leaders as Henry Harriman and Gerard Swope, replaced the previous emphasis on voluntarism with demands for enforceable regulatory powers granted to trade associations that would assure compliance with decisions collectively reached within industries. Much of NIRA was an outgrowth of a business movement that since the 1890s had sought the relaxation of antitrust laws so that businessmen could cartelize and contain competition through price controls, production limits, market allotments, and labor standards.

NIRA also embodied elements of various theories less motivated by the preservation of business interests and autonomy. These included calls from such figures as Rexford G. Tugwell for industrial planning and management by the state and for countercyclical federal spending, the idea that public works projects would prime the pump and encourage employment, purchasing power, and economic recovery. Finally NIRA included work-sharing proposals for the employment of more workers for fewer hours and at "living wages." These measures, it was thought, would break the underconsumptionist deadlock of a modern consumer economy and eliminate competitive advantages in aggressive wage cutting, particularly in labor-intensive industries such as aircraft. Worksharing proposals were advocated principally by organized labor and its allies in Congress, led by Sen. Robert F. Wagner. They argued that the expansion of mass purchasing power depended upon the reform and regulation of industrial relations and that these could come about only if workers were assured the right to collective bargaining through independent representatives.[6]

The idea of expanding purchasing power through shorter working hours was the impetus behind the legislative maneuvering that culminated in NIRA. Just before Christmas 1932, Sen. Hugo Black of Alabama introduced a radical bill outlawing in interstate commerce products of firms that employed workers for more than six hours per day or more than five days per week. During the New Deal's One Hundred Days the Roosevelt administration countered the heavy-handed Black bill, which had passed the Senate on April 6, 1933, with more flexible proposals for the control of wages and hours on an industry-by-industry basis. As the weeks passed and the clamor for action on industrial recovery increased, Roosevelt ordered a disparate group—Budget Director Lewis Douglas, labor lawyer Donald Richberg, Rexford Tugwell of the Department of Agriculture, Secretary of Labor Frances Perkins, Gen. Hugh Johnson, and Senator Wagner—to produce what finally emerged as the National Industrial Recovery Act on June 13.[7] NIRA consisted of three parts and was given an operational life of two years. Title III of the act concerned amendments to emergency relief programs, and Title II established the Public Works Administration with authority to spend $3.3 billion on employment-generating federal projects. Title I was the act's essence: It suspended the antitrust laws and authorized industries working through trade associations to draw up "codes of fair competition" that would regulate production, prices, and labor standards.[8]

NIRA appeared to confer significant new regulatory powers upon the president and collectivized industries, but in fact, the act's wording left these powers latent. NIRA was a "piece of enabling legislation" that offered a great deal of new power but did not even require its use. It put forth only the vaguest goals—"remove obstructions" to commerce, "provide for the general welfare," "reduce and relieve unemployment," effect "united action of labor and management"—and provided no concrete guides as to how those goals were to be achieved or how conflict over the act's interpretation was to be resolved. The nature of the act's administration was left to the president to decide; it was entirely up to FDR to judge the political room for maneuver. He could approve or reject codes based on whatever criteria or even ignore the act if he desired. The only clear requirements were that any code he did approve had to be formulated after public hearings and through fair representation of all affected. Every code also had to include Section 7a, which provided for the rights of workers "to organize and bargain collectively through representatives of their own choosing . . . free from the interference, restraint, or coercion of employers . . .," stipulations that were themselves open to wide interpretation.[9]

To administer the act, Roosevelt created the National Recovery Administration and appointed General Johnson as Administrator for Industrial Recovery and Donald Richberg as General Counsel, along with a number of deputy administrators recruited mostly from business. FDR and Johnson were conscious of NIRA's potential for radical steps in relations between business and government, yet both were sensitive to its vulnerability to constitutional challenge and to the ambivalence of most Americans toward positive government. They therefore downplayed NIRA's implicit powers of coercion and encouraged a view of the NRA as government supervision of industrial self-regulation on a scope only slightly more rigorous than previous arrangements. Adhering to the basics of Hooverian associationalism, FDR described the NRA as a means of building a cooperative partnership between business and government, not government control of business. "It is not the function of the National Recovery Administration," read an early NRA pronouncement, "to prescribe what shall be in the codes to be submitted by associations or groups. The initiative in all such matters is expected to come from within the industry itself."[10]

Thus, although NIRA incorporated important elements of those views that advocated extensions of federal authority through public-works spending and through federal guarantees of the ability of workers to improve their purchasing power, it was business, particularly businesses with effective trade associations, that set the agenda for the early New Deal's approach to industrial recovery. This development reflected the general biases of FDR and most of his advisers and the reality of the predominant influence of business, which was brought to bear upon the NRA most effectively by the new Business Advisory Council in the Department of Commerce.[11] It also reflected the fact that business possessed expertise and organizational advantages over those who advocated time-consuming extensions of state power or major new roles for organized labor. In the atmosphere of emergency built up through almost four years of depression, speed was essential; and it was inevitable that the views of businessmen, who had organizations and personnel already in place, would take precedence.[12]

Whatever businessmen thought, however, the primary function of the Recovery Act and the NRA was not to serve them. Rather, it was to serve the Roosevelt administration's immediate political need, which was to appear active in a crisis.[13] Somehow the federal government had to foster confidence, and it had to do so immediately. The path of least resistance, which FDR always had the keenest eye for, led naturally through business institutions. Performance rather than substance was the major impetus behind NIRA, and if the act reflected the aspirations of industry, they remained tenuous and vaguely formulated. They varied widely from industry to industry, and the means for realizing them left intact traditional voluntarism and promotion, best symbolized by the Blue Eagle campaign. Such means rarely departed from the customary methods used by the strongest industries and the strongest firms within them.[14]

The NRA may have offered industry "governmentally approved cartelism,"[15] but it never delivered. Industries that hoped the NRA spelled relief from competition and deflation did not receive the degree of control needed to make cartels effective. Generally, the NRA remained the "sprawling, poorly coordinated and relatively ineffective organization" that might have been anticipated in a polity as open and decentralized as the United States.[16] Customary struggles among various interest groups were simply raised to a higher plane by the NRA, which provided neither the administrative machinery nor the consensus for their settlement. Businessmen were not given a free hand because American law, political culture, and governmental structures would permit no clear victory for any single interest or particular ideology.

The Senate passed NIRA with only a slim majority (46 to 39), and it insisted on the inclusion of the Brandeisian Borah amendment protecting small business and prohibiting "monopolistic practices." Though this amendment was characteristically ambiguous, it sharply qualified the act's suspension of antitrust law and left the NRA wide open to constant attacks. Business' apparent victory began losing its lustre as economic indexes resumed their downward trends in late summer 1933 and as antitrust critics asserted themselves in a rising chorus of attacks on what seemed to them to be the anticompetitive thrust of most of the codes approved by the NRA. Meanwhile the perspectives of the planners and organized labor on NIRA's intentions continued to compete with business. FDR was obliged to make gestures to both, particularly to labor's goals on hours and wages, which were acknowledged most notably in the President's Reemployment Agreement—the voluntary Blanket Code. Denied a positive role in policy, labor and the planners had to be satisfied, however, with joining the antitrusters in Congress to obstruct the business agenda. By early 1934, industrial self-regulation with state sanction was well in retreat as an investigative panel chaired by Clarence Darrow aired the many conflicting expectations of NIRA.[17]

Through 1934 and until the NRA's demise in the Shechter case of May 1935, the NRA hobbled along, an expression of the contradictions of American industry and the limitations of U.S. political economy. The NRA's administrative structure ensured the representation of a plurality of groups throughout the process of code formulation. An Industrial Advisory Board was composed of business leaders appointed by the secretary of commerce; a Labor Advisory Board was appointed by the secretary of labor; and a Consumer Advisory Board by the NRA. Each served as the conduit through which traditional pressure groups participated in the hard bargaining that, in the absence of any clear guidelines in the Recovery Act, determined the codes' features. The advancement by these boards of their particular constituencies' interests and interpretations of NIRA or the obstruction of the advancement of another's depended upon the relative strength, organization, and bargaining clout that elements within and among the three constituencies brought to the NRA.[18] The NRA provided them, business included, with important new strength in its recognition of their right to function collectively; but it endowed them with no new organizational strength, nor did it alter the balance of power among them. On the contrary, the enormous diversity of American industry and the ability of innumerable interests within it to assert their claims in the political sphere were stamped upon the NRA. In its lack of clear functions and goals, the NRA could not cope with the multitude of external pressures and quickly evolved into a deadlocked "administrative colossus," driven by the "principle of muddle."[19]

The Recovery Act was designed to acknowledge but not to acquiesce in any one of the several aspirations that sought fulfillment through federal recovery legislation. Further evidence of NIRA's pushes-toward yet pulls-away-from the administrative state is contained in both the wording and the NRA's handling of Section 7a. The hopes of organized labor and their supporters, as well as those who saw strict labor standards as effective anticompetition mechanisms, were largely disappointed when the weaknesses of Section 7a became apparent along with early evidence that the Roosevelt administration's qualified commitment to the enforcement of any of the many principles behind NIRA extended most especially to the concept of mass trade unionism. NIRA's labor provisions were easily evaded by employers and did little to alter the old truism that the advancement of workers' interests depended upon their economic power within particular industries.

Nevertheless Section 7a amounted to an important shift in the federal government's administrative function within labor relations and was included in NIRA despite the vigorous opposition of businessmen. It represented the first acceptance in legislation of the federal government's role as the upholder of labor's rights on an industry-by-industry basis.[20] Whatever their effectiveness, the NRA, its Labor Advisory Board, and the other labor boards established during the NRA's life were the first institutionalizations of this role. No matter how ephemeral, they represented a distinct shift in national policy and legitimized the pursual of workers' interests as a class. Their methods and decisions laid the foundations for the evolution of more durable arrangements under the National Labor Relations Act of 1935. Indeed in terms of its impact upon an evolving American state and political economy, the NRA's departures in industrial relations are of much greater lasting significance than the steps taken toward the regulation of business practice.

Important as they may have been in the long term, the immediate, practical effects of these departures in industrial relations depended upon the policies of the administrators of NIRA and the power available to them to enforce those policies. Much like its approach to the cartelization of industry, NIRA encouraged but did not provide support for independent unionism. Union claims to workers that NIRA meant that "the President wants you to organize" were never backed up, either by presidential statements or action. The experiences of aircraft workers demonstrate that authentic collective bargaining, like the effective limitation of competition in industry, required as always independent organization and power (see chapters 6 and 7).

In its early months, the NRA's equivocation was limited mostly to questions of labor organization. Only later did its unwillingness and inability to utilize federal power to chart clear and coherent directions through the maze of conflicting interests that surrounded trade practice reform become apparent. Until then the NRA held great appeal to businessmen, particularly among those seeking order within competitive, labor-intensive industries. For aircraft manufacturers, the NRA appeared to offer what they could hardly have imagined possible. It held out the chance of wresting from Congress the power of regulation over their industry, which derived from its control of the market for military aircraft. Moreover, through the NRA the manufacturers might shift this power not to a sympathetic army and navy, as had been their goal in 1924–1926, but to their own trade association. The promises of strong trade practices seemed real enough as the NRA tempted all industries with them in the hope of securing their immediate cooperation. A number of industries—cotton textiles, lumber, and steel—were given early approvals for codes with apparently tight but as yet untested provisions for pricing and production.[21]

As the process of creating a code for aircraft manufacture unfolded, however, the ephemeral objectives and powers of the NRA became increasingly apparent, along with its function as merely a new battleground for old struggles. Seeming to offer so much for the industry, the NRA emerged instead as another confirmation that aircraft manufacture was Congress's business. Even worse, the NRA would come to threaten manufacturers with a new regulatory structure in their relations with their workers—the only sphere where they still made decisions autonomously. As increases in manufacturing costs associated with the technical leap from wood to metal aircraft were not matched by greater flexibility in procurement policies, the manufacturers' ability to impose shares of these burdens upon workers assumed greater importance yet came under challenge. Thus attitudes among manufacturers to the NRA shifted from initial enthusiasm, as a great opportunity was sensed, to defensiveness and resentment as the possibility grew that the government might use the NRA as yet another punitive mechanism against them.

The Aeronautical Chamber of Commerce was easily caught up in the flush of anticipation that surrounded Roosevelt's signing of NIRA. A month before, its Military Contractors Committee warned that "serious difficulties were again developing in relations between the industry and the services." It cited the bitter feelings toward the industry among contracting officers generated by the Wall Street boom and stressed that "to avoid or adjust these difficulties continuity of contact on a definite policy is necessary." It decried the manufacturers' indifference to collective action and recommended that "a special effort should again be made to enroll the Douglas, Martin, and Consolidated companies as members of the Chamber."[22] Its revenues and influence declining, the ACC gladly accepted the new role the NRA seemed to offer.

The ACC was largely dormant by 1933 and like many other trade associations felt new life breathed into it by the NRA. It was reorganized to accommodate the NRA, and a code of fair competition was swiftly produced. "The law is a fact," wrote the ACC's president Thomas A. Morgan in both an affirmation of NIRA and a warning to manufacturers. President of Sperry Gyroscope and the troubled Curtiss-Wright, Morgan had supported FDR's campaign. He told the chamber's members that the law "requires each industry to get together in its trade association and agree upon a 'code of fair competition' [which] if approved will have the force of law in the conduct of the industry." For the eager Morgan, the industry was about to embark upon an era of centralized control for the good of all its members. "Dissenting minorities will be heard, and an attempt will be made to establish compromise ground, but if this fails, minorities will be forced by application of the law into line." Central to this new control was the ACC, which would "act as a powerful representative of the industry . . . in close touch with those in Washington. . . . The Recovery Administration will cooperate in every possible way with the Chamber in working out this code, but they expect the industry to get together, take the initiative, and formulate its own regulations." Morgan told the manufacturers not to worry about what the press was saying the main goals of NIRA were, namely, "an immediate wage increase and increased employment." Countering this widely shared interpretation of NIRA's intent and staking out the position that the chamber would maintain throughout on labor issues, Morgan stated that "these probably will not apply to this industry with its specialized personnel."[23]

To coordinate the chamber's contacts with the NRA, Morgan hired Leighton Rogers, who had been replaced as director of the Aeronautics Trade Division of the Bureau of Foreign and Domestic Commerce with the change in administration. In that position he had helped manufacturers, especially subsidiaries of Morgan's Curtiss-Wright, expand their export markets. An eager "Hoover man," as the manufacturers described him, Rogers had been such an energetic advocate of the associationalist ethic for the industry that many manufacturers perceived his aggressive calls for its "sympathetic supervision" by the Department of Commerce as threats to their autonomy.[24] By mid-1933, however, the unemployed Rogers seemed suitably experienced and connected in Washington to represent the industry. He looked forward to the new powers of self-regulation that NIRA was expected to provide and immediately set about "concentrating the ideas of the entire industry." He persuaded the chamber's Board of Governors to center control over the association in its executive committee under his direction. Eleven days before NIRA was signed, Rogers began gathering a twenty-six-member code committee and started preparing a draft code. The committee included such industry leaders as Thomas Morgan and J. A. B. Smith of Curtiss-Wright, Sherman Fairchild, G. W. Vaughan of Wright Aeronautical, Philip G. Johnson of Boeing, Donald L. Brown of Pratt & Whitney, and G. M. Bellanca.[25]

The NRA generated much positive feeling and a new, uncharacteristic sense of common goals among aircraft manufacturers. One trade journal foresaw an "industry working unselfishly for the good of the whole," thanks to the NRA, despite the past difficulties of "many in the industry to think and act cooperatively" or to accept that "the trade of aeronautics is at last really to be represented by the Aeronautical Chamber of Commerce."[26] Manufacturers expected that the NRA would become a new clearinghouse for all the industry's dealings with the government. The NRA would assume Congress's and the military's power over the industry, which, it was thought, industrial self-determination meant. Promising an end to the industry's competitiveness and financial risks and to the military's denial of manufacturers' proprietary designs rights, the NRA pledged the beginning of a new era of steady, profitable military contracts and the orderly evolution of aeronautics. Consequently membership and active participation in the ACC swelled during summer 1933. For manufacturers such as Reuben Fleet of Consolidated, the time was ripe for expressions of support for the New Deal. Fleet had snubbed the chamber, except for a brief period when the Air Corps Act was passed, but joined again upon passage of NIRA to participate in the code-making process. He was most willing to offer his support to the "wonderful work of the NRA," along with his views on how that work might best be pursued in the interests of aircraft manufacturers.[27]

Having reorganized itself for the purpose, the chamber formally applied for the right to submit a code for the industry. Assuming that their goals for NIRA were the NRA's as well, Rogers and Morgan argued that the chamber was well poised to "effectuate for the industry the policies of the NRA and the policies of this Administration." The right to represent the industry came to it, they claimed, because it listed among its members more than 90 percent of the active capacity of the nation's aircraft industry. They also claimed for ACC members 3,100 workers among a total of 3,167 engaged in aircraft engine manufacture. As an afterthought, they provided a list of manufacturers still not affiliated with the ACC, which included Beech, Grumman, Lockheed, Martin, and Seversky.[28]

The scope of the draft code's provisions and the dispatch with which they were formulated by the chamber suggest how eagerly the industrial powers conferred by the NRA could be perceived by labor-intensive, competitive industries. The chamber put forth trade practice and labor proposals that embodied an aggressive strategy to concentrate control of the industry, contain competition, cut production costs, and assure themselves the ability to pass any cost increases on to their government consumers. A National Control Committee of the Aeronautical Chamber of Commerce was to police industry's compliance with fixed standards of wages, hours, prices, and business ethics. All industry members were to submit to an accounting system imposed by the control committee and were to provide statistics on wages, hours, costs, assets, inventory, orders, sales, and prices. They were also to defer to the control committee's power to amend and interpret the code and to arbitrate disputes arising from it. Expectations of such powers of self-control were further encouraged in preliminary conferences with NRA officials such as Edward R. Stettinius, Jr., "a coordinator in General Johnson's office," who sought the chamber's help in appointing technical advisers to the NRA and who stressed the need for strong provisions for anticompetition in whatever code the industry decided to submit for the NRA's approval.[29]

The manufacturers gladly complied. Their list of prohibited "unfair competitive practices" focused on the government's leverage over their industry in its nonrecognition of proprietary rights to military aircraft designs. Protection of these rights was at the heart of their proposed code. Member firms were to be forbidden from signing production contracts for aircraft that had been designed by another member unless the designer had been compensated to his and the control committee's satisfaction. The proposed provisions for trade practices called for an unlimited monopoly upon a design and for the prohibition of contracting for aircraft below cost.[30]

Despite these positive developments, by the time the public hearing on the code for the aircraft industry was finally scheduled and well before the industry began to act as a lightning rod for so much anger toward big business, much had transpired to suggest that the NRA was not to be the pliant servant that the manufacturers had initially expected. As early as August 1933 the NRA Code Analysis Division (CAD), the initial processor of codes submitted by industry, prepared a highly critical report on the manufacturers' draft code, which it found in breach of the representation provisions of NIRA Section 3a. For the democratic CAD, the chamber's representing 90 percent of the industry's active business did not "establish the right of the association to be considered representative of the industry." Its bylaws and constitution were found too restrictive and inequitable for those firms that carried on the remaining 10 percent of business and for those that for various reasons had not produced any aircraft during the preceding year. CAD suggested that the code was a device to ensure that the final 10 percent of independent production would be absorbed or at least prevented from growing. The various activities funded by the chamber, such as the organization of air shows and the production of an annual yearbook, were considered unfair burdens upon those who would seek membership in the chamber because of the code. Also considered unfair to nonmembers were voting privileges granted to chamber members who had only an indirect relation to aircraft manufacturing, such as banks and insurance companies interested in aviation, publishers of trade journals, manufacturers of fuels and lubricants, and aircraft distributers and dealers.[31]

The narrow issue of the chamber's representativeness hampered all attempts to produce a code for aircraft manufacture. The chamber tried to deflect challenges led by Eugene Vidal, the new director of the Commerce Department's Bureau of Aeronautics, who had irritated manufacturers with his widely publicized but unrealistic plan to encourage small aircraft manufacture through federal development of a mass producible "flivver plane." Before the NRA Vidal argued for builders of aircraft no matter how small or dormant. He claimed that 131 manufacturers were active in the United States and that the chamber represented only 28 percent of them.[32] The chamber found itself on the defensive, trying to show that inactive firms were not worthy of consideration. Without success, it tried to persuade such important holdouts as Glenn Martin and Leroy Grumman to join.

With the civilian leadership of the army and navy as allies, Vidal also attacked the chamber's proposals for restricting competition and protecting the manufacturers' design rights. For Vidal, these proposals "could be of untold harm to the aircraft industry by permitting the creation of a monopoly on unpatented designs."[33] Assistant Secretary of War H. H. Woodring appointed army attorneys to lobby the NRA against the chamber's proposals. Navy Secretary Claude Swanson attacked the proposals as threatening "a most disruptive effect on the Government's procurement policy." Ignoring the fact that manufacturers heavily subsidized them, he claimed the government's right to the full fruits of its experimental contracts with private industry and the right to let production contracts in a manner that "best serves the interests of the government." To restrict production contracts to those who had designed aircraft or their parts would open the navy to charges of favoritism, he argued. The chamber's trade practices would serve as an "extension of monopolies" and "seriously retard the development of an industry vital to the National Defense."[34]

The manufacturers insisted upon their design rights. For Reuben Fleet, the NRA had been "designed to eliminate unfair competitive practices" in industries "in need of rehabilitation." It was the NRA's responsibility to end "the policy under which firms in the industry are deprived of the products of their brains." The NRA could correct the Air Corps Act, which allowed the army and navy to continue its "piracy." The policy of seeking the lowest bidder for production contracts, which nonrecognition permitted, was "stifling invention and development." It "demoralizes designers and technical workers and deprives the government of the benefits of the proud workmanship of those who create and produce an airplane."[35]

CONGRESSIONAL WILL

Even if the military and the NRA had been more sympathetic to the manufacturers, little could have been done on their behalf as hostility toward aviation mounted on Capitol Hill. During the early New Deal, the air transport and aircraft industries became focal points for antitrust resentment that proved especially potent when directed toward aviation. In the views of many representatives of both parties' rural wings, the industry's recent behavior on Wall Street seemed to be part of a conspiracy to appropriate what was supposed to be a democratic technology. It also typified the greed and excesses of big business, its violations of economic egalitarianism, "natural" competitive laws, and independent innovation, which for many, summed up the sources of the depression. Even worse in their minds was the thought that if these corporate indulgences were not financed by bilked stock investors, they were underwritten by the taxpayer through federal assistance for air navigation and technical research, air-mail subsidies, and military contracts. The latter form of aid made the industry particularly vulnerable to antitrust sentiment, not only because it provided Congress a direct way to punish the industry but also because it rounded off the industry as a target for the antimilitarism and anti-imperialism, which along with indignation over big business, comprised the nodal points of Midwestern progressivism.

During the first half of the 1930s, the agrarian political current that had shaped the Air Corps Act was sustained at a high pitch in Congress by the Sons of the Wild Jackass, a group of Insurgent Republican senators that included William E. Borah of Idaho, George W. Norris of Nebraska, Hiram W. Johnson of California, Arthur H. Vandenberg of Michigan, and Gerald P. Nye of North Dakota. Of similar persuasion were a group of Democratic and farmer-laborite senators including Burton K. Wheeler of Montana, Bronson M. Cutting of New Mexico, Bennett Champ Clark of Missouri, Henrik Shipstead of Minnesota, and Robert M. LaFollette, Jr., of Wisconsin. Broadly, these senators and their many allies in the House opposed big business, big government, and imperialism, which from their perspectives worked hand in hand against the economic interests of farmers and workers and led the nation inevitably to war. They attacked "special privilege," Wall Street, banks, and utilities and denounced internationalist foreign policy and military, particularly naval, spending, which they viewed as the servants of northeastern financiers.[36]

Reflecting a broad consensus behind economic nationalism and distrust of big business, these agrarian-Progressives played key roles in the formation of public policy during the early New Deal. Senators Borah and Nye were the loudest critics of the NRA, attacking what they considered its aids to monopoly and increased consumer prices. By November 1933 Nye was calling for a "complete reversal of present NRA policies"[37] and for a National Recovery Review Board to scrutinize NRA codes and personnel. In March 1934 FDR was forced to appoint that board, and its investigation effectively emasculated whatever limited steps the NRA was willing to take on behalf of industry cartels.

However, like their restraints on the NRA and the aviation industry, the antitrusters' impact upon policy and legislation was largely negative and obstructionist. Thomas McCraw's remark on Louis D. Brandeis applies well to this group: Its critique of modern industrial society was an "aesthetic construct rather than an analytic or prescriptive one."[38] On the practical level, the group's most prominent Republican members were too self-righteous and placed too great a value on their personal independence to ever combine into an effectively led, cohesive bloc that could take the initiative in Congress. Despite agreement on the slogans and rhetoric of their brand of progressivism, they often disagreed on such particulars as trade legislation when local interests were affected. They quarrelled when one of them seemed to absorb too much of the spotlight or appeared to be taking leadership. They remained nominal members of a much weakened minority party and cultivated images of outsiders to Roosevelt's administration, in which some of them had been offered important posts. Their defense of states' rights and their opposition to government planning, subsidies, and deficits were contradicted by their support of federal welfare programs, assistance to farmers, and public electric-power projects. Also contradictory was their attraction to air power as a means for continental defense—supposedly free of the high costs, bureaucracy, and imperial ambition associated with the navy—yet their unwillingness to confront the problems of air power's industrial base.[39]

FDR was always ambivalent toward the group. He was conscious of their numerical presence in Congress, their role in keeping the GOP split, and the electoral support they had given him in the West and Midwest, yet he criticized their "complete unreliability." Still, such typical formulations as Borah's—"I look upon the fight for the preservation of the 'little man,' for the small, independent producer, and manufacturer, as a fight for a sound, wholesome, economic national life"—expressed deeply held, popular values and reserved for the group a high moral ground. Those values often appealed to FDR himself, and when they did not, could not be ignored, even if congressional assaults on the "curse of bigness" often had high costs for the "little man," such as workers who paid heavily for congressionally imposed price competition in aircraft manufacture.[40]

The latitude that had to be conceded to the populist Progressives helps explain the political ravaging of a weak aviation industry during the early New Deal. Made to do penance for the way it symbolized alleged corrupt manipulation of the national economy, the industry was also held responsible for the disappointment of the hopes that many Americans had attached to aeronautic technology since before World War I. Aeronautics had been widely expected to rescue the mythic American individual, who seemed more and more overwhelmed by the limited horizons, impersonal dynamics, and bureaucratic institutions of mature industrialism. It seemed to open a new and unlimited natural frontier that drew upon and redeemed basic skills of mechanical inventiveness and physical dexterity. Rapid technical change presumably offered endless room to new ideas and new participants and served as a natural barrier to monopolistic control. All the planning, organization, and complex engineering formulas that made aircraft possible paled beside the fact that only a single pilot could make an airplane come alive. The rejuvenation of the American man through aeronautics had been fundamental to the procompetition procurement provisions of the Air Corps Act. It was personified in such heroic individuals as Gen. Billy Mitchell, who used air power to attack military bureaucracy and to revive notions of the decisive, virile military act, and in Charles Lindbergh, who demonstrated that advanced technology could be mastered by a small-town boy in coveralls and that a huge realm outside business, politics, and formal education awaited personal conquest and offered social mobility.[41]

The faith in advanced technology as a redeemer of individualism was open to easy disappointment. The paradox was suggested in President Coolidge's references to Lindbergh's plane, the *Spirit of St. Louis*, as he pinned the Distinguished Flying Cross on the Lone Eagle's chest in 1927: "We are proud that in every particular this silent partner represented American genius and industry. I am told that more than 100 separate companies furnished materials, parts or service in its construction."[42] Yet rather than confront the contradictions of their faith and its growing irrelevance to actual conditions, aeronautical populists, like antitrusters, preferred to reassert threatened myths and to understand both unrealized hopes and genuine hardship in terms of calculating violators of values and law, hoarders of profit and power, builders of trusts.

Congress's attempts to return aviation to an ideal state of purity and free it from the clutches of an Air Trust under "bankers' control" began during the last months of the Hoover administration as Justice Ferdinand Pecora's investigation of the stock exchange uncovered market rigging in aviation stocks.[43] In summer 1933 Senator Black began his lengthy investigation of the distribution of air-mail contracts by Hoover's postmaster general, Walter F. Brown. Hoover's secretaries of war and navy felt compelled to regard "lowest" as the overriding adjective in the "lowest responsible bidder" clause of the legislation that governed their dealings with aircraft manufacturers. But in his efforts to build a rational and dependable national air-transport network, Brown had taken a similar clause in the McNary-Watres Air Mail Act of 1930 to the extreme on the "responsible" side.

By February 1934 Black's investigation revealed how successfully Brown had used air-mail contracts to impose an efficient network upon generally resistant airlines. Also clear was that though large profits had been made on aviation stocks, mainly losses had been made in air transport despite the air mail. If not for the enormous sums generated by aviation holding companies during the Wall Street boom, few airlines would have survived the depression or have been able continually to finance new equipment. Nevertheless indignation over the personal speculative gains made by such figures as William Boeing, who unrepentantly testified before the Black Committee, and outrage over Brown's "Spoils Conferences," in which air-mail contracts were distributed, led to their abrupt cancellation by Roosevelt on February 9. This led in turn to the disastrous performance of the Army Air Corps, ordered to fly the mail, and the first major political setback for the president as a campaign against his action led by Charles Lindbergh drew wide support even from Roosevelt's closest supporters.[44]

For aircraft firms these developments brought about new suspicions of their relations with the military, which resulted in aircraft that crashed when they attempted the seemingly simple task of air-mail delivery and the clauses of a new Air Mail Act that denied contracts to aviation holding companies or to airlines linked to aircraft manufacturers. Proposed by FDR, this clause scuttled the holding companies that had emerged in the late 1920s.[45] In September 1934, for example, United Airlines was spun off by United Aircraft and Transport. Its Connecticut manufacturing holdings—Pratt & Whitney, Hamilton-Standard, Chance Vought, and Sikorsky—were concentrated in a new United Aircraft Corporation, and Boeing operated independently in Seattle with a subsidiary in Wichita.

The mixture of personal conviction and political pragmatism that prompted FDR's approaches to the air-mail issue was also behind his earlier decision to appoint George H. Dern as secretary of war and Harry H. Woodring as assistant secretary of war, men who sparked fresh controversy over the methods used by the military in contracting for aircraft. Dern as governor of Utah and Woodring as governor of Kansas had been among the earliest supporters of FDR's bid for the presidency. Neither was particularly distinguished or qualified for their new positions, and both their appointments and FDR's cutbacks at the War Department reflected his long indifference toward the army and its problems. Woodring, strict and aggressive in his fiscal conservatism, his populist mistrust of big business, and his continentalist views of national security, was left much latitude in his role as overseer of army procurement and in the preparation of plans for industrial and economic mobilization. Replacing Secretary Dern who died in 1936, Woodring stamped his views on the War Department until 1940 when his opposition to aid for the Allies, to heavy bombers, and to negotiated contracts won him distinction as the first member of Roosevelt's cabinet to be fired.[46]

In 1933 Woodring grew nervous about Air Corps contracts presented to him for routine approval. The Air Corps advertised its "general requirements" among aircraft manufacturers, who produced design proposals on paper. These were assessed and a winner selected, who built a prototype under a bailment contract that provided government equipment such as engines and instruments for one dollar. The Air Corps then bought the prototype at a prearranged price, tested it, and when funds became available the Air Corps Procurement Board made a recommendation for quantity production. A production contract was usually negotiated with the prototype builder under authority of the old Army Regulation 5-240 because under the Air Corps Act such contracts were not permitted.[47] Woodring's discomfort grew as a number of disappointed and desperate bidders for contracts under a $7.5 million PWA army-aircraft grant complained about favoritism in their distribution. Air Corps officers protested that quality military aircraft and the need to avoid delays depended on their methods. They argued that the power of potential competition, which they wielded in their negotiations with manufacturers, had the same effect as open-price competition. Nevertheless in late 1933 Woodring informed them that he would not approve their contracts until they had been opened to advertised bidding.[48]

Rumors of Woodring's actions prompted a steady rise in public and congressional resentment for the aircraft industry that reached a crescendo in the early weeks of February 1934 with the cancellation of the air mail contracts. Reports that Pratt & Whitney regularly reaped 45 percent profit on its navy aircraft engine work, as well as a flurry of activity in aviation stocks in anticipation of the PWA aircraft grants and the naval expansion bill then under consideration in Congress, were enough to arouse even the suspicions of Carl Vinson, chairman of the House Naval Affairs Committee and one of the manufacturers' erstwhile friends in Congress. Admiral King produced evidence that the Pratt & Whitney profits were anomalous and had been brought down to 7 percent. He also showed that the industry averaged only 4.3 percent returns on its total naval business and that many contractors, particularly airframe manufacturers, regularly absorbed substantial losses. Nevertheless, as alleged profiteering made daily national headlines, Vinson sought to determine "whether there is favoritism or trickery in obtaining contracts" and appointed a subcommittee under John J. Delaney to investigate the navy's dealings with the industry.[49]

Testimony before the month-long Delaney hearings consisted largely of naval officers' defense of the status quo in aircraft procurement and only reserved criticisms of the system by manufacturers who were on the defensive, did not want to provoke Congress, and still held out hope for relief from such congressional scrutiny in an NRA code. They restated old complaints about their inability to "patent an airplane design that will hold water" and about competitive contracting as a time-consuming obstacle to keeping abreast with relentless technological change. In Leroy Grumman's words, "As soon as an airplane is finished and ready for production, by the time you get it into your squadron for flying, there is a new airplane built by someone which makes it obsolete." One congressman insisted that "there must be a starting and stopping place somewhere." But Glenn Martin repeated points he had made since the war, explaining that simple bidding on production work was futile because it presupposed the freezing of aircraft designs and the ability of any firm to develop the designs of another. "Even the final experimental model is not a developed airplane . . . we have never had an airplane that was perfected."[50]

Admiral King argued that rumors of profiteering were wildly exaggerated and that the navy was by far the major beneficiary of its relations with the industry. He warned the committeemen not to make changes that "would deny the benefit to the government of the contractor's losses on experimental aircraft." He proudly cited a recent experimental competition for a dive bomber in which Martin was paid only $80,000 for a prototype that cost $112,000 to build and Consolidated only $75,000 for its $225,000 sample. Even though "dozens" of firms had failed, King argued, the navy would always be able to take advantage of aircraft manufacturers who had an endless supply of motivation to build aircraft: "you know and I know that they are in business and eventually hope————." Acting Navy Secretary H. L. Roosevelt stressed the protection assured the government in the various options provided by the Air Corps Act. They provided the government the full benefits of new thinking in private design without having to give any "tangible consideration" in return. Moreover, "without further compensation to the designer, [the government] has the right to make, to have made for its use, and to use any number of aircraft embodying the design. This is the consideration flowing to the government."[51]

The investigating congressmen were unnerved by the intractability of the problems in procurement of military aircraft and by the irrelevance of the theories of conspiracy that had largely prompted their efforts and sustained the press' interest in them. But having painted themselves into a corner, they blamed probable corruption and offered snippets of conspiracy for public consumption. They argued that the financial crisis of various aircraft firms resulted from consolidation rather than from false hopes for commercial aviation, the depression, or the military's contracting methods. Chairman Delaney attacked consolidation as "the hand of death" and assailed the bankers "who started the depression" for "squeezing the life out of" small companies. He complained about what was later called the revolving door between the military and industry, decrying the large number of former naval officers at UATC. He lectured Commander Weyerbacher, chief of the Navy Bureau of Aeronautics Materiel Branch, who while on leave had shared his expertise with a small engine firm: "Do you not see the impropriety of a man who has your position . . . to turn against the government and go out and consult with people outside?" Suggestions were also made that the Aluminum Company of America, supplier of 90 percent of the industry's aluminum, must somehow be behind an aviation conspiracy.[52]

In the end, however, and with the advice of Edward Warner, editor of *Aviation* magazine and former assistant secretary of the navy for aeronautics, the committee produced a measured analysis of the problem of procurement. Warner told the congressmen that depending upon private enterprise for "a new and constantly changing product" inevitably "involves special and vexing problems" and "a substantial departure from the general rule of purchase of government supplies by unrestricted competitive bidding." In his view aircraft were best developed and built by their "originators," and the government had no choice but to negotiate contracts. He insisted that the government was adequately protected in the atmosphere of potential competition created by the Air Corps Act, by government auditors and inspectors, and by the yardstick at the Naval Aircraft Factory (NAF). "There comes a time when we must trust someone," he declared.[53]

The committee duly reported that the industry's profits had been exaggerated, that negotiated contracts were needed until "the art becomes stabilized," that the military aircraft business was best characterized as "keen competition in a limited market," and that the government's interests were safe. Nevertheless public expectations and the idea that a punitive environment for military contractors was necessary compelled the committee to recommend an expansion of activity at the navy's yardstick for costs and performance, the NAF at Philadelphia. Such measures, Chairman Delaney declared, "will tend to put these manufacturers and these men who have been supplying material to the navy and army on guard and to watch what they are doing in the future."[54]

In early February, as false rumors of excessive profits among aircraft firms were fanned by Senator Black's hearings, an investigation of War Department contracting was called for by the House Military Affairs Committee now chaired by the populist agrarian from South Carolina, John McSwain, who had been instrumental in the passage of the procompetition Air Corps Act. To hold hearings a subcommittee under William N. Rogers of New Hampshire was appointed.[55] Rumors of profiteering were dispensed with early as Air Corps officers presented audited evidence showing that the opposite was in fact true. Curtiss, for example, had lost $378,000 on $10.3 million in army business from 1928 to 1933.[56] Still, members of the Rogers Committee reiterated what was by then the traditional explanation in Congress for the troubles of military aircraft production in a context of private enterprise. They blamed conspiracy, collusion, and the violation of the values and methods of free competition. Manufacturers adroitly persuaded them to shift their attention from the industry to the Air Corps and in particular to its chief, Gen. Benjamin D. Foulois, who made little effort to sensitize the congressmen to the complexities of procurement and the problems of maintaining military aircraft production on a price-competitive basis. He did not try to explain the difficulties of providing for quality military aviation with severely limited funds or the reality that despite the predominant use of negotiated contracts under old army regulations, effective rivalry on the basis of both price and a rapidly evolving technology was maintained. He simply told the aghast committeemen that "there had been no significant contracting except by negotiation for the past three years."[57]

In the minds of the committee members, the crashes of Air Corps planes trying to move the air mail and an untimely crash of a Boeing P-26 were proof that negotiated contracts not only transgressed American values and defrauded the taxpayer but also resulted in lethargic trusts that produced inferior aircraft and poor contract performance. In January 1933 the Air Corps negotiated a $1.4 million contract with Boeing for 136 P-26 pursuits. As of June 1934 only ninety-three had been delivered and were already obsolete. Production had been held up after a crash that was fatal to the pilot because of a basic flaw in design, which the Air Corps and Boeing had been warned about well in advance. The highest points on the P-26 contour were its tail tip and the pilot's exposed head. On February 22, 1934, at the height of controversy for the aviation industry, a P-26 nosed over while landing, and the pilot's neck was broken. Particularly annoying for the committee members was that Foulois had made a "gentlemen's agreement" with Boeing for a more advanced pursuit, the P-29, buying the plane's prototype for only one dollar but promising Boeing its production contract. Because of the omissions of the officers who testified, the committee did not consider that contracts were negotiated with firms like Boeing for reasons other than favoritism, such as the special competence of a firm to produce and develop the aircraft it had designed or the advantages of focusing the energies of a single design group on a

These Boeing P-26As feature headrests eight inches higher than the original design to protect the pilot's head in case of nose-over. Popularly known as the "Peashooter," the P-26 made its first flight in January 1934. It had a maximum speed of 235 miles per hour and a ceiling of 27,000 feet.

particular aircraft type. Yet neither could the committee find evidence of what motivated the "collusion" that supposedly resulted in such tragedies as the P-26 crash. Claire Egtvedt gave evidence that Boeing had already lost $500,000 on the P-26.[58]

Still the Rogers Committee, like the Delaney Committee, blamed probable corruption and a failure to adhere to the principles of competitive equal access to government contracts, which alone could produce innovation, efficiency, and economy. It issued a unanimous and searing report on the Air Corps' contracting methods in June 1934, insisting upon "open unrestricted competition in the purchase of planes and materiel." Rogers told the House that he hoped the report marked the beginning of a "house cleaning" in the Air Corps. He called for disciplinary action against Foulois, who was singled out for engaging in "illegal procurement of aircraft and accessories" and "various subterfuges" designed to evade the procompetition intent of the Air Corps Act with such results as the P-26 and air mail crashes.[59]

In response to the challenges raised by privately produced military aircraft to the traditions of military-industrial relations, Congress once again chose to reaffirm tradition. A renewed emphasis on price competition for the development and production of military aircraft meant that aircraft firms were forced to restrain innovation whose costs could not be predicted and that might exclude them from contracts. They were also compelled to seek low-cost, repetitive, quantity production. Contracting officers had to reduce the technical requirements circulated among manufacturers in order to expand the number of firms that could realistically bid on contracts. Required minimum standards for bids on new types became the best standards of two years past, rather than the best achieved.[60]

Ironically the Rogers Committee complained that the lower technical standards that Woodring had already ordered for the PWA project protected firms that did not stay abreast of developments. The committee was uncomfortable with both negotiated contracts and the consequences of competitive contracts but offered no suggestions for resolving the dilemma. Most congressmen were much less interested in such vexing complications than in reasserting the old truths to satisfy theirs and the public's intuitions. They sought assurances from the army that its methods would place an even greater weight upon economy and competition—assurances gladly supplied by Assistant Secretary Woodring. The cause of competitive aircraft contracting received a further boost on May 21, 1934, when Comptroller General McCarl handed down a decision overturning a contract negotiated with the Great Lakes Aircraft Company of Cleveland. "No similar purchasing procedure may be accepted by this office as obligating appropriated moneys." Great Lakes' contribution to competition was ended by McCarl's decision, however, as it was forced to liquidate.[61]

The Delaney Committee—the subcommittee of the House Naval Affairs Committee—called for an increase in government competition in naval aircraft manufacture, but its recommendation was a dead letter as Congress had already passed the Vinson-Trammell Act mandating the use of government facilities for the supply of at least 10 percent of the navy's experimental and production aircraft. Vinson-Trammell also contained provisions limiting profits to 10 percent on all navy contracts worth more than $10,000. These provisions, apparently so minor in an act that

authorized a $470 million naval construction program, nevertheless con-
sumed the bulk of debate on the act, with the particular restrictions on
aircraft manufacturers figuring most prominently. Vinson-Trammell, or
the "Treaty Naval Bill," had two goals—relief and rearmament. The latter and lesser goal reflected a growing nervousness about mounting tensions in Europe and the Far East and the collapse of talks at the Geneva
Disarmament Conference. Citing the naval building holiday under President Hoover, Carl Vinson grimly announced that "disarmament by
example is a dismal failure." His bill called for a five-year program for
ship construction and modernization that would return American naval
strength to levels agreed upon at Washington in 1922 and London in 1930.
Vinson argued such a buildup would "do more to bring down naval armament than anything else the Congress could possibly do."[62]

Opposition came from pacifists who attacked "merchants of death" and
military spending of any type, from isolationists who criticized the navy's
global ambitions and preferred a continentalist defense that relied more
heavily upon the army, and from others who feared the threats to the
relation between congressional and executive authority contained in the
bill's various provisions for presidential discretion in the use of the funds.
The Vinson bill was strongly supported by FDR, who sought to make
"the navy an extension of his political personality," not only for the publicity and stature generated by his frequent excursions "at the helm," but
also for the power that came with construction assignments. In the Senate the bill was taken up by Park Trammell of Florida but was delayed for
almost two months by senators such as William Borah, Huey Long, and
Gerald Nye, who assailed the bill as an incitement to a new arms race
and, in Nye's words, as "a bill for the relief of the munitions makers of the
United States."[63]

What made their actions rearguard, however, were the attractions of
the labor-intensive, make-work projects that would quickly sprout
throughout the nation. "I know what every one of you is interested in,"
Carl Vinson assured his House colleagues, "you want work for your naval
yards." He promised that contracts for ships, armor, guns, and ordnance
would be distributed according to unemployment levels in various locales
across the land wherever there were naval yards and arsenals. Those who
wanted rapid reemployment but were opposed on principle to military
spending or military contractors were assuaged by the Tobey Amendment, which limited profits on navy contracts to 10 percent of costs and by
the president's expressions of support for Senator Nye's Special Investigation of Munitions Makers.[64]

The obstacles to passage of Vinson-Trammell hinged upon the extent of punitive measures deemed necessary against naval aircraft contractors. Curiously in retrospect, the most vitriolic assault on the industry was mounted by the senator from Washington State. Specifically attacking the personal stock profits of William Boeing, already a major Seattle employer, Democrat Homer T. Bone told the Senate that the "people of this country are weary of the spectacle of the Government being looted, literally looted, by private airplane companies." He called for the supply of at least 50 percent of the navy's aircraft needs by government plants as a first step toward freeing the taxpayer from "the absolute mercy of private manufacturers of airplanes."[65]

To get the Vinson bill through the Senate and into conference with the House, Trammell was forced to accept amendments sponsored by Senator Bone providing for 25 percent of naval aircraft requirements to be filled in government plants along with 10 percent profit limitations on all navy contracts above $10,000. In conference, with FDR's help, Vinson persuaded his Senate counterparts that the start-up costs and delays of completing 25 percent of the navy's aircraft work in government plants were unacceptable and could well destroy private aircraft manufacture. The navy had only twelve officers capable of designing aircraft and could never attract new men on the salaries Congress limited it to paying. With FDR's support, who as assistant secretary of the navy had worked for the establishment of the Naval Aircraft Factory in 1917, Vinson persuaded them to leave the amount of government manufacture to the president's discretion and to limit the 10 percent profit limitation to contracts above $50,000. The bulk of navy contracts were worth less than that amount and the cost of auditing so many would be much greater than any possible savings that might result.[66] Still, the Senate rejected the amendments its conferees returned. Finally a compromise was reached that reserved 10 percent of aircraft work to government plants and placed the floor for the 10 percent profit limitation at $10,000. While Senator Bone fumed that the new bill's "weazel words" on government aircraft production represented "servile worshipping of private interests," the Senate passed the bill by a margin of 65-19, and FDR signed it on the twenty-seventh of March.[67]

Vinson-Trammell's financial penalties intensified the negative effects of fifteen years of congressional regulation of the aircraft industry. Manufacturers bitterly protested that their industry was singled out for punitive measures and equated with criminal activity. They complained that profit limitations were not matched by profit guarantees and that profits were computed before federal taxes, which placed the actual profit limitation at 7 to 8 percent. They also complained that a firm's profits had to be computed on each separate contract, preventing the equalization of profits and losses among contracts and over time. Prior to the act, naval contractors at least had hope that losses on development work might be made up in production contracts. Especially galling and a particular obstacle to business planning and technical development was the refusal of the Internal Revenue Service, charged with auditing contractors and collecting excess profits, to state in advance acceptable elements of cost. Whether development costs, overhead, state and local taxes, interest on borrowed funds, and so forth would be accepted was to be determined only after the fact on "a case by case basis." "This of course means only one thing," commented Donald L. Brown, president of Pratt & Whitney, "the contractor will not know his profit or loss until the contract is audited by the Internal Revenue Department." Others argued that strict profit limitations would have all the negative effects of cost-plus contracts—the discouragement of efficiencies in design and production and higher unit costs—because manufacturers would do nothing that might increase their profits beyond the limitation only to have them returned to the Treasury.[68]

While reaffirming price-competitive aircraft procurement—the source of disorder, conflict, and waste in the industry since the war—Vinson-Trammell had the ironic effect of limiting the number of firms that would compete for navy contracts. The difficulties in attracting new investment, which aircraft firms had suffered since the stock market crash, were compounded. Bonding charges increased up to 400 percent for navy contractors, and some bonding companies refused to supply them at all. Boeing refused navy work through the 1930s, its executives decrying stringent government auditing of both their commercial and military work as "savoring of the Russian OGPU."[69]

The delays, rancor, and waste of price competition and the costs of auditing innumerable contracts and expanding government plants led to a feeling among military officers that matters had gone too far. Admiral King complained that profit limitations and 10 percent production in government plants created "administrative difficulties far out of proportion to the intangible benefits that might result." Officers in his bureau were convinced the Act would retard the development of naval aviation and tried until 1940 to offset its effects with little success. In March 1935 they persuaded Carl Vinson to introduce an amendment that would allow the transferral of losses on contracts in one year to profits in the succeeeding year, but it failed to pass.[70]

The navy also tried to minimize the effect of the 10 percent government-production clause by building only simple trainers at the Naval Aircraft Factory. This clause was especially worrisome for manufacturers as popular aversion to arms makers grew.[71] Congressmen intended the Naval Aircraft Factory to serve the same purposes that Josephus Daniels had in mind when he established it in 1917—the monitoring and maintenance of traditional competition within a private aircraft industry. Manufacturers, however, saw it as an opening wedge for the nationalization of their industry, which along with the public control of all weapons industries became a widely favored idea in America during the 1930s. Arms makers and their financiers were popularly understood to have fomented World War I and were now busily trying to spark new conflict in Europe, the Far East, and Latin America.[72] Exposure of these sinister manipulations and the desire for a shift of American diplomacy and military doctrine away from an internationalist orientation to isolationist continental defense prompted Senator Nye and his agrarian colleagues to launch a lengthy investigation of weapons makers and to recommend the nationalization of the weapons industry.[73]

The investigation drew support from such diverse sources as the 12-million-strong peace movement; the American Legion, who demanded that the government "take the profits out of war"; Eleanor Roosevelt; and conservative business voices such as Henry Luce, publisher of *Fortune*, who resented federal spending and internationalist diplomacy. In the wake of the collapse of the Geneva arms talks, Roosevelt too saw merit in the argument that arms makers provoked international conflict and did not want to aggravate agrarian Republicans. Later he would regret his support for the Nye Committee when in 1936 it began to impugn Woodrow Wilson's motives for going to war and succeeded in galvanizing a powerful isolationist sentiment that circumscribed his options in foreign policy.[74]

The committee began hearings in September 1934. The first group to be grilled by the committee's able staff members, Stephen Raushenbush and Alger Hiss, were aircraft industry executives including representatives of Curtiss-Wright and United Aircraft. The questioners made much of the firms' agents in areas where conflict loomed and of the role of the Bureau of Foreign and Domestic Commerce in promoting aircraft sales abroad; but the Committee and an eager press were disappointed by the forthrightness and conservatism of these "merchants of death" and by the inability, despite access to the companies' records, to make the case that their aircraft sales abroad incited war. With a similar lack of concrete results, hearings into all phases of the defense industry and into the role of American banks and corporations in World War I continued into 1936. The committee published many volumes of hearings and seven major reports, the final one recommending nationalization of military industries.[75] Opinion polls showed strong support for the idea, but the administration prevented passage of a bill for the purpose introduced by Nye.[76]

The Nye Committee produced no new legislation but was nevertheless significant in shaping popular attitudes toward American foreign policy, the defense industry, and war preparedness. In respect to the aircraft industry, the committee aided Congress's efforts to keep its business environment as restrictive as possible. In maintaining the competition that defined the industry's relations with the military until summer 1940, Congress operated effectively and independently. The views of aircraft manufacturers and private experts were ignored by Congress, and officers in the aviation wings opposed congressional policy with little effect.

Roosevelt, who earlier had done much to encourage sentiment against the aircraft industry, also tried unsuccessfully to move Congress toward a less ideological approach to the industry's problems. In December 1934 he appointed a board chaired by Bernard Baruch and including Hans Morgenthau, Jr., Frances Perkins, and Henry Wallace. He wanted the board to formulate new legislation for military-industrial relations, but the Nye Committee branded Baruch a "war profiteer" and nothing came of its proposals. FDR followed the pattern set by Wilson and Coolidge, who had tried to counter congressional investigations of the industry with quieter executive probes. In 1934 he appointed the Federal Aviation Commission under the Atlanta newspaper editor Clark Howell. With the manufacturers' strong approval, it called for an Air Commerce Commission to end bureaucratic duplication among the various federal agencies involved in commercial aviation. It also repeated the recommendation for an authorization of the army and navy secretaries "to make purchases by direct negotiation with the manufacturer best able to supply the desired equipment."[77]

The president declined to back the commission's calls for coordinated federal aviation activities. Largely because of Congressman McSwain's prodding, he also rejected its recommendations on procurement as well as similar suggestions by a 1934 War Department study under the venerable Newton D. Baker.[78] Referring to the World War I fiasco, McSwain insisted that "aircraft manufacturers have squandered millions" and warned that negotiated contracts "will bring about corruption and moral debauchery of a most deplorable sort." So out of touch was McSwain with the issues of privately produced military aircraft that he introduced a bill guaranteeing private design rights to military aircraft in an attempt to protect small designers from the "Aircraft Trust" that had tried for years to win such protection.[79]

The White House and the army and navy could do little more than limit the effects of Congress's efforts to shape the industry according to its ideological goals. Nor could the NRA do much to qualify Congress's control over the industry. It was forced to reject the chamber's draft code after its public hearing in December 1933, and the manufacturers' representatives began a long and futile process of bargaining with the NRA. In a revised code presented in January 1934, the chamber still insisted on the manufacturers' rights to their designs but lamely included disclaimers of any attempt to override whatever powers the military possessed for purchasing or seizing design rights in time of war. During February and March 1934 a series of conferences were held among chamber, NRA, army, and navy representatives, but the military men, according to Leighton Rogers, "were not permitted by their respective secretaries to come to an agreement" on "the one important trade practice which would make the code valuable to the industry."[80]

As the various congressional investigations proceeded it became obvious that the aircraft industry was not going to get a new deal. On May 10, 1934, the industry finally lifted the provisions for design rights from its proposed code. For one member of the NRA Industrial Advisory Board, the deletion of the "design piracy clause for political reasons," which "constitutes the meat of this code," was a complete repudiation of his version of the NRA's role—the rationalization of industry and the suppression of competition.[81] Given the frequent association of technically advanced industries with corporatist arrangements, as well as the interdependency between the state and the aircraft industry, it is striking that aircraft so clearly exposed the limits of the NRA. Because aeronautics was the period's high technology and because aircraft manufacture was a military industry, they inevitably became channels for cultural, ideological, and political currents with which corporatism could not cope. These currents clashed with the needs of a high-technology industry, but the resultant discord and dysfunctions were nevertheless institutionalized. Having surrendered the battle for corporatist self-regulation of their industry through the NRA, the manufacturers turned instead to the more modest goal of a cost-cutting labor code that might also impose some limits on competition.

CHAPTER SIX

Lost Opportunities:
Aircraft Workers
and the NRA

SECTION 7a

The story of the attempts to organize aircraft workers under the NRA is one of failure and lost opportunities with long-term consequences for the industry's development. As many underpaid and overworked aircraft workers realized, they bore much of the brunt of the competition maintained in their industry by Congress. A strong union offered a means of stabilizing the industry by denying military contractors and Congress the competitive space provided by differentials in wages and working conditions. Many worked hard for a national aircraft worker's union, but the obstacles proved too many and too large. Unorganized aircraft workers continued to function as primary variables in the battle for aircraft contracts and as underwriters of an industry kept competitive by congressmen for reasons of ideology.

The fate of the manufacturers' proposals for trade practice reform suggests that while the NRA may have reflected a broad agreement on how the nation's economic problems required detailed federal attention, this new consensus could not be made effective. The NRA did not represent a clear shift in the distribution of authority at the federal level or in attitudes as to what the precise nature of expanded government intervention should be. Even for aircraft manufacture, a product of special consideration by the state that might have acted as a model for the sort of intervention envisioned by many during the early New Deal, the NRA simply served as a new forum for the customary interplay of interests that comprised it. The NRA did little to alter the relative positions of these interests or the dynamics of the relationships among them. In a repeat of their experiences with the Air Corps Act, the manufacturers saw their proposals to the NRA for reforming their industry's trade practices easily quashed by Congress.

The NRA did, however, introduce a new variable in the equation of interests that shaped the aircraft industry. That variable had existed as long as aircraft had been built, but under the NRA it acquired an importance it had previously lacked. Section 7a made it clear that aircraft workers as a group had to be granted consideration as a factor in the conflict of interests even if the details of that consideration were left entirely vague. As the primary element in the actual process of producing aircraft, the workers held a potentially large leverage within the industry, but the NRA provided them no new powers beyond a concession of legitimacy. Aircraft workers were left to realize their potential on their own. They needed to bring organizational strength to the interplay of interests that the NRA was structured to facilitate.

Under Section 7a, workers' strength relied, as it always had, on independent organization. However, through its Labor Advisory Board (LAB), the NRA provided workers with a new and energetic base of support within the state. Although this board could do little to enhance the positions of workers, it did much to defend them. The LAB was the first of a series of similar boards, culminating in the National Labor Relations Board (NLRB), that marked the beginning of comprehensive intervention by the federal government in industrial relations, which were at the heart of the New Deal's regulatory innovations.

Section 7a's wording left FDR and Hugh Johnson much leeway for preserving the status quo of labor relations, which they preferred. It neither substituted collective bargaining for individual bargaining nor required workers to join unions. It stated that workers could bargain collectively and were to be assured of the right to join, organize, or assist unions if they chose, free from employer interference. For Johnson the priority was the speedy passage of codes, which necessitated business cooperation. To reassure business he announced on the NRA's first day that conferences between workers and employers were not required for the formulation of code provisions on wages, hours, and working conditions. Proposals for labor standards were reserved as the exclusive prerogative of employers. If codes for some industries did emerge from collective bargaining (mining, the building and needle trades, for example), it was only because those industries were already well organized by labor. Still, it was significant that whatever collective agreements predated NIRA achieved a new legal status, moving from the realm of private contract law to that of statute law.[1]

Employer "interference, restraint, or coercion" were not defined, leaving employers with many options in blocking the unionization of their workers. Section 7a did not outlaw company unions; it merely prohibited employers from making participation in a company union a condition of employment. Without a decisive policy to the contrary and effective means of enforcement, traditional heavy-handed methods of discharge and intimidation were not truly prohibited by NIRA. Indeed, they could only be encouraged by such statements as Johnson's to auto manufacturers that it was "emphatically not the intention that the administration shall be used as an instrument for promoting the interests of organized labor."[2]

During summer 1933 this sentiment helped trigger the largest wave of strikes since 1921 as workers realized that their aspirations for NIRA were being denied and that their new grant of legitimacy was worth little without its vigorous assertion. In August FDR tried to offset the NRA's provocative management of the state's new role in labor relations by appointing the National Labor Board (NLB), comprised of three labor members, three industry members, and Senator Wagner as chairman. The NLB more fully assumed the role of an impartial, quasi-judicial, federal arbiter of labor relations. It created a national system of regional labor boards that interpreted and tried to enforce Section 7a for the benefit of workers and in opposition to Johnson. It called for elections by secret ballot to help unions win recognition from employers, criticized company unions, and defended the majority rule for the exclusive representation of workers.[3]

But the NLB was denied the mechanisms for enforcement that would have given it the power to effect the revolution in industrial relations that its interpretations of Section 7a implied. There was little the NLB could do when employers fired union activists and otherwise intimidated workers or when they simply refused to permit elections, recognize majority rule, or bargain with their workers in good faith. Preservation of the open shop was nonnegotiable for most American industries, and anti-unionism assumed the proportions of a crusade throughout the NRA period. "It was not merely a question of individual employers, acting singly, but of an organized campaign of non-compliance in which entire industries acted in concert."[4]

The limitations of a toothless NLB were passed on to the NLRB established by FDR in June 1934. It shared its predecessor's interpretations of

Section 7a, but despite its expanded powers to invoke the jurisdiction of circuit courts, it could do little more to enforce them. The NLRB was denied the power to resolve the critical question of whether units for collective bargaining would be established through majority or proportional representation. "The NLB and then the NLRB became lone voices crying in the wilderness of non-compliance.[5]"

The fulfillment of workers' new claims under NIRA depended on the pressure they could bring to bear upon their employers, and the pressure aircraft workers could exert, if adequately organized, was enormous. Labor intensity defined the industry despite the shifts in aircraft construction to metal materials that lent themselves more readily to mechanization. Indeed the percentage of value-added by aircraft manufacture represented by wages increased with the shift to all-metal aircraft. In 1927 it stood at 50.3 percent; in 1931, at 56.9 percent; and in 1933, at 55.7 percent, figures very high relative to other manufacturing industries (see Table 3.2, p. 48). Market size remained limited while the technical developments associated with this period of rapid change increased the complexity of the product and its manufacturing process. Obsolescence rates of military aircraft were almost instantaneous. Many, such as the Boeing P-26, were useless except as trainers even before their production contracts were signed. Product change and complexity kept hopes for the stability of long production runs and mass-production techniques as distant as ever.[6]

For a sense of the relative importance of the various costs faced by aircraft manufacturers see Table 6.1 and Table 6.2. The manufacturers had no way to regulate new entry or price competition; these costs help to explain their hostility to independent unions, their meager offerings to

Table 6.1. Costs and Overhead at the Chance Vought Corporation (UATC), 1929–1933

	1933	1932	1931	1930	1929
Manufacturing	$670,101	756,147	579,716	684,258	469,597
General	81,611	90,095	47,806	84,823	76,887
Sales and service	36,886	29,373	29,080	32,380	30,081
Total	788,598	875,615	656,602	801,461	576,565
Production labor	706,384	584,842	321,853	559,598	688,004
Percentage overhead	112	149	204	143	84

Source: Hearings before the Subcommittee on Aeronautics . . . , 73rd Cong., 1st sess., 1934 (Delaney Hearings), 67.

Table 6.2. "Typical Case—Principal Navy Plane" Costs, 1933

	Experimental Fighter	Production Fighter
Engineering salaries and direct labor	$94,152	$4,926
Manufacturing overhead	36,051	4,149
Administrative overhead	2,863	36
Military development	329	0
Direct charges	10,781	168
Military sales expenses	10,972	12
Material	8,744	2,680
Total cost	153,940	11,999
Sales	18,410	12,150
Profit	—	159 (7.9%)
Loss	105,522 (−98.5%)	—

Source: Hearings before the Subcommittee on Aeronautics . . . , 73rd Cong., 1st sess., 1934 (Delaney Hearings), 309.

labor in their proposed code, and the extreme rigors imposed upon aircraft workers. Their proposed labor provisions suggest the manufacturers' early captivation with the NRA. The proposals were unanimously approved by the chamber's code committeemen, who were confident in their acceptance by the NRA and the inability of workers to oppose them. They were part of the manufacturers' search for the best of both worlds—the means for passing on increased costs to their consumers in the government through trade-practice rules restricting competition and the power to keep the major element of those costs as low as possible through control over wages, hours, and working conditions. Some of the committeemen also recognized that closely regulated labor standards were important supplements to trade-practice rules. But as approval of their trade-practice proposals became less and less likely, manufacturers were willing to settle for a strictly enforced, regressive labor code as a desirable outcome of their dealings with the NRA. In this approach they resembled most other industries that encountered deadlock over trade-practice proposals, as well as oligopolistic industries, such as auto manufacture, for which strong trade-practice provisions were unnecessary.[7]

The manufacturers bowed to Section 7a and its vague calls for the rights of workers to organize and bargain collectively free from employer interference. But they insisted upon the contentious inviolability of the "existing satisfactory relationships" clause and the "merit" clause, which the auto industry had successfully included in its code and had shown that

Table 6.3. Average Employment, Hours, and Wages in
Aircraft Manufacture, 1929–1933

	Employment	Average Hrs/wk.	Average Wage
1929	19,990	—	67.4
1931	11,603	—	—
1932	9,829	44.3	71.2
1933	11,562	42.8	64.6
1934	11,090	39.0	64.9
1935 (Jan.–Sept.)	12,811	39.6	64.2

Includes aircraft engines.

Source: Compiled from statistics in "AMC, Statistics," box 6046; C. A. Pearce, "Aircraft Manufacturing Industry," April 4, 1934, 25, "AMC, Documents," box 6046, NRA *Records,* RG 9, National Archives, Washington, D.C.; see also Bureau of Labor Statistics, "Wages and Hours in the Manufacture of Airplanes and Aircraft Engines 1929," Bulletin 523, November, 1930.

they could be used on behalf of company unions and to dismiss workers who attempted independent organization.[8] The proposed code's minimum wage of forty cents per hour was a special threat to workers (see Table 6.3). The manufacturers claimed it was not their intention to reduce established wages. However, few doubted that the industry's average of sixty-five cents would soon gravitate to the minimum if implemented in a code because of sharp price competition, the swings in hiring and layoffs driven by the cycles of military contracts, and the manufacturers' recent record of wage cuts.

The chamber felt less need to defend its low minimum-wage proposal than its call for a maximum forty-hour week and time and a third pay for overtime. Both were well outside the guidelines of the NRA's Blanket Code, or the President's Reemployment Agreement (PRA) of July 27, 1933. The PRA, and the Blue Eagle campaign spawned by it, grew out of the early discovery that producing codes and inducing reemployment among the innumerable fields that comprised American industry was a slow and complicated process, particularly since each interested party was entitled to "his day in court." FDR did not want to lose the momentum of his so-far successful display of presidential activism in the face of the depression. He worried that the initiative in measures for recovery might be assumed by Congress. Unwilling to speed the code-making process by forcing employers to participate, he instead appealed to their patriotism, asking each to "do his part" and voluntarily submit to the Blanket Code pending NRA approval of a code for his industry. The PRA restricted the employment of any artisan, factory, or mechanical worker to thirty-five hours per week except for any six weeks within that period during which workers could fill a forty-hour week. Signers of the PRA were entitled to display the Blue Eagle, identifying them with the national antidepression crusade directed by the NRA and featuring propaganda, parades, and peer pressure. If aircraft manufacturers were capable of ignoring these appeals to their social consciences they were less able, though most did, to ignore Executive Order 6246 of August 10, 1933, which required federal contractors to comply either with their industry's code or with the PRA.[9]

In defense of their proposals for hours, the manufacturers had strong arguments to make, given the unsuitability for a high-technology industry of an industrial-relations framework that rigidly regulated working patterns and hours. The broad prescriptions for economic recovery advanced by Senator Wagner and AFL leaders, who argued that work-sharing measures would reduce unemployment and expand purchasing power, were appropriate for many industries but inimical to aircraft. Manufacturers insisted that their industry be recognized as a "special case," not as a mass-production industry in which work-sharing measures might be effective. They demanded minimal overtime pay and the right to manage their plants in accord with the unique requirements of their products. These included "precision work to a superlative degree," the right to hire and fire according to merit, and "elasticity of hours" to cope with fixed-period contracts. More importantly they insisted on the right to continuously employ the "hands of the same men" to prevent the dilution by labor shifts of particular workers' knowledge of particular aircraft under construction. Their workers were "specialized" not because they built aircraft but because they built particular aircraft. Each was unique, even within the same production series. To prevent "slipshod workmanship" and a possibly "exacting toll in death," only a small number of employees could work on a particular aircraft at any given time and had to be available at all times to cope with "so much special engineering . . . necessary during construction" and the military's regular insistence upon design changes. Thus, the chamber argued, aircraft workers should be excluded from the maximum-hour provisions.[10]

The manufacturers had a good case for flexibility of hours. So confident were they in the NRA, however, that they put forth such arguments without suggestions for offsetting the workers' burdens. Instead, they proposed what amounted to a large wage cut. Manufacturers also made contradictory claims that helped turn the NRA against them. They argued that work-sharing was not necessary since "there exists no large amount of unemployment in the industry," but that if the government expanded its military aircraft program, employment could be found for "virtually all trained aircraft mechanics in the country."[11] Reuben Fleet, who had consented to the proposed code and its claim that no unemployment existed, could at the same time appeal for increased government aircraft spending on behalf of "at least 2,000 highly trained aircraft workers out of work in Buffalo." Fleet's general manager, Laurence D. Bell, also described such measures as "the only hope for the thousand men we have been forced to lay off during the last year" along with the "many thousands of employees who are suffering forced layoffs" throughout the nation.[12]

Manufacturers thus antagonized their workers and critics immediately and needlessly since they genuinely expected approval of their anticompetitive trade-practice proposals, which would have made labor costs largely irrelevant. On elasticity of hours, they would have been in accord with the majority of their workers, who understood the industry's needs better perhaps than the manufacturers. Sharing their employers' motivations in this unprofitable industry, most workers were happy to put in long hours to be part of the excitement of building better aircraft. Many had done so for years, supplying their valuable skills at wages well below what they commanded in other industries. Like their employers, they were willing to subsidize the development of aeronautics. Yet explorations and accommodation outside the formula of closely regulated work patterns to expand employment could not be made with their employers, who were unable to overcome the automatic hostility to labor generated by the competitive regime imposed by Congress. Manufacturers thus lost what could have been important allies in the pursuit of a new regulatory framework for their industry.

To the manufacturers it seemed that the NRA existed to serve them, but their workers too supposed that the NRA had been designed with their specific problems in mind and also made aggressive appeals to Washington. In a steady stream of letters individual workers, members of their families, new aircraft union locals, and their supporters in Congress pressured NRA administrators to act upon what they perceived to be the primary intent of NIRA—the betterment of working conditions, purchasing power, and living standards. They insisted that the promises of Section 7a be immediately fulfilled and that workers be provided the same pledges of collective power that their employers were receiving.

NRA administrators responded to these appeals, blocking at every turn NRA approval of the manufacturers' labor proposals. Their actions proved critical as various factors combined to prevent aircraft workers from effectively organizing and advancing their interests on their own. Like unorganized workers in other industries, initial enthusiasm among many aircraft workers during the early weeks of the NRA produced spontaneous organizations and responsiveness to American Federation of Labor campaigns.[13] In aircraft this new militancy surprised employers and in some plants resulted in temporary victories. But again as in other industries, initial enthusiasm cooled as organizing campaigns were sidetracked by the ambivalence of other aircraft workers toward unionization, by hesitant leadership and jurisdictional disputes among established unions, and by the dogged resistance of employers. In the absence of effective, independent representation for aircraft workers, without which the possibilities of Section 7a could not be realized, NRA administrators, particularly LAB officials, functioned as labor's bargaining agents. They could do little to advance the workers' interests, but they could assure that federal power would not be used to shift upon them an even greater share of the industry's burdens.[14]

RESISTANCE, INDEPENDENCE, AND OBSTRUCTIONISM

An effective presence for both businessmen and workers within the bargaining arena that defined the NRA code-making process depended upon organizational strength.[15] Such strength among aircraft workers depended upon the degree and durability of their loyalty toward unions and also upon connections between their unions and larger national labor bodies. These were perceived by the NRA as legitimate, experienced voices for labor that could offer workers legal and tactical guidance. Both loyalty and connections were only tenuously achieved by aircraft workers. To be effective the workers' loyalty to independent unions had to be stronger than their loyalty to their employers, who were uniformly hostile to unions. However, many aircraft workers strongly identified with their firms' names and products and shared with their employers emotional attachments to aircraft production and a sense of responsibility for furthering a new technology deemed crucial for the nation's prestige, economic development, and military defense.[16]

Their commitment to their work coupled with the threatening atmosphere maintained by their employers limited sustained collective militancy among aircraft workers. Hoping to survive the frequent and acute contractions in employment that defined their industry, they were reluctant to antagonize their employers.[17] When they did display militancy and a willingness to act collectively, they insisted upon their own independent organizations tailored to suit their special circumstances. Many aircraft workers considered themselves a breed apart, as members of a team that produced unique products by hand. Except for a few in various plants who maintained membership in one or another AFL affiliate, they had little experience with and were suspicious of outside unions that sought to organize them into separate craft unions. Consequently the upsurge of activism encouraged by Section 7a was diluted by conflict with AFL internationals, which opposed new unions organized along plant or industrial lines, and by the opposition of many workers within specific plants to affiliate with existing national organizations.

The AFL had been the major force behind the wording and passage of Section 7a but was in a poor position to take quick advantage of whatever potential it held for organized labor. The leaders of the internationals that comprised the federation would not support large-scale, industrially based organizing campaigns. They were jealous of their traditional prerogatives to organize workers along craft lines and fearful of the dilution of their privileged and proud ranks by millions of semi-skilled and unskilled workers. Emerging from a lengthy period of almost uninterrupted defeats and reversals, they were mindful of the hostility and power of the employers whom they faced and the limited resources that they themselves commanded. Historically they had reason to be suspicious of Washington and were wary of their sudden legitimacy. The power of these separate unions within its constitutional structure made the mass organization of workers extremely difficult for the AFL. Still, AFL president William Green and secretary Frank Morrison were willing to act quickly under NIRA and with limited regard for various jurisdictional claims. They utilized whatever limited resources the AFL national office could muster on its own to recruit industrial workers into Federal Labor Unions (FLUs) affiliated directly with the AFL, arguing that these would serve to take immediate advantage of the new eagerness among the unorganized who would later be allotted among the various craft unions.[18]

Even these minimal efforts at mass organization were perceived as threats by the old internationals, which protested the inclusion of workers under their jurisdictions within the rapidly proliferating FLUs. The International Association of Machinists (IAM), which claimed skilled aircraft workers, was a particularly determined defender of its jurisdiction. Over the years the IAM had developed its own measured organizational responses to an evolving industrial economy, tactics which seemed threatened by the sudden calls for the mass organization of workers under Section 7a. Traditionally the IAM had focused on skilled metalworkers but was willing to expand its jurisdiction over less-skilled workers to help maintain job control and a strategic presence within plants and industries where craft skills were being displaced by mechanization.[19] While this evolving semi-industrial organizational strategy displayed greater flexibility than the old craft internationals are usually credited with, the IAM's work in aircraft makes clear that it remained a conservative, job-conscious union, built upon a proud voluntary mutualism of craftsmen, skeptical of both government involvement in labor relations and the desirability of extending labor organization to workers simply as workers.

The IAM attacked Green for allowing FLUs' absorption of machinists in the auto and steel industries. With its endless claims it restrained the AFL and discouraged workers who did not want to see their plants divided into separate locals.[20] IAM President A. O. Wharton insisted that AFL organizers stop seducing workers who fell under his jurisdiction with the low initiation and monthly fees charged by FLUs. IAM officials, charging monthly dues of $1.75 and initiation fees ranging from $5.00 to $20.00, came across as "grafters and racketeers" as FLU organizers charged $1.00 per month and $2.00 for initiation. "This is absolutely destructive to our organizing work," complained Wharton.[21]

Only slowly would the Machinists respond to these challenges by launching all-inclusive industrial drives of their own. With its high concentration of skilled machinists and light dependence on unskilled workers, the aircraft industry provided an organizing target that helped ease the IAM's transition from craft to industrial unionism. But this change was long delayed by the endurance of old attitudes among the Machinists and by the resistance of aircraft workers to the IAM's organizational policies. The transition came only well after the NRA period, after the real opportunities it offered were lost, and when the workers' aversion to the IAM had multiplied, making the task that much more difficult.

The claims of the Machinists to aircraft workers went back to 1916, when they expanded their official work classification to include "the manufacture, repairing, and maintaining of automobiles, firearms, fire engines, locomotives, hydroplanes, and aeroplanes."[22] But the IAM did little in aircraft except to block the initiatives of others, particularly those who sought to organize aircraft workers along industrial lines. That idea was raised within the AFL during the heady days of 1928. Workers in Wichita and California, caught up in the intoxicating atmosphere then enveloping aviation, described the industry as a great opportunity for the AFL but warned against the conventional approach of craft organization. Wichita carpenters told Green that the nine plants in their city, including Cessna and Beech, "should be working union labor [but] we do not want to try and organize the plant in 5 different crafts such as Carpenters, Painters, etc. but want a union as airplane builders—one craft." A San Diego group with its eye on Douglas workers warned Green that "to organize the workers under our present craft union plan does not seem possible." Aircraft workers, although specialized tradesmen, considered themselves aircraft builders before machinists, carpenters, or electricians, they explained. "We must decide on a program immediately lest we find ourselves in the same position as we did in the automotive industry, with the result we all hate to contemplate." The IAM vetoed the idea. "We can see no good reason why the industry cannot be organized on a craft union basis." Green informed the Wichita carpenters that because of claims on the industry from unions ranging from the Machinists to the Electrical Workers and even the Bridge and Structural Iron Workers, the "Executive Council directs that in organizing the airplane builders and workers they should be organized by trades . . . they should apply for separate charters."[23]

The AFL's interest in aircraft workers during 1928 was discovered by the Aeronautical Chamber of Commerce, which surveyed its membership on the possibility of common action to thwart a union drive. At that time most manufacturers were fairly sanguine about their industry's prospects and displayed little anxiety over unionization. Edgar Gott of Keystone Aircraft in Bristol, Pennsylvania, accurately predicted that an AFL campaign in aircraft was unlikely to succeed because of the great diversity of trades. Reuben Fleet, surrounded by a "vast reservoir of skilled labor," could not see how the AFL could succeed in Buffalo. But Walter Beech, whose Wichita carpenters had proposed an industrial union, was disturbed by the prospects of organized aircraft workers. Anticipating what would be a basic approach among manufacturers to organized labor under the NRA and beyond, he suggested that they establish company unions in their plants with "the manufacturer being a part of the union. This gives control, more or less, of the situation."[24]

The IAM's first active interest in the industry came in 1930 during the strike at the Wright Aeronautical engine plant in Paterson, New Jersey. The IAM was more comfortable among engine workers, who were more naturally its constituents, while airframe manufacture was a minefield of jurisdictional disputes. Some IAM organizers saw aircraft as an industry of the future in which the Machinists could get a foothold through its key engine plants. However, their experiences in Paterson only served to confirm hesitancy toward the industry in the minds of IAM leaders. Paterson provided a sampling of the great difficulties of organizing aircraft workers—their independent-mindedness, the unsuitability of the IAM's traditional tactics, and the deep resistance to unionization among manufacturers in an industry kept artificially competitive by federal law and for whom wages were the key variable of costs.

Prompted by the company's speed-up measures in production, which amounted to a 40 percent wage cut, 1,000 workers began a strike at Wright Aeronautical in December 1930. The company's president, Guy W. Vaughan, hoped the dispute would provoke better contracting terms from the army and navy and was prepared to weather the lengthy strike, which the independent, committed, and well-organized Wright machinists seemed bent on sustaining (see p. 113–116). Officials of the local IAM Silk City Lodge 188 also saw opportunities in this determination, but at the time of the strike, they had only twenty-seven members at Wright. Like their employers, the engine workers had little but contempt for "outside unions" and felt compelled to counter their employers' charges that they were the dupes of "professional agitators" engaged in "communistic activities." They proudly insisted that theirs was a "spontaneous walkout . . . these men are not organized."[25]

Still, local IAM officials thought the Machinists could get "a big boost" at Wright and at other plants in the industry if it actively supported the strikers who were rapidly gaining national attention for embarrassing the Hoover administration. Workers were being forced to strike for restorations of wage cuts at a plant 90 percent dependent upon contracts from the government, whose major policy in response to the depression was to win business promises that wages would not be cut. All the dramatic elements were there: pickets in subzero temperatures, hired thugs to harass pickets, and a federal contractor who callously told the press that "hunger will soon drive the strikers back to work." The Paterson Machinists, in an appeal to the Grand Lodge, pointed out that, "if we lose this struggle it will be deplorable because it is undoubtedly the greatest opportunity we have ever had in the industry." Setting the pattern for his approach to aircraft through the 1930s, IAM President Wharton nevertheless ordered restraint. At heart he believed that workers should seek out the IAM rather than vice versa. He also sympathized with Curtiss-Wright's strategy of dramatizing the consequences for workers of Congress's attitudes toward procurement. Perhaps it was best, he wrote, to leave it to "the Department of Labor to establish whether the letting of contracts competitively resulting in cutting wages is productive for workers."[26]

The strike dragged on. The IAM leadership grew hostile to the strikers as proceedings for an injunction against the Machinists were launched by Wright despite their minimal involvement. Seeking financial aid for the strikers, the Paterson Machinists were informed from sunny Miami, where Wharton was at a convention, that the top Machinist "was not agreeable to spending any money in the Paterson strike as the men had ample time to become members of our Association before the crisis came." The Paterson local was instructed to seek any agreement that guaranteed nondiscrimination against the strikers, which meant no agreement at all since Vaughan had already offered them their jobs back after finding that his strike breakers were ruining equipment. The strikers insisted on wage increases and recognition of their committee, which Vaughan refused. He would not waver from his long-held "intention of running an open shop indefinitely," nor did he have to until late into World War II.[27]

As March approached, appeals went out again to Wharton for financial aid, but he reiterated his complaint that so many came to the IAM only in times of distress. Finally on April 17 the strike was called off as the workers conceded defeat. Vaughan agreed to rehire them but reserved the right to place them in any position and at any wage. Anxious to avoid future delays from work stoppages, the army, navy, and Labor Department conferred with Vaughan in an attempt to soften his approach to labor, but he would concede nothing more than vague promises to deal with workers' grievances so long as no "outside union" was part of the process.[28]

Conditions in Paterson were "worse than I have ever known them . . . not a job to be had." Yet the only lesson IAM leaders drew from the Wright strike was "the danger of striking before organizing." For them the solidarity and self-organization displayed for more than five months by the Wright workers was illegitimate because it was not IAM inspired. Organizing Wright thereafter was impossible for the Machinists. The depression, wide swings in employment, aversion for the IAM, company unions, and intimidation made all further attempts to build independent unions at Wright "a waste of time," as one IAM organizer put it in 1936. In December 1940 unorganized and underpaid workers at Wright were committed by the company union to a no-strike pledge for the war's duration.[29]

In securing whatever new rights were offered under Section 7a and in influencing in some way the formulation of an NRA code for their industry, aircraft workers received little but obstructionism from the AFL internationals who laid claim to them. Although the IAM restrained others, it too felt restrained from organizing aircraft workers while so many claimed their various trades. It was especially sensitive to conflict with the United Brotherhood of Carpenters and Joiners of America (UBCJA), with which it had finally negotiated a ceasefire in a seventeen-year jurisdiction battle and which had a toehold in aircraft.[30] After the IAM had spurned them and under pressure from its members in the Hollywood studios, the UBCJA reluctantly granted a charter in early 1932 to a small group of carpenters that had organized themselves in Santa Monica. Yet the UBCJA showed little interest in its Douglas Aircraft Mechanics 1557. It too was wary of exacerbating jurisdictional tensions for the minimal gains offered by organizing aircraft workers. Thus they were left to rely on self-organization, labor advocates in the NRA, and whatever the AFL could give under the limitations imposed by the AFL Executive Council.

EARLY SUCCESSES AND DEFEATS
UNDER SECTION 7a

For aircraft workers in Buffalo, NIRA suggested the time had come to challenge policies on wages, hours, and hiring at Curtiss and Consolidated. "I don't want revenge," one worker wrote FDR, "but I would like to see justice done . . . the men are chafing at the bit . . . but are helpless to do anything. Curtiss Aeroplane bears watching."[31] He and his fellows did not stay helpless for long, however, after they combined to form the independent Buffalo Aeronautical Workers Union. Its president, Chauncey J. Cook, and secretaries, John J. Murphy and Merle A. Benton, worked to assure their members' representation in Washington and to realize their vision of a national industrial union for all aircraft workers. The union's membership swelled to nearly 1,000 after a successful strike at Consolidated in late June 1933. Reuben Fleet had imposed a series of wage reductions since 1930, the latest a 12 percent cut in March 1933, defending them as necessary to stay competitive in the military aircraft market. But the strike persuaded him to reduce weekly hours from fifty-two to forty with no pay reduction, to raise the pay of salaried workers proportionately, and to hire 150 new workers.[32]

Anticipating early NRA approval of the manufacturers' code, Fleet saw these concessions as necessary only for the interim. He hoped this demonstration that he was "doing his part" would pay dividends in Washington through speedy passage of the code with its regressive labor standards and its end to the military's expropriation of aircraft designs. Moreover Consolidated's navy flying boats were candidates for PWA funds. Fleet was also negotiating with the Reconstruction Finance Corporation for assistance in expanding his plant and water terminal on Lake Erie. Regardless of Fleet's tactics, the strike produced an early and encouraging victory that served as an example to other workers of what was possible under the NRA.

After the strike Cook and Murphy led the Buffalo workers into an AFL Federal Labor Union. A strike threat by FLU 18286 reversed a 13 percent wage cut at Curtiss on September 19. Curtiss was undoubtedly motivated by the same faith as Fleet's in imminent relief from an NRA code; but the company had the added inducement of preserving its first tenuous margins of profit and a foreign market for its fighters, which began to expand rapidly in 1933. Nevertheless the threat of a strike was necessary to persuade Curtiss to institute even the Blanket Code's provisions for hours, which had been generously modified for aircraft manufacturers. Buffalo aircraft workers seemed to be on a roll as Cook was appointed to the NRA Labor Advisory Board, where he promoted a national industrial union. An Aeronautical Workers Convention with representatives of plants across the nation met in Buffalo in October.[33]

New self-confidence and early advances for aircraft workers under Section 7a were also evident at the United subsidiaries in Connecticut. C. W. Deeds, vice-president at Pratt & Whitney, detailed for the workers "certain facts about the NRA." These included the claim that the NRA "is designed to increase trade and business" and that though many might think the president wanted workers to join unions, "there is nothing in the bill that compels, or even encourages, employees to join any organization." Anger at these claims and the additional one that workers had to bear the burdens of low-cost foreign competition incited them to plan a strike for early September 1933.[34]

A local IAM agent persuaded them to back down until the company could respond to their demands for a forty-hour week with a 25 percent pay hike and time and a half for overtime. Anticipating quick action on an NRA code, United president D. L. Brown acceded to all the demands "until the permanent code is approved." These concessions led the IAM local to expect "a strong organization as a result," but it was disappointed as workers at Pratt & Whitney, Hamilton-Standard Propeller, Chance Vought, and Sikorsky conservatively "decided they had reached the top of their ladder." Their approaches to unionism were firmly within a cost-benefit framework. They mistrusted the IAM and could see no point in paying dues to it or even to a low-cost FLU. They realized their victory was tentative and represented only a redress of past losses. As a mechanic at Pratt & Whitney put it to General Johnson, "they claim that they did give us an increas of waiges but obvios i cannot see that way, We will go back to 1932 where they durning that summer slashed oure waiges from %25 to %41." But the United workers saw their fight in the NRA code-making process and thought that "the purpose of properly representing ourselves" could be served through their own independent union—the Industrial Aircraft Workers of America.[35]

At other plants aircraft workers did not fare as well, and the limits of the workers' new legitimacy without an effective organization behind them was more apparent. In August 1933 four IAM members at Martin in Baltimore fell victim to the "simplest and most direct weapon" available to anti-union employers—the summary discharge.[36] Martin, who was known to fire workers if he found them so much as talking on the job, was a resolutely independent and anti-union manufacturer. He ignored his industry's trade association, the NRA process, and its labor provisions and spent most of his time on the shop floor supervising a $2.5 million contract received in 1933 for forty-eight B-10 bombers. In contrast to other manufacturers whose overexpansion and errors had been financed by eager stock investors, Martin had borrowed funds to overbuild his facilities. When his five-year gold notes came due in 1934 he could not honor them and barely skirted bankruptcy.[37] To build the bombers he expanded his work force from 257 in February 1933 to 1,107 six months later and imposed a twelve-hour day upon his workers at an average of fifty cents per hour, 20 percent below the national average. They grew restive but displayed little interest in the IAM and its fees. Nevertheless in July 1933 when a handful of IAM members were fired and workers were informed that they would have to work Saturdays as well, two hundred Martin men appeared at the Machinists' meeting.[38]

Baltimore IAM officials realized that if the IAM's high fees and dues did not seal its fate with Martin's workers, its failure to win the reinstatement of the discharged men certainly would. With unemployment at 20 percent and one in six families on nearly exhausted relief programs in Baltimore, the workers would need assurances of job security before they antagonized Martin. But the IAM leadership's lukewarm efforts in Wash-

Martin B-10 bombers under construction at the Middle River plant near Baltimore in early 1936.

ington were unproductive. Secretary of War Dern claimed there was little he could do since Martin had signed the bomber contract before the advent of the NRA. The Martin workers consequently snubbed the IAM as well as an offer for a FLU charter and placed their hopes in the NRA, sending a delegation to the public hearing on the industry's code. A sampling of their hopes is provided by the besieged wife of a Martin machinist and mother of six small children who pleaded with General Johnson for rapid passage of an aircraft code embodying the workers' aspirations. She could not provide enough food, clothing, or heat for her family on her husband's wages. "I know lots of people the NRA has helped . . . what I want you to do is to inform me why the Glenn L. Martin Plane Company is not paying more money." As the code-making process stalled, some Martin workers turned to the AFL and hopes for a national union. They were given a FLU charter in early 1934, but Martin unceremoniously fired its entire organizing committee.[39]

Martin provided other manufacturers with a model of how NIRA's ambivalent gestures toward labor could be successfully ignored. He did not have to accommodate organized labor until a small majority of 60,000 workers was finally won over by the United Auto Workers in July 1943. At North American Aviation in Baltimore, controlled by General Motors, Martin's model was followed with similar results.[40] If some aircraft manufacturers needed a model for anti-unionism and non-compliance with federal labor law, Donald Douglas certainly did not. His predisposition against organized labor was well known, born of a deeply held personal animus and sustained by the fact that labor costs were the determinants of whether he turned profits or losses on his aircraft. His attitudes were militantly shared by employers in the Los Angeles area who, working through the "M&M"—the Merchants' and Manufacturers' Association—had made Los Angeles the "pioneer open-shop city of America . . . the chief stronghold and outstanding beneficiary of that system of industrial relations," as the *Los Angeles Times* boasted in August 1933. Its publisher, Harry Chandler, had led a group of local businessmen who provided the seed capital for Douglas in 1922. Encouraged by the *Times*, the M&M's response to Section 7a included the retention of a private army of police, an arsenal of tear gas, and studied noncompliance with any Washington directives on labor matters.[41]

Douglas workers were proud of the aircraft they built, but many despised Douglas, likening his arbitrary management to that of a "feudal baron." Section 7a seemed to offer relief. Stressing their pride in their skills, the members of UBCJA Local 1557 appealed to Johnson for "some immediate results so that we may quiet the anxiety" at Lockheed, Douglas, and its Northrop subsidiary.[42] Conditions were especially hard at Douglas. As *Fortune* later reported, the fabled DC-2 was selling well. Still, even excluding development costs ($182,000 to Douglas, $125,000 to TWA), the company lost $266,000 on the first twenty-five in 1933–1934. Douglas Aircraft was "operating on the principle of infinite pains," *Fortune* rightly concluded, neglecting to mention that most were borne by the workers.[43]

If the value of engines, off-the-shelf parts, and instruments are subtracted, wages represented about 65 percent of the DC-2's cost of manufacture.[44] In summer 1933 pay at Douglas averaged fifty-one cents, well below prevailing rates for skilled workers in Los Angeles, with higher rates going to those who "stand in well with the boss." Day shifts of eleven and a half hours on weekdays, Saturday afternoon shifts, plus eight hours on Sundays made up the work regime for six hundred workers. Another three hundred put in ten hours on the night shift, six days per week. Douglas paid no overtime, ability and seniority "amount to nothing," and "a man is fired for the least slander or remark." In August, despite the NRA and the Blanket Code, Douglas ordered an average pay cut of 17 percent and fired men for promoting the union and writing letters to the NRA.[45]

Unable to act independently, the Douglas workers were left with the NRA. Because of its many weaknesses and all the room for evasion by manufacturers, the value of the NRA for workers derived chiefly from the new expectations and sense of their rights as a group that the NRA created among workers, employers, the public, and government officials. No matter how ambivalent or widely ignored these rights might have been, they set new and real parameters on the options of employers even in as hostile an environment as Southern California. Robert E. Gross, president of Lockheed Aircraft in Burbank, cited the NRA along with the technical complications of the new Electra transport as the major elements of "what I am up against" in delivering the plane to impatient customers who held his performance bonds against delivery on set dates. Despite its feebleness in California, the NRA was "the one fly in the ointment. [The NRA] has been running up our costs and shortening our working hours so that we cannot work as long or as steadily as we used to be able to." Until Douglas pressured Gross to stop "harboring union members," his company made a real effort to conform to the labor provisions of the NRA. Lockheed limited overtime, paid time and a third when it was unavoidable, and engaged in genuine bargaining with its three hundred workers through UBCJA 1557.[46]

A SURROGATE AGENT FOR LABOR

Severe as life was for aircraft labor, without the new sense of expectation and legitimacy for workers as workers provided by Section 7a, conditions surely would have been driven down by employers like Douglas to the minimum level of sustenance needed to keep workers standing up in the plants. Another important outcome of NIRA on the workers' behalf was their de facto representatives on the Labor Advisory Board. Contemporary analysts at the Brookings Institution credited the LAB with developing "indirect representative bargaining" and identified it as a major step in the federal government's emerging regulatory role in labor relations. Still, in the absence of effective labor organization, the LAB was defensive in character, occasionally protecting workers from employers seeking cost-cutting mechanisms in the NRA codes and from larger pressures within the NRA for rapid code approval.[47]

The LAB could not create conditions in which genuine bargaining between aircraft manufacturers and workers could take place. If there ever had been a chance of exploring accommodation outside the work-sharing schemes of the theorists of underconsumption, which were so debilitating for aircraft manufacture, and of building a new alliance against congressional subversion of the industry, it disappeared in 1934. The manufacturers' obstinacy grew as the crisis over procurement unfolded on Capitol Hill, as demands for rigid work rules escalated, and as the IAM's sabotage of the industrial union reduced pressures to compromise. Over a period of eighteen months, until NIRA was struck down, the Aeronautical Chamber of Commerce and the LAB met at least thirty-four times but did not negotiate. They merely stood one another off with inflexible demands that were intolerable for both sides. Matching the manufacturers' obstinance, LAB demanded pay raises that the industry could not afford. Nor would the LAB abandon the vocabulary of work-sharing principles that were better suited for low-skilled, mass-production industries, threatening to what little control the manufacturers retained over their affairs and not really representative of aircraft workers' desires. It insisted on reduced hours rigorously monitored and bureaucratically enforced through strict classifications for jobs and skills and on binding contractual agreements, which were impediments to a dynamic aircraft industry.

The public hearing on the aircraft code began in Washington on December 20, 1933, and was presided over by Deputy Administrator K. J. Ammerman, a failed aircraft-engine manufacturer from Milwaukee whose new job was to produce a code as quickly as possible. Representing the LAB was Chauncey Cook of the Buffalo Aeronautical Workers Union and David Kaplan, the IAM counsel. Leighton Rogers opened the hearing with a statement on behalf of the chamber. Stressing the industry's role in national defense he argued that its unique problems forced manufacturers to seek the codification of such "controversial measures" as low minimum wages, elasticity of hours, and the right to hire and fire according to a worker's merit. Low minimum wages were needed, Rogers maintained, to produce competitive aircraft for the foreign market. Only more military contracts, not work-sharing measures, could increase employment in the industry. Rogers offered a forty-hour-maximum week but insisted that highly flexible overtime provisions were needed to prevent halts in production until specialized workers could legally work again.[48]

Briefs were presented on behalf of workers by agents of the Machinists, the AFL, and the independent Baltimore Aeronautics Union, who declared that the proposed code would impede the "true" purposes of NIRA—the reduction of unemployment and the expansion of purchasing power. Outlining an argument that would be made continually within the NRA against the manufacturers, the labor representatives suggested that the industry had responsibilities to society that transcended immediate business realities. Manufacturers selfishly refused to build up a large reservoir of aircraft workers needed in case of war and for aircraft's inevitable role as America's "industry of the future." Ignoring the well-known pitfalls of doing business with the government, the labor representatives insisted that the industry's dependency on federal contracts made it imperative that an "exemplary code" be produced that would do more to "further the Administration's program than the code for the average industry." A thirty-hour-maximum work week should be enforced and defined clearly as six hours per day, per seven-day period. Overtime pay should be at time and a half and strictly limited to "emergency conditions" when life or property was threatened. The labor representatives condemned the chamber's forty-cent minimum-wage proposal as "wholly inadequate for a minimum standard of living" and demanded sixty-five cents, health and safety provisions, representation on the code authority, and a national Joint Industrial Relations Board made up of employer and worker representatives.[49]

Led by Cook, the LAB also denounced the manufacturers' code, pointing out how its provisions for hours were "designed to make room for every possible evasion" and to confuse the workers in their complexity. Without a clearly stated hourly limit per day, the forty-hour week could easily be circumvented by staggering employment. By exempting from the code those engaged in supervisory and technical work "and the respective staffs of those so engaged," it would be easy to free skilled workers from the provisions whenever necessary. The exemption of maintenance and emergency workers would be a license for abuse since "it has become a practice in this industry to designate almost every job in a plant as an emergency job." Unlike other codes, which clearly stipulated that only managers and executives receiving more than thirty-five dollars per week were exempt, the chamber's code provided for the exemption of all salaried employees. The manufacturers could thus free workers from the code by rehiring them on a salaried basis. Even with all its loopholes, the code's provisions for hours were meaningless because of its final clause: "The maximum hours herein prescribed shall apply only in so far as practicable"—the manufacturer being judge of "practicable."[50]

Within a month of the hearing, Rogers and supportive NRA administrators produced another draft code that eliminated most of the loopholes detected by the LAB. Still, the chamber would not relent on the forty-hour weekly maximum, its complicated overtime provisions, and the forty-cent minimum wage. The LAB repeated its critique and stressed that the forty-cent "minimum is very quickly going to become the maximum for the majority of employees, due to the fact that we have a very high turnover of labor." Cook continued to insist that a thirty-hour maximum and a sixty-five-cent minimum wage were the only solutions to "severe unemployment in the industry" and the LAB refused to approve the manufacturers' code.[51]

The LAB's obstruction of the code was encouraged by an unjust report on the industry produced by C. A. Pearce of the NRA Division of Research and Planning. It reflected more the sentiment against the aviation industry raging in Congress than a reasoned, objective approach to the industry's problems. Without considering the industry's constant complaints about the government's methods of buying aircraft, Pearce painted a "sanguine picture" of its future and criticized its pleas for special consideration by the NRA. He granted that the majority of firms were in an "unfavorable earning situation" but claimed that the basis still existed for the industry to exercise its "responsibilities to the nation," which in his view were to provide military aircraft and economic recovery through higher wages.[52]

Repeating the error so often made by the industry's many detractors, Pearce argued that it was protected merely because its main client was the United States. The actual details of the relations between the industry and the government were irrelevant once the label "protection," or its variant, "collusion," were attached. Moreover the likelihood that government appropriations for military aircraft would be expanded, despite the industry's "present political difficulties," was sufficient to conclude, without considering how those appropriations would actually be spent, that the industry's prospects were bright. Pearce foresaw, quite unrealistically, "a cheap mass market airplane" and sensed the "natural thrust" of the industry toward oligopoly because of the rising costs of development and the growing ineligibility of most firms for essential military or airline contracts. Such concentration would likely have been the course for the industry had design rights been recognized by the government, a basic feature of the industry Pearce ignored. He concluded that the industry's trade-practice proposals were unacceptable and that there was "no room for tolerance of this industry in respect to limitations on hours of work." Furthermore, it was incumbent upon an industry so essential in a "national emergency" to prepare itself for "sudden calls for production." As for the proposed forty-cent minimum wage, it was "wholly inadequate to the end of increasing wage rates and purchasing power," which in Pearce's view were the "Administration's intentions."[53]

The Pearce report helped the LAB to check NRA approval of the chamber's third draft code in late April 1934. In May the Chamber was forced to relent on its demand for recognition of the manufacturers' design rights in its proposed code. It thus gave up all hopes for industrial self-regulation through NRA-sanctioned trade-practice rules. Some manufacturers retained interest in the possibility of self-regulation through an industry-wide labor code and reduced costs through low wages. However, their concern in the rest of their dealings with the NRA was defensive. In particular they hoped to avoid a code imposed by FDR under powers granted in NIRA's Section 3d as yet another punitive measure against the aircraft industry. FDR had never used this power, but if any industry seemed a likely candidate for its application in 1934 it was aircraft manufacture.[54]

The chamber's code committeemen thought their defense could be directed by one man and they appointed Rogers as their delegate to the NRA. Weary of futile meetings in Washington, they thought their time was better spent in managing their plants. For the next eight months, Rogers sparred alone with the NRA. For him the code was a matter of personal prestige. He had been hired by the chamber largely because of the NRA and his assumed connections in Washington. Rogers continued to approach the NRA in the hope that a favorable labor code, his reputation, and the associationalist ethic in aircraft manufacture might still be salvaged. He refused to relent on the provisions for labor desired by the manufacturers. "We must have elasticity of hours and we must have the right to retain our employees on the basis of merit alone." The LAB was just as adamant that workers would not bear the brunt of the industry's problems. During 1934 Rogers produced at least six draft codes—all to no avail. Despite the concurrence of the Industrial Advisory Board and the deputy administrator charged with producing a code for the industry, the LAB blocked approval of any code that did not rigidly limit hours and defend workers' income.[55]

Rogers had a formidable opponent in Dr. Carl Raushenbush of the LAB, who made the frustration of the aircraft manufacturers a personal project. Raushenbush, son of the famed Social Gospeler, absorbed the prevalent hostility for the industry and set out to show that years of plundering the Treasury had not satisfied aircraft manufacturers, who were now bent on extracting as much as they could from their workers. He eagerly consumed information and perspectives on the industry provided by his brother Stephen, secretary to the Nye Committee investigating munitions makers. Raushenbush compiled a profile of the industry as a virtual trust, but of an especially deplorable type, dependent upon federal largesse in the form of military contracts. He compiled figures showing workers at the Naval Aircraft Factory making time and a half for overtime and an average wage of eighty-two cents compared with sixty-two cents in private industry. Failing to note that the NAF did not compete for its work and had none of the financial risks of private firms, he drew upon these figures to help LAB defeat draft codes submitted by Rogers during summer 1934.[56]

Firmly at an impasse, the code was submitted for arbitration to the NRA Advisory Council in August. Made up of three representatives each of the Labor, Industrial, and Consumer's Advisory Boards, the council was designed to "break policy deadlock."[57] The LAB's brief to the council held that the "industry has failed to propose a code that is at all satisfactory" and attacked its proposals on overtime and wages as intolerable for "an industry that subsists on public funds." The LAB expressed the sense of the industry as a kind of public utility with an obligation to society but one that did not require special consideration from the state. It asked the council to consider the question: "Is the profitableness of the industry relevant, considering that the existence of an aircraft industry is important in time of war?"[58]

Conflicts between the manufacturers and LAB were hashed out in an informal meeting before the council met. In attendance were Raushenbush of LAB and John P. Frey and David Kaplan of the AFL Metal Trades Department. Rogers, E. H. Gilpin, chief engineer at Pratt & Whitney, and T. A. Morgan, president of the chamber, represented the industry. They argued that since the manufacturers could not get relief through patent law or an NRA code from the services' practice of opening production contracts for their designs to competitive bidding, they were forced to insist upon "elasticity of hours as only means of adjusting plants to difficulties with which encountered [sic]." Technical changes occurred "everyday" and strict delivery dates were imposed by the military, to whom the "NRA means nothing." The labor representatives admitted the dilemma but would not accept that workers bear its costs. "Why are these costs not passed on to the government?" asked Raushenbush.[59] The manufacturers might have answered that without effective regulation either by themselves, the government, or labor unions, the attractions of cutting wages and underbidding would always be too strong. And the army and navy, competing for air power missions and forced to operate with Congress's stingy appropriations and its insistence upon competitive contracting, would always seek the most from manufacturers.

The Advisory Council took the industry's side, agreeing that only elasticity of hours could protect it from the costs of research and development, strict performance requirements on military contracts, competitive bidding, and the military's "violation of design rights." It recommended wide latitude in the setting of hours for production and no limits on hours in experimental and emergency work, but it declined to set minimum wage or overtime pay rates. Instead it assured the preservation of controversy by recommending that these "be worked out in the usual way by the Deputy Administrator and the Labor Advisory Board."[60] If the NRA was only a higher, politicized forum for controversy within industry, then the NRA Advisory Council was just a step beyond that. Negotiations continued between the industry and the NRA and among NRA officials. Old differences persisted, and an approved code remained as elusive as ever. NRA Division II, responsible for the code, was embarrassed by its inability to deliver. I. D. Everitt, its administrator, began horse trading with the LAB on behalf of the manufacturers. He offered minimum-wage parity for women here and double time for overtime beyond certain limits there in the hope that the opposing parties would "concur, since this will close a long discussion on a considerably overripe code." However, neither Raushenbush nor Rogers would relent.[61]

The negative outcome of another conference of representatives of the NRA boards and the industry held in late November was predetermined by the circulation of another scathing NRA report on the industry. Its author displayed a much better understanding of the industry's dynamics and plight at the hands of Congress than did the earlier Pearce report, but in his view the manufacturers brought their troubles upon themselves. They made lawmakers believe that the government's price-competitive policy was viable by continually accepting onerous contracts and allowing themselves to be victimized by the procurement practices of the government. Consequently labor was forced to pay "quite a part of the penalty for 1) the federal government's ability to coerce the industry to perform work without proper compensation 2) management's errors of judgement and 3) industry's tolerance of the whims of buyers." The practice of not charging for work performed and agreeing to deliveries impossible to perform without excessive overtime had become systemic in the industry, and the NRA offered it the opportunity of codifying labor's role as a cushion against this "malpractice." The report insisted "that we cease expressing pity for this 'young' industry." The NRA could "help the industry to help itself by making it see that one of the first cardinal principles of business is to insure that compensation is received for work or service performed, regardless of who may be the buyer."[62]

At the final 1934 meeting, "negotiations broke down completely" and the code-making process hung in abeyance until January 1935 when Rogers presented a new draft "in one more last effort to obtain a code." He again made the case for the industry's "very precarious position." Higher wages and expanded employment were unthinkable when "90% of the industry was losing money" and its main problem was keeping the men it had employed. The "industry has no way of effectively passing on increased costs to the customer." Higher costs would only result in fewer aircraft and less work.[63]

The process of approval for Rogers's final draft began its circuitous route through the NRA bureaucracy, including five boards, the Industrial, Consumers', and Labor Advisory Boards, the Planning and Research Division, and the Legal Division. The turnover in NRA staff slowed the process even further as advisers had to learn anew about the industry and study the history of the attempts to formulate a code for it. By mid-March both Planning and Research and LAB still found the proposed definition of emergency work far too broad, and LAB insisted on overtime pay at time and a half and double time beyond the first eight hours. Finally, hopes for an aircraft manufacturing "code of fair competition" came to an end when the review officer for Division II judged Rogers's final proposal "not consistent with policy." Two months later the NRA was struck down in the *Shechter* case.[64]

AN ABORTED NATIONAL UNION

While the LAB directed these rearguard measures, the Buffalo aircraft workers' Federal Labor Union, led by Chauncey Cook, continued to seek the more positive advancement of workers' interests through a national industrial union. Contacts were made in Baltimore, Hartford, Los Angeles, Seattle, and St. Louis. During spring 1934 thinly coordinated strikes took place which only served, however, to confirm the weaknesses of the nascent national union, particularly in the face of IAM obstructionism. Martin had fired with impunity FLU's organizers in his plant; a brief strike at North American in Baltimore was easily defeated.

On April 10 the independent Industrial Aircraft Workers of America of Hartford struck Pratt & Whitney for better wages and the closed shop. The next day workers at Chance Vought and Hamilton-Standard followed suit, bringing the total number of United workers on strike to 1,500. They demanded a minimum wage of sixty cents with substantial increases for skilled workers and time and a half for overtime. United would not negotiate, despite the complaints of its customers whose engine deliveries were held up. After five weeks a settlement was arranged by the New England Regional Labor Board in which the company agreed only to rehire the workers without discrimination and to entertain individual wage grievances. Pratt & Whitney was not organized until February 1945.[65]

In March 1934 the 200 members of Douglas Aircraft Mechanics UBCJA Local 1557 struck, demanding $1.10 per hour for skilled workers and the abolition of the Douglas Employees Association, the company union. Widespread unemployment among Los Angeles aircraft workers, many of whom had recently migrated to Southern California, and Douglas's policy of gladly firing unionists combined to limit support for the strikers and easily brought about their defeat. Although trade unionism in Los Angeles was spurred by Section 7a, by mid-1934, local open-shop forces, encouraged by the brutal suppression of the San Pedro waterfront strike, had regrouped and dealt the labor movement major reversals. Los Angeles NRA agencies were controlled by local business, and the regional NLB branch was entirely ineffective.[66] Under Douglas's insistence Robert Gross at Lockheed moved to reverse his stance on labor. "Mr Douglas and I," he wrote, "are watching every move as carefully as we can and are prepared to the best of our ability." Collective bargaining at Lockheed had gone by the wayside. "We are increasing the number of men as fast as we can and are also putting in pay increases on a merit basis where justly deserved." Lockheed fired long-time employees and UBCJA activists such as Ashby McGraw, citing incompetence. McGraw sought redress through the Los Angeles Board of the NLB, but despite hours of corroborating testimony from fellow workers, it decided unanimously for the company.[67]

In this environment, and as the code process stalled in Washington, many Los Angeles aircraft workers came to recognize that a national industrial union was the prerequisite for building upon the foundation provided by Section 7a. Yet their senses of independence and superiority as builders of Douglas and Lockheed airplanes and as long-time members of the UBCJA left insufficient room for cooperation with the Buffalo work-

Douglas DC-2 transports under construction in Santa Monica in June 1934.

ers. Led by McGraw and T. H. Witham, they disparaged the AFL Federal Labor Unions as unionization on the cheap and preferred a national federation under their own direction. In October 1934 at the San Francisco AFL convention Witham presented a plan for a national union under his direction and the temporary jurisdiction of the AFL Executive Council. Its goal was the national standardization of wages and work conditions. But UBCJA president W. M. Hutcheson gave him no support and, reportedly happy to be rid of them, dealt away UBCJA claims to aircraft workers. IAM president Wharton persuaded the executive council to reject the Douglas Carpenters' plan, declaring, "I do not know of any organization that is in a better position to give leadership than our own." The AFL decreed that the industry would henceforth come under the exclusive jurisdiction of the IAM.[68]

In Buffalo independent unionism for aircraft workers was also sabotaged by the IAM, but there the Machinists' work was eased by the overconfidence of FLU 18286 and by the successes of a local employers' movement that took its cues from the notorious Houde Engineering Corporation, an auto-parts manufacturer dedicated to exposing all the weaknesses of federal labor law. As part of the coordinated national campaign in aircraft, FLU 18286 walked out in March 1934, calling for wage increases and equalization of pay at both Curtiss and Consolidated. Its aggressive demands included an increase to ninety cents per hour for assemblers, inspectors, and other semiskilled workers. Only a "bare majority" of the 2,000 workers actually went out. The companies ignored their demands, and the strike dragged on.[69]

On April 21 the Buffalo Regional Labor Board, though sympathetic to labor, found the strike in violation of the agreement signed by FLU in September 1933, which was in effect for another two months.[70] On May 15 Senator Wagner, chairman of the NLB, affirmed the decision, and the strikers voted to reduce their demands to the request that they be reemployed and the strike breakers discharged. An AFL agent in Buffalo who attended their meeting described the annoyance among the workers for Cook and Murphy, who had brashly led them to defeat. Curtiss and Consolidated were of course willing to take back their specialized and underpaid workers, and on May 23 they returned.[71]

Seeking the full rewards of its victory, Curtiss requested an election monitored by the NLRB (which replaced the NLB in June 1934), to redetermine the collective bargaining agent for its workers. The company made the request through its company union, the Aircraft, which it had established in fall 1933, following the lead of the Houde Welfare and Athletic Association. Indeed the Aircraft was managed by the attorney who was orchestrating Houde's $100,000 legal battle with the NLRB, which had decided to make a national test case out of the company's refusal to recognize representatives elected by a majority of its workers as the bargaining agent for all. The Justice Department took Houde to court in November 1934 but dropped the case when NIRA was struck down. The labor boards established during the NRA period held elections for representation, pursued the complaints of workers, and generally provided them with new self-consciousness as workers. But lacking power to compel compliance with their decisions, the boards could do little more for workers. In the face of hostile employers, workers were left to rely upon their ability to wield their economic power. As the agent for the Buffalo Regional Labor Board described the value of elections in establishing collective bargaining: "This is necessarily contingent upon the willingness of the company to accept the results of the elections. . . ."[72]

Through endless litigation, FLU 18286 managed to prevent a new election at Curtiss. Ralph P. Damon, president of Curtiss, was happy to see the union so occupied and in late August announced a wage increase of five cents per hour "in agreement with the company union, The Aircraft."[73] The obvious limits of federal labor boards in winning gains for aircraft workers led Cook to renew the pursuit of more effective national organization, only to be thwarted again by the Machinists. Another convention was held in Buffalo in July 1934. Present were workers from Boeing, the North American and Martin plants in Baltimore, the United Aircraft subsidiaries, and Great Lakes Aircraft in Cleveland, but none from Southern California. In September Cook persuaded the members of FLU 18286 to resume payments to the AFL and to make "every effort to prove themselves good members." Cook was encouraged by Meyer L. Lewis, an organizer assigned by AFL President Green to assess the prospects for a national aircraft campaign, despite the recent grant of exclusive jurisdiction to the Machinists.[74]

Lewis toured Hartford, Paterson, Baltimore, and Buffalo. He described weak organizations but was confident "that in every one of these cities a splendid local can be built up if it is the desire of the Federation to interest itself in this industry." Lewis found enthusiasm for the idea of a national union in each plant and blamed the Machinists for obstructing it. He recommended an organizational strategy that began at Boeing and the Paterson and Hartford engine plants, "the key points in the entire aeronautical industry." Lewis tempted Green by pointing out the industry's value as a "political weapon, since 95% of the business seems to be government business." Yet Green could only reiterate dismally "the jurisdictional claims of the Machinists," who were making it "well nigh impossible to inaugurate and carry forward an aggressive organizing campaign among aeronautical workers." An expectant Cook was disappointed and organizer Lewis was withdrawn from Buffalo. Left with nothing more than NLRB litigation in the struggle with Buffalo aircraft companies and their company unions, Cook felt betrayed and again cancelled payments to the AFL. "Let me impress upon you that we have sold you to our rank and file," he angrily wrote Green.[75]

Meanwhile Reuben Fleet at Consolidated had been ignoring FLU 18286 since its May 1934 defeat and the expiry of its contract at the end of June. The union, with 500 of Fleet's 850 workers organized, petitioned the NLRB for an election in August 1934; but with the help of Houde's lawyer, Fleet's counterpetitions prevented an election until December 5. The outcome was a resounding victory for the union as 795 workers voted for FLU, only 15 voted for the company union, the Aerotrade, and thirty-two voided their ballots. Nevertheless on the spurious claim that the fifteen and thirty-two denied FLU exclusive bargaining rights, Fleet prevented negotiations through endless proceedings in the courts and the

NLRB. This maneuvering continued into 1935 until Fleet settled the issue by moving his plant and about 300 supervisory workers to San Diego. There were other sound reasons for Consolidated's move, such as year-round fair weather and the concessions offered by the City of San Diego. Also, Fleet won a $5.4 million contract for flying boats in July 1935 and the navy preferred delivery at tidewater. Yet Fleet had long been committed to the Niagara Frontier and to a flying boat industry on Lake Erie. The open shop in the Southland, widely advertised in the trade journals, prompted his move. At a meeting with Sidney Hillman of the Office of Production Management in 1941, he remarked that "a 50-day strike in Buffalo sent him to Southern California." By July 1935 FLU 18286, the heart of the national campaign, had collapsed. Attempts by the San Diego Federated Trades and Labor Council to establish a new FLU for 1,000 Consolidated workers being paid 30 to 40 percent less than the national average were blocked by the IAM local.[76]

The strikes in aircraft during spring 1934 acted to further galvanize anti-union manufacturers behind the chamber, which began a series of bimonthly confidential reports on wages and labor conditions in the various plants. In the view of Boeing's management, the "general unrest in the industry, and particularly the efforts of the Aeronautical Workers Union [make it] highly essential that every manufacturer have in his possession information concerning the rates paid by other manufacturers," or in another manufacturer's words, "a file on the agitators." The value of anti-union cooperation, either through blacklists or an enforced, regressive NRA labor code, decreased, however, as the failures of the union movement accumulated and competition for scarce contracts persisted. Only a small number of manufacturers continued to divulge information on wages to one another after the defeats of the strikes, even though from Boeing's perspective, "such information is valuable not only in dealing with labor but also in giving the manufacturer a much better picture of the competitive picture in figuring prices and in estimating costs." Rogers also saw the self-regulatory benefits of such practices but admitted that there were always those manufacturers who "seem to think it good fun to lay little traps for us."[77]

Boeing executives had more reason than most to hope for industry-wide cooperation either to defeat labor or to ensure uniform labor standards throughout the industry. In 1933 Boeing's prospects for recovering the large development costs of its Model 247 airliner through a long production series were frustrated by the appearance of Douglas's superior product. As 247s accumulated in inventory the unprofitable Boeing was

This mid-1930s view of Boeing's Engineering Department suggests another aspect of the industry's labor intensity and high variable costs. Through the interwar years, aircraft firms maintained on average one white-collar worker for every three production workers. In May 1940 approximately 100,000 employees worked on airframes, 40,000 of whom were on salary. Draftsmen and engineers also unsuccessfully sought relief in an NRA code from the relentless pressure on their salaries caused by Congress's procurement rules.

also losing heavily on its P-26 army pursuits. At the same time Boeing officials, long intrigued by the concept of the "flying dreadnought," had committed $300,000 for the development of a four-engined, long-range heavy bomber, the XB-15, precursor to the B-17 Flying Fortress.

Greatly complicating Boeing's situation through the 1930s was the relative strength of trade unionism in the Seattle area and of independent unionization in its plant. Fortunately for Boeing, however, this strength was dissipated by the IAM. At Boeing the Buffalo men's attempts to forge links with other aircraft workers showed more promise than elsewhere. In early January 1934, 87 percent of 1,500 Boeing workers voted yes on a balloting arranged by the company union, which asked them "Do you want an organization?" A vote was then scheduled for February 20 to determine "what type of union" the workers desired.[78] IAM officials in Seattle saw the opportunity, and an organizer was assigned to the plant; but John Murphy of the Buffalo FLU "stole the show." Like many other activists in the AFL's FLU movement who roamed the nation trying to build national councils of industrial FLUs, Murphy believed that only "One Big Union," as he put it to the Boeing workers, could deliver the promise of NIRA. He conveyed an invitation from the Buffalo FLU to coordinate their activities and read them its recent resolution to halt payments to the AFL until it agreed "to dispense with all organizers in the industry advocating craft organization." Comparing them with the IAM's offerings, Murphy outlined the attractions of a FLU on the Buffalo pattern, where "all action takes place only with approval of the rank and file," who "control their own finances," pay monthly dues of only one dollar, and whose "officials are shop workers who receive the same pay as those on the bench." He pleaded for their "help to fight the code."[79]

Sensing that the Boeing workers were "partial to the Buffalo plan," the IAM in Seattle sought help from the Grand Lodge. Despite the possibilities of a situation in which William Boeing and his associate employers were at that moment the focus of a national scandal, the official IAM response was nothing more than complaints about industrial unionism and a condemnation of FLUs, which only produced "the usual fight to get the men who rightfully belonged to the Machinists, leaving to the AFL those not eligible." The Buffalo men were "trouble makers . . . an outlaw group."[80] In the election, 886 Boeing workers voted for Murphy's FLU 18886, 600 for Boeing's company union, and 50 spoiled their ballots. None voted for the Machinists, whose problem at Boeing was not so much the Buffalo "outlaws" as the simple fact that the workers, including the IAM's "eligible members," wanted representation by a single union even if it meant the company union. Nevertheless an AFL organizer in Seattle planned to place the men in a FLU and then "split them up" according to craft lines even though he expected that "most machinists will stay in the FLU." Not wanting to leave this to the choice of the Boeing workers, the IAM pressured AFL Secretary Morrison to revoke the FLU charter "until craft workers are removed from the list." The Machinists were cynically confident that although "it will be difficult for us to reverse what [Murphy] has done among the workers . . . we will at least have a chance if they are not permitted to join the AFL and pay cheap dues."[81]

The irrelevancy of the craft approach at Boeing was continually reported to the Grand Lodge. The Boeing workers wanted a "Federal Labor Charter to cover all or nothing," and 600 had made paid applications to the AFL. In defiance of Morrison's order, Murphy continued to urge the Boeing workers to resist craft stratification. He gave them a charter issued directly by the Buffalo local. The IAM warned Morrison that either the Buffalo local was to be "curbed" or "we'll have a new international to deal with." Morrison ordered payments made by Boeing workers for FLU membership returned and promised that only the Machinists would be allowed to organize them.[82] Real prospects for viable unionization under NIRA were thus aborted at Boeing as 200 workers in stiff competition with the company union barely managed to maintain the organization begun by the Buffalo local.

In the end and despite all its vagueness, NIRA held more promise for aircraft workers acting collectively than it did for their employers. Had workers been able to emulate the organizational cohesion that the manufacturers briefly displayed in response to NIRA, they would have been in a strong position to use Section 7a, particularly in view of their strategic role in aircraft production and the political traumas faced by their employers. Had they been able to establish an effective national system of collective bargaining, they could have helped their employers stabilize the industry in spite of themselves, by eliminating the bulk of the competitive space in wage differentials that the government took advantage of and by helping expose the contradictions and waste of the artificial business environment sustained by procurement law. But across the United States, the opportunities of Section 7a were denied aircraft workers and their industry mainly by the International Association of Machinists.

CHAPTER SEVEN

Patterns to World War II: Poised for Mass Production

EXPANSION, EXPORTS, AND WORKING CAPITAL

After 1935 and the NRA's demise the aircraft industry expanded rapidly, but its basic structural patterns persisted into the World War II period. These were determined mainly on Capitol Hill, where congressmen used procurement law to block an integrated and rationalized military-industrial complex for warplanes. Instead they continued to mold this growing complex into an expression of old antistate, antitrust political culture. After 1935 that culture was further institutionalized in the organization of expanding aircraft firms and in their relations to one another, to the military, and to their workers. It also continued to find material expression in the technology of aeronautics and the aircraft produced by these firms.

Sustained in these ways, the values of American republicanism would help set the terms for how the vast expansion of the aircraft industry would be managed, what weapons it would produce, and how they would be used in combat during the war. Between mid-1940 and Victory over Japan Day the United States spent $45 billion on military aircraft—a vast sum that included only the cost of planes and engines, not ordnance, government-financed factory expansion, machinery, equipment, housing for workers, and so on. That figure exceeds amounts spent on warships or any other category of munitions.[1] At the peak of production in spring 1944, over 3 million production workers were busy building aircraft, engines, and parts. The wartime experiences of many more Americans were shaped by the aircraft program as annual labor turnover was nearly 75

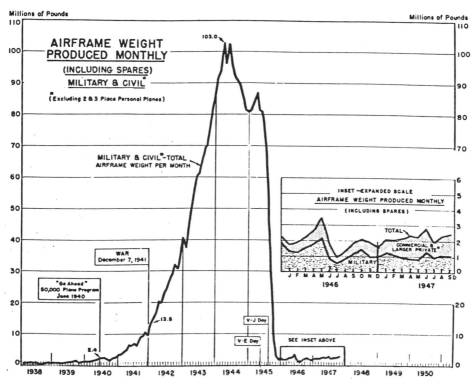

Figure 7.1. Airframe Weight Produced in the United States, 1938–1947.
American aircraft production by weight, less engines and accessories, during the
New Deal, World War II, and the early cold war.
Source: Box 39, Records of the President's Air Policy Commission (Finletter
Commission), Record Group 220, Harry S. Truman Library, Independence, Mo.

percent, and hundreds of thousands more worked in clerical and management positions or at the army and navy's modification centers. Congress's business—the prewar aircraft industry—was raw material for
the most extensive single episode in social intervention yet undertaken
by the federal government. The state agencies and policies that emerged
reflected this raw material as much as the shaping demands of total war
and a rapidly evolving technology.

During the 1930s the turbulent competition that had defined Congress's
business was checked to the extent that new entry became much more
difficult. Appendix 4 lists the large number of active firms in 1939. However, escalating design costs and the greater capital costs of larger
facilities and of tooling and retooling for metal production made positions

in the industry considerably more expensive. Firms more and more became identified with particular aircraft types. Their mainly military clients rarely had more than one or two immediate alternatives among suppliers of state of the art aircraft ranging from carrier fighters to heavy bombers. Yet despite the industry's "natural drift," as an NRA analyst had termed the thrust of its technology toward specialization and concentration, the army and navy were obliged by Congress to deal with the industry as if all firms were potential suppliers of every type, able to compete equally and solely on price. Thus manufacturers had to think of themselves in those terms and frame their business and technical plans accordingly. Artificial price competition and the long delays of the bidding process continued, as did losses on military work and the government's exploitation of the industry and its workers. Compared to earlier years, the financial constraints on aeronautics built into the industry's business environment proved much more difficult to overcome merely by private desires to stay in the industry, build the nation's air power, and prod technical advance. The negative effects of these constraints continued to be compounded by the inevitable hostility, suspicion, and secrecy generated by Congress's business environment among all concerned.[2]

The major firms are listed in Table 7.1 in the order of their sales for 1938. United Aircraft subsidiaries included Sikorsky, Chance Vought, Hamilton-Standard Propeller, and Pratt & Whitney. Pratt & Whitney and Wright Aeronautical of the Curtiss-Wright combine together split the market for high-performance engines. Unlike previous years when on average engine costs equaled airframe costs, by the mid-1930s airframe costs were soaring while engine costs remained relatively stable. In 1938 engines and propellers represented on average about 30 percent of total aircraft costs. Thus about 30 percent of total business listed in Table 7.1 was for engines. Halves of that third may be subtracted from the sales of United and Curtiss-Wright for a rough indication of a competitive airframe market among the major firms.

Large contracts for attack and medium bomber aircraft and the strong appeal at home and abroad for the DC-3 transport kept Douglas well ahead of a cluster of six firms. In any other year during the late 1930s Boeing would have been within this cluster, but 1938 was an especially bad year for the firm as the Air Corps dithered on the long-range B-17 Flying Fortress, finally signing a disappointingly small follow-on order for thirty-nine B-17s in mid-1938. Brewster and Bell were newcomers after 1935. Laurence Bell did not accompany his employer Reuben Fleet to California. In 1936, using abandoned Consolidated workers and facilities,

Table 7.1. Leading Aircraft Firms by Sales, 1938

United Aircraft	$36,700,000	(less engines)	$13,300,000
Curtiss-Wright	33,103,000	(less engines)	9,700,000
Douglas	28,347,000		
Martin	12,417,000		
Consolidated	12,245,000		
Lockheed	10,275,000		
North American	10,062,000		
Grumman	4,905,000		
Seversky	3,618,000		
Boeing	2,006,000		
Brewster	1,490,000		
Bell	1,200,000		
Total	156,368,000		

Source: See the charts and tables in Kennard W. Tibbitts, "Financial Summary," box 39, MG1-2, Records of the President's Air Policy Commission (Finletter Commission), RG 220, Harry S. Truman Library, Independence, Mo.

he established his own firm in Buffalo. Light plane companies such as Cessna, Beech, Fairchild, Bellanca, and Piper, only the first two of which did more than $1 million in sales in 1938, are excluded from Table 7.1.

The industry's expansion was due in part to increases in army and navy spending for aircraft (see Table 7.2). By 1936 the bitter atmosphere of scandal enveloping aviation had receded and fears of growing foreign air forces had increased, both to the points that lawmakers could with some comfort consider providing new planes for army and navy aviation, which seemed drastically undersupplied. Procurement of new army aircraft, for example, had averaged only 132 units per year in the period from June 1932 to June 1936. By the end of 1936 the number of front-line Air Corps aircraft was still 28 percent below the 1,800 authorized ten years earlier in the Air Corps Act's five-year expansion program. In the summer of 1936 FDR signed a bill increasing the authorization to 2,320. Still, as had been the case under the Air Corps Act, authorization was one thing, appropriations and contracts were others.[3]

Delays in the budgetary process and competitive contracting, the vulnerability of military funds to recurrent calls for economy and boycotts of the "merchants of death," ongoing suspicion of air power within the army and navy, and the relentless inflation of aircraft costs all conspired to keep the numbers of aircraft below authorized levels well into 1941. Despite the emphasis by most concerned on numbers of aircraft over quality and research and development, numerical shortfalls persisted.[4] Although

Table 7.2. American Aircraft Production, 1931–1944 (in $millions)

	Sales, Frames, Accessories, and Spares	Sales, Engines	Commercial Sales[1]	Exports and % of Total Sales	Army and Navy Aviation Procurement[2]
1931	32.6	14.5	15.2	4.9 (10)	31.0
1932	22.7	9.3	7.8	7.9 (25)	29.0
1933	23.8	9.7	13.6	9.2 (27)	25.0
1934	27.3	15.5	25.1	17.7 (41)	13.0
1935	32.5	12.7	22.4	14.3 (32)	23.0
1936	55.0	22.1	26.6	23.1 (30)	44.0
1937	84.2	30.1	48.5	39.4 (34)	58.0
1938	N.A.	N.A.	N.A.		N.A.
1939	194.2	74.3	27.8[3]	117.8 (44)	68.0
1940	223.0[4]	111.0[4]	N.A.	311.9	205.0
1941	1196.0	462.0	N.A.	626.9 (39)	587.0
1942	4329.0	1434.0	N.A.	N.A.	2915.0
1943	9924.0	2453.0	N.A.	N.A.	10072.0
1944	12907.0	3432.0	N.A.	N.A.	12828.0

[1]Includes commercial exports
[2]Includes items other than aircraft industry products
[3]Less engines
[4]1940 third and fourth quarters only

Source: Compiled from R. Modley, *Aviation Facts and Figures 1945* (New York: Aircraft Industries Association, 1945), 15, 54, 88; R. Modley and T. J. Cawley, *Aviation Facts and Figures 1953* (New York: Aircraft Industries Association, 1953), 22, 158; R. Modley et al., *Aviation Facts and Figures 1958* (New York: Aircraft Industries Association, 1958), 28; W. B. Harding, *The Aviation Industry* (New York: C. D. Barney, 1937), 33, all of which are based on Bureau of the Census and War Production Board statistics.

Congress's price-competitive contracting rules forced the industry toward high-volume production strategies, the level of funding actually provided by Congress joined the technical dynamism and complexity of the industry's product to thwart the industry's pursuit of the ideal of mass production. Still, the ideal was aggressively pursued despite all its antipathy to aeronautics and aircraft manufacture and to the small, sporadic, and specialized demand for the industry's output.[5]

This type of market stood in sharp contrast to the large, relatively predictable market for automobiles and other consumer products for which standard output could be almost continuously mass-produced in anticipation of sales. Obsession with the mass-production ideal, however, left fewer and fewer industry analysts who understood that apart from engine production, aircraft was less a manufacturing industry than a contracting business, like construction or shipbuilding.[6] During the later 1930s contractors either forgot this truth and their long histories of unprofitable "feast and famine" operations or were forced to ignore them by the imperatives of military contracting. Their options were limited, short of leaving the business, which for reasons of prestige and other emotional commitments few were willing to do. Also, higher fixed costs made exit from the industry much more difficult than it had been during the 1920s. And most manufacturers seemed confident in mass demand for their products and new treatment from Congress in a seemingly imminent war.

Whatever the case, contractors accepted larger and larger contracts, usually at losses. They expanded their plants, hired and trained new workers, bought sophisticated equipment, and reorganized shop floors and work patterns to facilitate rapid, volume production. Usually, however, contractors took such steps only to watch new models surpass theirs while competitors won the next large contract and to find themselves junking production equipment, again without work, and wondering when and from where the next order would come. The aircraft industry evolved at odds with itself—a mass-production industry with no mass-production product or market.

Had manufacturers been able to alter their regulatory environment along corporatist lines, or in terms of the "associative state," as proposed by Charles Lawrence and the Aeronautical Chamber of Commerce in 1924–1926 and again before the NRA, aircraft production might have approached the ideal of "flexible specialization": one or two aircraft firms specializing in one or two of the many types of aircraft needed, confident in the stability of a staff of designers and workers and in the prospect of small but continuous and remunerative demand for their output, even when inferior to a competitor's. Separate staffs would prod one another to take innovative steps and be much more willing to share advances with manufacturers concentrating on other types as well. One model would rarely be greatly inferior to another and only until both were rapidly made obsolete by the next model. The army and navy would still have had lean air forces, but these probably would have been equipped with greater numbers of more sophisticated aircraft, contributing to a better grasp of their possibilities and limits in combat. In relation to foreign aircraft and more importantly to the severe demands of militarily effective air power, the many deficiencies of American warplanes in the late 1930s almost certainly would have been avoided. Instead the emergency of war and the powerful institutional momentum built up within the industry by procurement law and the pursuit of the ideal of mass production compelled the hope that these deficiencies could be offset by sheer numbers.

By the eve of World War II Congress's business environment had produced an aircraft industry with more than 50 percent of its capacity not utilized (see Appendix 4). For a mass-production industrial power like America inactive aircraft plants suggested weakness, unpreparedness. It seemed essential to keep plants producing, even to expand them, particularly as this anxiety was usually coupled with the popular idea that effective and invincible air power was little more than a matter of getting "waves" of aircraft aloft—an idea as old and as captivating as the World War I vision of military aviation. Under-utilization of the aircraft industry in the late 1930s paralleled popular ideas of strategic necessity to encourage simple doctrines of air power that could employ mass output.[7] Unlimited demand during World War II temporarily relieved the tensions of a contracting business artificially geared to produce for a mass market. After the war it would be primarily up to cold war planners to produce such a market for a vastly expanded industry.[8]

Before wartime demand radically altered the industry's market, a burgeoning export market, mainly for military aircraft, was critical in sustaining and channelling toward volume production the industry that would later help determine what wartime demands upon it would be. Exports during the 1930s provided solid profits that allowed the industry at least marginal viability under Congress's regulatory framework. Grover Loening, aircraft-industry analyst at Chase National Bank discounted the commercial market as stagnant since airlines were unprofitable and largely had the planes they needed. Although the air-transport market was growing quickly, strides in range, speed, and payload kept down the numbers of aircraft needed to serve it. Given the situation under procurement law, in Loening's view the industry's best hope lay overseas. He estimated that exports were responsible for 80 percent of the industry's profits, which after 1935 were still small but at least materializing regularly. In complete contrast to their dealings with the army and navy, manufacturers "could set prices" for foreign buyers who paid "money on the table" in advance and "who can't wait to get their aircraft." Loening predicted that unless "war fever abates," the export market would continue to provide the industry's lifeblood.[9]

Guy Vaughan of Curtiss-Wright told congressmen that "the development of airplanes for the future comes from the export business." He estimated that exports provided for "two thirds of development costs." The significance of exports was viewed from a broader perspective by the Export Committee of the Aeronautical Chamber of Commerce. It cited export profits as "crucial to the industry and the national defense," not only because they provided for research and development but because they helped the industry in "cutting manufacturing costs," in buying costly hydropresses and other machines, and in building the mass-production aircraft industry that was equated more and more with national security. Exports also helped the pursual of mass-production output, the committee noted, because they called for repetitive output of "frozen designs." Until the great Allied purchases, beginning with a $25 million British order for the Lockheed Hudson in summer 1938, the military and State Department would allow exports of little else than obsolescent craft.[10]

Under the Roosevelt administration, international politics reinforced congressional politics in shaping the evolution of the aircraft industry and its technology toward quantity output. The "missionary work" of the Bureau of Foreign and Domestic Commerce, so important in building an export market for aircraft during the Hoover years, was eclipsed during the New Deal as these high-profile sales began playing a much more central role in the nation's foreign policy. Aircraft exports were particularly important as part of the Good Neighbor Policy toward Latin America, calculated in part to contain "outside" economic penetration of the Western Hemisphere. After the Neutrality Act of 1935 aircraft exports became a direct device of New Deal policy abroad. Both military and commercial aircraft were included on the Munitions Control list, mandated by the act and administered on a case-by-case basis by the White House. Until the Allied war purchases, most aircraft exports went to Latin America "in severe competition with Italy and Germany," whose positions in the South American aircraft and airline businesses the State Department wanted to overthrow. Key to U.S. foreign sales was the Export-Import Bank, which through three- to five-year credits underwrote deals with heavily indebted Latin American countries. In 1939, 100 percent financing for aircraft sales to Latin America was provided as part of the Hemispheric Defense Plan.[11]

So critical were foreign sales that at least one firm—Seversky Aircraft—falsified export applications and established a dummy corporation to forward aircraft, aluminum sheet, and machine guns to Japan in 1938–1939. As the war approached, the commercial and strategic goals of aircraft exports and airline expansion abroad continued to reinforce one another in government policy. Manufacturers agreed that the "export business is again, in 1940, writing the profit position of the industry . . . firms that do not continue to strive for exports will find their names on the list of OUR WAR DEAD." In 1940 lending authority for the Export-

Import Bank was extended, and $500 million was made available for use in the Western Hemisphere. Nelson Rockefeller, FDR's coordinator of commercial and cultural relations for the American republics, assumed oversight of promotion and finance for aircraft exports. To the industry's delight he reaffirmed what had been federal policy for years—"the complete Americanization of aviation in the entire Western Hemisphere with particular respect to Latin America." Such was the goal as well of Robert A. Lovett, recruited from Brown Brothers, Harriman, to become assistant secretary of war for air from 1941 to 1945. Lovett's hopes for American aviation were grander, however, extending to Asia, Africa, and Europe. Even while coordinating the army's share of the immense aircraft-production program of World War II and driving the new Army Air Forces toward his vision of a global colossus of American power, Lovett found time to integrate new foreign air bases and military air-transport routes into a plan for a preeminent American position in postwar commercial air transport.[12]

The importance of foreign sales in sustaining the American aircraft industry during the pre-war years is underscored when its shaky financial position, despite profitable exports, is considered. Through these years, manufacturers constantly contended with serious shortages of working capital. In 1935 increasing volume and low wages helped produce profits for the major military and commercial manufacturers that began replacing the deficits of the first half of the 1930s. They rose along a curve to 6.2 percent on sales in 1937 and 13.3 percent in 1940. These composite figures are misleading, however. They obscure the comparative strength of engine manufacturers and the disastrous situation faced by many individual aircraft firms such as Boeing, which in 1938 lost 27.7 percent on only $2 million in sales. Aircraft firms had much difficulty attracting the interest and capital of stockholders, which meant that working control within firms remained concentrated, especially in the case of such "owner-operated" firms as Douglas, Bell, Grumman, Martin, and Consolidated. At the end of 1939 shareholder investment equalled 53 percent of the year's sales, compared to 113 percent for American industry as a whole. Thus most of what was presented as profits was not paid out in dividends but reinvested in the business.[13] Plowing back profits is generally regarded as evidence of long-term commitment to competitiveness and growth, but the technological dynamics of this industry and the prior convictions of manufacturers made reinvestment of the bulk of any profits—primarily into new designs—less an option than a need. During the years 1935–1938, the 57 percent of the industry's profits that were reinvested covered only some of the immediate costs of doing business in this industry.[14]

A good sense of the dubious meaning of profits in aircraft manufacture and of why the industry had trouble attracting new investment is provided by the deferred development charges added annually to the industry's books. For the top eighteen firms these charges against anticipated future profits amounted to $3.1 million in 1937 and $5.9 million in 1938, or 41 and 39 percent of profit on sales for those years. Of the $5.2 million spent by twelve top firms in these two years, 44 percent was deferred. Presented as "intangible items" on the balance sheet, deferred charges in 1939 equalled .3 percent of net worth at International Harvester, 1.8 percent at General Electric, and 7.2 percent among the eighteen top aircraft companies. Deferring development costs against profits on hoped-for future sales was a flexible accounting technique that had always been practiced in the industry despite the attempts at accounting reform by the army, navy, and Aeronautical Chamber of Commerce beginning in 1933. Deferred charges allowed the books of aircraft firms "to be juggled at will," making it "possible to show a profit or loss in any given year almost according to desire."[15]

The ambiguity of profit in this high-technology, military industry—not only as a measure of business strength but in the industry's appeal to participants—had always been at the heart of the dilemmas surrounding its organization, its relations with the state, and the orderly development of its technology. Aircraft production presented unique problems that would have been difficult to cope with under any arrangement, including the corporatist alternative. These difficulties revolved around the unpredictabilities of a uniquely complex product that existed initially only on paper and in the minds of engineers and workers, then continually evolved while being manufactured until quickly becoming obsolete and discarded. The profit factor, a consequence of relying on private enterprise to supply these products, was a significant additional complication, much exacerbated by Congress's resistance to associationalist reforms, by its insistence that aircraft contracting adhere to ancient rules, and by its false suspicions that aircraft manufacturers were motivated mainly by big profits. The problems of financing the supply of high-technology weaponry by competitive private industry were never solved.[16] However, they became less pressing, less a month-by-month source of crisis for the industry, less a direct constraint on technological change with the demand for American air and space power during World War II and the postwar years of the cold war and global expansion.

The industry's current ratio, one of the best bellwethers of financial health, further highlights the plight of aircraft firms and the impact of the industry's business environment on aeronautic technology. The current ratio compares current assets—cash, inventory, receivables—to current liabilities—notes and accounts payable—giving a good measure of liquidity and the availability of working capital for such expenses as research and development. The lower the ratio, the closer the break-even point. In 1939 the current ratio for American manufacturers as a whole stood at 4.2; for the aircraft industry it stood at 1.7. In the same year working capital per dollar of sales was ninety cents at International Harvester, fifty-two cents at General Electric, and twenty-eight cents among the top eighteen aircraft firms.[17] The negative consequences for new development were compounded because much of the industry's working capital was invested in tooling for quantity output and greater floor space. Also, inventory turnover, the length of time required to complete contracts and receive final payment, was much longer in aircraft than in most other industries—an aspect of the industry's financial condition that also compelled streamlined, repetitive production.

Still, as it always had, the aircraft industry plodded through. Firms overcame the apathy of the banking and securities communities, relying on federal trade credits, reinvestment of export earnings, low wages, and as U.S. entry into the war neared, on grants for plant expansion from the army, navy, and the Reconstruction Finance Corporation, advance payments on production contracts, and tax deferrals. Yet even during the days of apparent prosperity in 1941, the industry, in the confidential view of navy financial analysts, was "technically bankrupt." A "public utility" dependent on the government as "ultimate obligator," aircraft offered "little basis for private investment confidence." Its fate at war's end posed a broad imponderable. Surveying its financial history, these analysts noted the industry's "constant disadvantage in bargaining power" with the military, observing that any approach toward financial health for aircraft firms would have been and would continue to be "political anathema." "No business man in his right mind, with a free choice, would make a career of aircraft manufacture," they concluded. But happily for American air power and the roles it would play for the United States, the aircraft industry "has appealed to the very few who had the sporting instinct to wrestle with an outrageous fortune and pit their wits against insuperable obstacles."[18]

CONGRESS'S BUSINESS: FOUNDATIONS
FOR A NEW MILITARY POLITICAL ECONOMY

During the late 1930s manufacturers, officers, and their supporters on Capitol Hill tried again to reform Congress's regulation of the aircraft industry, seeking amendment of Vinson-Trammell's profit limitations and especially the Air Corps Act's provisions on design rights and advertised bidding. These, in the view of one Wall Street investment house, meant losses and "skimping in the production of an article in which quality rather than price should be the prime consideration." Until the blitzkrieg in Western Europe, however, Congress easily deflected these efforts. In 1937, Cong. John Costello, a California Democrat friendly with Reuben Fleet and Donald Douglas, introduced a bill that would have provided manufacturers full rights to their designs and effectively ended price competition, but it failed to reach the hearing stage. Unsuccessfully reintroduced in 1938 and 1939 it was cynically dubbed the "annual design rights bill" by the counsel to the Aeronautical Chamber of Commerce.[19]

Attempts were also made to amend Vinson-Trammell's 10 percent profit limitation beyond H.R. 5730, a 1936 amendment sponsored by Carl Vinson, chairman of the House Naval Affairs Committee, that released from the act's provisions makers of "scientific equipment" for naval aircraft—gyroscopes, automatic pilots, bombsights, and the like. H.R. 5730 also allowed aircraft firms to apply losses on naval contracts to profits on contracts completed in the following year. This was minimal help, however, since contractors' commitments were usually multi-year in length. As the Nye Committee released reports calling for the nationalization of defense industries, the ACC felt relief from procurement law was best pursued not through the public sphere of legislative reform but through quiet lobbying of the military and the Internal Revenue Service, charged with monitoring compliance. Carl Vinson, eager for reform and one of the most powerful figures in the House, nevertheless advised against the legislative route, telling the ACC that "amendment would provoke great controversy in Congress." A rare occasion for high-level dialogue on procurement matters was a March 1937 meeting in New York that included representatives of all the major firms, Generals Oscar Westover and H. H. Arnold of the Army Air Corps, and Comdr. H. C. Richardson of the Navy Bureau of Aeronautics. Yet after two days of listening to the manufacturers' pleas and expressing anxiety over the comparative weaknesses of U.S. military aircraft, the military men could give the manufacturers nothing beyond a hearty "thank you for your views." And despite the ACC's tactful presentations to the Internal Revenue Service, carefully designed to alter its regulations on allowable costs while "not incurring the animosity of those who have been concerned with their preparation," the chamber's efforts again went nowhere. The issue was forced on Capitol Hill.[20]

One bill pushed in 1937 by Cong. Byron Scott of California, also a friend of Fleet and Douglas, simply sought to exempt aircraft from Vinson-Trammell. By a vote of twelve to four, H.R. 7777 was passed by the House Naval Affairs Committee after Vinson "told the committee to report it out favorably as soon as possible" and after lengthy presentations by military officials and manufacturers in support of the bill. Charles A. Edison, secretary of the navy, complained that the "Navy suffers because manufacturers are reluctant to take its business." He argued that an aircraft industry taking on various "experimental" contracts "in the hope that the law of averages will allow them some contracts for amortization" of their design costs was not the way to build a dependable and advanced production base for naval air power.[21]

Adm. A. B. Cook, chief of the Bureau of Aeronautics, provided data from the three-year period 1934–1936, showing that manufacturers' losses on navy work averaged 71 percent on development contracts and profits of 2.8 percent on production work. Since only a "negligible" amount in excess profits had been recovered in all naval contracting under Vinson-Trammell, the act in Cook's view was counterproductive. To show how naval aviation suffered and became more costly under the law, he offered the following hypothetical situation based on reports from contracting officers and inspectors: A manufacturer lost $100,000 on $1 million in work during one year and made $200,000 on $1 million the next year. He could deduct the loss from the profit, reducing it to a $100,000 return on $2 million in business over two years, or five percent. Since no further amount of profit in the second year could improve his position and since he could not include losses from army or commercial work, he had no incentive to make other customers' contracts carry some of the losses on navy work. Apart from whatever personal desire he had to produce superior naval aircraft, he would direct his most inefficient resources, tools, workers, and so on to navy work and in fact would avoid navy work. Cook argued that with all their powers of audit and inspection, his officers were perfectly capable of keeping profits "reasonable" without Vinson-Trammell's debilitating help.[22]

Leading manufacturers presented much evidence of the wastes, delays, financial hardships, and impediments to aeronautics caused by price competition generally and by Vinson-Trammell specifically. Still, H.R. 7777 drew only reserved support from the services in the end. As they had since the battle over the Air Corps Act in 1925–1926, the army and navy air wings feared stirring up issues that might provoke Congress into even more restrictive legislation. In a political atmosphere shaped by the popular idea that "merchants of death" were again pushing the world into war and by the deep recession of 1937–1938 which President Roosevelt blamed on a "strike" by capital against the New Deal, H.R. 7777 became "involved in legislative snarls." It languished on the House calendar and was finally stricken from it in June 1938 after objections by two familiar Texas Democrats on the Naval Affairs Committee, Clyde L. Garret, who with John J. McSwain had led the campaign against aircraft procurement reform in 1926, and W. D. McFarlane, who had dissented from the 1934 *Delaney Report* on the industry and had helped revive the myth of the Aircraft Trust for the 1930s.[23]

Some examples suggest the results for manufacturers and their aircraft. After 1934 Douglas designed five new aircraft for the navy at a total cost of $730,000 but recovered only $259,000 through development contracts. Of the five, only one resulted in a production contract, a $3.7 million order for 118 Devastator torpedo bombers. At the hearings on H.R. 7777, Douglas's comptroller predicted a loss of $275,000 on this contract, without including development costs. Although the production contract was negotiated, Douglas felt pressed to minimize its price even at the risk of turning a loss, for fear of provoking the navy to turn to open bidding for the Devastator. Douglas's comptroller argued that the Vinson-Trammell amendment allowing the forwarding of losses in one year to profits in the next was of little use to the company. Even if on the few occasions contracts were completed in succeeding years, losses on development contracts could not be recovered in production contracts because the Treasury had simply decided that that was forbidden.

> Mr Scott: There is no way in the world under the present regulations for you to recover those experimental plane losses?
> Mr Lewis: No . . . the only loss you can carry forward against . . . future profit is a loss on a production contract.

Lewis complained that finding outside financing for expansion—employment had increased 100 per cent at Santa Monica to 6,800 workers in twelve months—was hampered because 80 percent of the company's $36 million backlog were military orders, suspect in the eyes of investors

Electricians at work on two-engine Douglas B-18s in Santa Monica, November 1938. A major attraction of these bombers to the Air Corps, operating under Congress's rules, was their low cost relative to the four-engine Boeing B-17, which was much larger, more sophisticated, and built by workers in Seattle paid substantially more. The B-18 program, however, proved to be a false economy. First designed in 1934 as a military derivative of the DC-2, B-18s served minor roles in World War II, such as patrolling for submarines in the Caribbean.

because of procurement law. Thus working capital had to be diverted to fixed assets. In his view the heart of his firm's problems with the Vinson-Trammell Act and the Treasury's conservative interpretations of it was that profit, if it came, acquired a new meaning: No longer was it something added to the surplus account or distributed in dividends; rather, it was a fund to cover the costs of performance—costs that the government simply refused to recognize.[24] For the navy's Devastator, the sacrifices of Douglas Aircraft, its owners, and especially its employees were significant. Yet they paled beside those of navy fliers who at the battle of Midway in 1942 were killed flying futile missions in these obsolete craft because the constraints of procurement policy had prevented the development and deployment of something better.

Over a twenty-year period to mid-1937 Glenn Martin sold aircraft worth $36 million—95 percent to the military. Sixty percent of sales went to payrolls; net profit amounted to only 1.6 percent of sales. If not for the brief prosperity in Cleveland during the late 1920s, his company would have reported a substantial overall deficit, had it survived at all. Martin consistently turned losses on military contracts during the 1930s. A $1.5 million loan in 1935 from the Reconstruction Finance Corporation sustained him long enough to take advantage of the export market for military aircraft. In 1937, for example, Martin sold abroad flying boats and obsolete two-engine B-10 bombers worth $15 million, while his combined business with the army and navy totaled less than $500,000.[25]

From 1928 to mid-1937 Curtiss-Wright spent $10.5 million on military development beyond sums received for such work in government contracts. During that time Wright engine horsepower leapt from 575 to 1,500 and Curtiss fighter speed increased from 180 to 300 miles per hour. Curtiss-Wright's president, Guy Vaughan, argued that price competition, enforced by the government's denial of design rights, and Vinson-Trammell's restrictions on the distribution of losses among contracts and over periods beyond one taxable year meant that the $10.5 million was largely "contributed" by his firm to the nation's air power. In 1932–1936, Curtiss Aeroplane lost 29 percent on army sales and 12.5 percent on navy sales. Exports returned 17.7 percent for a net loss on total business of 4.6 percent. In 1933–1934 Curtiss Aeroplane lost $154,000 on a $121,000 development contract for a failed army design. In 1935 it signed a 136-plane contract for a navy observation plane, the SOC-1 Seagull, based substantially on the failed design. Curtiss asked the Internal Revenue Service to allow its loss as an element of cost on the navy contract. "No part of the loss sustained by your company . . . may be considered for the purpose of determining profits under Vinson-Trammell" was the ruling. Performance cost disallowances by the Treasury, Vaughan claimed, put the act's profit limitations at an actual 6 percent, wholly inadequate even when achieved, for such a "speculative business." Year-by-year statements from the holding company and its Wright and Curtiss subsidiaries showed that profit limitations were irrelevant. Yet innovation was hampered and new investors discouraged. During the five-year period 1937–1941, the airplane, engine, and propeller divisions of Curtiss-Wright together spent $25.6 million on military development but recovered only $5.8 million through their contracts.[26]

Only the manufacturers' commitments to improved designs, on behalf of technical advance and a somewhat credible American air power, offset the business distractions and financial disincentives of government contracts. Chance Vought, a United Aircraft subsidiary, "almost solely occupied with Navy work," lost $934,000 on $4.8 million in sales during 1934–1937, thanks to a "keenly competitive situation," and the "low prices" the navy was able to pay. J. F. McCarthy, United's controller, protested that Vinson-Trammell "cramps our style in going forward with experimental and development work."[27] Reuben Fleet, building navy flying boats, testified that "we had no profit, . . . had not paid dividends in 9 years," and that "no one in San Diego would buy our stock. . . . Our industry is changing, it is going ahead, and this [procurement law] is crucifying us."[28]

Leroy Grumman, a leading naval innovator at Bethpage, Long Island, argued that Vinson-Trammell dampened his "inventive zest," not only because of losses but because it required minute scrutiny of costs, which forced the hiring of cadres of accountants and the rearrangement of work patterns. Grumman showed that his losses made Vinson-Trammell "inoperative" and complained of "the very complicated accounting system" it required. Prior to the act the firm "more or less charged things as they came along to certain jobs," but now design and production were becoming increasingly bureaucratized as everyone was filling out forms to trace labor time and the cost of innumerable items to specific contracts. Coping with accounting was forcing him to run an organization far different from the small, flexible, and administratively lean business relatively able to cope with rapid technical change that he oversaw until Vinson-Trammell. Still he boldly reassured congressmen that "we will keep on trying."[29]

After the demise of H.R. 7777, hopes for procurement reform were again raised in late 1938. Hitler's successful political uses of the Luftwaffe intimidated FDR, and in November 1938 he announced to his cabinet his desire for 10,000 aircraft for the Air Corps and annual capacity for 20,000. Whether he too was a victim of the popular promises and fantasies of air power or recognized the symbolic power of large numbers of aircraft for diplomatic purposes and for mobilizing domestic opinion, FDR was the main player in the military aircraft "numbers racket" through the war. The 10,000 figure was pulled from the air by the president.[30] It was reluctantly reduced to 3,000 in his January 1939 message to Congress, not in line with what seemed necessary for a credible military force but with what seemed politically realistic, given its $1.2 billion price tag and Congress's greater fiscal conservatism and isolationism after the 1938 elections. Rather than any military determination of what was needed to defeat the Axis, the White House's sense of what might be hoped for from

American industry set the numbers of aircraft ordered, the way production was planned, and the resources allocated throughout the war. The army and navy followed this lead, their input centering on the types of aircraft built, the firms best suited for these, and how air power doctrine would be shaped to utilize them.

Even FDR's shrunken post-Munich request for warplanes meant large new demands on the industry and seemed unlikely to be met without a new dispensation in military-industrial relations. As they had under similar prospects in 1925 and 1933, the manufacturers turned again to the Aeronautical Chamber of Commerce, hoping for a favorable accommodation with the government along associationalist lines. After the NRA failure, the ACC had reassumed its basic role as a trade association in name only, despite its continued hopes, as old as the World War I associationalist dream for aeronautics, that it could coordinate technical change, market development, and business-government relations for the aircraft industry. During the later 1930s it performed valuable functions in the State Department on behalf of exports and in the crucial area of suppressing federally ordered wage increases. Yet separate contacts between individual firms and government bureaucrats overwhelmingly defined the industry's relations with the military and with other government agencies such as the State Department and the Reconstruction Finance Corporation. In altering the central fact of the industry's business environment—"the iron clad insistence heretofore enforced by fiscal officers of the Government that price is substantially the controlling factor in aircraft contracts"[31]—the chamber could do little. Thus manufacturers continued to give it little of their time or money. The major firms either refused to join or indifferently maintained their membership, paying dues but rarely providing the chamber with a quorum at its policy-making meetings. Aircraft associationalists blamed the lack of interfirm cooperation on the "young prima donna nature of many people in the industry."[32] In fact, secrecy and independence were inevitable in Congress's business.

The sudden rise in 1938–1939 of large-scale air power in perceptions of national security greatly increased attention in Washington to the industry's problems, and many hoped the chamber would serve as a meeting ground and clearing house between it and the government. In January 1939 John H. Jouett of Fairchild Aircraft became president of the ACC, replacing Leighton Rogers. Consolidated, Douglas, North American, Seversky, and Grumman joined. Martin still refused formal participation, but he and representatives of the others met frequently, hoping to "bring to bear the industry's point of view on the new legislation" that would fund FDR's defense requests and determine how those funds would translate into contracts.[33]

However, the ACC could not assume the authoritative, representative voice for the industry, so reluctant were firms to provide it with detailed information on their capacity, back orders, development projects, or any other data that might be useful to competitors. At the prompting of Donald Douglas, always suspicious of Washington and the eastern manufacturers, the California firms—Lockheed, Northrop, Consolidated, Vultee, Ryan, and North American, which had moved West from Baltimore in 1935—insisted upon formal reorganization of the chamber so that West Coast members could meet separately and impose upon policy as a bloc. Under Douglas and Guy Vaughan respectively, West and East Coast ACC Committees were established, setting a pattern in which mobilization of the industry for the war—pricing, wages, subcontracting, material allocations, distribution of man- and woman-power, social services—was pursued along scattered regional lines. By late 1942 the ACC's weak claim as the industry's national voice was forfeited to the pressures of regionalization and to the concerns of geographically distinct groups of manufacturers for their postwar competitive positions. Indicative of the durability of the industry's prewar structure, in November 1942 manufacturers deserted the chamber en masse and made their claims in Washington through three separate bodies, the East Coast, West Coast, and Central Councils of the new National Aircraft War Production Council, Incorporated. These three advocate groups found stiff rivalry from the Automotive Council for War Production, a Detroit-based group of manufacturers producing aircraft, parts, and subassemblies.[34]

Of concern to the manufacturers in 1938–1940 was a false but widespread sense that the industry was in no position to absorb large new orders from the army and navy. Beliefs that the industry was "loaded down" with foreign orders or too small and primitive to apply the techniques of mass production deemed essential for FDR's program led many to argue for reliance on the auto industry or on "air arsenals"—new government plants. The ACC countered with statistics detailing the industry's under-utilization and the large sums that were nevertheless still being "put into brick and mortar" and production equipment to replace skilled labor and to reorganize the shop floor.[35] It argued that no help or production lessons were needed from the auto industry and that the industry was poised for mass production, needing only mass-production orders. By most of the rules of business history and industrial organization it makes little sense to talk about an industry as merely poised for mass production. Mass-production techniques and mass markets are mutually dependent and develop in tandem. But in aircraft the rules of industrial and market development do not apply since Congress patterned this industry's formation in accord with ideological and political rules.

A desperate Reuben Fleet telegraphed from San Diego: "We are in a wonderful position to produce large volume of aircraft . . . business on hand consists of service trial orders occupying approximately five percent capacity . . . we could go to town for you . . . waiting for production. . . . " Like Martin in Baltimore, Consolidated was virtually at a standstill in late 1938 and the first half of 1939, and few of the other plants had orders beyond three to six months. Under-utilization of plant space (see Appendix 4) and the likelihood that this situation would continue at least until July–September 1939 because of the delays of appropriating funds and contracting under "the usual competitions" led one securities analyst to advise his clients to pay close attention to manufacturers of trainers and heavy bombers. Unlike most army and navy fighters and attack craft, American heavy bombers were "state of the art" in comparison to foreign offerings, thanks to Boeing's persistence in this field. Trainers were basic and could be produced in large numbers. As with the B-17, production would begin immediately upon signing the contract, "while production of advanced fighters will not begin for months after the orders." Bombers and trainers were thus likely to be emphasized in the program, the analyst suggested, because public reassurances dictated a stress on numbers and the scale of air power rather than on its sophistication. Bombers also used more floor space, making contractors look stronger financially—a fact that had impressed Clement Keys in the mid-1920s.[36]

Louis B. Johnson, assistant secretary of war, defended the industry's claims to adequate capacity at the White House and argued for keeping its capacity fully occupied. He also consulted with the ACC on new contracting rules to be recommended to the Military and Naval Affairs Committees that would allow the army and navy to allocate aircraft orders. The manufacturers again insisted on noncompetitive, negotiated production contracts with aircraft designers. They wanted provisions for liberal advance payments to help them finance expansion; the right "to lump profits and or losses on all Government business whether Army or Navy"; and "accounting measures" with acceptable costs of contract performance "established before hand" rather than after legislation by the

Internal Revenue Service as had been the case under Vinson-Trammell. A corollary but burning concern for manufacturers was how they and their expanded facilities would fare after completion of the program.[37]

Gen. "Hap" Arnold, chief of the Air Corps, lobbied on the industry's behalf, insisting in particular on the power "to negotiate contracts for airplanes and other aircraft equipment." Unlike most of his predecessors in both the army and navy, Arnold wanted negotiating powers more to facilitate mass production than technical progress. Competitive bidding meant endless delays and for the large orders planned would have the effect of perverting Congress's procompetitive intentions. Bidding advantages would go to the largest, most active firms, Arnold argued, whose models the Air Corps had firmly committed itself to—the Curtiss P-36 and P-40, the Douglas B-18 and A-20—which were achieving economies of scale on foreign orders. Full employment of all aircraft firms would be legally impossible. Boeing, Consolidated, Seversky, Martin, and Vultee had few orders, were heavily burdened by inactive overhead, and faced large tooling costs. Without the power to negotiate contracts it was impossible to plan properly, and the Air Corps would be unable to restructure the industry into one "capable of meeting a war emergency," away from the disorder produced by "the competitive method of procurement employed during the past. . . ."[38]

If there were still aircraft manufacturers and air power experts who thought their recommendations would be followed by Congress or who believed that they at last held the upper hand in a world on the brink of war, they were set right when Vinson-Trammell's profit limitations for naval aircraft were "jammed into the authorization bill at the last moment" and extended to army contracting. No provisions were made for negotiated contracts in the National Defense Act of April 3, 1939, which authorized $300 million for the Air Corps. The only concessions the industry won were rejection of the idea of the air arsenal, an increase in the profit cap from 10 to 12 percent, and the right to carry forward any return on a contract below 12 percent as a credit in future profit computations. The Air Corps was also authorized to purchase prototypes beyond just the winner of design competitions but only at 75, 60, and 50 percent of the actual cost to the first, second, and third losing manufacturer. As for specifics on the costs of contract performance, the manufacturers were still left to hope for the best from the Treasury.[39]

The ACC pleaded for recognition of complete development costs and the cumulative application of the profit limitation to both army and navy contracts. The first point was critical as "existing methods are definitely

The Curtiss P-36C. The P-36 design was begun by Curtiss in November 1934 and competed with the Seversky P-35 until an Air Corps order for 210 P-36s was signed with Curtiss in July 1937. Entering service in 1938–1939, these models were wholly outclassed by British, German, and Japanese fighters. Only the Curtiss P-40, designed in 1937 and first appearing in American and British squadrons in mid-1940, even approached the abilities of foreign models.

retarding development and the best evidence of it is our present status in world military aircraft performance. . . ." Donald Douglas threatened to quit the ACC because of the Act's failure to provide clearly for development costs. Paralleling their response to the Air Corps Act in 1926, he and other manufacturers assumed that some kind of conspiracy against them was afoot—perhaps led by the auto industry. For them the pro-competition attitudes of the "hillbillies" on the congressional committees could not possibly be genuine. Douglas believed the ACC was under the sway of Pratt & Whitney and Wright Aeronautical, engine builders who enjoyed patents on their products, could easily recoup their design costs, and did not want to see funding legislation held up by provisions that would only favor airframe companies.[40]

A panel under Gen. W. G. Kilner, appointed to reformulate the Air Corps' research and development plans, stressed again the crippling effect of the government's unrealistic approach to the costs of aircraft design and the technical strides that could be expected if contracting was used to help the industry concentrate. Louis Johnson was of a similar view and convened a War Department board to establish accounting rules, but progress was slow and its recommendations nonbinding on the Treasury. Rules were finally approved by the Treasury, War, and Navy departments on June 28, 1939. By the end of July "the growing feeling" among manufacturers was "that the regulations are far too restrictive," failing to encompass the real costs of performance. No provisions were made for combining all government work to determine excess profits or for amortizing development costs. The army advocate general would not permit a cost index, or "escalator clause," to cover inflation. Arguing that the security given the government on development contracts was insufficient, the Treasury rejected the Air Corps' concession on advance payments for such contracts and even demanded a share of the royalties on designs that manufacturers were able to charge foreign buyers![41] General Arnold continued to press for the power to negotiate, stressing "the critical situation in this respect" and reiterating the point that competitive contracts under the Air Corps Act would not only deter new development but would also have to go to a few firms with order books already filled while others faced bankruptcy. All attempts to amend the law in 1939 were unsuccessful, however.[42]

Manufacturers grew deeply anxious about their inability to live up to the ideal of mass production, constantly pointed out and interpreted as primitivism by the press. Anxiety combined with anger as they invested and expanded, only to find even a rapidly growing market inadequate for steady production and the coverage of design, plant, and equipment overhead. Moreover all their proposals for stabilizing the industry and helping it along to the levels of concentration that mass production presupposed were invariably rejected. The air forces, too, were frustrated. Their visions of preeminent air power were dependent first of all on massive aircraft production, and they wanted to avoid being tagged with a repeat of the production fiasco of World War I. Yet military-industrial relations had been so restricted by Congress that no institutional base for interaction with the industry existed. Through the interwar years these relations had consisted almost entirely of adversarial contract negotiations and ad hoc contacts on technical matters at the services' testing facilities. Consultation and planning on business matters were rare and generally understood as illegal and immoral. Powers for planning industrial mobilization granted the assistant secretary of war (ASW) under the Defense Act of 1920 were underfunded, understaffed, and went undeveloped. They had little impact as manufacturers ignored time-consuming ASW surveys, which continued to focus on likely problems during a war emergency rather than on those that existed in the present for aircraft firms. The attitude that "the buyer is not responsible for production," first expressed by Admiral Taylor during World War I, prevailed until 1939.[43]

A July 1939 meeting with the industry called by General Arnold in an attempt to build new bridges revealed how the military was still grasping for a basic understanding of the industry's dimensions and dynamics. The Army Air Corps had little in the way of a scheme for industrial mobilization as part of an overall strategy for air power. The industry's capabilities as they existed, as they had evolved under Congress's direction, would do much to determine that strategy. Arnold complained about American airplanes "with performance equal only to those of foreign nations produced five years ago" and insisted that "there is definitely a need for change." Nevertheless the discussion only touched upon new development. The underlying almost desperate concern was that the industry would be able "to handle the load" of current orders and the huge new orders expected. The discussion focused on questions of mass production. Gen. George H. Brett, chief of the Air Corps Materiel Division, told manufacturers that "productivity" would be the "Number 1" consideration. For him the Air Corps' main problem was distributing contracts for only 2,600 planes among all available plants so that they could develop mass production. Stating the maxim that would largely govern not only America's approach to air power but its overall strategy as the "arsenal of democracy," during the war, Brett announced that "the ability to produce is more valuable than the equipment."[44]

The discussion centered on how to "judge productive capacity" in so complex an industry. Arnold wanted some way "to make my case . . . to my superiors," a "yardstick" to measure output of aircraft, a statistical base that could be used in easily understood tables and graphs. "If we do not produce those planes . . . I will get hell." He groped for ways to wrap the "Aviation Expansion Program" within some net of control and predictability. As bids from the manufacturers were opened during spring and summer 1939, Arnold and his associates were staggered to find that the Air Corps' best-laid plans were irrelevant since it had no real sense of the actual and rapidly accelerating costs of advanced aircraft and the new accessories, instruments, and hours of engineering that went into them. That situation was inevitable, given the weak links in military-industrial relations. The Air Corps had to take the publicly announced numbers of aircraft desired by FDR and translate these figures into cost estimates for presentation to Congress, which appropriated the funds. Yet the Air Corps was not allowed to confer with manufacturers on prices until bids had been opened, and bids could not be taken until funds were made available.[45]

The manufacturers disputed various versions of Arnold's yardstick, but on other matters they could easily agree, such as on their immediate needs—markets for a nascent mass-production industry. They concurred in Glenn Martin's view that the best way to solve their problems was by "increasing the number of airplanes purchased. . . . We do not see sufficient markets in peacetime," he complained. "Fifty percent of the men in this room are looking for business." Martin called for an even more aggressive campaign to find export outlets for aircraft and described the spiral that manufacturers now seemed caught in: "It is impossible to produce satisfactory [numbers of] aircraft without trained personnel. They can only be trained by having production orders." Manufacturers could also agree on how they wanted to be approached by the military. "Would the industry individually prefer that we treat their firm as a separate confidential problem or have it all come out in open session?" asked General Arnold. With competitive bidding still the rule and the postwar business environment always a source of anxiety, no one contested the response of United Aircraft's Donald Brown that the firm-by-firm approach was preferable. "I don't think the industry wants competitive information to get into the hands of competitors."[46]

Long before 1939 the price-competitive rules and practices defining the regulatory framework for aircraft manufacture were striking for their consistency; they remained unaltered year after year despite deep and outspoken opposition among the businessmen being regulated and their numerous supporters in the government. Congress ensured that regulation of the industry continued unchanged into 1940. Army and navy officials were regularly called to account for how contracts were let and to reassure congressmen that "the method of purchase of airplanes and engines in quantity for the Aviation Expansion Program is strictly in accordance with both the letter and the spirit of the Air Corps Act of 1926. . . ." Also on watch for Congress, the Internal Revenue Service remained "fully alert to protect the interest of the Government in audits of costs and computations of excess profits."[47]

The sudden collapse of the Low Countries and France in May and June 1940, along with FDR's stirring May 16 call for annual output of 50,000 aircraft, at last persuaded congressmen to acknowledge the pleas of contracting officers and put aside their suspicions of the industry to speed aircraft supply. Again, FDR pulled the figure out of the air, hoping to generate the largest possible emotional commitment to preparedness.[48] Congressmen fell into line even faster than their predecessors had in 1917. They made appropriations for aircraft totaling $2.9 billion by mid-summer and changed the procurement laws. Carl Vinson led the way, sponsoring a bill passed in late June that temporarily repealed the Vinson-Trammell Act and gave the navy discretionary power to negotiate with aircraft firms. It was also authorized to make 30 percent advance payments and to sign cost-plus, fixed-fee contracts. In early July Congress passed a bill extending these powers to the War Department.[49]

How to use these new laws to cope with the accumulated disorders of the aircraft industrial base and to erect upon it a framework for enormous output were problems for those FDR was obliged to recruit from among America's business elite.[50] In existing plants multiplied in size and in new, giant, "greenfield" plants across the land—Long Beach, Omaha, Willow Run, Buffalo, Columbus, Marietta, Dallas, and so on—it took these men only two years to achieve massive output, in large part because politics and ideology as applied through procurement law had been pushing firms and their work forces in that direction against the grain for some time. Significantly, new competition, associationalism, or the other designations of an American political economy of corporatism were not revived. They were not enlisted on behalf of the wartime aircraft program—the heart of America's war economy—as they had been continually in the industry from World War I through the failure to win a code of fair competition under the NRA. By 1940 America's corporate elite was extremely wary in matters of political economy. Notably absent was the sense of experimentation in business-government relations, of building new and permanent patterns of cooperation between private and public spheres, and of the special roles of technology-driven industries such as aircraft on behalf of these goals. In the crisis of the early 1930s such aspirations, even proposals for comprehensive state planning, found a receptive if unenthusiastic audience among businessmen. However, after years of mainly negative experiences with various New Deal agencies and innovations, most businessmen realized that the American state threatened as much as it promised. By the late 1930s they hoped to turn the tide of increasingly extensive government intervention in business affairs, and the conservative Seventy-sixth Congress was only too eager to help.[51]

Of special concern were New Deal measures infringing directly upon day-to-day business decisions and traditional business prerogatives. Labor laws were of first importance here. Nevertheless the limits of New Deal labor laws, compounded in aircraft by the Machinists' obstructions to effective worker organization, helped ensure that of all the difficulties faced by the aircraft program's "dollar-a-year" managers, those connected with labor would be the most vexing. From labor turnover and strikes to absenteeism and the distribution of man- and womanpower, the complexity of each was a legacy of industrial relations during the interwar years.[52] The failure of unionism in aircraft during the period of the NRA denied the industry a stabilizing mechanism and a new, organized constituency with which Congress's regulation might have been countered and the problems of manpower mobilization eased. Instead the open shop in aircraft prevailed almost everywhere well into the war, and labor relations were marked by constant turbulence and animosity. Still the major factor of production costs during the late 1930s (see Table 3.2), wages and working conditions remained the chief determinants of profitable or losing aircraft contracts. Until cost-plus contracting in 1940 relieved the pressure, unregulated wages and working conditions continued to provide the manufacturers critical maneuvering room in Congress's competitive business environment.

For keeping labor relations unregulated after the NRA, manufacturers could credit their own resolute opposition to unionization, their illegal intimidation of workers, actions against industrial unionism on the part of the Machinists, and effective representation of the industry on labor matters in Washington by the Aeronautical Chamber of Commerce. Until 1939 the chamber's main function for the industry was antilabor, curbing federally mandated increases in labor costs and deflecting other labor policy initiatives, which were "of mounting importance . . . to the members."[53] The only time between the NRA and the war when the ACC acted genuinely on behalf of the industry as a whole came during a brief period in 1938. The Walsh-Healy Act of 1936, the "little NRA," mandated time and a half overtime pay and the fixing of minimum wages for workers on federal contracts. When the new Public Contracts Board in the Department of Labor finally got around to aircraft in December 1938, the chamber with the industry's full support successfully pressed for a minimum wage of a mere fifty cents and exemption of those who worked on development contracts. So low were the base minimum-wage provisions of the Fair Labor Standards Act of June 1938, the last major piece of New Deal social legislation, that the ACC felt it could be safely ignored.[54]

As the war neared, much of the chamber's energy was absorbed by trying to contain other government initiatives on aircraft labor, which it grimly described as part of "a broad program of control of business activities under centralized government regulation." Particularly disturbing were "grave" attempts by bureaucrats in the Labor Department, the Civilian Conservation Corps, and the National Youth Administration to assume control over aircraft worker recruitment, apprenticeship, training, distribution, and housing. Manufacturers preferred local control over their labor supply and either their own, municipal, or private technical and trade schools. Federal involvement, they insisted, should go no further than providing subsidies. Companies like Curtiss in Buffalo found that containing federal efforts in the supply of skilled workers was yet another inducement toward trimming their reliance on the skilled and toward pushing the "functionalization of procedure at our factory." They were happy to report that proposed federal training programs were unnecessary. "With this change in operations, by localizing operations, we find that the number of skilled employees are not as great as we first expected" and that local, unemployed, and unskilled workers could meet hiring needs. Manufacturers hoped that emphasis on the scale of expansion, on numbers of workers, and on the "marked freezing of designs for mass production" would diffuse federal attempts at "barging into our personnel expansion picture."[55]

For their great leeway in relations with their workers, manufacturers could also thank a residue of proud resistance among skilled workers in particular plants to the idea of working for aircraft workers as a whole. Also, the constant drain on activists' energies persisted in the ongoing feuds within the labor movement, now between the Machinists-AFL and the new Congress of Industrial Organizations (CIO) and within both groups as well. Under the NRA, the Machinists had done everything necessary to thwart the movement for an industrial union. During the later 1930s its initiatives in the industry were driven mainly by the desire to thwart or match the CIO's drive in aircraft, efforts made difficult by the IAM's bitter reputation among aircraft workers since the NRA years.

At least one manufacturer could also thank the United States Army for its direct intervention in labor organization at a timely moment. Federal labor law became much more explicit than it had been under the NRA after congressional passage and Supreme Court approval of the Wagner Act in 1935 and 1937. Moreover, the new National Labor Relations Board's "vigorous and uncompromising enforcement" of a national "common law of labor relations" was critical to the successes of industrial unionism during 1937–1939 throughout American industry.[56] Still, Glenn

Welders and machinists at the Glenn L. Martin Company in Baltimore, July 1937. In the foreground are engine mounts and a jig for the gun-turret nose of the obsolete B-10 bomber, then being produced in quantity for export.

Martin was able to serve the industry as a model of how to deny workers their rights. In August 1937 the IAM responded to rumors that the CIO was organizing at the Martin plant in Baltimore by launching a drive of its own. It confidently expected that Martin "would prefer us rather than the CIO," which was supposedly guided by "communistic thinking." But the plant proved to be a "dead area" for both the IAM and the CIO, each respectively signing up only sixteen and fifty of 2,300 workers after six months' effort. Constant sniping between them repelled workers, and skilled workers who received their training at community polytechnicals felt that "they are way ahead of labor organizations." If some workers were not contemptuous of professional organizers and their less skilled fellows or intimidated by employment patterns of constant turnover and continuing deprivation in the Baltimore area, they had to contend with Martin's spies and the company union.[57]

Only after NLRB decisions outlawing company unions in other local plants and an aggressive effort at Martin by local IAM agents who pointedly declared their independence from the IAM Grand Lodge did Martin workers show enough interest in unionization to justify an NLRB representation election. In September 1938, however, the 12th Infantry encamped on the plant's lawn on election day. The "Army had set up machine guns and [were] packing 45s on the hips." Referring to the 1937 Memorial Day Massacre on the south side of Chicago in which ten strikers were shot by police, the Martin workers "wondered if they were going to have a repeat of the Republic Steel situation" and voted the company union. The IAM again collapsed at Martin. Its organizers and their families were harassed by the company, and its constituency was becoming even less likely as the factory and production process were being reorganized for mass production of exports and the much greater use of regimented unskilled labor. It was difficult to "counteract the timidity of the new boys who . . . are not indignant at the company . . . whose standard of living has always been very low . . . when they make $18 a week they are nigger rich and content." By late 1939, eleven thousand worked at Martin, mostly "country boys . . . who have never worked before and have never heard of an organization." According to *Fortune*, "Martin has had to organize his plant almost along military lines." There was a "protection force of 40 uniformed men . . . to prevent sabotage" but also to monitor union activists. There were dozens of foremen and supervisers, and "hundreds of 'pushers' or 'leaders' who are the nerve endings of the labor control system."[58] The main output of this regime was the obsolescent Martin Model 167 attack bomber for export mainly to the French. High profits from these export sales, enhanced by low wages and preserved by a strict policy of no dividend payments, provided Martin with the resources to design one of the nation's outstanding wartime aircraft, the B-26 Marauder.

Satisfied that its efforts in aircraft during the NRA years had obstructed organization of aircraft workers by anyone, the Machinists ignored the industry until 1936 when Boeing's management sought them out. Since its attempts in 1928-1930 to impose some measure of order on the aircraft industry through corporate integration, Boeing had led the search for anticompetitive mechanisms. Its executives continued to view uniform working conditions as central to industry-wide stability. In 1936 they hoped to avoid the labor strife then plaguing much of American industry ànd stabilize their work force for production of the B-17 bomber. Having received the first production order for thirteen in January 1936 and expecting many more orders, they had constructed a new plant on the Duwamish Waterway. Boeing offered IAM Lodge #751 a closed shop

Some of the first 13 production B-17s in formation over Manhattan for the American Legion parade, September 21, 1937.

and an average wage of eighty-one cents—highest in the industry—in exchange for no-strike pledges, promises of an end to disruptive battles for craft jurisdiction, job classifications kept few and vague, and most importantly, assurances that vigorous efforts would be made to organize Martin and the Southern California plants of Douglas at Santa Monica, Consolidated in San Diego, and North American beside the Los Angeles airport at Inglewood.[59]

These firms actively competed in the bomber market, and their underpaid labor maintained heavy pressure on the prices Boeing could command for the B-17. Neither firm had a four-engine bomber design as an alternative to Boeing's Flying Fortress, but Air Corps doctrine had not yet congealed around the heavy bomber. The Martin B-10 and Douglas B-18 two-engine medium bombers had their adherents, and their lower labor costs added to their attractiveness. Still, even had the B-17 been the Air Corps' unrivaled choice, the pressure from low wages at Boeing's competitors would have continued since each could build the B-17, and

Boeing had no legal claim to its design, whose cost amounted to $650,000 by May 1939.[60]

In spring 1939 the Air Corps took full advantage of the pressure on aircraft prices stemming from Congress's nonrecognition of design rights by doing little to dispel rumors that it was entertaining bids for forty B-17s from such firms as the United subsidiary, Sikorsky Aircraft. By then, however, the emergence in the mock-up stage of the Consolidated B-24 Liberator provided the Air Corps all the leverage it needed with Boeing, which it naturally preferred for B-17 work. General Brett explained the situation to General Arnold: "this means of bringing in an additional source of supply for heavy bombers [B-24s] will react as an advantage in negotiation with the manufacturer of the B-17 model airplane. It is to be noted that the prices quoted by Boeing Aircraft Company in quantity production are in excess of production prices quoted by Consolidated . . . ," and were 40 percent higher than estimates presented to Congress.[61]

In view of FDR's urgent call for large numbers of combat aircraft and the hundreds of millions of dollars soon to be so freely spent on the Flying Fortress, one can only marvel at the months of haggling and delays during spring and summer 1939 as the Air Corps tried to shave $2,000 to $3,000, or 1–2 percent, from the B-17's unit cost—unless one had a sense of how Congress had imposed a culture of suspicion and explicit legal strictures upon contracting officers. Boeing's contract for thirty-eight B-17s worth $8.1 million was not signed until September 20. The company soon found that it was not possible "to produce the aircraft without a loss." By spring 1940 the Air Corps wanted forty-two more B-17s from Boeing, but the prices it insisted upon were rejected by the consortium of banks that had participated in a 1939 Reconstruction Finance Corporation loan for Boeing and that held a veto over Boeing contracts.[62]

Unfortunately for Boeing, its investors, and its workers but happily for taxpayers who received the B-17 below cost well into the war, the assurances in 1936 of a national IAM campaign in aircraft were made by local Machinists in Seattle and were empty without the full support of the IAM Grand Lodge and the AFL. Through the second half of the 1930s IAM officials on the West Coast complained bitterly to their president, A. O. Wharton, about his "complete lack of true cooperation." They wanted a single district lodge for all West Coast aircraft workers, but Wharton insisted that "all plans for District Lodges on an industry wide basis must be fought to prevent national organization . . . District Lodges were de-

Finishing a zinc die in 1937 at the Boeing plant in Seattle for use in a drop-hammer press to form one of the thousands of sheet aluminum parts for the B-17. Returns on such operations depended on the quantity of aircraft ordered and the prices that could be extracted from Air Corps contracting officers.

Boeing workers prepare a B-17 cabin in 1937.

signed for all industries within communities." No organizers were appointed for California until 1938 and only then to counter the United Auto
Workers of the CIO. The Boeing IAM Lodge warned that its wage scale,
even if it was still only on a par with unskilled lumber workers in the area,
was undermining Boeing's competitiveness, threatening their members'
jobs, and preventing any improvements for them. "We are stalemated
with Boeing until other plants are organized and a basic scale is set for the
industry . . . our present scale already interferes with competitive bidding."[63]

Had these local officials received the full support of the IAM in 1936–
1939, the difficulties of organizing plants apart from Boeing probably
would have been insurmountable. Activists at Douglas despised the
Machinists for their 1934 obstructions and were not about to let them
benefit from a "lot of hard work in an uphill battle with Douglas." Adding
to such grudging feelings were the conservatism and elitism of most
skilled aircraft workers, their resentment for the growing numbers of
unskilled workers—"celery pickers"—and the fact that the struggle for

organization seemed nothing more than endless squabbling among different unions. Time, energy, and resources were wasted in battles between IAM locals and the CIO. Workers "have been kept dizzy by affiliation disputes."[64] The extreme fluidity of work forces further complicated the situation as the military's procurement methods brought about wide expansions and contractions in employment.

Yet in the eyes of local Machinists, the "lack of interest of the workmen [in unions] in the aircraft industry here," was due mainly to the Southern California manufacturers' open shop belligerence, the result of years of exacting price competition for military contracts and of a regional business culture of particularly virulent and effective anti-unionism, bent on keeping Southern California "the white spot of the open shop." In his crusade against the "industrial termites"—much aided by the Los Angeles district attorney and sheriff—Donald Douglas set the pace and ideological tone for the other manufacturers who flouted federal law and "cowed and intimidated" their workers with spies, agents provocateurs, private police forces, yellow-dog contracts, firings, and red-baiting propaganda. Despite the view among his executives that labor agreements meant greater efficiencies and far less disruption, Douglas insisted that "they fight to the end," that they "only meet with and enter into agreements when they have no recourse, when they are whipped." To head his "protection force" and direct the battle against organized labor, Douglas hired in 1938 James Davis, former chief of the Los Angeles Police Department, a "burly, dictatorial, somewhat sadistic, bitterly anti-union man," who had fathered the L.A.P.D.'s notorious Red Squad.[65]

The IAM collected some successes in Southern California, gaining brief and limited recognition and contracts at Lockheed in Burbank and Consolidated in San Diego. Even if these were not the "sweetheart deals" or IAM-sanctioned company unions as the United Auto Workers charged, they were still tenuous and of limited value for workers so long as Douglas, Northrop, Ryan, Vultee, and North American remained unorganized and continued to pay "sweatshop" wages averaging 20–25 percent less than the competition. Through the secretive Southern California Aircraft Industry Association, these firms used a "scientific blacklist" to take advantage of the flow of labor in and out of each other's plants, driven by the cycles of military contracts and supplied by the steady migration of youthful workers mainly from rural areas to the east. After being laid off, a worker's clearance papers were stamped with a numerical code that only personnel managers understood and that provided a measure of the worker's competence, past involvement with unions, and last wage. If deemed acceptable as a new hiree, he or she was offered a take-it-or-leave-it position at ten to twenty cents less than his or her previous rate. The Walsh-Healy Public Contracts law provided a minimal base of fifty cents per hour but it applied only to army and navy work, not to export or commercial orders. Another way southern California manufacturers maintained marginal profits on their rapidly streamlining factory operations was to get new workers to pay to work in their plants. Union organizers continually complained about "gip schools" that recruited eager young men from high school and from out of state with promises of "aeronautical training." Tuition ran as high as $600, and students were merely shown how to rivet, sent to the plants, paid a minumum wage for a few months, and then laid off to make way for the next graduate.[66]

These illegal activities and the manufacturers' ability to engage in them with impunity suggest the limits of New Deal departures in industrial relations, even after the Wagner Act. At the same time they suggest the threat of those departures to aircraft manufacturers and what might have been accomplished for workers and the industry had they been able to build effective organizations under NIRA. Labor relations in other industries during this period were of a similar tone, but among aircraft employers hostility was unique. Douglas was not organized until 1944; Curtiss-Buffalo not until 1942; Martin-Baltimore and Wright-Patterson finally in 1943; Pratt & Whitney in 1945. Grumman was never organized. While the demands of mobilization for war did much to shore up the broad position of industrial unionism,[67] its impact in aircraft was long delayed. Mirroring the situation under the NRA, when workers' representatives with no organizational base had minimal influence over the industry's response to crisis, the labor movement played an incidental role in planning the wartime expansion. The results were the preservation of the industry's centrifugal structural patterns, the great unattractiveness of the wartime industry to workers, and constant dilemmas for firms trying to recruit and keep a stable and reliable work force.[68]

Limiting federal intervention in labor markets was of prime concern to dollar-a-year men bent on containing the New Deal, but they were also committed to holding the line across the field. For the men from Wall Street like Secretary of War for Air Robert Lovett, the government's tremendous new national presence through army and navy purchasing was both essential for the nation's military survival and economic growth and convenient for the preservation of an independent business system which they led.[69] Practically unlimited funds for procurement meant that the still unresolved economic dilemmas and social conflicts that had given rise to corporatist thinking and the New Deal could be substantially quelled. A new culture of state intervention on a vast scale and more attuned to the preferences and needs of private enterprise could be erected upon the spending powers of the War and Navy departments, which in 1939 were "about to be converted into a kind of gigantic Bourse," according to Eliot Janeway. So far these powers had been left largely latent in the face of chronic depression. A new military-industrial complex could help curb the accomplishments of liberal New Deal progressives, social Keynesians, and the labor movement; mitigate the economic conditions that had paved the way for these accomplishments; and contain new proposals from the Left for the use of emergency war powers to further advance its agenda. That agenda found notable expression in the much publicized Reuther Plan of 1940, a proposal by Walter Reuther of the United Auto Workers for a tripartite labor-, business-, and state-managed reordering of the aircraft and auto industries to fulfill not only FDR's call for 50,000 planes but also a vision of greater social equity and industrial democracy.[70]

The Reuther Plan and similar schemes were deflected, however, by the war economy's managers, for whom the practices of military Keynesianism posed much less of a challenge to American traditions of political culture, market capitalism, and business voluntarism. Military Keynesianism meant the active use of the state's monetary and fiscal powers, as proposed by John Maynard Keynes, but the jettisoning of those parts of his program that urged careful administration and ongoing planning for full employment and redistribution of the nation's wealth. This curtailed Keynesianism proved a potent and attractive solution to the contradictions between voluntarist American political culture and the need for ongoing state intervention to encourage demand, which the depression had made clear. Its attractions persisted through the postwar decades, as the bulk of those federal dollars not generated by self-financed programs such as Social Security were spent by the military and as planning or administrative intervention went little further than imposing upon national life ideas and assumptions about the size and scope of military needs and the directions of military technology. Also, there were the powerful yet collateral shaping demands of bureaucratic politics at the Pentagon and constituency politics on Capitol Hill.

Thus even though complaints of delays, cross-purposes, and waste were frequent throughout industrial mobilization for World War II, there were sound political and ideological reasons for not altering the haphazard and administrative backwardness of military supply left over from the interwar years. As in World War I, America's military emergency was never so critical that rigorous central direction and the adjournment of "politics as usual" were necessary. Even when the crises in production of 1941–1942 forced greater centralization, direction of the "warfare state" remained bureaucratically divided, ad hoc, and essentially responsive to the traditional voluntarist values of American business.[71] Again, the scale of funding and resources available subsumed the disorder, which the dollar-a-year-men preferred to the coercions of a state they could not necessarily control.

The particular disorders of military aircraft supply were similarly not solved but overwhelmed—and thus preserved—by a combination of unlimited demand, highest priority granted aircraft workers and materials, more realistic contracting terms, and the superhuman efforts of plant managers, workers, and bureaucrats in the contracting bureaus and offices of the war and navy assistant secretaries for air. Production planners were much more pragmatic than their World War I predecessors had been, much less driven by desires to prove new theories of political economy. They were considerably aided in that metal construction made mass output of aircraft more feasible than it had been during the stick, wire, and glue days of World War I. And the industry had already taken important steps in mass-production techniques. Aircraft, too, were more powerful, more durable, more tolerant of imperfect construction. When imperfections or enemy improvements could not be adequately offset by sheer numbers, the program's managers were willing and able to scrap whole assembly lines and turn to new models. They had the time and resources that their enemies could never match. And again unlike their World War I predecessors, they had channelled good shares of these toward the kind of research and development that Congress's interwar industry could never afford and which produced such inimitable craft as the Superfortress, Mustang, Hellcat, and Corsair.[72]

The World War II managers of aircraft production did not see their task as an exercise in reformist social intervention. They accepted the framework of Congress's business and the social vision it embodied. They were willing to work within these and were able to because of funding and demand that were given no boundaries either by Congress, the Treasury, or military doctrine. Their general approach is suggested by their response to the inherited fragmented pack of separate aircraft firms, always suspicious of the government and jealous of their independence and competitive positions when hostilities ended. Instead of the new competition of the associationalist state championed by Howard Coffin during

World War I or the concentration and rationalization of the industry that animated Charles Lawrence's efforts during the New Era and early New Deal, the managers of the aircraft program pursued the firm-by-firm approach, the tradition in the government's dealings with the industry. The conservative business leaders and high contracting officers who oversaw the program had no reason for structural reform of the industry. Every firm now had plenty to do, and the resources were there for the expansion and financial stability of all the industry's participants, no matter how poorly managed. The War and Navy departments rarely intervened directly in the organization and management of aircraft firms, even though their sudden transformation into giant defense contractors was often beyond their abilities. The military pressed for new management at Republic Aviation in spring 1941 and for the ouster from Consolidated of the obstreperous Reuben Fleet, who was replaced in late 1942 by Thomas Girdler, former president of Republic Steel and bête noire of the labor movement. These moves were exceptions illustrating the rule of business autonomy and voluntarism that guided the policies of the aircraft program's managers. Otherwise, wartime spending solidified the competitive, unwieldy, and overbuilt structure of Congress's interwar aircraft industry.

CHAPTER EIGHT

Conclusion

This study stresses the role of political culture in the formation of the American aircraft industry, in the early development of aeronautic technology, and in the origins of the contemporary military-industrial complex. It suggests the limits of institutional or technological approaches to business and industrial history and the history of political economy. The key factors in aircraft were ideology and traditional ways of government. Because aircraft manufacture was a military enterprise—a political industry—congressmen were able to use funding and contracting law to make it a bastion of free-market enterprise, antitrust, and antistatism—values and practices more attuned to a seemingly bygone era of proprietary, competitive capitalism.

Political culture applied through contracting rules proved stronger than the imperatives of a powerful technology and the tendencies toward concentration of an industry so reliant on complex and high-cost research and development. It also proved stronger than the pressures toward an integrated, mutually supportive framework of military-industrial relations, which high-technology weapons need. Congress's influence over the early aircraft industry underscores the resiliency of traditional values and arrangements and their power in shaping the challenges of economic and technological change as much as they were shaped by them. The old tension within American politics between democratic ideals and concentrated economic and social power was reproduced and given institutional momentum in the early military-industrial complex for aircraft.

During the 1920s and 1930s the social vision of economic individualism remained potent in Congress, especially on its military and naval committees. The aircraft industry, high profile and directly dependent on them for its essential military business, offered congressmen a unique opportunity to act on their views. Given these factors, Congress would surely have insisted on price competition for aircraft and on highly restricted links between the industry and the air forces, regardless of its assessment of the industry's performance in World War I. Unfortunately for the industry and its technology, the broad but erroneous conclusion that America's costly wartime failure to mass-produce advanced aircraft was due to some business conspiracy led to an even stricter adherence to Congress's onerous terms for the military aircraft business.

To be sure, Congress's success in having its way in this industry was possible because of the noneconomic goals and dedication of aircraft entrepreneurs and designers who, like William Boeing, Donald Douglas, Glenn Martin, and Clement Keys, accepted Congress's terms, wanting to be part of this new technology, build better aircraft, develop the nation's air power, and perhaps profit in some distant future. Aircraft workers, too, were a critical factor. They sacrificed much to stay in this low-wage industry, whether out of economic necessity, infatuation with its unique products, or for a chance to use old craft skills and be part of the manufacturing process in ways that were becoming increasingly rare on the nation's assembly lines. Investors also carried the burden, underwriting Congress's business at a crucial point in the evolution of aeronautics during the Hoover administration and allowing the government to continue exploiting aircraft firms and workers into the New Deal era. When funds generated by the 1927–1929 stock boom were depleted, a profitable export market for military aircraft emerged to help carry the industry until the explosion of demand during World War II. Together, these kept the industry and American aeronautics competitive during the interwar years and often the leader internationally. Without them Congress would have had to pursue a much less wasteful and disruptive approach to the industry, assuming its desire for a viable aircraft industry was sufficiently compelling.

The role of an old social vision, of political choice, in the development of the aircraft industry and its relations with the state is underscored by the alternative for development proposed by industry leaders but regularly rejected by Congress, most importantly in the Air Corps Act of 1926 and the industry's attempt to win a New Deal from the National Recovery Administration. This corporatist or associationalist alternative was based on the idea that the most effective way to pursue aeronautics and provide for the nation's air power was to let manufacturers, designers, and military experts plan and manage an exclusive group of producers, free from the financial and market pressures of commercial enterprise. In the aircraft industry's case, with its meager commercial opportunities and overwhelming dependence on specialized military sales, such pressures existed only because Congress imposed them through contracting law, creating an artificial commercial market. Had Congress tolerated just one element of the associationalists' proposals—full recognition of the manufacturers' rights to their designs—much of the rest of their program would have fallen into place. Particularly after the end of the low-cost, stick-and-wire biplane days during the 1920s, the industry probably would have concentrated into a stable, exclusive group of firms with more effective and less bitter labor relations.

This alternative would have had its limitations too, as must any framework for managing so dynamic a technology as aeronautics and the endless complications of producing a wide range of militarily effective warplanes. A basic difficulty would have been that in the associationalist framework, aeronautics would have been freer to develop more quickly, with greater sophistication, and with clearer direction. It would have been harder to coerce military aeronautics into the patterns of design and production needed to satisfy the powerful idea of continuous-flow mass production as the way America worked best and the equally unshakable perception of air power as a large-scale weapon used overwhelmingly. Congress's business was well suited for accommodating these prevailing views. Two decades of contracting law's constant pressure for simple, low-cost, quantity output resulted in an industry in need of little more than massive expansion to achieve staggering wartime production. Many writers have pointed out the logic of America's industrial approach to fighting World War II and the bureaucratic, intellectual, and cultural history of the doctrine of large-scale, destructive air power.[1] Along with the shaping role of political culture in the development of the warfare state, defense industries, and their technologies, the early experiences suggest the connections among war strategy, military doctrine, and the social base of weapons supply.

Top Contractors with the U.S. Army Air Service, 1919–1925

Company	Main Product	Total Contract Value
Aeromarine Plane and Motor Hammondsport, N.Y.	airplanes, engines	$1,161,151
Atlantic Aircraft Hasbrouck Heights, N.J.	engine accessories	366,977
Boeing Airplane Seattle	airplanes	3,945,547
Chance Vought Long Island City, N.Y.	airplanes	397,870
Consolidated Aircraft Buffalo	airplanes	740,946
Curtiss Aeroplane Buffalo	airplanes, engines	3,326,315
Dayton Engineering Labs Dayton, Ohio	engine parts	168,310
Douglas Aircraft Santa Monica, Calif.	airplanes	456,882
Eberhart Steel Products Buffalo	airplanes	988,731
Elias & Bros. Buffalo	airplanes	426,421
Fairchild Aerial Camera New York City	cameras	114,543
Gallaudet Aircraft Norwich, R.I.	airplanes	893,643
General Electric Schenectady, N.Y.	electrical equipment	128,560
Goodyear Tire & Rubber Akron	airships	381,696

Company	Main Product	Total Contract Value
Huff Daland Ogdensburg, N.Y.	airplanes	456,402
Irving Airchute Buffalo	parachutes	395,735
Loening Aero Engineering Long Island City, N.Y.	airplanes	879,874
Glenn L. Martin Cleveland	airplanes	1,780,320
National Steel Products Dayton	hardware	222,122
Ordnance Department Rock Island Arsenal, Ill.	spares, guns	294,369
Packard Motors Detroit	engines	1,235,399
Steel Products Engineering Springfield, Ohio	spares	305,263
Thomas Morse Ithaca, N.Y.	airplanes	1,431,323

Source: "Statement Showing Manufacturers and Location . . . ," Feb. 24, 1925, Office of the Chief of the Air Service, Procurement Section, Planning Branch Records, box 1, entry 276, AAF Records, RG 18, National Archives, Washington, D.C.

Major Army and Navy Production Contracts before the Air Corps Act

		Model	Qty.	Cost/Unit	Method of Contracting
1921	Curtiss	TS-1	11	$9,569	negotiated
1921	Curtiss	TS-1	23	9,975	open bidding
1922	Douglas	DT-2	18	16,925	negotiated
1922	Vought	VO-1	18	10,065	negotiated
1923	LWF	DT-2	20	15,510	open bidding
1923	Douglas	DT-2	20	15,585	open bidding
1923	Vought	VO-1	13	11,540	negotiated
1923	Martin	MO-1	30	26,072	negotiated
1924	Vought	VO-1	24	11,650	negotiated
1924	Boeing	NB-1	50	7,700	negotiated
1924	Martin	CS-1	35	25,200	open bidding
1924	Boeing	NB-1	22	7,265	negotiated
1924	Vought	VO-1	20	9,300	negotiated
1925	Martin	CS-2	40	19,836	open bidding
1925	Vought	VO-1	40	10,111	negotiated
1925	Vought	VO-1	20	9,200	negotiated
1926	Loening	OL-3	10	22,115	negotiated
1926	Martin	T3M-1	24	23,711	negotiated
1926	Boeing	FB-5	27	22,250	open bidding
1926	Curtiss	F6C-3	35	12,938	negotiated
1926	Consol.	NY-1	20	8,630	negotiated
1926	Consol.	NY-1	16	8,150	negotiated
1926	Martin	T3M-2	100	12,256	open bidding
1926	Consol.	NY-1	10	8,240	negotiated
1926	Vought	FV-1	20	10,313	negotiated
1927	Curtiss	F6C-4	31	11,808	negotiated
1927	Boeing	F2B-1	32	12,650	negotiated

Source: Hearings before the Subcommittee on Aeronautics . . . , 73rd Cong., 1st sess., 1934 (Delaney Hearings), 427.

Navy Aircraft Contracts Valued above $100,000, by Firm and Method of Contracting, 1926–1933

Firm	Year	Aircraft Quantity	Contract Value[1]	Method of Contracting
Bellanca Aircraft	1932	4	$114,507	not advertised
B/J Aircraft	1931–33	19	369,518	advert. and negot.
Boeing Airplane	1927–33	531	8,421,095	advert. and negot.
		136	1,414,227	open competition
Chance Vought	1927–33	300	8,402,799	advert. and negot.
Consolidated	1931–33	52	1,127,817	advert. and negot.
		23	1,726,249	open competition
		21	1,799,500	not advertised
Curtiss Aeroplane	1926–33	670	6,208,839	not advertised
		626	12,454,740	advert. and negot.
		68	297,061	open competition
Detroit Aircraft	1931	5	166,332	advert. and negot.
Douglas Aircraft	1927–33	425	7,691,918	advert. and negot.
		20	244,792	not advertised
Fokker Aircraft	1929–31	32	1,221,387	advert. and negot.
Great Lakes	1932	1	128,630	advert. and negot.
Grumman Aircraft	1931–33	23	1,430,211	advert. and negot.
		34	687,771	not advertised
Martin, Glenn L.	1927–33	136	6,093,125	advert. and negot.
		10	1,676,394	not advertised
Sikorsky Aviation	1930	10	427,337	advert. and negot.
		3	165,562	open competition

[1]Includes spare parts, engines, services, and materials

Source: Compiled from "Navy Contracts on File in Comptroller's Office Showing Method of Procurement of Aircraft," *Hearings before the Subcommittee on Aeronautics . . . ,* 73rd Cong., 1st sess., 1934 (*Delaney Hearings*), 1481–88.

Overcapacity in the U.S. Airframe Industry by Plants in Man-Hours per Month, December, 1939

Plant	Man-Hours per Month, December 1939	Potential Man-Hours per Month,[1] December 1939
Martin	1,784,990	2,772,800
Douglas-Northrop (El Segundo)	291,144	374,674
Douglas (Santa Monica)	1,050,000	1,530,000
Lockheed	884,870	1,325,745
Boeing	685,400	1,299,750
Consolidated	354,399	1,213,100
Curtiss-Wright (Buffalo)	398,590	1,039,800
Curtiss-Wright (St. Louis)	0	285,450
North American	646,410	814,510
Vought-Sikorsky	207,960	693,200
Beech	93,582	311,940
Bell	129,975	701,865
Bellanca	14,400	285,000
Brewster	341,000	439,200
Cessna	13,691	151,638
Fairchild	55,629	225,290
Fleetwings	32,407	779,850
Grumman	129,975	381,260
Porterfield	10,745	69,320
Republic	103,000	259,950
Ryan	67,587	207,960
Spartan	9,705	43,325
St. Louis	10,398	173,300
Stearman	58,922	168,000
Stinson	49,217	121,310
Vega	25,648	155,970
Vultee	55,725	100,000
Waco	19,065	129,975

Plant	Man-Hours per Month, December 1939	Potential Man-Hours per Month,[1] December 1939
Arrow	21,316	415,920
Burnelli	3,466	103,980
Culver	10,398	48,524
ERC	11,438	95,315
Kellet Autogiro	9,358	51,990
Piper	16,983	200,162
Pitcairn	0	103,980
Taylorcraft	15,944	67,587
Totals	7,613,337	17,141,640

[1]Based on 40-hour week

Source: From AAG Records 1939–1942, 452.1, series 2, classified, box 792, RG 18, National Archives, Washington, D.C.

CHAPTER ONE. INTRODUCTION

1. F. Braudel, *Wheels of Commerce* (New York: Harper & Row, 1982), 461.

2. W. H. McNeill, *The Pursuit of Power: Technology, Armed Force, and Society since A.D. 1000* (Chicago: University of Chicago Press, 1982), chaps. 7, 8. See also Thomas L. McNaugher, *New Weapons, Old Politics: America's Military Procurement Muddle* (Washington, D.C.: Brookings, 1989), and Benjamin Franklin Cooling, *Gray Steel and Blue Water: The Formative Years of America's Military-Industrial Complex, 1881–1917* (Hamden, Conn.: Archon Books, 1979), esp. 159 and chap. 8.

3. Studies of political economic reform in modern America that stress the predicaments Americans encountered as they pushed forward institutional change while retaining commitments to individualism, popular control, decentralization and the limited state include Stephen Skowronek, *Building a New American State* (New York: Cambridge University Press, 1982); Martin J. Sklar, *The Corporate Reconstruction of American Capitalism, 1890–1916* (New York: Cambridge University Press, 1988); Melvin I. Urofsky, *Big Steel and the Wilson Administration* (Columbus: Ohio State University Press, 1969); Robert D. Cuff, *The War Industries Board* (Baltimore: Johns Hopkins University Press, 1973); Ellis W. Hawley, *The New Deal and the Problem of Monopoly* (Princeton, N.J.: Princeton University Press, 1966); Barry D. Karl, *The Uneasy State* (Chicago: University of Chicago Press, 1983); Robert F. Himmelberg, *The Origins of the National Recovery Administration* (New York: Fordham University Press, 1976).

4. For this fluid conception of federal business regulation see Thomas K. McCraw, "Regulation in America: A Review Article," *Business History Review* 49 (Summer 1975): 159–183, and David Vogel, *Fluctuating Fortunes: The Political Power of Business in America* (New York: Basic Books, 1989).

5. Maintaining the historical pattern, in the mid-1980s the military generated 66 percent of American aerospace demand. If NASA's demands are included, the figure rises to 75 percent. D. Todd and R. D. Humble, *World Aerospace: A Statistical Handbook* (London: Croom Helm, 1987), 146.

6. Barry Bluestone et al., *Aircraft Industry Dynamics* (Boston: Auburn House, 1981), 9–10; H. O. Stekler, *The Structure and Performance of the Aerospace Industry* (Berkeley: University of California Press, 1965), 154–155; R. Schlaifer and S. D. Heron, *The Development of Aircraft Engines and Fuels* (Boston: Harvard University Graduate School of Business Administration, 1950), 8, 28. For similar conclusions on the defense industry as a whole see J. F. Gorgol, "A Theory of the Military-Industrial Firm," Ph.D. dissertation, Columbia University, 1969, chap. 1, and Seymour Melman, "From Private to Pentagon Capitalism," in Melman, ed., *The War Economy of the United States* (New York: St. Martin's Press, 1971).

CHAPTER TWO. A NEW DILEMMA

1. For a similarly misguided mass-production approach to warships see David A. Hounshell, "Ford Eagle Boats and Mass Production during World War I," in Merritt Roe Smith, ed., *Military Enterprise and Technological Change* (Cambridge, Mass.: MIT Press, 1985), 175–202. For the limits of assembly-line mass production in aircraft see Tom Lilley et al., *Problems of Accelerating Aircraft Production during World War II* (Boston: Harvard University Graduate School of Business Administration, 1947), 32–41.

2. This formulation relies on the "flexible specialization" mode of manufacturing described in Michael J. Piore and Charles F. Sabel, *The Second Industrial Divide* (New York: Basic Books, 1984), 29–31, 268–272, and in Charles F. Sabel and Jonathan Zeitlin, "Historical Alternatives to Mass Production: Politics, Markets and Technology in Nineteenth Century Industrialization," *Past and Present*, no. 108, Aug. 1985, 144.

3. Quoted in "History of the Aircraft Production Board" (1920), 51, box 1, entry 107, Army Air Force (AAF) Records, Record Group 18, National Archives, Washington, D.C.; see also "Reasons and Excuses, If Any, Assigned for Failure to Produce," May 27, 1918, box 1, entry 22, AAF Records; Alfred Goldberg, *A History of the United States Air Force 1907–1957* (Princeton, N.J.: Van Nostrand, 1957), 13; Arthur Sweetser, *The American Air Service* (New York: D. Appleton & Co., 1919), 251–252; Benedict Crowell and Robert F. Wilson, *The Armies of Industry* (New Haven, Conn.: Yale University Press, 1921), 325–332; Frederick L. Paxson, *America at War 1917–1918* (Boston: Houghton, 1939), 111: "The provision of aircraft was not a matter of question, but of creation. The industry did not exist in the United States." For a better sense of the aircraft program's failure see C. F. O'Connell, Jr., "The Failure of the American Aeronautical Production and Procurement Effort during the First World War," M.A. thesis, Ohio State University, 1978, and C. J. Gross, "George Owen Squier and the Origins of Military Aviation," *Journal of Military History* 54 (July 1990): 281–305.

4. Goldberg, *Air Force*, 1–13; Archibald D. Turnbull and Clifford C. Lord, *History of United States Naval Aviation* (New Haven, Conn.: Yale University Press, 1949), 1–105; Irving B. Holley, Jr., *Ideas and Weapons* (New Haven, Conn.: Yale University Press, 1953), 25–38.

5. *Aviation*, Dec. 1, 1916, 295; *New York Times*, July 28, 1916, Jan. 1, 2, 21, 1917; Grover Loening, *Takeoff into Greatness* (New York: Putnam, 1968), 7–95.

6. Belief in the supremacy of American scientific and manufacturing expertise for war purposes was encouraged by Thomas A. Edison, chairman of the Naval

Consulting Board, and by Henry Ford. Upon the break in U.S. relations with Germany on Feb. 3, 1917, Ford assured the press that he would place his company, which had produced 600,000 cars in 1916, "at the disposal of the United States government" and would provide 1,000 submarines per day. Hounshell, "Ford Eagle Boats," 177–180.

7. Sweetser, *American Air Service*, 75–91; Michael S. Sherry, *The Rise of American Airpower* (New Haven, Conn.: Yale University Press, 1987), 17–19; "The Conquering Air Fleet," *Washington Post*, July 14, 1917. In 1916 the optimistic Coffin told NACA that "the problems confronting the aircraft industry are wonderfully simple compared with those of the automobile industry." Quoted in Alex Roland, 2 vols. *Model Research: The National Advisory Committee for Aeronautics 1915–1958* (Washington, D.C.: NASA, 1985) 1:35.

8. For a history of these politics that spoofs its title see Seward W. Livermore, *Politics Is Adjourned: Woodrow Wilson and the War Congress 1916–1918* (Middletown, Conn.: Wesleyan University Press, 1966).

9. *Congressional Record*, 65th Cong., 1st sess., July 14, debate on H.R. 5326, "A bill to authorize the President to increase temporarily the Signal Corps of the Army, and to purchase, manufacture, maintain, repair, and operate airships, and for other purposes," 5105–5143. During 1917 $59 million was appropriated for naval aviation and by the end of the war another $840 million for army aviation.

10. Morris Sheppard quoted in *Aviation*, Aug. 15, 1917, 111; Hearings on S.80, "A Bill to Establish a Department of Aeronautics and for Other Purposes," 65th Cong., 1st sess., June 12–July 2, 1917. For Coffin's testimony see 33–37. Turnbull and Lord, *Naval Aviation*, 96. Sweetser, *American Air Service*, 68–69; H. H. Arnold, *Global Mission* (New York: Harper, 1949), 54.

11. Sherry, *Rise of American Airpower*, 1–21; Joseph J. Corn, *Winged Gospel: America's Romance with Aviation, 1900–1950* (New York: Oxford University Press, 1983), 3–71; Dale Carter, *The Rise and Fall of the American Rocket State* (London: Verso Press, 1988).

12. David Kennedy, *Over Here: The First World War and American Society* (New York: Oxford University Press, 1982), 93–98; Cuff, *War Industries Board*; Ellis W. Hawley, *The Great War and the Search for a Modern Order* (New York: St. Martin's Press, 1979), 18–23.

13. A. J. Eddy, *The New Competition* (New York: D. Appleton & Co., 1912); William Appleman Williams, *The Contours of American History* (Chicago: Quadrangle, 1961), 425–438; Hawley, *Great War*, 3–15; E. W. Hawley, "Herbert Hoover, the Commerce Secretariat, and the Vision of an Associative State," *Journal of American History* 61 (June 1974): 116–140; Robert D. Cuff, "Herbert Hoover, the Ideology of Voluntarism and War Organization during the Great War," *Journal of American History* 64 (Sept. 1977): 358–372; see also Robert F. Himmelberg's untitled essay in *Herbert Hoover and the Crisis of American Capitalism*, J. J. Huthmacher and W. I. Susman, eds. (Cambridge, Mass.: Schenkman, 1973), 59–85, and Charles S. Maier, "Society as Factory," *In Search of Stability: Explorations in Historical Political Economy* (New York: Cambridge University Press, 1987) 19–69.

14. Howard Coffin, "Aircraft Industry Needs Standardization," *Aviation*, May 1, 1917, 309; Coffin to Walcott, Jan. 8, 30, 1917, box 15; S. S. Bradley to Coffin, Nov. 23, 1917; Coffin to Bradley, Jan. 8, 1918, box 14, entry 87, AAF Records; "Suggestions for Increasing Publicity, Conserving Good Will, and for Laying the Foundations of After the War Business," memo of the Curtiss Aeroplane and Motor Co.,

Sept. 9, 1918, series 1, box 3, Clement M. Keys Papers, Archives of the National Air and Space Museum, Smithsonian Institution, Washington, D.C.

15. Cuff, *War Industries Board*, 16–27, 40–42.

16. *New York Times*, July 9, 1916; *Aerial Age Weekly*, Sept. 18, Oct. 30, 1916; Roland, *Model Research*, 17–20, 33–37.

17. *New York Times*, Oct. 21, Dec. 19, 20, 1916.

18. Orville Wright, *How We Invented the Airplane*, ed. Fred C. Kelly, (New York: Dover, 1953) 3–22; Tom D. Crouch, *The Bishop's Boys: A Life of Wilbur and Orville Wright* (New York: Norton, 1989), 411–423; Fred Howard, *Wilbur and Orville: A Biography of the Wright Brothers* (New York: Knopf, 1987); *Aerial Age Weekly*, Aug. 14, 1916, 653; *New York Times*, Dec. 31, 1915, June 8, July 30, Aug. 8, 1916.

19. Edward M. Hagar, Wright-Martin president, to "All Manufacturers," Dec. 16, 1916, box 8, entry 87, AAF Records; *New York Times*, Dec. 20, 1916.

20. The aircraft and aviation industries' experiences during the interwar years suggest some qualification of Martin Sklar's argument that the trust question was settled during the Wilson years and became thereafter a merely "histrionic" political issue. Sklar, *Corporate Reconstruction*, 15, 20, 90, 173. Indeed the military-industrial complex for aircraft became a stronghold of the antitrust ethic.

21. Cuff, "Herbert Hoover," 369; Cuff, *War Industries Board*, 148; Austin K. Kerr, "Decision for Federal Control: Wilson, McAdoo, and the Railroads," *Journal of American History* 54 (Jan. 1967): 550–560; Lewis Gould, *Regulation and Reform* (New York: Knopf, 1986) 190–91.

22. Walcott to Coffin, Dec. 21, 1916; Coffin to Walcott, Jan. 4, 1917, box 8; Coffin to Walcott, Jan. 8, 30, 1917; Walcott to Coffin, Jan. 25, 1917; box 15; Arthur C. Cable, "The Aircraft Production Board: Report of its Activities during its First Four Months," box 2, entry 87, AAF Records; *Aerial Age Weekly*, Feb. 19, 1917, 650; Roland, *Model Research*, 34; *New York Times*, Dec. 29, 1916.

23. *Aerial Age Weekly*, Feb. 5, 1917, 525.

24. Cable, "The Aircraft Production Board"; Walcott to Wright Martin Corp., Feb. 6, 1917, box 12, entry 87, AAF Records; "Advisory Committee Report on Patent Situation," *Aviation*, Apr. 15, 1917, 268; Roland, *Model Research*, 37–43; Walcott to Daniels, Mar. 29, 1917, box 15, entry 87, AAF Records.

25. Walcott to Mingle, Apr. 25, 1917, box 8; Mingle to Coffin, May 5; AMA "News Item," May 11, 1917, box 18; Waldon to Coffin quoted, May 23; Walcott to Benton Crisp, May 23, 1917, box 8, entry 87, AAF Records.

26. "Suggested Outline of Work to be Undertaken . . . ," box 2, entry 87, AAF Records; Coffin's civilian appointees were Sydney Waldon, R. L. Montgomery (a Philadelphia financial consultant), and Edward A. Deeds of National Cash Register, Dayton Engineering Laboratories, and the recently formed Dayton-Wright Airplane Company. Deeds, who would become the focus of later efforts to blame the aircraft program's failure on scandal, quickly accepted his appointment but not until expressing some prophetic apprehension. "The public might not understand," he cabled. Deeds to Coffin, May 10, 1917, box 10, entry 87, AAF Records.

27. Goldberg, *Air Force*; Turnbull and Lord, *Naval Aviation*, 1–105.

28. Russell F. Weigley, *History of the United States Army* (New York: Macmillan, 1967), xii.

29. Holley, *Ideas and Weapons*, 63–64, 82–102.

30. Roland, *Model Research*, 10, 35–36.

31. Restrictions under Sec. 3648 of the Revised Statutes—"no advances of public

money shall be made in any case whatever"—were temporarily lifted in August 1917 but were made only in amounts that did not exceed 30 percent of the value of contracts involved and carried a 5 percent interest charge. See H.R. 5566, *Congressional Record*, 65th Cong., 2d sess., 5570, and "Organization, History of Finance," box 1, entry 111, AAF Records.

32. For the army's inexperience with private contractors see Anne Trotter, "Development of the Merchants of Death Theory," in B. F. Cooling, ed., *War, Business and American Society* (Port Washington, N.Y.: Kennikat Press, 1977), 77, and Roland, *Model Research*, 35–36.

33. James E. Hewes, Jr., *From Root to McNamara: Army Organization and Administration, 1900–1963* (Washington, D.C.: Center for Military History, 1975), 5; Cuff, *War Industries Board*, 62; see also Elias Huzar, *The Purse and the Sword: Control of the Army by Congress through Military Appropriations, 1933–1950* (Ithaca, N.Y.: Cornell University Press, 1950).

34. Turnbull and Lord, *Naval Aviation*, 10, 31, 45, 97–99.

35. Skowronek, *Building A New American State*, 212–234.

36. Livermore, *Politics is Adjourned*; Cuff, *War Industries Board*, 64–67, 111–137, 141–147; Cuff, "An Organizational Perspective on the Military-Industrial Complex," *Business History Review* 50 (Summer 1978): 254–255, 265; Hawley, *Great War*, 23–24; Karl, *Uneasy State*, 38; Skowronek, *Building a New American State*, 234–247.

37. Resolutions, June 12, 22, 1917, box 7; undated memo, box 2, entry 87, AAF Records.

38. B. J. Williams, AMA secretary to Coffin, June 4, 1917; Coffin to Russell, June 8, 1917; "Partial Statement of Mr. Howard E. Coffin to Aircraft Manufacturers' Association," July 11, 1917, box 14, entry 87, AAF Records.

39. "Memo for the Chief Signal Officer," Aug. 4, 1917; "Organization Chart, Equipment Division Air Service," box 10, entry 87, AAF Records; "History of Administrative Work in the Equipment Division of the Signal Corps," July 26, 1919, box 2, entry 111, AAF Records; Sweetser, American Air Service, 68–69.

40. "Minutes of the Subcommittee on Patents," June 18, 1917; "Resolution of the Board, Wright-Martin Aircraft Corporation," June 21, 1917; "Cross-License Agreement," box 8, entry 87, AAF Records.

41. "Protest of the Aeronautical Society of America against the Formation under Government Auspices of an Aircraft Trust, the Stifling of the Spirit of Invention in America and the Squandering of Public Monies," *Journal of the Aeronautical Society of America* 2 (Sept. 1917), box 4, entry 87, AAF Records; *New York Times*, Oct. 3, 1917.

42. Minutes of Coffin's meeting with the manufacturers, Sept. 10, 1917, box 14; Resolutions, Sept. 21, 1917, box 7, entry 87, AAF Records. Cost-plus bogey contracts were cost-plus contracts with an efficiency incentive—a provision for a percentage added to the manufacturer's fee of any reduction of anticipated costs.

43. Coffin to Baker, Aug. 20, 1917, box 2, entry 87, AAF Records; E. David Cronon, ed., *The Cabinet Diaries of Josephus Daniels 1913–1921* (Lincoln: University of Nebraska Press, 1963), 206, 215–218.

44. "Minutes of Special Meeting of the Executive Committee," Oct. 2, 1917, box 8; Gregory to Baker, Oct. 6, 1917, box 14, entry 87, AAF Records.

45. "Reorganization, Plans, and Sections," Feb. 6, 1918, box 2, entry 22, AAF Records; "Organization of Finance," Mar. 27, 1920, box 1, entry 111, AAF Records; quoted in *Aviation*, Apr. 15, 1918, 384. For a typical sample of army contracting

officers' suspicions see a memo signed by Maj. F. E. Smith, commander of the Finance Division, Mar. 8, 1918, box 17, entry 22, AAF Records: "There is in the undersigned's opinion no question about the intent of the Wright-Martin Corporation to take every possible advantage of the Government under the contract, and we are watching the situation very carefully to checkmate every move on their part." A major source of conflict between manufacturers and military accountants was the latter's surprising refusal to recognize interest on debt as an element of cost in cost-plus contracts.

46. S. S. Bradley, general manager of the MAA, to Aircraft Board, Oct. 23, 1917; Colonel Thompson, Finance Branch, to the judge advocate general, Nov. 19, 1917; Patent Committee to Aircraft Board, Jan. 14; Coffin to Daniels and Baker, Jan. 23, 1918; Daniels to Bradley, Mar. 28, 1918; "Supplemental Cross-License Agreement," box 8, entry 87, AAF Records; Clement Keys to Coffin, Dec. 20, 1917, box 9, entry 87, AAF Records. In the end the army paid out $750,000 to the MAA during the war. Maj. W. H. Frank to Joseph Ames, NACA chairman, Jan. 8, 1921, box 13, entry 22, AAF Records. The army and navy continued to pay the MAA one hundred dollars per aircraft during the interwar years.

47. Ryan to Baker Aug. 28, 1918, box 2, entry 22; "Reasons and Excuses, if Any, Assigned for Failure to Produce," May 27, 1918, box 1, entry 22, AAF Records.

48. See Crowell and Wilson, *Armies of Industry*, 333–416; Sweetser, *American Air Service*, chaps. 6–11; G. W. Mixter and H. H. Emmons, *United States Army Aircraft Production Facts* (Washington, D.C.: GPO, 1919), 33–46.

49. "The objectives of more weapons and of better weapons tend to pull in opposite directions . . . standardization brings stultification." Holley, *Ideas and Weapons*, 121, 123.

50. Piore and Sabel, *Second Industrial Divide*, 44, 47.

51. Quoted in *Aviation*, Aug. 15, 1917, 389. A visit to the support facilities of the National Air and Space Museum in Silver Hill, Md., where World War I aircraft are refurbished, conveys a sense of the overconfidence of those who hoped to mass-produce them. Ford quoted in Sweetser, *American Air Service*, 182. Sweetser noted that "the fine hand tooling abroad was entirely different from standardized machine work here," *American Air Service*, 172.

52. Henry Still, *To Ride the Wind: A Biography of Glenn L. Martin* (New York: 1964), 124–137; Loening, *Takeoff*, 101–107; Holley, *Ideas and Weapons*, 106.

53. Lybrand Ross Bros. & Montgomery, "Curtiss Aeroplane & Motor Corporation," July 2, 1917, box 16, entry 22, AAF Records.

54. Willys to Coffin, June 14, Aug. 21, 1917; Curtiss's suppliers refused to make any more deliveries except "on a spot-cash basis." Willys to Deeds, Sept. 12, 1917, box 9, entry 87, AAF Records; *Aerial Age Weekly*, Aug. 13, 769; *Aircraft Production, Hearings before the Subcommittee of the Senate Committee on Military Affairs*, 65th Cong., 2d sess., June 3–7, 1918; minutes of Coffin's meeting with the manufacturers, Sept. 10, 1917, box 14, entry 87, AAF Records.

55. "History of the SPAD—Single Pursuit Plane" (Jan. 1920), box 4, entry 111, AAF Records. The $30 million contract included 500 Italian Caproni bombers that were never built.

56. Ibid.; Willys to Coffin, Oct. 10, 19, 1917; Aircraft Board Resolution, Nov. 22, 1917; Morgan to Coffin, Nov. 26, 1917; Morgan to Coffin, Nov. 27, 1917, box 9, entry 87; "History of the Bristol Fighter," n.d., box 2, entry 111, AAF Records.

57. "Minutes of Meeting," Jan. 17, 1918, box 2; Coffin to Baker, Jan. 2, 1918, box 3, entry 87, AAF Records.

58. "Minutes of Meeting," Jan. 17, 1918, box 2, AAF Records.

59. J. E. Cole to A.B., Feb. 15; "Observations at Buffalo," Apr. 26; Major Smith, "Memo of Visit to Curtiss," May 17; N. T. Harrington to Benedict Crowell, Apr. 1918, box 16, entry 22; "Reorganization, Plans and Sections," Feb. 6, 1918, box 2, entry 22, AAF Records.

60. "History of the Bristol Fighter," box 2, entry 111, AAF Records.

61. Paxson, *America at War*, 79.

62. *New York Times*, May 2, 1918; for the constant attacks of Theodore Roosevelt, Henry Cabot Lodge, and other Republicans on the Wilson administration's mobilization efforts see Livermore, *Politics Is Adjourned*, 62–91.

63. Sweetser, *American Air Service*, 215; Paxson, *America at War*, 267; Livermore, *Politics Is Adjourned*, 125–137; judge advocate general to Aircraft Board, Feb. 14, 1918, box 1, entry 87, AAF Records; *Aircraft Production, Hearings before the Subcommittee of the Senate Committee on Military Affairs*, May 29–Aug.16, 1918, and Report no. 555, 65th Cong., 2d sess., Aug. 22, 1918; U.S. Department of Justice, *Report of the Hughes Aircraft Inquiry*, Oct. 25, 1918, copy in the *Congressional Record*, 65th Cong., 3d sess., 883–914.

64. Ryan to Baker, Aug. 28, 1918, box 2, entry 22, AAF Records.

65. Ryan testimony, *Aircraft Production, Hearings*, Aug. 15, 1918; Gray quoted in "History of the Administrative Work of the Equipment Division" (1919), box 2, entry 111, AAF Records; Holley, *Ideas and Weapons*, 68–80.

66. Ryan to Baker, Aug. 28, 1918, box 2, entry 22, AAF Records; Nash testimony, *Aircraft Production, Hearings*, Aug. 8, 1918.

67. "Diagram 36," box 3, entry 111, AAF Records; the Thomas Report, the result of the House investigation of aircraft production, in *Aviation*, July 1, 1918; Loening, *Takeoff*, 109–110, 116; Holley, *Ideas and Weapons*, 121, 126–132; O'Connell, "Failure," 58–62, 84. Unfortunately, records of the striking feat of production at Dayton-Wright do not seem to survive.

68. Mixter and Emmons, *Aircraft Production Facts*, 5, 29; Benedict Crowell and R. F. Wilson, *Demobilization* (New Haven, Conn.: Yale University Press, 1921), 199–213.

69. See esp. Hawley, *Great War*, 20, 26; William E. Leuchtenberg, "The New Deal and the Analogue of War," in John Braeman et al., eds., *Change and Continuity in Twentieth Century America* (Columbus: Ohio State University Press, 1964), 81–143.

CHAPTER THREE. CONGRESS'S BUSINESS

1. David A. Hounshell, *From the American System to Mass Production, 1800–1932* (Baltimore: Johns Hopkins University Press, 1984), 303.

2. Keys to Bradley, Mar. 30, 1925, series 4, box 5, Keys Papers; for samples of similar hostility within the postwar Air Service toward the "Aircraft Trust" see "History of the Development of Aircraft Production During the War of 1917," (1920), box 1, entry 111, AAF Records, and Maj. R. M. Jones to Gen. Mason Patrick, Apr. 24, 1923, box 66, entry 276, Records of the Planning Branch, Procurement Division, Office of the Assistant Secretary of War, 1921–1941, Record Group 107, National Archives, Washington, D.C.

3. G. R. Simonson, "The Demand for Aircraft and the Aircraft Industry, 1907–1958," *Journal of Economic History* 20 (Sept. 1960): 365.

4. William B. Stout, quoted in *Automotive Industries*, May 15, 1919, 1089.

5. For John Willys's complaints on Curtiss's debt load and failure to profit from the war and his fruitless appeals to the government's "sense of fairness" see Willys to W. C. Potter of the Bureau of Aircraft Production, Nov. 12, 1918, box 16, entry 22, AAF Records; for sketchy information on the status of wartime aircraft contracts see "Liquidation," July 1919, box 59, entry 22, AAF Records. The government held a Curtiss mortgage until 1929.

6. On this point see I. B. Holley, Jr., *Buying Aircraft: Materiel Procurement for the Army Air Forces* (Washington, D.C.: Office of the Chief of Military History, 1962), 35–36. On large deferred-development charges as a central accounting feature of high-tech weapons industries see McNeill, *Pursuit of Power*, 288–290.

7. Raskob to Keys, Dec. 26, 1922; see also Alfred P. Sloan to Keys, Jan. 18, 1923, series 4, box 19, Keys Papers.

8. C. M. Keys, *Hearings before the Select Committee of Inquiry into Operations of the United States Air Service*, House, 68th Cong., 1st sess., 1924 *(Lampert Hearings)*, 1132–1133; Reuben H. Fleet, *Hearings before the Subcommittee on Aeronautics Making Investigation into Certain Phases of the Manufacture of Aircraft and Aeronautical Accessories as They Refer to the Navy Department*, 73rd Cong., 1st sess., 1934 *(Delaney Hearings)*, 1092; G. L. Martin, *Delaney Hearings*, 728; "Douglas Aircraft Company, Inc., Special Circular," 1928, series 3, box 3, Keys Papers; Paul A. Dodd, *Financial Policies in the Aviation Industry* (Philadelphia: University of Pennsylvania, 1933), 47, 76. Boeing made an average of $140,000 per year from the end of 1921 to the end of 1926, the bulk of its returns coming during two profitable years, 1925–1926. "Official Circular," July 1, 1927, series 3, box 1, Keys Papers.

9. Holley, *Buying Aircraft*, 80. "Like barnacles on an ocean-going vessel, a superfetation of statutes, court decisions, administrative regulations . . . had developed to slow down or prohibit the Army's effective purchase of . . . materiel." R. Elberton Smith, *The Army and Economic Mobilization* (Washington, D.C.: Office of the Chief of Military History, 1959), 68.

10. Holley, *Buying Aircraft*, 86.

11. Keys, *Hearings on H.R. 11249, A Bill to Permit the Purchase of Naval Aircraft and Aircraft Engines without Advertisement and for Other Purposes*, House Naval Affairs Committee, 69th Cong., 1st sess., Apr. 1926 *(Butler Hearings)*, 2431; Stekler, *Structure and Performance*, 71; M. J. Peck and F. M. Scherer, *The Weapons Acquisition Process* (Boston: Harvard University Graduate School of Business Administration, 1962), 344–345.

12. Baker to Senate Committee on Military Affairs, Aug. 28, 1919, box 16, entry 22, AAF Records; Francis A. Callery, "Aircraft Finance," *Air Affairs*, Summer 1947, quoted 484; John B. Rae, *Climb to Greatness* (Cambridge, Mass.: MIT Press, 1968), 8; Bluestone et al., *Aircraft Industry Dynamics*, 17.

13. Almarin Phillips, *Technology and Structure: A Study of the Aircraft Industry* (Lexington, Mass.: Heath Lexington Books, 1971), 1–22; A. H. Cole, "An Approach to the Study of Entrepreneurship," in *Enterprise and Secular Change*, F. C. Lane and J. C. Riemersma, eds. (Homewood, Ill: R. D. Irwin, 1953), 181–195.

14. McNeill, *Pursuit of Power*, 293; Keys, *Lampert Hearings*, 989, 1130–1131, and *Butler Hearings*, 2413; Keys to Fleet, Nov. 7, 1923, series 4, box 1, Keys Papers; Peter M. Bower, *Curtiss Aircraft 1907–1947* (Annapolis, Md.: Naval Institute Press, 1987).

15. On Ford's losses see *Fortune*, May 1935, 79.

16. Keys spent $1.2 million on engineering from 1920 to 1924, $340,000 of which were losses on development contracts with the army and navy. Keys to Russell, Nov. 10, 1925, series 1A, box 2, Keys Papers; *Lampert Hearings*, 1132; Holley, *Buying Aircraft*, 36.

17. Section 7 of *An Act Making Appropriations* . . . , H.R. 12280, June 4, 1918. Settlement was usually made only upon final completion of a contract. *Lampert Hearings*, 885–887.

18. In 1934 Glenn Martin claimed there were "fifty different trades" involved in aircraft production. *Delaney Hearings*, 741.

19. *Aerodigest*, Feb. 1936, 24; June, 1938, 39; Holley, *Buying Aircraft*, 26–33. In 1921 the only machinery used to construct the first airplane built by Donald Douglas and James Kindleberger, a large passenger ship called the *Cloudster*, was a simple hand drill press. E. Cassagneres, *Spirit of Ryan* (Blue Ridge Summit, Pa.: Tab Books, 1982), 38. According to the Aeronautical Chamber of Commerce (ACC), in 1922 the work force in aircraft factories was 75 percent skilled. "Memo Summarizing the Replies . . . ," May 20, 1922, ACC Reel 5.38.9, Records of the ACC, Library of the Aerospace Industries Association, Washington, D.C.

20. For a description of the complexities of metal aircraft manufacture see F. P. Laudan, factory superintendent at Boeing, "Factory Procedure in the Fabrication of All-Metal Aircraft," *Aerodigest*, Jan. 1936, 26; R. E. Chandler, "The Personnel Problem in Aircraft Manufacture," *Aerodigest*, May 1936, 24, June 1936, 30; Lilley et al., *Problems of Accelerating Aircraft Production*, 32–41.

21. Piore and Sabel, *Second Industrial Divide*, esp. 29–31, 268–272; S. Tolliday and J. Zeitlin, eds., *The Automobile Industry and Its Workers: Between Fordism and Flexibility* (New York: St. Martin's Press, 1987), 1–25; Keys quoted, Keys to Raskob, Jan. 2, 1923, series 4, box 19, Keys Papers.

22. William G. Cunningham, *The Aircraft Industry: A Study in Industrial Location* (Berkeley: University of California Press, 1951).

23. Quoted in *Automotive Industries*, June 2, 1921, 1089.

24. Bluestone et al., *Aircraft Industry Dynamics*, 123; Keys to Frank Russell, June 26, 1921; Keys to C. Roy Keys, his brother and Buffalo factory manager, Sept. 5, 1922, series 1A, box 2, Keys Papers.

25. Lilley et al., *Problems of Accelerating Aircraft Production*, 32–41; Holley, *Buying Aircraft*, 28; on "natural monopoly" in engine manufacture see the testimony of Charles L. Lawrence, president of the engine firm Wright Aeronautical, in *Butler Hearings*, 2450.

26. *Lampert Hearings*, 1132; Holley, *Buying Aircraft*, 127; Schlaifer and Heron, *Development of Aircraft Engines*, 32, 43–44, 76–77, 172.

27. Keys to Frank Russell, series 1A, box 2, May 8, 1926, Keys Papers.

28. Lester H. Brune, *The Origins of American National Security Policy* (Manhattan, Kans.: MA/AH Pub., 1981), chap. 2; James P. Tate, "The Army and Its Aircorps" (Ph.D. dissertation, Indiana University, 1976).

29. For example, Keys described the manufacturers' roles in the annual interservice competition at the Pulitzer air races during the early 1920s in *Lampert Hearings*, 988–990. He claimed that the navy's 1923 victory in the coveted Schneider Cup races cost his firm $10,000. *Lampert Hearings*, 1134.

30. Kennedy, *Over Here*, 96–97; Urofsky, *Big Steel and the Wilson Administration*, 119, 147–148; Cooling, *Gray Steel*, chap. 8; William O. Shanahan, "Procurement of Naval Aircraft 1907–1939," unpublished document, Naval Aviation History

Unit, 1946, vol. 27, 296, Washington Naval Yard Library; "Memorandum Concerning Relative Cost for Similar Planes Carried on at McCook Field and at Private Factories," 1925, series 1, box 7, Keys Papers; for a study of the NAF see William F. Trimble, "The Naval Aircraft Factory, the American Aviation Industry, and Government Competition, 1919–1928," *Business History Review* 60 (Summer 1986): 175–198.

31. "Air Transport and the Aircraft Industry," *Aviation*, Jan. 1, 1919, 682; *Aviation*, Jan. 15, 1919, 747; Mar. 1, 1919, 166.

32. Uppercu, "To all members" of the Aeronautical Chamber of Commerce, Aug. 7, 1922, ACC Reel 5.16.4; see W. M. Leary, Jr. "At the Dawn of Commercial Aviation: Inglis M. Uppercu and Aeromarine Airways," *Business History Review* 53 (Summer 1979): 191.

33. Keys, *Butler Hearings*, 2433; Keys, *Lampert Hearings*, 1156; *Moody's Industrials* (1921), 1138.

34. "Consolidated Aircraft Corporation 1923–1927," ACC Reel 5.73.0; Rae, *Climb to Greatness*, 11–13; Fleet, *Butler Hearings*, 2394; Chester Cuthell, counsel for Curtiss, *Butler Hearings*, 2399.

35. Keys to Raskob, Dec. 6, 1924, series 4, box 19, Keys Papers.

36. Contract clause in series 1A, box 1, Keys Papers. See the provision on design rights in a contract between Curtiss and the Army Air Service in the *Congressional Record*, 68th Cong., 1st sess., Jan. 29, 1924, 1636–1637. Comptroller General J. R. McCarl to the secretary of the navy, Feb. 18, 1925, copy in *Butler Hearings*, 2485. The decision was in connection with a Martin aircraft.

37. Fleet, *Butler Hearings*, 2392; Lawrence, *Butler Hearings*, 2450, 2431.

38. Keys, *Butler Hearings*, 2419.

39. See Sen. Hiram Bingham's account in *Congressional Record*, 69th Cong., 1st sess., 1926, 10496; Keys, *Butler Hearings*, 2407; Reuben Fleet to Cong. John J. McSwain, Nov. 13, 1933, quoted in Edwin H. Rutkowski, *The Politics of Military Aviation Procurement, 1926–1934* (Columbus: Ohio State University Press, 1966), 287. Keys to Frank Russell, May 12, 1921; Keys to C. Roy Keys, Dec. 13, 1922, series 1A, box 2, Keys Papers; Holley, *Buying Aircraft*, 84–86.

40. Fleet quoted in Rutkowski, *Politics of Military Aviation Procurement;* Keys to C. Roy Keys, May 25, 1922, series 1A, box 2, Keys Papers.

41. Keys, *Butler Hearings*, 2432; "Status of Airplane Factories since July 1st, 1923," ACC Reel 5.68.1.

42. Harold Mansfield, *Vision: A Saga of the Sky* (New York: Duell, Sloan, and Pearce, 1956), 1–48 (an official history of Boeing Airplane).

43. ACC Reel 6.89.5.

44. Section 3718, Revised Statutes, quoted in Shanahan, "Procurement of Naval Aircraft," 294.

45. Moffett, *Butler Hearings*, 2469.

46. Keys, memo, Feb. 3, 1922; series 1A, box 1, Keys Papers; *Lampert Hearings*, 1133–1134, 1144–1145, 1629, 2801; "Curtiss Aeroplane and Motor Company to the Stockholders," Mar. 8, 1924, *Lampert Hearings*, 1388–1389; Moffett, *Lampert Hearings*, 1628; Martin, *Lampert Hearings*, 2278–2281; Keys, *Butler Hearings*, 2433; Shanahan, "Procurement of Naval Aircraft," 312.

47. Hawley, *Great War*, 38, 45–53, 70; William H. Becker, *The Dynamics of Business-Government Relations* (Chicago: University of Chicago Press, 1982), chap. 9.

48. On Hoover's encouragement of an aviation industry trade association in 1921 see Thomas W. Walterman, "Airpower and Private Enterprise: Federal-Industrial Relations in the Aeronautics Field, 1918–1926" (Ph.D. dissertation, Washington University, 1970), 323–328, and David D. Lee, "Herbert Hoover and the Development of Commercial Aviation, 1921–1926," *Business History Review* 58 (Spring 1984): 87, 93–94.

49. Samuel S. Bradley, general manager of the ACC, "What is to Be Done?" Jan. 8, 1923, ACC Reel 5.10.0; "Memo Summarizing the Replies . . . ," May 20, 1922, ACC Reel 5.38.9; see also *Aircraft Year Book 1923*, 6.

50. Howard Mingos, "The Birth of an Industry," in *The History of the American Aircraft Industry*, ed. G. R. Simonson, (Cambridge, Mass.: MIT Press, 1968), 50; Walterman, "Airpower and Private Enterprise," 43; Roland, *Model Research*, 58, 62–63; Bradley, "Speech to Special Meeting of the Board of Governors," Feb. 24, 1922, ACC Reel 5.10.0; Loening to the Packard Motor Co., June 30, 1922, ACC Reel 5.16.4.

51. Bradley to "Captain Turin," Sept. 21, 1923, ACC Reel 5.30.5; memo, 1922, ACC Reel 5.16.4; Bell to E. N. Gott, Sept. 22; Oct. 25, 1922, ACC Reel 5.57.3; Bradley to Russell, Mar. 4, 1922, ACC Reel 5.78.7; Bradley to G. M. Williams, Mar. 15, 1923, ACC Reel 5.81.4; "Aeronautical Chamber of Commerce Organizes," *Aviation*, Jan. 1922, 6; Walterman, "Airpower and Private Enterprise," 265–267.

52. Bradley to Russell, Mar. 4, 1922, ACC Reel 5.78.7; Martin to Bradley, Mar. 16, 1920, Oct. 6, 1921, Jan. 3, 1922, June 8, 1923, ACC Reel 6.29.2.

53. Bell to Vincent, Oct. 21; Vincent to Bradley, Oct. 29, 1921, ACC Reel 6.41.7; Williams to F. H. Russell, July 17, 1922, ACC Reel 5.16.4; Fleet to Bell, Aug. 1, 1923; Fleet to Lawrence, Mar. 6, 1925, ACC Reel 5.73.0.

54. Bradley to Gott, Nov. 12, Dec. 1, 1921, Aug. 3, 1922; Gott to Bradley, Oct. 31, 1921, July 18, 1922; Gott, "Outline of [Boeing] Activities for the Year 1922," Jan. 3, 1923, ACC Reel 5.57.3.

55. Bill Henry of Douglas Aircraft and the *Los Angeles Times* to Bell, May 8, 1922; Bell to Douglas, July 3, 1922, July 6, 1923; Russell to Douglas, Oct. 18, 1923, ACC Reel 5.83.6; Robert Gottlieb and Irene Wolf, *Thinking Big: The Story of the Los Angeles Times* (Putnam's: New York, 1977), 156.

56. Nick A. Komans, *Bonfires to Beacons* (Washington, D.C.: Department of Transportation, 1978), 177–178; Bradley Behrman, "Civil Aeronautics Board," in *The Politics of Regulation*, James Q. Wilson, ed. (New York: Basic Books, 1980), 75–120; R. E. Caves, *Air Transport and Its Regulators* (Cambridge, Mass.: Harvard University Press, 1962).

57. See esp. Walterman, "Airpower and Private Enterprise," 352–425.

58. E. W. Hawley, "Three Facets of Hooverian Associationalism: Lumber, Aviation, and Movies, 1921–1930," in *Regulation in Perspective*, Thomas K. McCraw, ed. (Boston: Harvard University Press, 1981), 95–123; Hawley, *New Deal and the Problem of Monopoly*, 240–244, and Lee, "Herbert Hoover and the Development of Commercial Aviation," 81–82, 85–86, 95.

59. On these limitations see Gabriel Kolko, *Main Currents in Modern American History* (New York: Pantheon, 1976), 100–117.

60. Weigley, *History of the United States Army*, 407.

61. *Army Reorganization Hearings before the Committee on Military Affairs on H.R. 7925*, 66th Cong., 1st sess., Oct. 7, 1919, 933. Explaining to senators the new logistics of air power, Keys remarked, "Here you are in a game that changes every

six months; it does not change only once in ten or twenty years [as with rifles, ships, and ordnance]." *Reorganization of the Army, Hearings before the Committee on Military Affairs on S. 2693*, 66th Cong., 1st sess, Aug. 20, 1919, 489.

62. See Paul A. C. Koistinen, "The 'Industrial-Military Complex' in Historical Perspective: The InterWar Years," *Journal of American History* 56 (March 1970): 819–839, and Randolph P. Kucera, *The Aerospace Industry and the Military* (Beverly Hills, Calif.: Sage, 1974), 11–26.

63. Skowronek, *Building a New American State*, 243–247, quoted, 243; Holley, *Buying Aircraft*, 43; Hewes, *From Root to McNamara*, passim.

64. Weigley, *History of the United States Army*, 402–412; "Administrative History of the Planning Branch," in *Preliminary Checklist of the Records of the Planning Branch, Procurement Division*, Planning Branch Records; Fowler W. Barker, "Procurement Work: Air Corps and Industrial Collaboration in Planning for Wartime Needs," *Airway Age*, August 1931, 140.

65. Menoher to ASW, July 15, 1921, box 69, Planning Branch Records; Mars to Bradley, June 8, 1922, ACC Reel 6.82.4; Bradley's "Memo Summarizing the Replies," in response to the questionnaire circulated among aircraft firms by the IWPD through the chamber, which includes his apology for the lack of "consideration and response from the manufacturers," May 20, 1922, ACC Reel 5.38.9. For surveys of the military's plans for industrial mobilization during the interwar years see Smith, *Army and Economic Mobilization*, 35–97; Holley, *Buying Aircraft*, chap 7; Albert A. Blum, "Birth and Death of the M-Day Plan," in *American Civil-Military Decisions*, Harold Stein ed. (Birmingham: University of Alabama Press, 1963), 63–96.

66. Bradley, "Statement of the General Manager," Jan. 8, 1924, ACC Reel 5.10.0.

67. "Curtiss Aeroplane and Motor Company to the Stockholders," Mar. 8, 1924; Keys to F. G. Allen, Apr. 5, 1924, series 1, box 4, Keys Papers.

68. Gott to Bell, Feb. 21; Bradley to Boeing, Dec. 29; ACC memo, Apr. 8; Gott to Bell, May 29; Lawrence to Martin, Oct. 20, 1924; Lawrence to Boeing, Mar. 9, 1925; P. G. Johnson, vice-president at Boeing, to Owen A. Shannon of the ACC, July 6, 1925; Paul Henderson to Boeing, Oct. 26, 1926, ACC Reel 5.57.3; Douglas to Keys, Sept. 24, 1924, series 4, box 2, Keys Papers; Fleet to Bradley, Sept. 20, 1925; Bradley to Fleet, Sept. 14, 1926, ACC Reel 5.73.0.

69. "An Outline with Reference to the Procurement of Aircraft for the U.S. Government which Will Reduce Price, Speed up Development, Guarantee a Constant Supply, and Sustain the Creative Elements of the Industry," May 16, 1924, ACC Reel 5.68.1; "Procurement of Aircraft for the United States Government: Some of the Existing Problems and Suggested Changes for Improving the Future," n.d., ACC Reel 5.63.5; Bradley to Martin, Jan. 17, 1924, ACC Reel 6.29.2.

70. "An Outline," ACC Reel 5.68.1; "Procurement of Aircraft," ACC Reel 5.63.5; Lawrence, *Butler Hearings*, 2450.

71. Moffett, *Butler Hearings*, 2469; Patrick, *Lampert Hearings*, 168–170, 811; Campbell, quoted in *Butler Hearings*, 2482; Hoover to Cong. J. M. Morin, Mar. 19, 1926, ACC Reel 6.53.4. For other statements of support for procurement law reform along the lines proposed by the manufacturers see Secretary of War D. W. Davis in *Butler Hearings*, 2325–2485; Secretary of the Navy C. D. Wilbur, quoted in Shanahan, "Procurement of Naval Aircraft," 293; *Tenth Annual Report of the National Advisory Committee on Aeronautics, 1924* (GPO: Washington, D.C., 1925); and *Report of the President's Aircraft Board* (GPO: Washington, D.C., 1925), 28–29, known as the Morrow Board after its chairman, Dwight W. Morrow. The

Morrow recommendations on procurement reform read as a brief of the industry's proposals.

72. See *Report of the Select Committee of Inquiry into Operations of the United States Air Service*, House, 68th Cong., 1st sess., Dec. 14, 1925 *(Lampert Report)*. The result of efforts of a group of Republican "Insurgents," including John M. Nelson of Wisconsin and Fiorello LaGuardia of New York, the Lampert Committee was intended to expose corruption in military aircraft contracting. H.R. 192, 68th Cong., 1st sess., Feb. 25, 1924. After eighteen months of hearings it found no evidence of malfeasance and reported that on the contrary the industry was rapidly "dwindling" due to the government's procurement practices. Fiorello H. LaGuardia, *The Making of an Insurgent* (Philadelphia: J. B. Lippincott, 1948), 161–191.

73. *Congressional Record*, 68th Cong., 2d sess., 738; William Allen White, *A Puritan in Babylon* (New York: Macmillan, 1938), 257, 433.

74. Weigley, *History of the United States Army*, chap. 17; Harry Howe Ransom, "The Air Corps Act of 1926: A Study in the Legislative Process" (Ph.D. dissertation, Princeton University, 1953), 81–82, 119–120, Coolidge quoted, 87; Margaret and Harold Sprout, "The Popular Revolt against Navalism," in *Toward a New Order of Seapower* (Princeton, N.J.: Princeton University Press, 1940), 100–117; Robert H. Ferrell, *Peace in Their Time* (New Haven, Conn.: Yale University Press, 1952); Selig Adler, *The Isolationist Impulse* (New York: Macmillan, 1966), 90–150.

75. Carl P. Parrini, *Heir to Empire: United States Economic Diplomacy, 1916–1923* (Pittsburgh: University of Pittsburgh Press, 1969), 248–276; Robert F. Smith, "Republican Policy and Pax Americana 1921–1932," in *From Colony to Empire: Essays in the History of American Foreign Relations*, W. A. Williams, ed. (New York: J. Wiley, 1972), 253–292; Michael J. Hogan, *Informal Entente* (Columbia: University of Missouri Press, 1977), 1–12.

76. Sherry, *Rise of American Airpower*, 34–35, 38, 53.

77. Ransom, "Air Corps Act," 112–117.

78. Lawrence, *Lampert Hearings*, 1017.

79. "Principles of Business Conduct," n.d., ACC Reel 6.53.4; Lawrence to Secretary of War Weeks and Secretary of the Navy C. D. Wilbur, Nov. 18, 1924, ACC Reel 5.68.1.

80. Bradley to Martin, Jan. 17, 1924, ACC Reel 6.29.2; Bradley to General Patrick, Aug. 15, 1924, ACC Reel 5.68.1; Lawrence to Martin, Oct. 20, 1924, ACC Reel 5.57.3.

81. See "Hays, William H.," ACC Reel 5.95.2; Will H. Hays, *The Memoirs of Will Hays* (Garden City, N.Y.: Doubleday, 1955), 310–319.

82. Lawrence to L. D. Gardner, Nov. 19; "Suggested Discussion," n.d.; Lawrence to "Gentlemen," Dec. 6, 1924, "Minutes of the Fourth Meeting of the Special Committee of the Aircraft Industry, Dec. 20th, 1924"; Bradley to Hays, Dec. 23, 1924, ACC Reel 5.68.1.

83. "Minutes of Second Meeting of the Aircraft Industry with Hon. Will B. Hays at the Yale Club, New York City, January 5, 1925," ACC Reel 5.63.5.

84. Special Committee to "Gentlemen," Jan. 16, 1925, ACC Reel 5.63.5.

85. Lawrence to Bradley, Feb. 8, 1925, ACC Reel 13.81.7; Bradley to Lawrence, Jan. 28, 1925, ACC Reel 6.53.4.

86. Keys to Russell, Nov. 10, 1925, series 1A, box 2; Mar. 15, 1925, series 1, box 2; Keys to Cong. Randolph Perkins, Feb. 14; Keys to Secretary Wilbur, Mar. 2, 1925, series 1, box 7; Keys to Hays, Feb. 3, 1925, series 1, box 4, Keys Papers.

87. John D. Hicks, *Republican Ascendency* (New York: Harper, 1960), 84–102, Progressive platform quoted, 98; Kenneth C. McKay, *The Progressive Party of 1924* (New York: Columbia University Press, 1947), 219; Walterman, "Airpower and Private Enterprise," 492; White, *Puritan*, 261–263.

88. Secretary Baker, *Reorganization of the Army, Hearings before the Committee on Military Affairs on S. 2693*, 66th Cong., 1st sess, Aug. 18, 1919, 181; for studies of the debates on the role of air power in national security doctrine see Ransom, "The Air Corps Act," and Tate, "The Army and Its Aircorps."

89. Holley, *Buying Aircraft*, 48–51, 63–67, 69; Rutkowski, *Politics of Military Aviation Procurement*, 216. The expansion of naval aviation was authorized in the Aircraft Procurement Act, *Public no. 446*, 69th Cong., 1st sess., 1926.

90. House Rep. 1396, 1395 on H.R. 12471 and 12472, *To Encourage Development of Aviation and Secure Advancement of Army Aeronautics*, 69th Cong., 1st sess., June 7, 1926, 5.

91. See James V. Martin, "Aircraft Conspiracy," *Libertarian* (March 1924): 119–167.

92. On these traditional views of technical development see Thomas P. Hughes, *Elmer Sperry, Inventor and Engineer* (Baltimore: Johns Hopkins University Press, 1971), 254–255, and Daniel J. Kevles, *The Physicists* (New York: Knopf, 1978), 102–138. On popular myths of the inventor-hero and of invention as a means to social mobility, see Susan J. Douglas, *Inventing American Broadcasting, 1899–1922* (Baltimore: Johns Hopkins University Press, 1987). Quotations from Cong. M. A. Madden, Butler Hearings, 2359.

93. Rutkowski, *Politics of Military Aviation Procurement*, 231–233; Henry C. Ferrell, "John J. McSwain: A Study in Political Technique" (Master's thesis, Duke University, 1957).

94. *A Bill to Regulate the Manner of Purchasing Aircraft, Aircraft Parts, and Aircraft Accessories, and to Promote and Encourage the Industry*, H.R. 11950, 69th Cong., 1st sess., 1926; McSwain, *Butler Hearings*, 2372, 2431; for McSwain's defense of his bill see *Congressional Record*, 67, pt. 11, 11756.

95. Keys, *Butler Hearings*, 2438; Keys to McSwain, Apr. 26, 1926, series 1, box 5, Keys Papers.

96. Rutkowski, *Politics of Military Aviation Procurement*, 227.

97. Bell to Bradley, Feb. 22, 1926, ACC Reel 6.53.4.

98. *Congressional Record*, 69th Cong., 2d sess., May 5, 1926.

99. *Butler Hearings*, 2340.

100. Bradley to Hays, Mar. 27, 1926, ACC Reel 5.95.2; Bradley to Paul Henderson, Apr. 12, 1926, ACC Reel 6.32.3.

101. *Conference Report 1527, To Increase the Efficiency of the Air Corps*, 69th Cong., 1st sess., June 22, 1926.

102. *United States Statutes at Large*, 44, pt. 2, sec. 10, 784–89.

103. Keys to Carl Vinson, Jan. 31, 1927, quoted in Holley, *Buying Aircraft*, 115.

104. Rutkowski, *Politics of Military Aviation Procurement*, 208; see also Rae, *Climb to Greatness*, 32–33, and Holley, *Buying Aircraft*, 89–93, 146.

CHAPTER FOUR. CARRYING CONGRESS'S BUSINESS

1. R. D. Weyerbacher and T. P. Wright of Curtiss Aeroplane, quoted March 1934, in typed, unpaged transcript of unpublished hearings, *Committee of the*

House Relating to an Investigation of the War Department 1934–1936, 73rd Cong., 2d sess., 1934 *(Rogers Hearings)*, box 1, Record Group 233, National Archives, Washington, D.C. Before the same committee Donald Douglas stated that "we have got so we do not read the fine print when we need a contract and the work."

2. Ronald Miller and David Sawers, *The Technical Development of Modern Aviation* (London: Routledge and Kegan Paul, 1968), 47–94; P. W. Brooks, *The Modern Airliner* (London: Putnam, 1961), 67–90; E. P. Warner, *Technical Development and Its Effect on Air Transportation* (Norwich, Vt.: Norwich University, 1938), 1–37.

3. *Delaney Hearings*, 1108. The costs of manufacture grew less steeply at 50 to 100 percent because of the ability to use a greater amount of tooling in metal construction. Holley, *Buying Aircraft*, 20–21. For figures on the costs of prototypes see Peck and Scherer, *Weapons Acquisition Process*, 344–345.

4. On the tendency toward oligopoly of industries producing advanced products for a monopsonistic military client see Clive Trebilcock, "The British Armaments Industry 1890–1914," in G. Best and A. Wheatcroft, eds., *War, Economy and the Military Mind* (London: Croom Helm, 1976), 92.

5. Moffett, "Memo to all officers," Oct. 19, 1932, quoted in Shanahan, "Procurement of Naval Aircraft," 35, 359; "no true picture of the procurement possibilities would warrant any assumption other than the dependence of naval aviation upon the engineering resources of the private aircraft manufacturers," ibid., 254; Holley, *Buying Aircraft*, 114, and Schlaifer and Heron, *Development of Aircraft Engines and Fuels*.

6. Moffett, memo, Shanahan, "Procurement of Naval Aircraft"; Holley, *Buying Aircraft*, 116; see H.R. 9359, 70th Cong., 1st sess., 1928, and H.R. 11569, 72nd Cong., 1st sess., 1932, for attempts to repeal the Air Corps Act's provisions for open competition on production contracts.

7. The majority of Air Corps contracts from 1926 to 1934 were negotiated under Army Regulation 5-240. Holley, *Buying Aircraft*, 116; Rutkowski, *Politics of Military Aviation*, 158–174.

8. V. E. Clark, general manager of Consolidated, to Chief, Materiel Division, Air Corps, Dec. 30, 1926, box 19, Keys Papers; *House Report No. 1506, Rogers Hearings*, 43–44; Shanahan, "Procurement of Naval Aircraft," 348–349.

9. Moffett, memo, Shanahan, "Procurement of Naval Aircraft"; Admiral King's testimony, House Committee on Naval Affairs, *Information as to the Method of Awarding Contracts for Ships and Aircraft for the United States Navy*, Jan. 24, 1934 *(Vinson Hearings)*, 274. Prices for aircraft were negotiated on the basis of previous and comparable performances and costs for labor, material, and overhead.

10. Morgan, Apr. 5, 1934, *Rogers Hearings*; King, *Delaney Hearings*, 1041. For an example of reminders to the military that its actions on behalf of Congress's vision of a properly regulated aircraft industry were being closely followed, see Cong. McSwain, to F. Trubee Davison, assistant secretary of war for air, in ASW Air, General Correspondence, 1926–1933, box 4, RG 107 (Davison Papers), National Archives, Washington, D.C.

11. Fleet, *Delaney Hearings*, 1090.

12. William Wagner, *Reuben Fleet and the Story of Consolidated Aircraft* (Fallbrook, Calif.: Aero Publishers, 1976), 117.

13. Basic doctrinal differences over the military uses of aircraft—strategic bombing, coastal defense, or close air support, and so on—persisted into World

War II as did the military establishment's efforts to check the rising influence of air power. "As a result of organizational uncertainty and instability, the system for procurement was forever in flux," Holley, *Buying Aircraft*, 104; Tate, "Army and its Aircorps," 89–124; Sherry, *Rise of American Airpower*, 49–52.

14. Curtiss Aeroplane to Chief of the Air Corps, Apr. 11, 1928, Rogers Committee Records, box 30.

15. Gen. W. E. Gillmore, chief, Materiel Division, Air Corps, to the Chief of the Air Corps, Apr. 27, 1928, in Rogers Committee Records, box 30.

16. *Rogers Hearings*, May 2, 1934, box 1.

17. Keys to Russell, Apr. 27, 1927, series 1A, box 2, Keys Papers.

18. Corn, *Winged Gospel*, 94–95.

19. Corn, *Winged Gospel*, 17–27; J. W. Ward, "The Meaning of Lindbergh's Flight," *American Quarterly*, 10 (Spring 1958): 3–16; the flight was "the occasion of a public act of regeneration in which the nation momentarily rededicated itself to something, the loss of which was keenly felt," Ward, 6.

20. Dodd, *Financial Policies*, 3–5, 35–41; Dodd's study is probably more reliable, but another later study pegged the total investment in aviation during 1927–1929 at $550 million, plus $90 million in municipal airports. See the confidential report, "A Review of the American Aviation Industry," National Aviation Corp., Aug. 9, 1935, copy in the Library of the National Air and Space Museum, Washington, D.C.

21. "Report of the Aviation Securities Committee," Oct. 30, 1931, series 5, box 23, Keys Papers; "The Aviation Industry," Pynchon & Co., Feb. 1929, copy in the Library of the National Air and Space Museum; G. W. Vaughan, president of Curtiss-Wright, who later told congressmen, "they sold a terrific amount of stock and the public took it, and they had plenty of reserves." *Hearings on H.R. 7777*, . . . Act to Establish the Composition of the U.S. Navy . . . , 75th Cong., 1st sess., Aug. 5–12, 1937 *(Scott Hearings)*, 1793.

22. Dodd, *Financial Policies*, 14.

23. NAT file, series 1A, box 1, Keys Papers; Henry Ladd Smith, *Airways* (New York: Knopf, 1942), 107–108, 112.

24. Keys to Gen. J. E. Fechet, Sept. 8, 1928, series 1A, box 1, Keys Papers.

25. J. A. B. Smith to Keys, Aug. 14, 1928, series 1A, box 1, Keys Papers.

26. *Buffalo Courier Express*, June 16, 1929; *Buffalo Times*, Jan. 6, 1929; Dodd, *Financial Policies*, 37; Rae, *Climb to Greatness*, 42.

27. *Buffalo Courier Express*, June 21, 1929, 24.

28. Dodd, *Financial Policies*, 55–56.

29. *Airway Age* criticized the outcome of Keys's corporate moves as "a dispersion rather than a unification." "Merger Groupings in Aviation," *Airway Age*, Apr. 1929, 426; Dodd, *Financial Policies*, 147; E. E. Freudenthal, *The Aviation Business: From Kitty Hawk to Wall Street* (New York: Vanguard Press, 1940), 97.

30. Smith, *Airways*, 145–146.

31. *Aviation*, May 25, 1929.

32. Dodd, *Financial Policies*, 48.

33. Rae, *Climb to Greatness*, 44–45, 50–51; Dodd, *Financial Policies*, 58; *Aerodigest*, Dec. 1933, 52.

34. Curtiss-Wright Corp., Report to the Stockholders, Mar. 24, 1931; Dodd, *Financial Policies*, 60.

35. *Aviation*, Mar. 16, 1929, 812; Mar. 23, 1929, 915; Apr. 20, 1929, 1336.

36. Smith, *Airways*, 153; Dodd, *Financial Policies*, 59, 82.

37. *Fortune*, Feb. 1939, 115.

38. "The Cord Corporation," *Aerodigest*, Nov. 1933, 22.

39. *Aerodigest*, Sept. 1933, 54; *Fortune*, Jan. 1933, 108; *Aerodigest*, May 1934, 69.

40. *Hearings on Stock Exchange Practices*, Banking and Currency Committee, Senate, 72nd Cong., 1st sess., pts. 6, 16, March 1933, March 1934 *(Pecora Hearings); Pecora Report*, 107–109. For the fortune amassed by William Boeing in these dealings, see *Hearings of the Senate Special Committee Investigating the Munitions Industry*, 1934–1936, pt. 6 *(Nye Hearings)*; Pratt & Whitney Aircraft Co. and United Aircraft Exports, Inc., Sept. 17, 18, 1934; Freudenthal, *Aviation Business*, 93–95.

41. D. L. Brown, *Delaney Hearings*, 870; Dodd, *Financial Policies*, 59–84.

42. Congress discovered another incentive for the integration of aviation firms. The consolidated tax returns that UATC submitted for its subsidiaries from 1929 to 1932 shaved $855,000 or 30 percent from the taxes they would separately have been liable for. *Congressional Record*, Apr. 9, 1934, 6433–6434.

43. "Merger Groupings in Aviation," *Airway Age*, Apr. 1929, 425; *Aviation*, May 25, 1929, 1804; the new plant in East Hartford covered 500,000 square feet and was designed by the Detroit architect Albert Kahn. Sikorsky was near by in Bridgeport. Moritz Kahn, "Aircraft Engine and Factory Layout," *Aerodigest*, Jan. 1936, 20.

44. D. L. Brown, *Delaney Hearings*, 870, 1540. A combined 1925 Pratt and Whitney investment of $1,000 by Rentschler, C. W. Deeds, and the engineer George Meade was worth $11.4 million in 1932 and was lavishly supplemented by high salaries. See also *Nye Hearings*, pt. 6.

45. "No. 1 Airplane Company," *Fortune*, Apr. 1932, 46–51.

46. Brown, *Delaney Hearings*, 1542.

47. Ibid., *Aerodigest*, May 1932, 96; *Airway Age*, Oct. 1930, 1364.

48. *Aerodigest*, Sept. 1934, 34, Apr. 1935, 141, Sept. 1935, 25.

49. See *Delaney Hearings*, 934–935, for a graphic portrayal of the interrelations among the various firms and their directors.

50. Freudenthal, *Aviation Business*, 117; Dodd, *Financial Policies*, 34, 108–110, 115–116, 149–150; "Aviation Begins to Earn Money," *Magazine of Wall Street*, Oct. 10, 1936, 760–762.

51. Dodd, *Financial Policies*, 9, 44–47, 70; James H. Kindleberger, vice-president, Douglas Aircraft, *Delaney Hearings*, 831. On the DC-2 as a bomber see undated copy of a letter from Douglas to chief of the Air Corps, Gen. B. D. Foulois, in *Rogers Hearings*, box 1.

52. Fleet, *Delaney Hearings*, 1088; "Summary of net income . . . ," *Delaney Hearings*, 719–720, 1092; Consolidated sold 72 trainers to China and 20 to Rumania in 1932–1933, *Aerodigest*, Mar. 1934, 61, Apr. 1934, 76.

53. "Preliminary Circular," Nov. 1929, General Correspondence, box 1, Glenn L. Martin Papers, Library of Congress; the Martin Company received its RFC loan on Jan. 17, 1935, entry 75, Records of the Reconstruction Finance Corp., Record Group 234, National Archives, Washington, D.C.; *Fortune*, Dec. 1939, 73–77.

54. Rae, *Climb to Greatness*, 30–31, 47.

55. The RFC took quite a risk with Lockheed, lending it $150,000 with only the Electra's patterns, dyes, and fixtures as collateral. For details on this loan and on the new Lockheed's early financial status see box 759, RFC Records, Record Group 234; Rae, *Climb to Greatness*, 66.

56. R. E. Gross to R. H. Gross, Oct. 20, 1933, Personal Correspondence, box 1;

R. E. Gross to Courtland S. Gross, Jan. 18, 1933, Business Correspondence, box 1, Robert Ellsworth Gross Papers, Library of Congress.

57. *Delaney Hearings*, 631.

58. J. D. Alexander, president of the Alexander Aircraft Co. of Colorado Springs, "Minutes of the Detroit Meeting of the Commercial Aircraft Manufacturers Section of the ACC," Apr. 28–29, 1929, ACC Reel 9.09.2.

59. "Minutes of the meeting of the Board of Governors," Oct. 17, 1929, ACC Reel 9.50.5.

60. Holley, *Buying Aircraft*, 10.

61. "Minutes of the Detroit Meeting . . . ," ACC Reel 9.09.2.

62. "Minutes of the Cleveland meeting of the Commercial Aircraft Manufacturers Section," Aug. 1929, ACC Reel 9.56.6, 9.04.8, 11.17.9.

63. ACC Reel 9.20.3, 8.54.4.

64. "Statement by F. B. Rentschler," n.d., ACC Reel 9.62.0; Rentschler, "Is Aviation Overexpanded?" *Magazine of Business*, July 1929, 37.

65. Freudenthal, *Aviation Business*, 88.

66. "Memorandum On the State of the Aircraft Industry: Report to the President of the United States," Dec. 1929, ACC Reel 8.89.4, 9.62.4.

67. Comdr. S. M. Krause, memo, May 31, 1931, quoted in Shanahan, "Procurement of Naval Aircraft," 351.

68. *Vinson Hearings*, 307.

69. ACC Reel 13.59.8, 11.17.9.

70. ACC Reel 11.13.1, 11.17.9, 11.33.2.

71. ACC Reel 12.27.5, 12.33.5; "The Aircraft Industry and the National Defense," addressed to President Hoover, Mar. 5, 1931; "Status of the Aircraft Industry," to the secretaries of war and navy, Mar. 3, 1932, ACC Reel 12.22.4; Payne to ACC, Oct. 20, 1930, ACC Reel 10.91.2.

72. Moffett to Lawrence, Mar. 16, 1932; Moffett and General Foulois to Lawrence, Aug. 25, 1932, ACC Reel 13.11.7; "Proposed System for Uniform Cost Accounting by Air Corps Contractors," Apr. 11, 1932, ACC Reel 13.0.1; Temple Joyce, *Delaney Hearings*, 691; Lawrence, "Status of the Aircraft Industry," to the war and navy secretaries, Mar. 3, 1932, ACC Reel 12.22.4.

73. "Minutes of Special Meeting of the ACC Board of Governors," Dec. 12, 1932, ACC Reel 13.11.7; Moffett and Foulois to ACC, Oct. 25, 1932, ACC Reel 14.70.5.

74. *Aerodigest*, Apr. 1932, 54.

75. Curtiss-Wright Exports lost large sums in 1930–1931, expanding for a large export market for commercial aircraft that failed to materialize. Dodd, *Financial Policies*, 88.

76. Warren I. Cohen, *Empire without Tears* (New York: Knopf, 1987), 3–4, 8, 19; Frederick C. Adams, *Economic Diplomacy* (Columbia: University of Missouri Press, 1976), 26; L. F. Schmeckebier and G. A. Weber, *The Bureau of Foreign and Domestic Commerce* (Baltimore: Johns Hopkins University Press, 1924).

77. *Aircraft Yearbook*, 1923, quoted, 10; "DOC Release," Apr. 12, 1924, ACC Reel 6.91.6 and box 2751, 2755, entry 561, Records of the Bureau of Foreign and Domestic Commerce, Record Group 151, National Archives, Washington, D.C.

78. ACC Reel 8.34.6; L. W. Rogers, "Exports of Aeronautic Products," *Aerodigest*, Apr. 1933; D. L. Brown, United Aircraft Corp. president, "Export Volume and Its Relation to Aviation Progress and Security," *Aerodigest*, Dec. 1934, 15.

79. *Aerodigest*, Mar. 1934, 62. For Curtiss's losses, see *Rogers Hearings*, April

5, 1934, box 1; Edward Deeds of Simmons Aircraft to ACC, June 13, 1930, ACC Reel 11.79.2.

80. Warner, "Buying Military Airplanes," *Aviation*, Nov. 1931, 667.

81. Lt. Comdr. W. Nelson, USN, "Cardinal Factors in Aircraft Production," *Airway Age*, May 1929, 641.

82. Warner, "Buying Military Airplanes"; Warner to Davison, Dec. 30, 1931; Davison to Warner, Mar. 14; Warner to Davison, Mar. 23; Davison to Warner, Apr. 11, 1932, box 30, Davison Papers.

83. "Curtiss-Wright Corporation Report to the Stockholders for Year Ended December 31, 1930," series 3, box 2, Keys Papers; "Comparative Balance Sheets of Wright Aeronautical Co.," *Delaney Hearings*, 533; "The American Aviation Industry," office memo, Carl M. Loeb & Co., New York, Apr. 11, 1935, 96–106, copy in the Library of the National Air and Space Museum; G. W. Vaughan, "Brief Outline of the Strike," box 3, Davison Papers.

84. See copies of *Tradewind* and *Wright Engine Builder* for 1928–1929, box 4, Davison Papers.

85. Vaughan to Secretary of Labor J. J. Davis, Nov. 13, 1930, copy in box 3, Davison Papers.

86. J. J. Connoly, International Association of Machinists Grand Lodge representative, to IAM president A. O. Wharton, Nov. 22 1930; Connoly to R. Fechner, IAM general vice-president, Dec. 12, 1930; E. W. Jersek, Silk City Lodge 188, "Petition to IAM Lodges," Feb. 27, 1931; "Statement of the General Committee," Dec. 14, 1930, Reel 341, Records of the International Association of Machinists, International President's Records, State Historical Society of Wisconsin, Madison.

87. Connoly to Conlon, Feb. 21; Connoly to Wharton, Feb. 21; Conlon to Connoly, Feb. 24; Jersek to Wharton, Feb. 26; Wharton to Jersek, Feb. 28; Connoly to Wharton, Apr. 17; copy of agreement in Connoly to Wharton, Apr. 25; Connoly to Davison, May 9, 1931, Reel 341, IAM Records.

88. On LaGuardia's involvement see Connoly to H. J. Carr, IAM general vice-president, June 9, 1931, Reel 341, IAM Records, and LaGuardia to Secretary of War Patrick J. Hurley, box 3, Davison Papers; "Audit, Wright Aeronautical Corporation," in C. E. Orton to Maj. H. H. Arnold, Dec. 29, 1930, Davison Papers. The Air Corps' main hope in regard to the strike at Wright was to demonstrate its strict adherence to the Air Corps Act. See memo, June 22, 1931, Davison Papers.

CHAPTER FIVE. THE NRA,
THE AIRCRAFT INDUSTRY, AND CONGRESS

1. Charles Lawrence to FDR, Mar. 5, 1933, President's Personal File, 669, FDR Papers, Presidential Library, Hyde Park, N.Y.

2. Executive Order 6174, signed by FDR on June 13, 1933, allocated $238 million in money from the Public Works Administration for new warships, and by early August contracts had been awarded for two aircraft carriers.

3. Sklar, *Corporate Reconstruction*, 1–14; Kolko, *Main Currents*, 129–138; Michael A. Bernstein, *The Great Depression* (New York: Cambridge University Press, 1987), 185–187.

4. Leverett S. Lyon et al., *The National Recovery Administration* (Washington, D.C.: Brookings, 1935), chap. 4; James P. Johnson, *The Politics of Soft Coal*

(Urbana: University of Illinois Press, 1979), chap. 5; William R. Childs, *Trucking and the Public Interest* (Knoxville: University of Tennessee Press, 1985), chap. 6; Norman E. Nordhauser, *The Quest for Stability* (New York: Garland, 1979), 117.

5. Hawley, *New Deal and the Problem of Monopoly*, chap. 2; Karl, *Uneasy State*, 115–122; Himmelberg, *Origins of the National Recovery Administration*, 181–218; Stanley Vittoz, *New Deal Labor Policy and the American Industrial Economy* (Chapel Hill: University of North Carolina Press, 1987), 78–82, 94–95; Thomas K. McCraw, "The New Deal and the Mixed Economy," in *Fifty Years Later: The New Deal Evaluated*, Harvard Sitkoff, ed. (New York: Knopf, 1985), 63.

6. Sidney Fine, *The Automobile under the Blue Eagle* (Ann Arbor: University of Michigan Press, 1963), 30; Joseph J. Huthmacher, *Senator Robert F. Wagner and the Rise of Urban Liberalism* (New York: Atheneum, 1968), 137–153.

7. Fine, *Automobile*, 31–33; Himmelberg, *Origins*, 196.

8. For a copy of NIRA see Lyon, *National Recovery Administration*, 889–899.

9. Ibid., 14, chap. 3; Hawley, *New Deal and the Problem of Monopoly*, 19. NIRA provided that violations of codes by firms would be an "unfair method of competition," pursuable in district courts under the Federal Trade Commission Act. But only those who had formally agreed to codes could be considered violators and, as Henry Ford demonstrated at an early stage, there was no power to make a firm sign its industry's code. Lyon, *National Recovery Administration*, 8–12.

10. *NRA Bulletin No. 2*, quoted in C. L. Dearing et al., *The ABC of the NRA* (Washington, D.C.: Brookings, 1934), 79.

11. Himmelberg, *Origins*, 201, 206–207, 219; Kim McQuaid, *Big Business and Presidential Power: From FDR to Reagan* (New York: Morrow, 1982), 21–37.

12. Dearing et al., *ABC*, 1, 10; Arthur R. Burns, *The Decline of Competition* (New York: McGraw-Hill, 1936), 464–465, 512–513; Jerold S. Auerbach, "New Deal, Old Deal, or Raw Deal: Some Thoughts on New Left Historiography," *Journal of Southern History* 35 (Feb. 1969): 21; Theda Skocpol, "Political Response to Capitalist Crisis," *Politics and Society* 10, no. 2 (1980): 155–201.

13. Albert U. Romasco, *The Politics of Recovery* (New York: Oxford University Press, 1983), 1–12, 186–215; Karl, *Uneasy State*, 111–130; Lyon, *National Recovery Administration*, 40–47; Hawley, *New Deal and the Problem of Monopoly*, 51.

14. Kolko, *Main Currents*, 129–130; Vittoz, *New Deal Labor Policy*, 97–134; Hawley, *New Deal and the Problem of Monopoly*, 56, 136; Lyon, *National Recovery Administration*, 258, 273, 647. For the importance of the "political-economic coalitions" that various industries could muster as determinants of their fortunes under the New Deal see Bernstein, *Great Depression*, 193.

15. Himmelberg, *Origins*, 76.

16. Lyon, *National Recovery Administration*, 85–88; quoted, 67.

17. Ronald L. Feinman, *Twilight of Progressivism* (Baltimore: Johns Hopkins University Press, 1981), 68–73. For the Darrow Board Report see *New York Times*, May 21, 1934.

18. Lyon, *National Recovery Administration*, 122–123.

19. Ibid., quoted, 29, 298; Hawley, *New Deal and the Problem of Monopoly*, 97, 137.

20. Lyon, *National Recovery Administration*, 18, 444–445, 527; Himmelberg, *Origins*, 207; Fine, *Automobile*, 48, 77; Vittoz, *New Deal Labor Policy*, 137; David Brody, *Workers in Industrial America* (New York: Oxford University Press, 1980), 125–126; Skocpol, "Political Response," 167; Howell Harris, "The Snares of Liberalism?" in *Shop Floor Bargaining and the State*, Steven Tolliday and

Jonathan Zeitlin, eds. (New York: Cambridge University Press, 1985), 164–168.

21. Lyon, *National Recovery Administration*, 53, 93.

22. "Minutes of the Meeting of the Military Contractors Committee," May 13, 1933, ACC Reel 13.81.7.

23. Morgan to FDR, Oct. 19, 1932, President's Personal File, 6631, FDR Papers; T. A. Morgan to members of the Board of Governors, June 21, 24, 1933, ACC Reel 13.59.8.

24. See the circular sent to all manufacturers by Clarence M. Young, assistant secretary of commerce for aeronautics, May 8, 1930, and Rentschler to Young, May 26, 1930, ACC Reel 10.17.2.

25. Memo to Board of Governors, July 13, 1933, ACC Reel 13.62.6; "Minutes of the Meeting of the Board of Governors," June 30, 1933; "Constitution and Bylaws of the Aeronautical Chamber of Commerce of America, Amended Aug. 1, 1933," ACC Reel 13.64.6; "Application," Aug. 3, 1933, "Aircraft Manufacturing Code (AMC), Documents," box 6045, Records of the National Recovery Administration, Record Group 9, National Archives, Washington, D.C.

26. *Aerodigest*, July 1933, 13.

27. Fleet to FDR, July 18, 1933, ACC Reel 14.95.0; Fleet to Hugh Johnson, Oct. 3, 1933, ACC Reel 13.62.2. For Consolidated's and Douglas Aircraft's application for ACC membership, inspired by the NRA, see ACC Reel 13.64.6 and ACC Reel 13.66.6. H. H. Wetzel represented Donald Douglas on the ACC's code committee.

28. "Application," Aug. 3, 1933, "AMC, Applications," box 6045, NRA Records. Both Beech and Lockheed joined the Chamber in fall 1933.

29. "Suggested Code," ACC Reel 13.63.6; memo, Aug. 8, 1933, ACC Reel 13.59.8. Charles Lawrence was appointed to the Industrial Advisory Board.

30. "Application" and "Proposed Code," Aug. 3, 1933, "AMC, Documents," box 6045, NRA Records.

31. "Report on Examination of Code of Fair Competition for the Aircraft Manufacturing Industry," Aug. 7, 1933, "AMC, Reports," box 6047, NRA Records.

32. *Business Week*, Feb. 3, 1934, 12; "Digest of Meeting Advisory Committee on Light Airplane," Jan. 9, 1934, ACC Reel 14.54.1, 14.63.2; Eugene Vidal to Johnson, Dec. 22, 1933, "AMC, Trade Practices," box 6047, NRA Records.

33. Vidal to Johnson, Dec. 22, 1933, box 6047, NRA Records.

34. H. H. Woodring to Johnson, Nov. 28, 1933; Claude Swanson to Milton Katz, assistant counsel, NRA, Nov. 7, 1933, "AMC, Procurement Contracts," box 6047, NRA Records. During the period 1928–1932, the twelve leading manufacturers spent $5.5 million on designs but received only $3 million in payments through development contracts. Rogers to Board of Governors, Nov. 27, 1933, ACC Reel 19.15.0.

35. Fleet to Johnson, Nov. 11, 1933, "AMC, Trade Practices, Design Piracy," box 6047, NRA Records.

36. Ray Tucker and F. R. Barkley, *Sons of the Wild Jackass* (Boston: L. C. Page & Co., 1932); Russell B. Nye, *Midwestern Progressive Politics* (New York: Harper & Row, 1959); Wayne S. Cole, *Roosevelt and the Isolationists* (Lincoln: University of Nebraska Press, 1983), 37–38.

37. Cole, *Roosevelt and the Isolationists*, 46.

38. Thomas K. McCraw, "Louis D. Brandeis Reappraised," *American Scholar* (Autumn 1985): 525–536; see also Hawley, *New Deal and the Problem of Monopoly*, 302.

39. Feinman, *Twilight*, 47–57, 65, 75; Cole, *Roosevelt and the Isolationists*,

188–191; Ronald L. Mulder, *The Insurgent Progressives in the United States Senate and the New Deal, 1933–1939* (New York: Garland, 1979), 33–34. For the isolationists' attractions to air power see Sherry, *Rise of American Airpower*, 84–85, 92.

40. FDR quote, Feinman, *Twilight*, 54; Cole, *Roosevelt and the Isolationists*, 46. In the election campaign FDR abandoned Wilsonian internationalism to win the support of agrarian progressives and the Hearst papers. During his first term he would do little in foreign affairs that might alienate their support for his domestic program. Robert Dallek, *Franklin D. Roosevelt and American Foreign Policy 1932–1945* (New York: Oxford University Press, 1979), 19, 70–71.

41. Sherry, *Rise of American Airpower*, 39–40; Stuart Chase, *Men and Machines* (New York: Macmillan, 1929), 178–179; Corn, *Winged Gospel*, 17–27.

42. Quoted in John W. Ward, "The Meaning of Lindbergh's Flight," *American Quarterly* 10 (Spring 1958): 12.

43. *Congressional Record*, Mar. 2, 1934, 3617; *Hearings on Stock Exchange Practices*, Banking and Currency Committee, Senate, 72nd Cong., 2d sess., pts. 6, 16, Mar. 1933, Mar. 1934.

44. *Hearings before the Special Senate Committee on the Investigation of Air Mail and Ocean Mail Contracts*, Senate, 73rd Cong., 2d sess., pts. 1–9, 1934, *(Black Hearings)*; see the editorials, telegrams, and letters protesting both FDR's action and the public challenges by FDR's staff to Lindbergh's integrity (Lindbergh was associated with TWA) in box 11, Official Files 19, FDR Papers; F. A. Spencer, *Air Mail Payment and the Government* (Washington, D.C.: Brookings, 1941); Paul Tillett, *The Army Flies the Mails* (Birmingham: University of Alabama Press, 1955); Arthur Krock, *New York Times*, Feb. 18, 1934, pt. 4, 1. Air mail was returned to the airlines in May 1934.

45. S. 3170, 73rd Cong., 2d sess., Public No. 308, June 12, 1934; FDR to Hugo Black, Mar. 7, 1934, box 11, Official Files 19, FDR Papers.

46. Keith D. McFarland, *Harry H. Woodring* (Lawrence: University Press of Kansas, 1975), 59–82.

47. For the Air Corps' procurement method see House Military Affairs Committee, *Investigation under H.R. 275* (Rogers Hearings), H. Rept. 1506, 73rd Cong., 2d sess., May 7, 1934; Rutkowski, *Politics*, 158–161.

48. Holley, *Buying Aircraft*, 128–129; Rutkowski, *Politics*, 81, 95, 140, 213–217; for an example of manufacturers' complaints see Curtiss Aeroplane to Colonel Crain and Colonel North, Dec. 9, 1933, box 30, Rogers Committee Records.

49. House Committee on Naval Affairs, *Information as to the Method of Awarding Contracts for Ships and Aircraft for the United States Navy*, 73rd Cong., 2d sess., Jan. 24, 1934 *(Vinson Hearings)*, 275; Vinson quoted in *New York Times*, Jan. 30, 1934.

50. Grumman, *Delaney Hearings*, 631; Martin, ibid., 728.

51. King, *Delaney Hearings*, 472; Roosevelt, ibid., 487.

52. *Delaney Hearings*, 693.

53. Ibid., 972.

54. See ibid., 550, for Delaney's comment, and 1469–1536 for the committee's report and a lengthy dissenting report filed by W. D. McFarlane. This Texas Democrat, father of Ronald Reagan's national security adviser, argued that the "aviation industry is really a single company," an "Air Trust" subject to "Wall and Pine Street," committed to "maximum reproduction with minimum improvement,"

responsible for "disastrous airplanes" and weak air defense. For FDR's attractions to McFarlane's interpretations and his desire to retain his report for "his file of speech material," see Stephen Early, assistant secretary to the president to Secretary Roper, Mar. 23, 1934, box 1, Official File 249, FDR Papers.

55. H. R. 275 in *Congressional Record*, 73rd Cong., 2d sess., Mar. 2, 1934, 3613.

56. See the testimony for Apr. 5, 1934, box 1, transcript of the *Rogers Hearings*, Record Group 233, National Archives, Washington, D.C. These hearings were held in executive session and were not published.

57. Ibid., no date or page.

58. Egtvedt, *Rogers Hearings*, Apr. 30, 1934.

59. H. Rept. 2060, 73rd Cong., 2d sess., reprinted in *Congressional Record*, 73rd Cong., 2d sess., June 18, 1934, 12474–12484.

60. Rutkowski, *Politics of Military Aviation*, 73–75, 103–104, 120–122, 135–137; Holley, *Buying Aircraft*, 128–131.

61. Shanahan, "Procurement of Naval Aircraft," 366.

62. Vinson, *Congressional Record*, 73rd Cong., 2d sess., Jan. 9, 1934, 1599.

63. Dallek, *Franklin D. Roosevelt*, 75–76; Henry C. Ferrell, Jr., *Claude A. Swanson of Virginia*, (Lexington: University Press of Kentucky, 1985), quoted 204, 208; *Congressional Record*, 73rd Cong., 2d sess., 3780; for pressure on FDR from unions, congressmen, and so on, for naval building to relieve unemployment in specific localities, see box 16, Official File 18, FDR Papers.

64. Ferrell, *Claude Swanson*, 205; for Vinson's comments see *Congressional Record*, 73rd Cong, 2d sess., Jan. 30, 1934, 1624, 1629.

65. *Congressional Record*, 73rd Cong, 2d sess., Feb. 20, Mar. 6, 1934, 2875, 3796.

66. Ibid., 3813; "I cannot see why we can't build our own aeroplanes in the factory that was a particular pet of ours," James Howe to FDR on Feb. 16, 1934, box 1, Official File 249, FDR Papers; see also box 16, Official File 18, for Assistant Navy Secretary H. I. Roosevelt to FDR, Feb. 24, 1934, complaining of the "enormous hardship and delays" threatened by the Bone amendment. *Conference Report*, H. Rept. 1024 and S. Doc. 156 in *Congressional Record*, 73rd Cong., 2d sess., Jan. 30, 1934, 5024; March 6, 1934, 3813; Mar. 21, 1934, 5024; *Vinson Hearings*, 5027.

67. *Second Conference Report*, S. Doc. 157, Mar. 21, 1934.

68. J. E. Schaefer, president of the Boeing subsidiary, Stearman Aircraft in Wichita, to W. J. Skelly, Feb. 21, 1935, ACC Reel 16.17.5; *Treasury Department Bulletin 4434*, May 19, 1934; Brown to C. Parker, ACC secretary, June 15, 1934. Vigorous lobbying of the Treasury by the ACC did nothing to alter its policy. L. W. Rogers, memo, Aug. 23, 1934, all in ACC Reel 16.43.1. For the Treasury's narrow attitude toward acceptable elements of cost in navy contracts see *Internal Revenue Bulletin 7*, 1935, ACC Reel 15.82.5. Allowable research and development costs in production contracts were highly limited and interest on borrowed funds used to complete a contract were not allowed. For profit limitations as "cost-plus merely designated by another name," see F. B. Rentschler to Foulois, Mar. 24, 1934, box 55, Rogers Committee Records, and E. P. Warner's statement, *Delaney Hearings*, 972.

69. J. D. Jones, United States Guarantee Co. to the General Aviation Corp., Nov. 16, 1934, ACC Reel 15.84.6; James P. Murray, Boeing vice-president, to C. E. Parker of the ACC, Apr. 17, 1935, ACC Reel 15.82.5.

70. King to Secretary of the Navy Swanson, Aug. 14, 1934, in Shanahan, "Procurement," 371; for Vinson's failed amendment see H.R. 5730, 74th Cong., 1st sess., Feb. 14, 1935.

71. For the chamber's nervousness see "Attacks on the Industry," ACC Reel 19.23.7.

72. Trotter, "Development of the Merchants of Death Theory," 93–104.

73. Adoption of S. 206 on Apr. 12, 1934, created the Nye Committee, which was instructed to "study the feasibility of efforts to thwart the commercial motive in war . . . and consider the desirability of a government monopoly on manufacture of munitions," *Congressional Record*, 73rd Cong., 2d sess., Mar. 12, 1934, 4228–4229. It included Nye, Walter F. George of Georgia, Homer T. Bone of Washington, Bennett Champ Clark of Missouri, Morris Sheppard of Texas, James P. Pope of Idaho, Arthur H. Vandenberg of Michigan, and W. Warren Barbour of New Jersey.

74. Cole, *Roosevelt and the Isolationists*, 69, 141–143; Wayne. S. Cole, *Senator Gerald P. Nye and American Foreign Relations* (Minneapolis: University of Minnesota Press, 1962), 85; Dallek, *Franklin D. Roosevelt*, 70–71.

75. Campaigns for the nationalization of the aircraft industry were led by the Nye committee members, particularly Senator Bone, and the Air Defense League. On Jan. 28, 1935, Cong. W. I. Sirovich, Democrat from New York City and chairman of the House Patent Committee, introduced a bill to establish the United States Air Transport System, which would exclusively carry the air mail and build transport and military aircraft in a new $15 million plant. H.R. 4880, 74th Cong., 1st sess. For the ACC's fears of nationalization see ACC Reel 16.0.7. "Aircraft Manufacture: A Description of the Industry and Proposals for Socialization," a 1935 pamphlet produced by the British New Fabian Research Bureau, was widely discussed in the U.S. See for example *New York Times*, Sept. 16 1935.

76. Cole, *Roosevelt and the Isolationists*, 161; *Hearings Before the Special Committee Investigating the Munitions Industry*, Senate, 73rd Cong., 2d sess., pt. 6: *Pratt & Whitney Aircraft Co. and United Aircraft Exports Inc.*, Sept. 17, 18, 1934; *Munitions Industry, S. Rept. 944*, pt. 7, June 19, 1936; Records of the Special Committee Investigating the Munitions Industry *(Nye Committee)*, Record Group 46, National Archives, Washington, D.C.

77. *Report of the Federal Aviation Commission* (Washington, D.C.: GPO, 1934); L. W. Rogers, "Annual Report for 1935," ACC Reel 16.49.3.

78. *Final Report of War Department Special Committee on Army Air Corps* (Washington, D.C.: GPO, 1934); FDR was impressed by the Baker Board's recommendations for the coordination of army and navy aircraft procurement. In Executive Order 6166, he established an Aviation Procurement Committee in the Procurement Division of the Treasury Department to consider the problem as well as ways to lessen the burdens of Vinson-Trammell's profit limitations for the industry. Little came of the committee, however, and it left no records.

79. McSwain to FDR, Jan. 26, 1935, box 1, Official Files 249b, FDR Papers; H. R. 5057, 74th Cong., 1st Sess., Jan. 30, 1935; L. W. Rogers, "Annual Report for 1935," ACC Reel 16.49.3.

80. Rogers to NRA, Jan. 7, 1935, "AMC, Documents," box 6045, NRA Records.

81. Rogers to deputy administrator, K. J. Ammerman, May 29, 1934, "AMC, Amendments, Trade Practices, Design Piracy"; A. F. Bassett, Industrial Advisory Board, memo, Aug. 14, 1934, Box 6045, NRA Records.

CHAPTER SIX. LOST OPPORTUNITIES

1. Lyon, *National Recovery Administration*, chap. 17, 444.

2. Jerold S. Auerbach, *Labor and Liberty* (Indianapolis: Bobbs-Merrill, 1966), 50; Fine, *Automobile*, 37, and Lyon, *National Recovery Administration*, 413–548; Johnson, quoted in Fine, 47. On the attitudes of Johnson and Donald Richberg toward NIRA's labor provisions see James A. Gross, *The Making of the National Labor Relations Board* (Albany: State University of New York Press, 1974), 33–130.

3. Lyon, *National Recovery Administration*, 466–470; Vittoz, *New Deal Labor Policy*, 138–141; Fine, *Automobile*, 184.

4. Lyon, *National Recovery Administration*, 483.

5. Ibid., 482–486, 523–526; Vittoz, *New Deal Labor Policy*, 94; James O. Morris, *Conflict within the AFL: A Study of Craft versus Industrial Unionism, 1901–1938* (Ithaca, N.Y.: Cornell University Press, 1958), quoted 148.

6. For the ongoing dominance of skilled labor and handwork in aircraft manufacture, see F. P. Laudan, factory superintendent at Boeing, "Factory Procedure in the Fabrication of All-Metal Aircraft," *Aerodigest*, Jan. 1936, 26–29 and R. E. Chandler, "The Personnel Problem in Aircraft Manufacture," *Aerodigest*, May, June 1936.

7. Lyon, *National Recovery Administration*, 141–149.

8. Fine, *Automobile*, 72–73.

9. Dearing, *ABC of the NRA*, 60–76, PRA copy, 131–133. Executive Order 6246 was aimed primarily at Henry Ford, who ignored the NRA. Fine, *Automobile*, 79.

10. "Application," Aug. 3, 1933, "AMC, Documents," box 6045; "Oral Testimony at the Public Hearing," Hearing no. 402, Dec. 20, 1933, box 7264, NRA Records.

11. "Application," Aug. 3, 1933, "AMC, Documents" box 6045, NRA Records.

12. Fleet to FDR, July 18, 1933, ACC Reel 14.95.0; Fleet to Hugh Johnson, Oct. 3, 1933; L. D. Bell to Johnson, Oct. 3, 1933, ACC Reel 13.62.2.

13. Brody, *Workers in Industrial America*, 96.

14. LAB functioned as "the spokesman within NRA of the organized labor movement in the United States," Fine, *Automobile*, 57; Lyon, *National Recovery Administration*, 428–429.

15. On the failure of steelworkers under NIRA as primarily the failure to organize nationally see Staughton Lynd, "The Possibility of Radicalism in the Early 1930s: The Case of Steel," *Radical America* 6 (1972), 37–64.

16. Mark Perlman noted the industry's "romantic aura," which helped it "attract and hold part of its labor force." *The Machinists* (Cambridge, Mass.: Harvard University Press, 1961), 109. For examples of attempts by manufacturers to cultivate this aura, see such company journals as *The BeeHive*, published for its employees by Pratt & Whitney, and *Contact*, published during the late 1920s by Lockheed Aircraft. Lewis H. Michenor, a Southern California organizer, described a "superiority complex . . . the aircrafter felt as though he was quite a different individual than the average auto worker," even though West Coast autoworkers averaged better than twenty cents per hour in wages. Oral History Transcript, June 21, 1960, Walter Reuther Library, Detroit.

17. For the cultural and economic constraints on worker militancy in other industries during the New Deal see Brody, *Workers in Industrial America*, 134–135; James A. Hodges, *New Deal Labor Policy and the Southern Cotton Textile Indus-*

try 1933–1941 (Knoxville: University of Tennessee Press, 1986), 33–36; Robert Zieger, "The Limits of Militancy: Organizing Paper Workers, 1933–36," *Journal of American History* 63 (Dec. 1976): 638–657; Zieger, *Madison's Battery Workers, 1934–1952* (Ithaca: New York State School of Industrial and Labor Relations, 1977), esp. 3; Melvyn Dubofsky, "Not So 'Turbulent Years': Another Look at the American 1930's," *Amerikastudien* 24 (1982): 5–20.

18. Brody, *Workers in Industrial America*, 83–84, 135; Morris, *Conflict within the AFL*, 150–153, 162–163, 173–177; Lyon, *National Recovery Administration*, 509; for the bitter experiences of organized labor in the 1920s, see Irving Bernstein, *The Lean Years* (Boston: Houghton Mifflin, 1960), and Auerbach, *Labor and Liberty*, chap 1.

19. Perlman, *Machinists*, 148; Christopher L. Tomlins, "AFL Unions in the 1930s: Their Performance in Historical Perspective," *Journal of American History* 65 (Mar. 1979): 1033.

20. Brody, *Workers in Industrial America*, 91–93; Fine, *Automobile*, 143–145; Morris, *Conflict*, 164; Irving Bernstein, *Turbulent Years* (Boston: Houghton Mifflin, 1969, 94–95.

21. Morris, *Conflict*, 154, 164–165. It should be noted that the IAM's defensiveness and jurisdictional claims during the NRA period also derived from serious financial troubles. In 1932–1933, 26 percent of its approximately sixty-one thousand members were unemployed. In early 1933 its funds had either been frozen or lost because its banks had failed. Perlman, *Machinists*, 206, 82–83.

22. A. O. Wharton to William Green, Apr. 19, 1928, "Jurisdiction Aircraft Mechanics, AFL Executive Council," Reel 341, IAM Records.

23. Ira McGlasson, Local 301, UBCJA Wichita to Green, n.d.; Green to McGlasson, Apr. 16, 30, 1928; Federated Trades and Labor Council of San Diego to Green, copy in Green to Wharton, Aug. 16, 1928; IAM general vice-president P. J. Carr to Green, Aug. 21, 1928, Reel 341, IAM Records.

24. Edgar Gott to S. S. Bradley, Aug. 8; Fleet to Bradley, Aug. 11; Walter Beech to Bradley, Aug. 10, 1928, ACC Reel 8.43.4.

25. J. J. Connoly, IAM Grand Lodge representative, to Wharton, Nov. 22, 1930; Connoly to R. Fechner, IAM general vice-president, Dec. 12, 1930; E. W. Jersek, Silk City Lodge 188, "Petition to IAM Lodges," Feb. 27, 1931; "Statement of the General Committee," Dec. 14, 1930, Reel 341, IAM Records; G. W. Vaughan, "Brief Outline of the Strike," Box 3, Davison Papers.

26. Connoly, Report, Nov. 15, 1930; Connoly to Wharton, Dec. 1, 1930; Wharton to Connoly, Dec. 3, 1930; Fechner to R. J. Conlon, IAM general vice-president, Dec. 30, 1930; Guy Vaughan's remark appeared in *Morning Call*, quoted in Connoly to Conlon, Dec. 16, 1930, Reel 341, IAM Records.

27. Connoly to Conlon, Jan. 13; Conlon to Connoly, Jan. 14, Jan. 30, 1931, Reel 341, IAM Records; Vaughan to Bradley, Aug. 14, 1928, ACC Reel 8.43.4.

28. Copy of agreement in Connoly to Wharton, Apr. 25; Connoly to Wharton, July 2, 18, 1931, Reel 341, IAM Records; Box 3, Davison Papers.

29. Brown to Jersek, Apr. 29; J. Richardson, secretary, Lodge 188, to Carr, Aug. 28, 1931; G. J. Bowen to Arthur Alten, Mar. 25, 1936, Reel 341, IAM Records.

30. Perlman, *Machinists*, 90, 100, 238.

31. Louis Maciejenski to FDR, July 14, 1933, "AMC, Employment, Skilled Workers," box 6047, NRA Records.

32. *Buffalo Courier Express*, July 24, 1933, 18; Fleet to Johnson, Oct. 3, 1933; J. J. Murphy, "Speech to Fellow Workers at the Boeing Plant," Reel 355, IAM

Records; Fleet claimed the strike settlement increased his wage bill by 28 percent, *Delaney Hearings*, 714.

33. Buffalo Aeronautical Workers Union, "Resolution," Sept. 15; Murphy and C. J. Cook to General Johnson, Sept. 15, 1933, "AMC, Employment," box 6046, NRA Records. By June, Curtiss's exports for 1933 were worth $2.5 million, due mainly to orders from China, *Aerodigest*, Mar. 1934, 62; copy of an invitation to the Buffalo convention signed by Murphy to the Seattle Central Labor and Trades Council, Oct. 24, 1933, Reel 355, IAM Records. Buffalo aircraft workers had a powerful ally in Cong. James M. Mead, chairman of the Committee on the Post Office and Post Roads, who lobbied high NRA officials on behalf of a thirty-hour week for aircraft workers at a minimum wage of sixty-five cents. Mead to Johnson, Nov. 28, 1933, "AMC, Manufacturing and Employment," box 6047, NRA Records.

34. "Notice to Employees," signed by C. W. Deeds, Aug. 23, 1933, "AMC, Employment, Wages and Hours," box 6047, NRA Records.

35. G. Bowen to Wharton, Aug. 25, Sept. 11, 1933, Reel 333, IAM Records; Brown to Frank Morrison, May 10, 1935, Reel 337, IAM Records; Eli Walker, Pratt & Whitney mechanic, Oct. 5, 1933; C. T. LaVista, president, Industrial Aircraft Workers Union, to Cong. H. P. Koppleman, Jan. 14, 1934, "AMC, Statistics," box 6047, NRA Records.

36. Auerbach, *Labor and Liberty*, 50.

37. Thomas Morgan to G. L. Martin, Nov. 2, 1934, Glenn L. Martin Papers, box 2, Library of Congress; Holley, *Buying Aircraft*, 37; *Fortune*, Dec. 1939, 73–77.

38. F. N. Kershaw, business agent, District Lodge 12, to Carr, July 1; Carr to Kershaw, July 6; Kershaw to Wharton, July 15; Wharton to John P. Frey, head of the AFL Metal Trades Department, July 17; Kershaw to Secretary of War Dern, Aug. 28, 1933, Reel 332, IAM Records; Martin to the ACC, Mar. 26, 1934, Martin Papers, box 2. Martin's attitudes toward organized labor and his willingness to take advantage of high unemployment and flout federal labor laws were widely shared by Baltimore employers. See Jo Ann E. Argersinger, *Toward a New Deal in Baltimore* (Chapel Hill: University of North Carolina Press, 1988), 146, chap. 6. For the weakness of the NRA's machinery for compliance in Baltimore see Argersinger, 59–60, 147–150.

39. Argersinger, 19; M. L. Kerwin, director of conciliation, Department of Labor, "Report on the Glenn L. Martin Company," Dec. 26, 1933, Reel 332, IAM Records; Evelyn Lanham to Johnson, Dec. 18, 1933, and to E. E. Hughes, Feb. 2, 1934; "AMC, Employment, Wages, and Hours," box 6047, NRA Records; NLB Release no. 3642, Mar. 5, 1934, in "Air Transport Code, Compliance," box 530, NRA Records.

40. NLB Release No. 2858, Jan. 22, 1934, "AMC, Conferences," box 6045, NRA Records.

41. Louis B. Perry and Richard S. Perry, *A History of the Los Angeles Labor Movement 1911–1941* (Berkeley: University of California Press, 1963), 197–201, quote, 250; Gottlieb and Wolf, *Thinking Big*, 185–215; Rae, *Climb to Greatness*, 11–12; David F. Selvin, *Sky Full of Storm: A Brief History of California Labor* (San Francisco: California Historical Society, 1975), 54–55; *Hearings before a Subcommittee of the Committee on Education and Labor*, Senate, 76th Cong., 3d sess., Jan. 1940, pursuant to S. Res. 266, 74th Cong.: *A Resolution to Investigate Violations of the Right of Free Speech and Assembly and Interference with the Right of Labor to Organize and Bargain Collectively (LaFollette Hearings)*, "Los Angeles Industrial Background, Open Shop Activities," Pts. 52, 53, 57, 58, 64.

42. W. E. Johnson, secretary, UBCJA 1557, to Hugh Johnson, Aug. 10, 1933, "AMC, Employment, Hours and Wages," box 6047, NRA Records.

43. "Success in Santa Monica," *Fortune*, May 1935, 79. Despite record sales of $5.3 million in 1934, Douglas returned only $39,000.

44. For the DC-2's costs see ibid., 190. Wages do not include engineers' salaries. Underpaid engineers and designers in Southern California also sought relief through the NRA. They objected to the exclusion of technical employees from the code's provisions and unsuccessfully tried to organize a national union. M. Carlson and George Hisbso to General Johnson, Mar. 13, 1934, "AMC, Amendments," box 6045, NRA Records; L. C. Porter, secretary of Seattle Association of Technicians, Engineers, and Architects, an AFL affiliate, to Congressman Zioncheck, Mar. 16, 1934, "AMC, Wages and Hours," box 6046, NRA Records.

45. H. C. Bard, a Douglas machinist, to J. T. Thorpe, IAM general vice-president, May 9; Carr to Thorpe, May 22, 1933, Reel 330, IAM Records; T. H. Witham, secretary, UBCJA 1557, to Cong. John F. Dockweiler, Sept. 7; Dockweiler to Johnson, Sept. 14, 1933, "AMC, Originals and Revisions," box 6046, NRA Records. For Los Angeles wage rates see *Monthly Labor Review*, Sept 1933, 660, and Perry and Perry, *Los Angeles Labor Movement*, 246. The best-paid sheetmetal workers in Los Angeles received $1.12.

46. Gross to Courtland S. Gross, Nov. 20, Dec. 1, 1933, and Gross to R. C. Walker, Apr. 18, 1934, Business Correspondence, box 1; Gross to R. H. Gross, Nov. 26, 1934, Personal Correspondence, box 1, Robert Ellsworth Gross Papers, Library of Congress; memo, "Lockheed and the NIRA," signed by Gross, Sept. 28, 1933; "Lockheed Aircraft InterDepartmental Communication," Sept. 28, 1934; "To All Employees," Gross et al., n.d., "Lockheed Aircraft, Misc. Papers, 1933–34," box 8, Ashby C. McGraw Collection, Walter Reuther Library, Detroit.

47. Lyon, *National Recovery Administration*, 430, 443.

48. "Transcript of Oral Testimony at the Public Hearing, Code of Fair Competition for the Aircraft Manufacturing Industry," Hearing no. 402, Dec. 20, 1933, "AMC, Hearings," box 7264, NRA Records.

49. Ibid.

50. LAB, "Analysis of the Brief Presented by the Industry," Dec. 21, 1933; "AMC, Amendments," box 6045; see also William Green to Johnson, Jan. 3, 1934, "AMC, Labor Provisions," box 6047, NRA Records.

51. "Post-Hearing Aircraft Conference on Wages and Hours"; "Latest Draft," Jan. 24, 1934, "AMC, Conferences," box 6045, NRA Records.

52. Pearce, "Aircraft Manufacturing Industry," Apr. 4, 1934, "AMC, Documents," box 6045, NRA Records.

53. Ibid.

54. "Upon his own motion, or if a complaint is made to the President that abuses inimical to the public interest and contrary to the policy herein declared are prevalent in any trade or industry or subdivision thereof, and if no code of fair competition therefore has theretofore been approved by the President, the President . . . may prescribe and approve a code of fair competition for such trade or industry . . . ," NIRA, sec. 3d, quoted in Lyon, *National Recovery Administration*, 892.

55. Rogers to I. D. Everitt, assistant deputy administrator, Apr. 23, 1934, "AMC, Documents," box 6047. Six draft codes are dated Jan. 24, Apr. 28, June 1, July 18, Aug. 8, and Nov. 27, 1934. Rogers to the NRA, Jan. 7, 1935, "AMC, Documents," box 6045, NRA Records.

56. C. Raushenbush's penciled notes, n.d., "AMC, General," box 6047; memo,

Board on Wages (Navy), to Commandant, United States Navy Yard, Philadelphia, Feb. 13, 1934, "AMC, Employment," box 6046; Rogers to Everitt, Aug. 9; Raushenbush to Everitt, Aug. 14. 1934, "AMC, Documents," box 6045, NRA Records.

57. Hawley, *New Deal and the Problem of Monopoly*, 98; Lyon, *National Recovery Administration*, 66.

58. Gates to C. E. Adams, division administrator, Aug. 28, 1934, "AMC, Reports," box 6046; Raushenbush to Advisory Council, Aug. 29, 1934; John Frey and Sidney Hillman to Advisory Council, Sept. 12, 1934, Central Record Section, Advisory Council, General Correspondence, box 8148, NRA Records.

59. Penciled notes of a meeting, n.d., Central Record Section, box 8148, NRA Records.

60. E. B. George, executive officer, Advisory Council, to Everitt, Sept. 13, 1934, "AMC, Reports," box 6046, NRA Records.

61. Raushenbush to Gates, Sept. 26; Everitt to Raushenbush, Sept. 26; Rogers to Everitt, Oct. 18, 23, 1934; "AMC, Employment, Wages, and Hours," box 6046; Murray to Everitt, Oct. 24, 1934, "AMC, Overtime," box 6047, NRA Records.

62. William Lawson, "Aircraft Manufacturing Industry," Nov. 30, 1934, "AMC, Conference," box 6045, NRA Records.

63. Rogers to the NRA, Jan. 7, 1935, "AMC, Documents," box 6045, NRA Records.

64. F. P. Evans, Research and Planning, to Everitt, Jan. 16, Feb. 14; LAB to Everitt, Jan. 15, Feb. 4; A. Brown, review officer, to Everitt, Mar. 9, 1935, "AMC, Reports," box 6046, NRA Records.

65. Temple N. Joyce, general manager at North American Aviation, to the ACC, Apr. 20; list of workers' demands signed by "committee"; Agreement signed by Joyce and the workers' committee, Apr. 28; D.L. Brown, to the ACC, Apr. 19; "Memorandum Agreement," May 16, 1934, ACC Reel 15.66.0.

66. J. F. Grover to Johnson, Feb. 16, Mar. 8, 1934; F. L. Scrogings to the secretary of commerce, Mar. 23, 1934, "AMC, Wages and Hours," box 6046, NRA Records; Perry and Perry, *Los Angeles Labor Movement*, 258–266, 272–275, 311–315.

67. T. Nylander of the NLB to Lockheed Aircraft, Jan. 15; Gross memo, Jan. 24; NLB Hearings, transcripts, Feb. 2, 16, 19; decision, Feb. 20, 1935 in McGraw v. Lockheed Aircraft Company, box 8, McGraw Papers; Bruce Nelson, *Workers on the Waterfront: Seamen, Longshoremen and Unionism in the 1930s* (Urbana: University of Illinois Press, 1988), 130–132.

68. "Excerpts from the Minutes of the Meeting of the Executive Council, AFL, San Francisco, Oct. 14, 1934"; Witham, "The Plan," Reel 334, IAM Records; McGraw, "Confidential News Bulletin, United Aircraft Mechanics," Sept. 1, 1934, "Lockheed Aircraft, Misc. Papers, 1933–34," box 8, McGraw Papers; Perlman, *Machinists*, 106–107.

69. *Buffalo Courier-Express*, Apr. 4; Morrison to Carr, Mar. 29, 1934, Reel 355, IAM Records; Weekly Report, Apr. 21, 1934, in Buffalo Regional Board Weekly Reports, tag 24, Records of the National Labor Board, Record Group 25, National Archives, Washington, D.C.

70. NLB decision, May 1, 1934, case no. 64, NLB, RG 25. For the sympathy of the Buffalo board to labor's hopes for NIRA, see copies of the speeches of its executive secretary, Daniel B. Shortal, ibid., and Fine, *Automobile*, 205.

71. NLB Release, No. 5066, May 15, 1934, NLB, RG 25; report of Organizer

Conroy, Buffalo, May 25, 1934, records of FLU 18286, AFL Records, Pt. 1: Strikes and Agreement File, 1898–1953, University Publications of America, P86–1659; Lawrence Bell to Rogers, Apr. 27; May 2; T. P. Wright, general manager at Curtiss, to the ACC, May 28, 1934, ACC Reel 15.66.0.

72. Hamilton to D. B. Shortal, "Petition of the Aircraft for Election," July 2, 1934; Shortal to Lloyd K. Garrison, chairman, NLRB, July 26, 1934, tag 24, NLB Records. On the Houde case and the issue of majority rule for the establishment of collective bargaining agents see Fine, *Automobile*, 205–206, 227, 310–311; Vittoz, *New Deal Labor Policy*, 144; Lyon, *National Recovery Administration*, 483.

73. *Buffalo Courier-Express*, Aug. 26, Sept. 22, 1934.

74. Buffalo Aeronautical Workers to Raushenbush, July 9, 1934, "AMC, Employment, Labor Provisions," Box 6047, NRA Records; J. C. Johnston, Buffalo Central Labor Council, to Green, Sept. 12, 1934, records of FLU 18286, AFL Records.

75. Lewis to Green, Oct. 22; Green to Lewis, Oct. 24; Cook to Green, Oct. 25; Cook to Lewis, Oct. 24; Lewis to Green, Nov. 1; Green to Cook, Nov. 20, 1934, records of FLU 18286, AFL Records. See the company union publication, *Aircraft News*, in Buffalo administration files, box 117, NLB Records.

76. Weekly Report, Dec. 15; Shortal to R. B. Watts, NLRB Counsel, Dec. 21, 1934; Weekly Report, Jan. 12, Mar. 23, 1935, tag 24, NLB Records; Brown to G. E. Edmonds, business agent, Local 1235, Long Beach, July 18; Leo Imblum to Wharton, Nov. 25, 1935, Reel 329, IAM Records; Fleet quoted by J. Carlton Word, president of Fairchild Aircraft, notes of meeting, July 15, 1941, ACC Reel 32.3.0.

77. G. W. Carr of Boeing, to the ACC, Apr. 10; T. N. Joyce to the ACC, Apr. 20; Rogers to H. H. Wetzel, vice-president at Douglas, Apr. 24, 1934, ACC Reel 15.66.0. See the bimonthly "Labor Reports" from March to September 1934 in ACC Reel 15.66.0 and ACC Reel 14.69.0.

78. Carl Sandvigen, business agent, IAM Hope Lodge 79, report for the week ending Jan. 9, 1934, Reel 355, IAM Records.

79. Copy of speech by Murphy in Sandvigen to Wharton, Jan. 18; Sandvigen to H. J. Carr, Feb. 21, 1934, Reel 355, IAM Records.

80. Ibid., Sandvigen to Wharton, Feb. 6; Carr to Sandvigen, Feb. 8, 26; Carr to Morrison, Feb. 26, 1934.

81. Ibid., Sandvigen to Carr, Feb. 21; Sandvigen, report, Mar. 3; Morrison to Carr, Mar. 7, 1934.

82. Ibid., R. Watson to Morrison, Mar. 18; Sandvigen to Carr, Mar. 22; Carr to Morrison, Mar. 26, 28; Morrison to Carr, Mar. 29, 1934.

CHAPTER SEVEN. PATTERNS TO WORLD WAR II

1. Smith, *Army and Economic Mobilization*, 7.

2. On the persistence of price competition and company losses see Holley, *Buying Aircraft*, 138–143. On the services attempts to get "the last pound of flesh out of each and every" manufacturer, see "Curtiss-Wright: Warrior," *Fortune*, Sept. 1938, 84–85. For insights on the results of procurement regulations for aeronautic development see the commentaries of Cy Caldwell, particularly "Major General Difficulties," *Aerodigest*, Jan. 1936, 15.

3. Holley, *Buying Aircraft*, 53–63, 66, 69–79, 169–175.

4. One critic claimed that during the first half of 1937 the army had only 270

state-of-the-art, combat-ready aircraft, the rest being unserviceable or useful only as trainers. Cy Caldwell, "Phantom Wings of the Air Corps," *Aerodigest*, July 1937, 30. Numbers were still well below the 1936 target in fall 1941. Under stiff competition with Lend-Lease, the Army Air Forces could field 1,392 modern combat craft, including 555 P-40 pursuits, 112 B-17s, and 386 B-25, B-26, A-20 and A-24 medium and light bombers. Most of these, however, lacked some or all of the combat essentials: armor, leak-proof tanks, and turrets. See Brig. Gen. Carl Spaatz, memo to Lovett, Nov. 25, 1941, "Combat Planes Available . . . October 31, 1941," box 155, entry 39, Records of the Office of the Assistant Secretary of War for Air, Robert A. Lovett, 1941–1945 (Lovett Records), Record Group 107, National Archives, Washington, D.C.

5. Concerned that it appeared primitive by America's standards of production, the industry's trade journals regularly featured the manufacturers' halting attempts to institute mass production. See for example A. C. Falk, "Reduction of Aircraft Costs by Engineering Planning," *Aerodigest*, July 1937, 42, or G. E. Barton, " 'Flow Processing' Method of Aircraft Production," *Aerodigest*, Jan. 1938, 28.

6. Grover Loening, an industry pioneer, was one exception who warned against investment in aircraft in expectation of high-output mass production. He cited the mass-production efforts of World War I, pointing out that "this system failed miserably." Aircraft was "really a contract business . . ., [it] never has been a real production industry and is not likely to be." Loening, "Aviation and Banking," confidential report prepared for the Chase National Bank, Oct. 1938, copy in the Library of the National Air and Space Museum, Washington, D.C.

7. "Owing to the intense feeling of horror which the civilian public feels regarding possible air raids . . . it would probably feel more comfortable if the War Department were known to be receiving large numbers of airplanes and foreign nations would probably regard the position of the U.S. in a different light." Donald Ross, "The Aviation Manufacturing Industry in the United States," Dec. 20, 1938, prepared for the securities firm, White, Weld & Co., 14, 9. Copy in the Library of the National Air and Space Museum.

8. The Finletter Commission was charged with advising President Truman on a comprehensive approach to national security, aircraft manufacture, and air transport; its 1947 records reveal the struggles of its participants with this dilemma. As the Finletter Commission deliberated on the nature of America's new commitments and the threats it faced, it is difficult to determine which served which in their minds: a healthy aircraft industry the needs of meeting a military threat or a military threat the needs of a healthy aircraft industry. That ambiguity seems unavoidable in an age of high-tech weaponry, but it was skewed by the commission, which assumed that a healthy aircraft industry was one with continuous, large-scale output. Records of the President's Air Policy Commission, Record Group 220, Harry S. Truman Library, Independence, Mo.

9. Loening, "Aviation and Banking," 9.

10. Vaughan, Aug. 10, 1937, *Hearings on H.R. 7777, Further Amending Section 3 . . .* , 75th Cong., 1st sess., Aug. 5–12, 1937 *(Scott Hearings)*, 1791; "Export Committee, Minutes," Mar. 25, 1938, ACC Reel 17.72.4; see also ACC Reel 19.06.9.

11. "Minutes of the Executive Committee Meeting," Mar. 21, 1939; ACC Reel 19.08.3; "Exports, Financing," ACC Reel 19.34.0. On the Export-Import Bank in Latin America during the 1930s see Adams, *Economic Diplomacy*, chaps. 5, 7.

12. For evidence of Seversky's subterfuges and at least $1.1 million in illicit deals with Okura & Co., New York agents for the Japanese navy and army, see photo-

stats of Okura documents in box 50, entry 131, Records of the Assistant Secretary of the Navy for Air, Artemus L. Gates, 1941–1946 (Gates Records), Record Group 72, National Archives, Washington, D.C.; for quotations, see memo, Sept. 12, 1939, ACC Reel 19.34.0; "Exports, West Coast Export Conference, L.A., Oct. 1940," ACC Reel 21.43.1; Lovett Records, passim. On the challenges of German aviation in Latin America see I. F. Gellman, *Good Neighbor Diplomacy* (Baltimore: Johns Hopkins University Press, 1979), 108–109.

13. Charts and tables in box 39, Finletter Commission Records; Holley, *Buying Aircraft*, 33–34; Lynn L. Bollinger and Tom Lilley, *Financial Position of the Aircraft Industry* (Boston: Harvard University Graduate School of Business Administration, 1943), 8.

14. Holley, *Buying Aircraft*, 35; thirty-seven manufacturers of aircraft, engines, and accessories spent $44 million on development during a five-year period ending Jan. 1, 1939, or 9.4 percent on $468 million in sales. "What Does the Future Hold?" Hirsch, Lilienthal & Co., Aviation Securities Department, New York, 1940, in the Library of the National Air and Space Museum.

15. Charts and tables in box 39, Finletter Commission Records; "An Engineering Interpretation of the Economic and Financial Aspects of American Industry," vol. 1, "The Aviation Industry," George S. Armstrong & Co., Consultants, New York, 1941, 36, copy in the Library of the National Air and Space Museum; Holley, *Buying Aircraft*, 33–36, quoted, 35.

16. McNaugher, *New Weapons, Old Politics*.

17. Bollinger and Lilley, *Financial Position*, 8–9; Holley, *Buying Aircraft*, 39–41; "An Engineering Interpretation," 35.

18. Capt. S. J. Zeigler and Special Assistant J. W. Meader, "An Investigation of the Financial Condition and Recent Earnings of Aircraft Contractors," for Artemus Gates, May 14, 1942, 12, 24–25, box 9, entry 131, Gates Records.

19. "The American Aviation Industry," office memo, Carl M. Loeb & Co., New York, Apr. 11, 1935, 44, copy in the Library of the National Air and Space Museum; H.R. 9327, 75th Cong., 1st sess., 1937; H.R. 10071, 75th Cong., 3d sess., 1938; Hotchkiss to Rogers, Feb. 9, 1939, ACC Reel 19.51.3. See also H.R. 6101, 75th Cong., 1st sess., 1937, seeking to prohibit the Naval Aircraft Factory from competing with the industry.

20. "Design Rights," ACC Reel 19.27.3; "Minutes of the Executive Committee," Nov. 4, 1938; "Minutes of the Procurement Committee," June 20, 1937, ACC Reel 17.22.3.

21. Edison to Scott, July 28, 1937, copy in *Hearings on H.R. 7777*, 75th Cong., 1st sess., Aug. 5–12, 1937, (*Scott Hearings*), 1697; see also H. Rept. 2149, 75th Cong., 3d sess., Apr. 18, 1938 (*Scott Report*), and ACC Reel 23-A.20.9., 23-A.36.0. For a copy of the relevant IRS regulations, see *Treasury Department Bulletin 4723*, ACC Reel 23-A.38.3.

22. Admiral Cook, *Scott Hearings*, 1698–1708; for a letter in support of H.R. 7777 from Gen. Oscar Westover, chief of the Air Corps, see *Scott Hearings*, 1796.

23. "Digest of the Minutes of the Executive Comm.," Mar. 24, Nov. 4, 1938, ACC Reel 17.22.3. "Some don'ts for testimony," Aug. 4, 1937, ACC Reel 18.16.2; L. W. Rogers, "ACC Annual Report," Jan. 1939, ACC Reel 19.12.0; *Congressional Record*, June 6, 1938.

24. W. H. Lewis, *Scott Hearings*, 1709–1748, quoted, 1743.

25. Glenn. L. Martin Corp. to Scott, Aug. 10, 1937, *Scott Hearings*, 1828–1830;

Loening, "Aviation and Banking." Sixty percent of sales in payrolls includes salaries for engineers, draftsmen, supervisers, accountants, clerks, and so on. The numbers of these nonproduction employees were very large in aircraft. In May 1940 there were 100,000 employees in airframes, 40,000 of whom were on salary. T. P. Wright, "An Analytical Discussion to Determine the Size of Aircraft Industry Required . . . ," May 25, 1940, copy in ACC Reel 23.35.8.

26. Vaughan, *Scott Hearings*, 1752–1813; Treasury Department to Curtiss Aeroplane, July 23, 1936, ibid, 1789.

27. C. J. McCarthy, Vought general manager, *Scott Hearings*, 1836–1841; J. F. McCarthy, ibid., 1843.

28. Fleet, ibid., 1718–1720.

29. Grumman, ibid., 1824–1828; for claims by manufacturers that Vinson-Trammell forced "pioneering steps" in cost accounting, see "Notes on Conference with War Department Board, April 12, 13, 1939," ACC Reel 19.82.1. For the abuse by contracting law of another leading innovator see Alexander P. Seversky to Louis Johnson, June 7, 1938, box 3A, entry 207, Secretary of War, General Correspondence, 1932–1942, Record Group 107, National Archives, Washington, D.C.

30. Sherry, *Rise of American Airpower*, 76–83, 97; Dallek, *Franklin D. Roosevelt*, 172–173. At a post–Pearl Harbor conference of top production planners including Lovett, Gates, Col. B. E. Meyers, and T. P. Wright, "none of those present . . . had any idea of how the President arrived at his objective for the aircraft program," which FDR had just pegged at 125,000 aircraft per year. Meyers to Col. L. W. Miller, Jan. 9, 1942, box 792, entry 293, Central Decimal Files 452.1, Army Adjutant General, 1939–1942 (AAG Records), series II, classified, Records of the Army Air Forces, RG 18, National Archives, Washington, D.C.

31. Hotchkiss to Rogers, Apr. 26, 1937, ACC Reel 17.14.4.

32. Leighton Rogers complained that he had been unable to muster a quorum for over two years. Rogers to Board of Governors, Apr. 11, 1938, ACC Reel 17.25.7, 20.25.5.

33. "Minutes of the Executive Committee," Jan. 16, 31, 1939, ACC Reel 19.03.0.

34. Jouett to "all manufacturers," Apr. 7, 1939, ACC Reel 19.89.0. For the manufacturers' resignations see ACC Reel 34.50.6; see the Records of the National Aircraft War Production Council, Harry S. Truman Library, Independence, Mo.

35. Rogers to Maj. F. G. Borum, Dec. 9, 1938, ACC Reel 18.15.0; "Annual Meeting," Jan. 26, 1939, ACC Reel 19.12.0.

36. Fleet to the ACC, May 16, 1939, ACC Reel 19.87.7; Fleet to chief of the Air Corps, May 12, 1939, box 64, 004.4, series 1, unclassified, AAG Records; Ross, "The Aviation Manufacturing Industry in the United States."

37. Johnson to Stephen Early, secretary to the president, Feb. 4, 1939, box 74A, Records of the Office of the Assistant Secretary of War, Louis Johnson, subject file, 1937–1940, RG 107, National Archives (Johnson Records); Jouett to Egtvedt, Mar. 17, 1939, ACC Reel 19.63.3; Jouett to Johnson, Mar. 22, 1939, ACC Reel 19.54.5; Fleet's Mar. 1939 telegrams to Jouett, ACC Reel 19.81.7.

38. Arnold, memos to Johnson, Mar. 13, 22, 1939, box 74A, Johnson Records; for Johnson's Mar. 17 plea to FDR for support of negotiated contracts and a draft bill for the purpose, see ibid.

39. Jouett to L. E. Graham of the Aero Supply Mfg. Co., Mar. 17, 1939, ACC Reel 19.06.9; Public No. 18, 555, H.R. 3791, *An Act to Provide More Effectively for the National Defense . . .* , 76th Cong., 1st sess., sec. 14, Apr. 3, 1939. "Materiel

Division Bull. no. 30A, Procurement Policy and Procedure for Aircraft, Aircraft Accessories and Aeronautical Equipment and Administrative Procedure," July 1, 1939, Book 18, box 8, Col A. J. Lyon's Project Files, 1939–1941, entry 219, Record Group 18, National Archives, Washington, D.C.

40. Vaughan to Jouett, Apr. 10, 1939; Douglas to the ACC, Apr. 7, 1939, ACC Reel 19.66.9. This slur against agrarian congressmen crops up regularly in the private documents. See for example Edgar Gott, Consolidated vice president, to Jouett, Jan. 22, 1940, ACC Reel 21.16.9.

41. "Final Report of the Air Corps Board on Revision to the 5-Year Experimental Program," June 28, 1939, box 219, 400.112, series 2, classified, AAG Records; "Notes on Conference with War Department Board, April 12, 1939," ACC Reel 19.82.1; Jouett to War Department, Apr. 14, 1939; "Draft of Proposed Treasury Regulations," ACC Reel 19.57.1; Jouett to W. H. Lewis, vice-president at Douglas, July 20, 1939; "ACC Accounting Committee Critique," July 20, 1939, ACC Reel 19.66.9; "ACC Executive Committee Meeting," June 14, 1939, ACC Reel 19.06.9.

42. Arnold, memos to Johnson, May 18, July 8, 1939, box 74A, Johnson Records.

43. See Rogers to Maj. F. G. Borum, Dec. 9, 1938, ACC Reel 18.15.0; "War Plans Survey 1936–1939," ACC Reel 20.25.5; the ASW, the Air Corps Planning Section, and the Army-Navy Munitions Board tried to coordinate plans and allocations for industrial facilities beginning in 1937. Their success can be measured by the response from Johnson, assistant secretary of war, to a request for basic information on the industry from the writers of "An Engineering Interpretation" cited in note 15, this chapter. It was Johnson's "feeling that such a request might prove embarrassing to the War Department at this time," and so the consultants agreed "to obtain such information elsewhere." D. S. Loudon of George S. Armstrong & Co., Jan. 30, 1939, to Col. H. W. Harms of the Planning Section, who penciled in this letter's margin, "It was also embarrassing to me," Box 64, 004.4, series 1, unclassified, AAG Records.

44. "Procurement Conference," transcript, July 10, 1939, ACC Reel 19.53.7. On America's war plans as a struggle of industrial might, see A. S. Milward, *War, Economy and Society 1939–1945* (Berkeley: University of California Press, 1977), 50–53; see also Sherry, *Rise of American Airpower*, 97: Mobilization was "the lowest common denominator of thinking about airpower."

45. The Air Corps "Yardstick Board" set pounds per square foot of factory floor space per month as the measure of production. On the Air Corps' frustration on cost-planning and the turn to Vannevar Bush and the National Research Council (NRC) for ways to cope with and reduce costs see Col. F. M. Kennedy to Arnold, Apr. 5, 1939; Brett to Arnold, Sept. 12, 1939; memo for Arnold, Mar. 29, 1940; Bush to Arnold, Sept. 28, 1939; on cost inflation see "Factors which Affect Increased Production and Unit Costs of Military Aircraft, Engines, and Accessories," July 9, 1940, NRC, all in box 793, 452.1, series 2, classified, AAG Records.

46. "Procurement Conference," ACC Reel 19.53.7. Echoing Martin's remedy for the industry, Robert Gross, president of Lockheed, told a reporter that "there are very few things in this industry that orders would not cure." "How Many Planes When?" *Fortune*, Aug. 1940, 49.

47. "Criticisms Made against Aircraft and Engine Procurement Aviation Expansion Program," n.d., 1940; Col. J. W. Schulz to Louis Johnson, Mar. 26, 1940, "Aircraft and Airplanes," box 74A, Johnson Records.

48. R. J. Overy, *The Air War 1939–1945* (New York: Stein and Day, 1980), 153.

"Where the 50,000 figure came from was at the time and still remains a mystery . . . it dwarfed all existing procurement plans of the Services." J. C. Sitterson, "Aircraft Production Policies Under the National Defense Advisory Commission and Office of Production Management," Special Study no. 21, Civilian Production Administration, May 30, 1946, 1.

49. *54 Statute 676*, 76th Cong., 3d sess., June 28, 1940; *54 Statute 712*, 76th Cong., 3d sess., July 2, 1940. Details on allowable costs, fees, taxation, and profit limitations awaited further controversy, lengthy negotiation with the National Defense Advisory Commission and the Treasury, and more legislation in the autumn.

50. On FDR's limited options here, see R. D. Cuff, "Commentary," in *The Home Front and War in the Twentieth Century*, James Titus, ed., (Washington, D.C.: Office of Air Force History, 1984), 111–118.

51. Richard Polenberg, "The Decline of the New Deal, 1937–1940," and David Brody, "The New Deal and World War II," in *The New Deal: The National Level*, J. Braeman, R. Bremner and D. Brody, eds. (Columbus: Ohio State University Press, 1975); Alan Wolfe, *America's Impasse: The Rise and Fall of the Politics of Growth* (Boston: South End Press, 1981), 15–18.

52. In 1943 labor turnover averaged 100 percent per year in most plants. "Conference Memo on Aircraft Production: Prospects Under Present Conditions," box 2, entry 38, Lovett Records.

53. H. G. Hotchkiss, ACC counsel, to Rogers, May 10, 1937, ACC Reel 17.14.4, and Nov. 6, 1935, ACC Reel 16.2.1. The ACC provided manufacturers this service despite their continued unwillingness to divulge data on wages and working conditions.

54. Rogers to all members, May 27, 1937, ACC Reel 17.87.9.

55. Jouett to all members, June 2, 1939, ACC Reel 19.06.9; "Minutes of Annual Meeting," Jan. 26, 1939, 19.12.0; Kindleberger to Jouett, June 5, 1939, 19.37.4; "Executive Committee," Jan. 1940, ACC Reel 20.32.5; J. A. Williams of Curtiss to Jouett, Jan. 30, 1940; ACC Reel 22.40.5; Bureau of Labor Statistics, "Confidential Survey of Aero-Engine and Aircraft Industries," June 1939, copy in ACC Reel 22.40.5; Jouett to J. E. Schaefer, general manager at Boeing's Stearman Aircraft in Wichita, Mar. 26, 1941, ACC Reel 22.44.8.

56. James A. Gross, *The Reshaping of the National Labor Relations Board* (Albany: State University of New York Press, 1979) 2, 16–17, 108.

57. Brown to Kershaw, Aug. 14; Kershaw to Brown, Aug. 20, 1937; R. C. Lehde to Brown, Jan. 1; P. Hutchings, memo, Nov. 16, 1938, Reel 332, IAM Records.

58. P. Hutchings, IAM Lodge 774, to W. M. Aicher, regional director, 5th Region, NLRB, Sept. 8, 1938. The Baltimore board held the election valid despite the army's presence. Aicher to Hutchings, Sept. 27, 1938; C. Cooke to Hutchings, Feb. 13, 1939, Reel 332, IAM Records; "Glenn L. Martin Co.," *Fortune*, Dec. 1939, 128.

59. I. A. Sandvigen, IAM business representative in Seattle, "Report for the Week Ending April 25, 1936"; Brown to members of the Executive Council, July 3, 1936; Sandvigen to Wharton, Aug. 19, 1937, Reel 355, IAM Records; on Boeing's new plant see *Aerodigest*, Feb. 1937, 32–34.

60. Tate, "Army and its Air Corps," 209–224; Robert Vander Linden, "The Struggle for the Long Range Heavy Bomber: The United States Army Air Corps, 1934–39," Master's Thesis, George Washington University, 1981. The figure did not include the cost of engineering work "of a general nature" or Boeing's costs in developing the original XB-15. Boeing lost $641,000 less $167,000 in insurance on

the B-17 prototype when it crashed because of human error while undergoing Air Corps evaluation tests in 1935. For these and other B-17 costs, see box 739, 452.1, series 1, unclassified, AAG Records.

61. Even Homer T. Bone, the senator from Washington State who had attacked Boeing in 1934 as a "looter" of the taxpayer, complained about the possibility of letting the B-17 to competitors. See Johnson to Bone and Sen. Rufus C. Holman, Mar. 30, 1939, box 739, 452.1, series 1, AAG Records. Cost differentials were significant: $153,668 per B-24 and $200,678 per B-17 based on a 100-unit order. These figures did not include $35,000 for four engines and about $50,000 for "government furnished equipment" per plane. Figures and quote in Brett to chief of the Air Corps, Mar. 25, 1939, ibid., and "Airplane Cost Data," Apr. 15, 1939, box 793, 452.1, series 2, classified, AAG Records. See also Wright Field to Arnold, Feb. 21, 1939, box 250, 452.1, series 2, classified, AAG Records. The XB-24 first flew in December 1939.

62. P. G. Johnson, Boeing president, to Arnold, Mar. 28, 1940, Box 745, 452.1, series 1, unclassified, AAG Records.

63. Sandvigen to Wharton, Dec. 9; T. McNett, Secretary, Lodge #751, to Wharton, Mar. 28, 1937; E. L. Lynch to Wharton, Apr. 17, 1938, Reel 339, IAM Records; Wharton to all vice-presidents, Apr. 19, 1937, Reel 330, IAM Records. In 1938 Boeing was in serious trouble as B-17 orders materialized only slowly. Eighteen hundred workers accepted demands for concessions. "They say they might as well fold up. . . . They say they had to be able to show their customers that . . . they are competitive." Sandvigen to Wharton, Oct. 28, 1938, Reel 355, IAM Records.

64. H. B. McMurray to Brown, Mar. 8, 1935, Reel 330, IAM Records; Lynch to Lundquist, May 22, 1939; Lynch to Wharton, June 24, 1938, Reel 329, IAM Records.

65. C. F. Grow to Brown, Sept. 19, 1937; Lynch and McNett to Wharton, Mar. 14, 1938, Reel 329, IAM Records; McNett to David Behncke, Mar. 22, 1938, Reel 341, IAM Records; Lew Michenor, quarterly report, spring 1939, United Auto Workers Region 6, box 15, Henry Kraus Collection, Walter Reuther Library, Detroit; "industrial termites" and "fight to the end," are Douglas, quoted in *Los Angeles Evening News*, Sept. 8, 1937, and *Los Angeles Examiner*, Apr. 23, 1938. On Chief Davis, Gottlieb and Wolf, *Thinking Big*, 199, 225.

66. Lynch to Wharton, July 11, 1938, Reel 341, IAM Records. The Boeing Company was not party to this scheme or other collective antilabor mechanisms among west coast manufacturers. McNett to Poesnecker, Nov. 26, 1938, Reel 355, IAM Records; McNett to Frank Weaver, Boeing personnel manager, July 19, 1938, box 1, Tom McNett Collection, Walter Reuther Library, Detroit; Wyndham Mortimer, "Report on Aircraft Situation," Oct 3, 1939, box 15, Kraus Collection.

67. Brody, *Workers in Industrial America*, 115–116, 136. Aircraft workers reached parity with auto and steel workers only during the Vietnam War, and then for only a brief while. Bluestone et al., *Aircraft Industry Dynamics*, 152.

68. For a sense of these dilemmas at one plant, the burdens for workers and their families, and the general waste and demoralization that ensued when such giant projects as the new bomber plants proceeded in accord with unqualified business prerogative, see L. J. Carr and J. E. Stermer, *Willow Run: A Study of Industrialization and Cultural Inadequacy* (New York: Harper, 1952).

69. For Lovett's fiscal orthodoxy see his "Gilt-edged Insecurity," *Saturday Evening Post*, Apr. 3, 1937, 20.

70. On the decline during the late 1930s of that faction of New Dealers advocating

an activist, regulatory state for economic and social reform see Nelson Lichtenstein, *Labor's War at Home* (New York: Cambridge University Press, 1982), 26–46, 82–83; Kolko, *Main Currents*, 155; and Alan Brinkley, "The Idea of the State," in *The Rise and Fall of the New Deal Order*, S. Fraser and G. Gerstle, eds. (Princeton, N.J.: Princeton University Press, 1989), 100–101. For a useful distinction between social and commercial Keynesianism see T. Skocpol and M. Weir, "State Structures and the Possibilities for Keynesian Responses . . ." in *Bringing the State Back In*, Evans et al., eds. (New York: Cambridge University Press, 1985), 108. Eliot Janeway, *The Struggle for Survival* (New Haven, Conn: Yale University Press, 1951), 43. For the Reuther Plan see box 144, entry 39, Lovett Records; Lichtenstein, *Labor's War at Home*, 83–89; Brody, "The New Deal and World War II," 282–286.

71. Janeway, *Struggle for Survival*; Bruce Catton, *Warlords of Washington* (New York: Harcourt, Brace, 1948); Smith, *Army and Economic Mobilization*, 35–118; Holley, *Buying Aircraft*, 247–273.

72. War Department spending for development of new airframes and equipment (engines and materials excluded) ballooned from $2 million in FY 1939 to $82 million in FY 1943 as the air force assumed its contemporary role as the nation's leading institution for technological change. "Research and Development Program, Fiscal Year 1940," Air Corps, Subtitle "B" Funds, July 28, 1939, box 192, 400.112, Bulkies, series 2, classified, AAG Records; "Research and Development Program, Fiscal Year 1943," Feb. 13, 1942, box 219, 400.112, series 2, classified, AAG Records.

CHAPTER EIGHT. CONCLUSION

1. See esp. Sherry, *Rise of American Airpower*.

ARCHIVAL SOURCES

Aeronautical Chamber of Commerce. Records. Library of the Aerospace Industries Association, Washington, D.C.

American Federation of Labor. Federal Labor Union 18286. Records. Part 1: Strikes and Agreements File, 1898–1953. University Publications of America, P86-1659.

Army Adjutant General, Army Air Forces, 1939–1942. Central Decimal Files. Record Group 18, National Archives, Washington, D.C.

Army Air Forces. Records. Record Group 18, National Archives, Washington, D.C.

Bureau of Foreign and Domestic Commerce. Records. Record Group 151, National Archives, Washington, D.C.

Davison, F. Trubee, Assistant Secretary of War for Air, 1926–1933. Office Files. Record Group 107, National Archives, Washington, D.C.

Gates, Artemus L., Assistant Secretary of the Navy for Air, 1940–1946. Office Files, Entry 131. Record Group 72, National Archives, Washington, D.C.

Gross, Robert Ellsworth. Papers. Library of Congress.

International Association of Machinists. International President's Records. State Historical Society of Wisconsin, Madison.

Johnson, Louis B., Assistant Secretary of War, 1937–1940. Office Files. Record Group 107, National Archives, Washington, D.C.

Keys, Clement M. Papers. Archives of the National Air and Space Museum, Washington, D.C.

Kraus, Henry. Collection. Walter Reuther Library, Detroit.

Lovett, Robert A., Assistant Secretary of War for Air, 1941–1945. Office Files. Record Group 107, National Archives, Washington, D.C.

McGraw, Ashby C. Collection. Walter Reuther Library, Detroit.

McNett, Tom. Collection. Walter Reuther Library, Detroit.

Martin, Glenn L. Papers. Library of Congress.

Michenor, Lewis H. Oral History Transcript, June 21, 1960. Library of Labor History and Urban Affairs, Wayne State University, Detroit.

National Aircraft War Production Council. Records. Harry S. Truman Presidential Library, Independence, Mo.

National Labor Board. Records. Record Group 25, National Archives, Washington, D.C.

National Recovery Administration. Records. Record Group 9, National Archives, Washington, D.C.

President's Air Policy Commission (Finletter Commission). Records. Record Group 220, Harry S. Truman Presidential Library, Independence, Mo.

Reconstruction Finance Corporation. Records. Record Group 234, National Archives, Washington, D.C.

Special Committee Investigating the Munitions Industry (Nye Committee). Records. Record Group 46, National Archives, Washington, D.C.

Roosevelt, Franklin Delano. Papers. FDR Presidential Library, Hyde Park, N.Y.

Secretary of War, 1932–1942, General Correspondence, Entry 207. Record Group 107, National Archives, Washington, D.C.

GOVERNMENT DOCUMENTS

American Aviation Mission (Crowell Commission). *Report.* Washington, D.C.: GPO, 1919.

Congressional Record. 1914–1940. Washington, D.C.

Federal Aviation Commission. *Report.* Washington, D.C.: GPO, 1934.

National Advisory Commission on Aeronautics. *Tenth Annual Report, 1924.* Washington, D.C.: GPO, 1925.

President's Aircraft Board (Morrow Board). *Report.* 1925.

Special Committee of the House Relating to an Investigation of the War Department, 1934–1936 (Rogers Hearings) (unpublished hearings), 73rd Cong., 2d sess., 1934, Box 1, Record Group 233, National Archives, Washington, D.C.

U.S. Congress. House. *A Bill to Regulate the Manner of Purchasing Aircraft, Aircraft Parts, and Aircraft Accessories, and to Promote and Encourage the Industry,* H.R. 11950, 69th Cong., 1st sess., 1926.

———. *Conference Report 1527, To Increase the Efficiency of the Air Corps,* 69th Cong., 1st sess., June 22, 1926.

———. House. *Hearings on H.R. 7777, Further Amending Section 3 of the Act to Establish the Composition of the United States Navy with Respect to the Categories of Vessels (Scott Hearings),* 75th Cong., 1st sess., Aug. 5–12, 1937.

———. *H.Rept. 1396, 1395 on H.R. 12471 and 12472,* 69th Cong., 1st sess., June 7, 1926.

———. *H.Rept. 1506 (Rogers Report),* 73rd Cong., 2d sess., July 17, 1934.

———. *H.Rept. 2060 (Delaney Report),* 73rd Cong., 2d sess., June 18, 1934.

———. *H.Rept. 2149 (Scott Report),* 75th Cong., 3d sess., April 18, 1938.

U.S. Congress. House. Committee on Military Affairs. *Army Reorganization Hearings on H.R. 7925,* 66th Cong., 1st sess., 1919.

U.S. Congress. House. Committee on Naval Affairs. *Hearings on H.R. 11249, A Bill to Permit the Purchase of Naval Aircraft and Aircraft Engines without Advertisement and for Other Purposes (Butler Hearings),* 69th Cong., 1st sess., 1926.

——. *Information as to the Method of Awarding Contracts for Ships and Air-craft for the United States Navy (Vinson Hearings)*, Jan. 24, 1934.

U.S. Congress, House. Select Committee of Inquiry into Operations of the United States Air Service. *Hearings (Lampert Hearings)*, 68th Cong., 1st sess., 1924.

——. *Report (Lampert Report)*, 68th Cong., 1st sess., Dec. 14, 1925.

U.S. Congress. House. Subcommittee on Aeronautics. *Hearings Making Investigation into Certain Phases of the Manufacture of Aircraft and Aeronautical Accessories as They Refer to the Navy Department (Delaney Hearings)*, 73rd Cong., 1st sess., 1934.

U.S. Congress. Senate. *Hearings before a Subcommittee of the Committee on Education and Labor*, 76th Cong., 3d sess., Jan. 1940, pursuant to S.Res. 266 (74th Cong.): *A Resolution to Investigate Violations of the Right of Free Speech and Assembly and Interference with the Right of Labor to Organize and Bargain Collectively (LaFollette Hearings)*, "Los Angeles Industrial Background, Open Shop Activities," Pts. 52, 53, 57, 58, 64.

——. *Hearings of the Special Committee Investigating the Munitions Industry (Nye Hearings)*, 74th Cong., 2d and 3d sess., 1934–1936.

——. *Second Conference Report*, S.Doc. 157, March 21, 1934.

——. *S.Rept. 555*, 65th Cong., 2d sess., Aug. 22, 1918.

U.S. Congress. Senate. Banking and Currency Committee. *Hearings on Stock Exchange Practices (Pecora Hearings)*, 72d Cong., 1st sess., 1933–1934.

U.S. Congress. Senate. Committee on Military Affairs. *Reorganization of the Army Hearings on S. 2693*, 66th Cong., 1st sess., 1919.

U.S. Congress. Senate. Special Committee on the Investigation of Air Mail and Ocean Mail Contracts. *Hearings. (Black Hearings)*, 73rd Cong., 2d sess., pts. 1–9, 1934.

U.S. Congress. Senate. Subcommittee of the Senate Committee on Military Affairs. *Hearings on Aircraft Production*, 65th Cong., 2d sess., 1918.

U.S. Department of Commerce. *Statistical Abstract of the United States*. Washington, D.C.: GPO.

U.S. Department of Justice. *Report of the Hughes Aircraft Inquiry*, Oct. 25, 1918.

U.S. War Department. Special Committee on the Army Air Corps (Baker Board). *Final Report*. 1934.

BOOKS AND ARTICLES

Adams, Frederick C. *Economic Diplomacy: The Export-Import Bank and American Foreign Policy 1934–1939* (Columbia: University of Missouri Press, 1976).

Adler, Selig. *The Isolationist Impulse* (New York: Macmillan, 1966).

Argersinger, Jo Ann E. *Toward a New Deal in Baltimore: People and Government in the Great Depression* (Chapel Hill: University of North Carolina Press, 1988).

Arnold, H. H. *Global Mission* (New York: Harper, 1949).

Auerbach, Jerold S. *Labor and Liberty: The LaFollette Committee and the New Deal* (Indianapolis: Bobbs-Merrill, 1966).

——. "New Deal, Old Deal, or Raw Deal: Some Thoughts on New Left Historiography," *Journal of Southern History* 35 (February 1969), 18–30.

Becker, William H. *The Dynamics of Business-Government Relations: Industry and Exports 1893–1921* (Chicago: University of Chicago Press, 1982).

Behrman, Bradley. "Civil Aeronautics Board." In James Q. Wilson, ed., *The Politics of Regulation* (New York: Basic Books, 1980), 75–120.

Bernstein, Irving. *The Lean Years: A History of the American Worker 1920–1933* (Boston: Houghton Mifflin, 1960).

———. *Turbulent Years: A History of the American Worker 1933–1941* (Boston: Houghton Mifflin, 1969).

Bernstein, Michael A. *The Great Depression: Delayed Recovery and Economic Change in America 1929–1939* (New York: Cambridge University Press, 1987).

Bluestone, Barry, et al. *Aircraft Industry Dynamics: An Analysis of Competition, Capital and Labor* (Boston: Auburn House, 1981).

Blum, Albert A. "Birth and Death of the M-Day Plan." In Harold Stein, ed., *American Civil-Military Decisions* (Birmingham: University of Alabama Press, 1963), 63–94.

Bower, Peter M. *Curtiss Aircraft 1907–1947* (Annapolis, Md.: Naval Institute Press, 1987).

Braudel, Fernand. *Wheels of Commerce* (New York: Harper & Row, 1982).

Brinkley, Alan. "The Idea of the State." In S. Fraser and G. Gerstle, eds., *The Rise and Fall of the New Deal Order, 1930–1980* (Princeton, N.J.: Princeton University Press, 1989).

Brody, David. *Workers in Industrial America* (New York: Oxford University Press, 1980).

———. "The New Deal and World War II." In J. Braeman, R. Bremmer, and D. Brody, *The New Deal: The National Level* (Columbus: Ohio State University Press, 1975), 267–309.

Brooks, P. W. *The Modern Airliner* (London: Putnam, 1961).

Brune, Lester F. *The Origins of American National Security Policy: Sea Power, Airpower and Foreign Policy* (Manhattan, Kans.: MA/AH Pub., 1981).

Burns, Arthur Robert. *The Decline of Competition: A Study of the Evolution of American Industry* (New York: McGraw-Hill, 1936).

Carr, L. J., and J. E. Stermer. *Willow Run: A Study of Industrialization and Cultural Inadequacy* (New York: Harper, 1952).

Carter, Dale. *The Rise and Fall of the American Rocket State* (London: Verso Press, 1988).

Cassagneres, E. *Spirit of Ryan* (Blue Ridge Summit, Pa.: Tab Books, 1982).

Catton, Bruce. *Warlords of Washington* (New York: Harcourt, Brace, 1948).

Caves, R. E. *Air Transport and Its Regulators–An Industry Study* (Cambridge, Mass.: Harvard University Press, 1962).

Chase, Stuart. *Men and Machines* (New York: Macmillan, 1929).

Childs, William R. *Trucking and the Public Interest: The Emergence of Federal Regulation 1914–1940* (Knoxville: University of Tennessee Press, 1985).

Cohen, Warren I. *Empire without Tears: United States International Relations, 1921–1933* (New York: Knopf, 1987).

Cole, A. H. "An Approach to the Study of Entrepreneurship." In F. C. Lane and J. C. Riemersma, eds., *Enterprise and Secular Change: Readings in Economic History* (Homewood, Ill.: R. D. Irwin, 1953).

Cole, Wayne S. *Roosevelt and the Isolationists* (Lincoln: University of Nebraska Press, 1983).

———. *Senator Gerald P. Nye and American Foreign Relations* (Minneapolis: University of Minnesota Press, 1962).

Cooling, Benjamin Franklin, ed. *War, Business and American Society: Historical Perspectives on the Military Industrial Complex* (Port Washington, N.Y.: Kennikat Press, 1977).

———. *Gray Steel and Blue Water: The Formative Years of America's Military-Industrial Complex, 1881–1917* (Hamden, Conn.: Archon Books, 1979).

Corn, Joseph J. *Winged Gospel: America's Romance with Aviation, 1900–1950* (New York: Oxford University Press, 1983).

Cronon, E. David, ed. *The Cabinet Diaries of Josephus Daniels 1913–1921* (Lincoln: University of Nebraska Press, 1963).

Crouch, Tom D. *The Bishop's Boys: A Life of Wilbur and Orville Wright* (New York: Norton, 1989).

Crowell, Benedict, and R. F. Wilson. *Demobilization: Our Industrial and Military Demobilization after the Armistice 1918–1920* (New Haven, Conn.: Yale University Press, 1921).

———. *The Armies of Industry* (New Haven, Conn.: Yale University Press, 1921).

Cuff, Robert D. *The War Industries Board: Business-Government Relations during World War I* (Baltimore: Johns Hopkins University Press, 1973).

———. "Herbert Hoover, the Ideology of Voluntarism and War Organization during the Great War." *Journal of American History* 64 (September 1977): 358–372.

———. "An Organizational Perspective on the Military-Industrial Complex." *Business History Review* 50 (Summer 1978): 250–267.

———. "Commentary." In James Titus, ed., *The Home Front and War in the Twentieth Century: The American Experience in Comparative Perspective* (Washington: Office of Air Force History, 1984), 111–118.

Cunningham, William G. *The Aircraft Industry: A Study in Industrial Location* (Berkeley: University of California Press, 1951).

Dallek, Robert. *Franklin D. Roosevelt and American Foreign Policy 1932–1945* (New York: Oxford University Press, 1979).

Dearing, C. L., et al. *The ABC of the NRA* (Washington, D.C.: Brookings, 1934).

Dodd, Paul A. *Financial Policies in the Aviation Industry* (Philadelphia: University of Pennsylvania, 1933).

Douglas, Susan S. *Inventing American Broadcasting, 1899–1922* (Baltimore: Johns Hopkins University Press, 1987).

Dubofsky, Melvyn. "Not So 'Turbulent Years': Another Look at the American 1930's," *Amerikastudien* 24 (1982): 5–20.

Eddy, A. J. *The New Competition* (New York: D. Appleton & Co., 1912).

Feinman, Ronald L. *Twilight of Progressivism: The Western Republican Senators and the New Deal* (Baltimore: Johns Hopkins University Press, 1981).

Ferguson, Thomas. "From Normalcy to New Deal: Industrial Structure, Party Competition, and American Public Policy in the Great Depression." *International Organization* 38 (Winter 1984): 41–94.

Ferrell, Henry C., Jr. *Claude A. Swanson of Virginia* (Lexington: University Press of Kentucky, 1985).

Ferrell, Robert H. *Peace in Their Time* (New Haven, Conn.: Yale University Press, 1952).

Fine, Sidney. *The Automobile under the Blue Eagle: Labor, Management, and the Automobile Manufacturing Code* (Ann Arbor: University of Michigan Press, 1963).

Freudenthal, E. E. *The Aviation Business: From Kitty Hawk to Wall Street* (New York: Vanguard Press, 1940).

Gellman, I. F. *Good Neighbor Diplomacy: United States Policies in Latin America, 1933–1945* (Baltimore: Johns Hopkins University Press, 1979).

Goldberg, Alfred. *A History of the United States Air Force 1907–1957* (Princeton, N.J.: Van Nostrand, 1957).

Gottlieb, Robert, and Irene Wolf. *Thinking Big: The Story of the Los Angeles Times* (New York: Putnam's, 1977).

Gould, Lewis. *Regulation and Reform* (New York: Knopf, 1986).

Gross, Charles J. "George Owen Squier and the Origins of Military Aviation." *Journal of Military History* 54 (July 1990): 281–305.

Gross, James A. *The Making of the National Labor Relations Board* (Albany: State University of New York Press, 1974).

———. *The Reshaping of the National Labor Relations Board* (Albany: State University of New York Press, 1979).

Harding, W. B. *The Aviation Industry* (New York: C. D. Barney & Co., 1937).

Harris, Howell. "The Snares of Liberalism? Politicians, Bureaucrats, and the Shaping of Federal Labor Relations Policy in the United States, ca. 1915–47." In Steven Tolliday and Jonathan Zeitlin, eds., *Shop Floor Bargaining and the State: Historical and Comparative Perspectives* (New York: Cambridge University Press, 1985).

Hawley, Ellis W. *The New Deal and the Problem of Monopoly: A Study in Economic Ambivalence* (Princeton, N.J.: Princeton University Press, 1966).

———. "Herbert Hoover, the Commerce Secretariat, and the Vision of an Associative State," *Journal of American History* 61 (June 1974): 116–140.

———. *The Great War and the Search for a Modern Order: A History of the American People and Their Institutions 1917–1933* (New York: St. Martin's Press, 1979).

———. "Three Facets of Hooverian Associationalism: Lumber, Aviation, and Movies, 1921–1930." In Thomas K. McCraw, ed., *Regulation in Perspective* (Boston: Harvard University Press, 1981), 95–123.

Hays, Will H. *The Memoirs of Will Hays* (Garden City, N.Y.: Doubleday, 1955).

Hewes, James E., Jr. *From Root to McNamara: Army Organization and Administration, 1900–1963* (Washington, D.C.: Center for Military History, 1975).

Hicks, John D. *Republican Ascendency* (New York: Harper, 1960).

Himmelberg, Robert. *Untitled essay.* In J. J. Huthmacher and W. I. Susman, eds., *Herbert Hoover and the Crisis of American Capitalism* (Cambridge, Mass.: Schenkman, 1973).

———. *The Origins of the National Recovery Administration* (New York: Fordham University Press, 1976).

Hodges, James A. *New Deal Labor Policy and the Southern Cotton Textile Industry 1933–1941* (Knoxville: University of Tennessee Press, 1986).

Hogan, Michael J. *Informal Entente: The Private Structure of Cooperation in Anglo-American Diplomacy 1918–1928* (Columbia: University of Missouri Press, 1977).

Holley, I. B., Jr. *Ideas and Weapons* (New Haven, Conn.: Yale University Press, 1953).

———. *Buying Aircraft: Materiel Procurement for the Army Air Forces* (Washington, D.C.: Office of the Chief of Military History, 1962).

Hounshell, David A. *From the American System to Mass Production, 1800–1932* (Baltimore: Johns Hopkins University Press, 1984).

———. "Ford Eagle Boats and Mass Production during World War I." In Merritt Roe Smith, ed. *Military Enterprise and Technological Change* (Cambridge, Mass.: MIT Press, 1985), 175–202.

Howard, Fred. *Wilbur and Orville: A Biography of the Wright Brothers* (New York: Knopf, 1987).

Hughes, Thomas P. *Elmer Sperry, Inventor and Engineer* (Baltimore: Johns Hopkins University Press, 1971).

Huthmacher, Joseph J. *Senator Robert F. Wagner and the Rise of Urban Liberalism* (New York: Atheneum, 1968).

Huzar, Elias. *The Purse and the Sword: Control of the Army by Congress through Military Appropriations, 1933–1950* (Ithaca, N.Y.: Cornell University Press, 1950).

Janeway, Eliot. *The Struggle for Survival: A Chronicle of Economic Mobilization in World War II* (New Haven, Conn.: Yale University Press, 1951).

Johnson, James P. *The Politics of Soft Coal: The Bituminous Industry from World War I through the New Deal* (Urbana: University of Illinois Press, 1979).

Jones, Bryn. "Controlling Production on the Shop Floor: The Role of State Administration and Regulation in the British and American Aerospace Industries." In S. Tolliday and J. Zeitlin, eds., *Shop Floor Bargaining and the State: Historical and Comparative Perspectives* (New York: Cambridge University Press, 1985), 219–256.

Karl, Barry. *The Uneasy State* (Chicago: University of Chicago Press, 1983).

Keller, Morton. "The Pluralist State: American Economic Regulation in Comparative Perspective, 1900–1930." In Thomas K. McCraw, ed., *Regulation in Perspective* (Boston: Harvard University Press, 1981).

Kennedy, David. *Over Here: The First World War and American Society* (New York: Oxford University Press, 1982).

Kerr, Austin K. "Decision for Federal Control: Wilson, McAdoo, and the Railroads." *Journal of American History* 54 (January 1967): 550–560.

Kevles, Daniel J. *The Physicists* (New York: Knopf, 1978).

Koistinen, Paul A. C. "The 'Industrial-Military Complex' in Historical Perspective: The InterWar Years." *Journal of American History* 56 (March 1970): 819–839.

Kolko, Gabriel. *Main Currents in Modern American History* (New York: Pantheon, 1976).

Komans, Nick A. *Bonfires to Beacons: Federal Civil Aviation Policy under the Air Commerce Act, 1926–1938* (Washington, D.C.: Department of Transportation, 1978).

Kucera, Randolph P. *The Aerospace Industry and the Military: Structural and Political Relationships* (Beverly Hills, Calif.: Sage, 1974).

LaGuardia, Fiorello. *The Making of an Insurgent* (Philadelphia: J. B. Lippincott, 1948).

Leary, William M., Jr. "At the Dawn of Commercial Aviation: Inglis M. Uppercu and Aeromarine Airways." *Business History Review* 53 (Summer 1979): 189–203.

Lee, David D. "Herbert Hoover and the Development of Commercial Aviation, 1921–1926." *Business History Review* 58 (Spring 1984): 78–102.

Leuchtenberg, William E. "The New Deal and the Analogue of War." In John

Braeman et al., eds., *Change and Continuity in Twentieth Century America* (Columbus: Ohio State University Press, 1964), 81–143.

Lichtenstein, Nelson. *Labor's War at Home: The CIO in World War Two* (New York: Cambridge University Press, 1982).

Lilley, Tom, and Lynn Bollinger. *Financial Position of the Aircraft Industry* (Boston: Harvard Graduate School of Business Administration, 1943).

———. *Problems of Accelerating Aircraft Production during World War II* (Boston: Harvard Graduate School of Business Administration, 1947).

Livermore, Seward W. *Politics Is Adjourned: Woodrow Wilson and the War Congress 1916–1918* (Middletown, Conn.: Wesleyan University Press, 1966).

Loening, Grover. *Takeoff Into Greatness* (New York: Putnam, 1968).

Lynd, Staughton. "The Possibility of Radicalism in the Early 1930s: The Case of Steel." *Radical America* 6 (1972): 37–64.

Lyon, Leverett S. et al. *The National Recovery Administration: An Analysis and Appraisal* (Washington, D.C.: Brookings, 1935).

Maier, Charles S. "Society as Factory." In *In Search of Stability: Explorations in Historical Political Economy* (New York: Cambridge University Press, 1987), 19–69.

Mansfield, Harold. *Vision: A Saga of the Sky* (New York: Duell, Sloan, and Pearce, 1956).

Martin, James V. "Aircraft Conspiracy." *Liberation* (March 1924): 119–167.

McCraw, Thomas K. "Regulation in America: A Review Article." *Business History Review* 49 (Summer 1975): 159–183.

———. "Louis D. Brandeis Reappraised." *American Scholar* (Autumn 1985): 525–536.

———. "The New Deal and the Mixed Economy." In Harvard Sitkoff, ed., *Fifty Years Later: The New Deal Evaluated* (New York: Knopf, 1985), 37–67.

McFarland, Keith D. *Harry H. Woodring: A Political Biography of FDR's Controversial Secretary of War* (Lawrence: University Press of Kansas, 1975).

McKay, Kenneth C. *The Progressive Party of 1924* (New York: Columbia University Press, 1947).

McNaugher, Thomas L. *New Weapons, Old Politics: America's Military Procurement Muddle* (Washington, D.C.: Brookings, 1989).

McNeill, William H. *The Pursuit of Power: Technology, Armed Force, and Society since A.D. 1000* (Chicago: University of Chicago Press, 1982).

McQuaid, Kim. *Big Business and Presidential Power: From FDR to Reagan* (New York: Morrow, 1982).

Melman, Seymour. *The War Economy of the United States: Readings on Military Industry and Economy* (New York: St. Martin's Press, 1971).

Miller, Ronald, and David Sawers. *The Technical Development of Modern Aviation* (London: Routledge and Kegan Paul, 1968).

Milward, Alan S. *War, Economy and Society 1939–1945* (Berkeley: University of California Press, 1977).

Mingos, Howard. "The Birth of an Industry." In G. R. Simonson, ed., *The History of the American Aircraft Industry: An Anthology* (Cambridge, Mass.: MIT Press, 1968).

Mixter, G. W., and H. H. Emmons. *United States Army Aircraft Production Facts* (Washington, D.C.: GPO, 1919).

Modley, R., and T. J. Cawley. *Aviation Facts and Figures* (New York: Aircraft Industries Association, 1953).

Morris, James O. *Conflict within the AFL: A Study of Craft versus Industrial Unionism, 1901–1938* (Ithaca, N.Y.: Cornell University Press, 1958).

Mulder, Ronald L. *The Insurgent Progressives in the United States Senate and the New Deal, 1933–1939* (New York: Garland, 1979).

Nelson, Bruce. *Workers on the Waterfront: Seamen, Longshoremen and Unionism in the 1930s* (Urbana: University of Illinois Press, 1988).

Nordhauser, Norman E. *The Quest for Stability: Domestic Oil Regulation 1917–1935* (New York: Garland, 1979).

Nye, Russell B. *Midwestern Progressive Politics: A Study of Its Origins and Development* (New York: Harper & Row, 1959).

Overy, R. J. *The Air War 1939–1945* (New York: Stein and Day, 1980).

Parrini, Carl P. *Heir to Empire: United States Economic Diplomacy, 1916–1923* (Pittsburgh: University of Pittsburgh Press, 1969).

Paxson, Frederick L. *America at War 1917–1918* (Boston: Houghton, 1939).

Peck, M. J., and F. M. Scherer. *The Weapons Acquisition Process: An Economic Analysis* (Boston: Harvard University Graduate School of Business Administration, 1962).

Perlman, Mark. *The Machinists: A New Study in American Trade Unionism* (Cambridge, Mass.: Harvard University Press, 1961).

Perry, Louis B., and Richard S. Perry. *A History of the Los Angeles Labor Movement 1911–1941* (Berkeley: University of California Press, 1963).

Phillips, Almarin. *Technology and Structure: A Study of the Aircraft Industry* (Lexington, Mass.: Heath Lexington Books, 1971).

Piore, Michael J., and Charles F. Sabel. *The Second Industrial Divide: Possibilities for Prosperity* (New York: Basic Books, 1984).

Polenberg, Richard. "The Decline of the New Deal, 1937–1940." In J. Braeman, R. Bremner and D. Brody, eds., *The New Deal: The National Level* (Columbus: Ohio State University Press, 1975), 246–266.

Rae, John B. *Climb to Greatness: The American Aircraft Industry, 1920–1960* (Cambridge, Mass.: MIT Press, 1968).

Roland, Alex. *Model Research: The National Advisory Committee for Aeronautics 1915–1958* 2 vols. (Washington, D.C.: NASA, 1985).

Romasco, Albert U. *The Politics of Recovery: Roosevelt's New Deal* (New York: Oxford University Press, 1983).

Rutkowski, Edwin H. *The Politics of Military Aviation Procurement, 1926–1934* (Columbus: Ohio State University Press, 1966).

Sabel, Charles F., and Jonathan Zeitlin. "Historical Alternatives to Mass Production: Politics, Markets and Technology in Nineteenth Century Industrialization." *Past and Present*, no. 108, August 1985, 133–176.

Schlaifer, R., and S. D. Heron. *The Development of Aircraft Engines and Fuels* (Boston: Harvard University Graduate School of Business Administration, 1950).

Schmeckebier, L. F., and G. A. Weber. *The Bureau of Foreign and Domestic Commerce* (Baltimore: Johns Hopkins University Press, 1924).

Selvin, David F. *Sky Full of Storm: A Brief History of California Labor* (San Francisco: California Historical Society, 1975).

Sherry, Michael. *The Rise of American Airpower: The Creation of Armageddon* (New Haven, Conn.: Yale University Press, 1987).

Simonson, G. R. "The Demand for Aircraft and the Aircraft Industry, 1907–1958." *Journal of Economic History* 20 (September 1960): 361–382.

Sklar, Martin J. *The Corporate Reconstruction of American Capitalism, 1890–1916: The Market, Law, and Politics* (New York: Cambridge University Press, 1988).

Skocpol, Theda. "Political Response to Capitalist Crisis: NeoMarxist Theories of the State and the Case of the New Deal." *Politics and Society* 10, no. 2 (1980): 155–201.

———, and M. Weir. "State Structures and the Possibilities for Keynesian Responses." In P. B. Evans, D. Rueschemeyer, and Theda Skocpol, eds., *Bringing the State Back In* (New York: Cambridge University Press, 1985).

Skowronek, Stephen. *Building a New American State: The Expansion of National Administrative Capacities, 1877–1920* (New York: Cambridge University Press, 1982).

Smith, Henry Ladd. *Airways: The History of Commercial Aviation in the United States* (New York: Knopf, 1942).

Smith, Robert Freeman. "Republican Policy and Pax Americana 1921–1932." In W. A. Williams, ed., *From Colony to Empire: Essays in the History of American Foreign Relations* (New York: J. Wiley, 1972), 253–92.

Smith, R. Elberton. *The Army and Economic Mobilization* (Washington, D.C.: Office of the Chief of Military History, 1959).

Spencer, F. A. *Air Mail Payment and the Government* (Washington, D.C.: Brookings, 1941).

Sprout, Margaret, and Harold Sprout. *Toward a New Order of Seapower* (Princeton, N.J.: Princeton University Press, 1940).

Stekler, H. O. *The Structure and Performance of the Aerospace Industry* (Berkeley: University of California Press, 1965).

Still, Henry. *To Ride the Wind: A Biography of Glenn L. Martin* (New York: Messner, 1964).

Sweetser, Arthur. *The American Air Service* (New York: D. Appleton & Co., 1919).

Tillett, Paul. *The Army Flies the Mails* (Birmingham: University of Alabama Press: 1955).

Todd, Daniel, and R. D. Humble. *World Aerospace: A Statistical Handbook* (London: Croom Helm, 1987).

Tolliday, Stephen, and Jonathan Zeitlin, eds. *The Automobile Industry and Its Workers: Between Fordism and Flexibility* (New York: St. Martin's Press, 1987).

Tomlins, Christopher L. "AFL Unions in the 1930s: Their Performance in Historical Perspective." *Journal of American History* 65 (March 1979): 1021–1042.

Trebilcock, Clive. "The British Armaments Industry 1890–1914." In G. Best and A. Wheatcroft, eds., *War, Economy and the Military Mind* (London: Croom Helm, 1976).

Trimble, William F. "The Naval Aircraft Factory, the American Aviation Industry, and Government Competition, 1919–1928." *Business History Review* 60 (Summer 1986): 175–198.

Tucker, Ray, and F. R. Barkley. *Sons of the Wild Jackass* (Boston: L. C. Page & Co., 1932).

Turnbull, Archibald D., and Clifford C. Lord. *History of United States Naval Aviation* (New Haven, Conn.: Yale University Press, 1949).

Urofsky, Melvin I. *Big Steel and the Wilson Administration: A Study in*

Business-Government Relations (Columbus: Ohio State University Press, 1969).

Vittoz, Stanley. *New Deal Labor Policy and the American Industrial Economy* (Chapel Hill: University of North Carolina Press, 1987).

Vogel, David. *Fluctuating Fortunes: The Political Power of Business in America* (New York: Basic Books, 1989).

Wagner, William. *Reuben Fleet and the Story of Consolidated Aircraft* (Fallbrook, Calif.: Aero Publishers, 1976).

Ward, J. W. "The Meaning of Lindbergh's Flight." *American Quarterly* 10 (Spring 1958): 3–16.

Warner, E. P. *Technical Development and Its Effect on Air Transportation* (Norwich, Vt.: Norwich University, 1938).

Weigley, Russell F. *History of the United States Army* (New York: Macmillan, 1967).

White, William Allen. *A Puritan in Babylon* (New York: Macmillan, 1938).

Williams, William Appleman. *The Contours of American History* (Chicago: Quadrangle, 1961).

Wiltz, John E. *In Search of Peace: The Senate Munitions Inquiry, 1934–36* (Baton Rouge: Louisiana State University Press, 1963).

Wolfe, Alan. *America's Impasse: The Rise and Fall of the Politics of Growth* (Boston: South End Press, 1981).

Wright, Orville. *How We Invented the Airplane.* Edited by Fred C. Kelly (New York: Dover, 1953).

Zieger, Robert. "The Limits of Militancy: Organizing Paper Workers, 1933–35." *Journal of American History* 63 (December 1976).

———. *Madison's Battery Workers, 1934–1952: A History of Federal Labor Union 19587* (Ithaca: New York State School of Industrial & Labor Relations, 1977).

UNPUBLISHED DOCUMENTS AND DISSERTATIONS

Armstrong, George S. and Co., Consultants. "An Engineering Interpretation of the Economic and Financial Aspects of American Industry." Vol. 1, "The Aviation Industry," New York, 1941. Copy in the Library of the National Air and Space Museum, Washington, D.C.

Ferrell, Henry C. "John J. McSwain: A Study in Political Technique." Master's thesis, Duke University, 1957.

Gorgol, J. F. "A Theory of the Military-Industrial Firm." Ph.D. diss., Columbia University, 1969.

Loening, Grover. "Aviation and Banking." Confidential report prepared for the Chase National Bank (October 1938). Copy in the Library of the National Air and Space Museum, Washington, D.C.

O'Connell, C. F., Jr. "The Failure of the American Aeronautical Production and Procurement Effort during the First World War." Master's thesis, Ohio State University, 1978.

Ransom, Harry Howe. "The Air Corps Act of 1926: A Study in the Legislative Process." Ph.D. diss., Princeton University, 1953.

Ross, Donald. "The Aviation Manufacturing Industry in the United States." White, Weld & Co., New York, Dec. 20, 1938. Copy in the Library of the National Air and Space Museum, Washington, D.C.

Shanahan, William O. "Procurement of Naval Aircraft 1907–1939." Naval Aviation History Unit, 1946. Vol. 27. Washington Naval Yard Library.

Sitterson, J. C. "Aircraft Production Policies under the National Defense Advisory Commission and Office of Production Management." Special Study 21, Civilian Production Administration, May 30, 1946.

Tate, James P. "The Army and Its Aircorps: A Study of the Evolution of Army Policy toward Aviation, 1919–1941." Ph.D. diss., Indiana University, 1976.

Vander Linden, Robert. "The Struggle for the Long Range Heavy Bomber: The United States Army Air Corps, 1934–39." Master's thesis, George Washington University, 1981.

Walterman, Thomas W. "Airpower and Private Enterprise: Federal-Industrial Relations in the Aeronautics Field, 1918–1926." Ph.D. diss., Washington University, 1970).

JOURNALS AND NEWSPAPERS

Aerial Age Weekly
Aerodigest
Air Affairs
Aircraft Yearbook
Airway Age
Automotive Industries
Aviation
Buffalo Courier-Express
Buffalo Times
Business Week
Fortune
Magazine of Business
Magazine of Wall Street
Monthly Labor Review
Moody's Industrials
New York Times
Saturday Evening Post
Washington Post

INDEX